D1710040

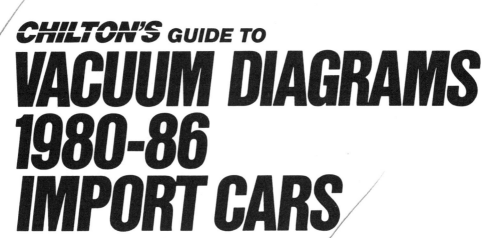

# CHILTON'S GUIDE TO
# VACUUM DIAGRAMS
# 1980-86
# IMPORT CARS

**Vacuum diagrams for 1980-86 import cars**

| | |
|---|---|
| **President** | Lawrence A. Fornasieri |
| **Vice President & General Manager** | John P. Kushnerick |
| **Editor-In-Chief** | Kerry A. Freeman |
| **Managing Editor** | Dean F. Morgantini |
| **Senior Editor** | Richard J. Rivele |

**CHILTON BOOK COMPANY**
**Chilton Way, Radnor, PA 19089**

Manufactured in USA
© 1988 Chilton Book Company
ISBN 0–8019–7822–X
Library of Congress Card Catalog No. 87–47942
1234567890   7654321098

# SAFETY NOTICE

Proper service and repair procedures are vital to the safe, reliable operation of all motor vehicles, as well as the personal safety of those performing repairs. This manual outlines procedures for servicing and repairing vehicles using safe effective methods. The procedures contain many NOTES, CAUTIONS and WARNINGS which should be followed along with standard safety procedures to eliminate the possibility of personal injury or improper service which could damage the vehicle or compromise its safety.

It is important to note that repair procedures and techniques, tools and parts for servicing motor vehicles, as well as the skill and experience of the individual performing the work vary widely. It is not possible to anticipate all of the conceivable ways or conditions under which vehicles may be serviced, or to provide cautions as to all of the possible hazards that may result. Standard and accepted safety precautions and equipment should be used when handling toxic or flammable fluids, and safety goggles or other protection should be used during cutting, grinding, chiseling, prying, or any other process that can cause material removal or projectiles.

Some procedures require the use of tools specially designed for a specific purpose. Before substituting another tool or procedure, you must be completely satisfied that neither your personal safety, nor the performance of the vehicle will be endangered.

Although information in this manual is based on industry sources and is as complete as possible at the time of publication, the possibility exists that some car manufacturers made later changes which could not be included here. While striving for total accuracy, Chilton Book Company cannot assume responsibility for any errors, changes, or omissions that may occur in the compilation of this data.

TL
210
.C538
1988
cop.1

# CONTENTS

## CAR SECTIONS

R00682 0094

# Audi

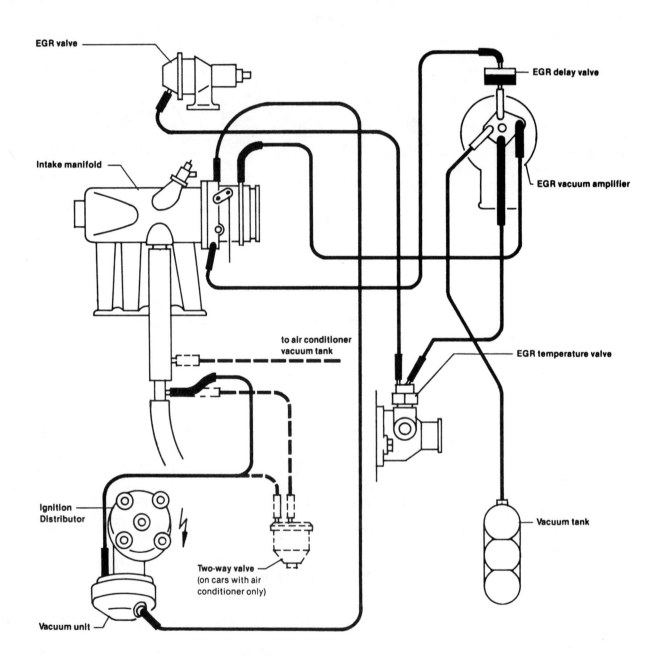

EGR valve

Intake manifold

to air conditioner
vacuum tank

Ignition
Distributor

Two-way valve
(on cars with air
conditioner only)

Vacuum unit

EGR delay valve

EGR vacuum amplifier

EGR temperature valve

Vacuum tank

Vacuum hose layout—w/CIS fuel injection—w/auto. trans—United States and Canada

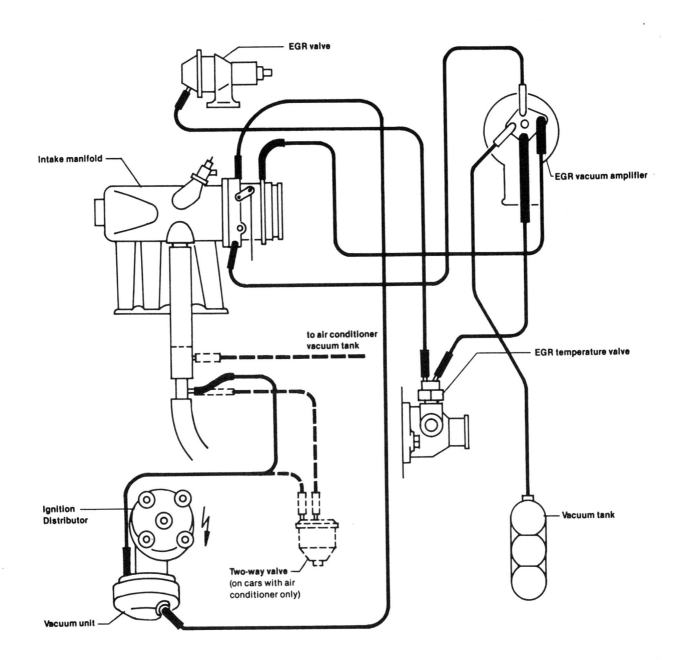

Vacuum hose layout—w/CIS fuel injection—Canada w/auto trans—California w/manual trans

3

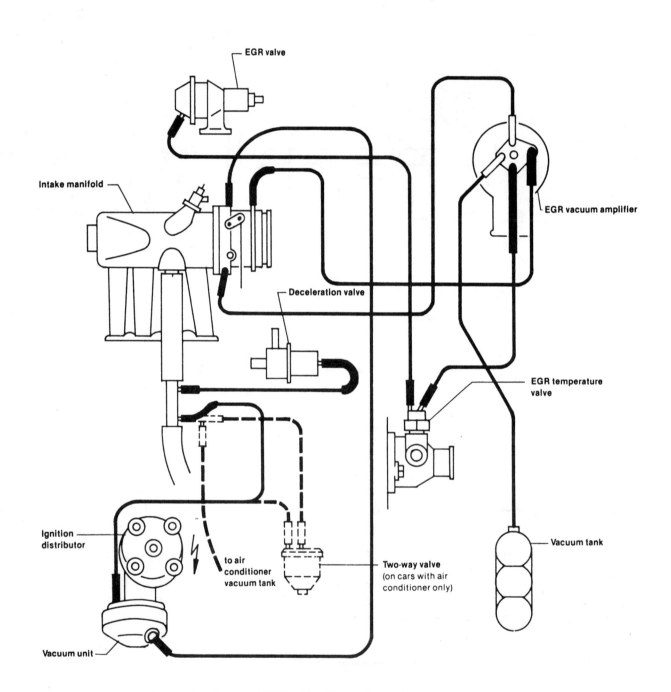

EGR valve

Intake manifold

EGR vacuum amplifier

Deceleration valve

EGR temperature valve

Ignition distributor

to air conditioner vacuum tank

Two-way valve (on cars with air conditioner only)

Vacuum tank

Vacuum unit

Vacuum hose layout—w/CIS fuel injection—w/manual trans—United States only

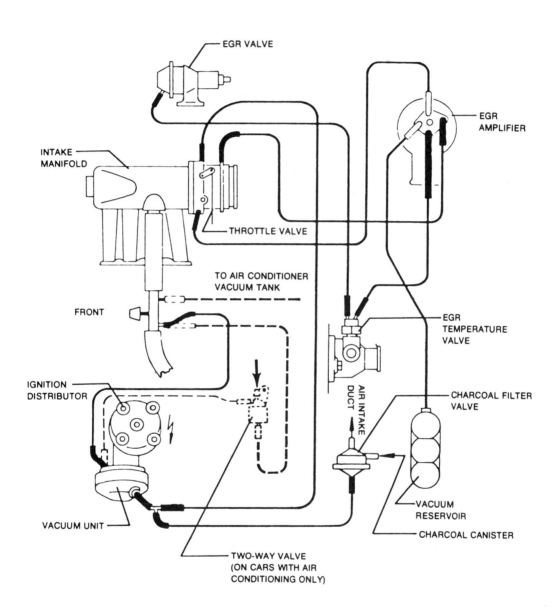

Vacuum hose layout—4000 series

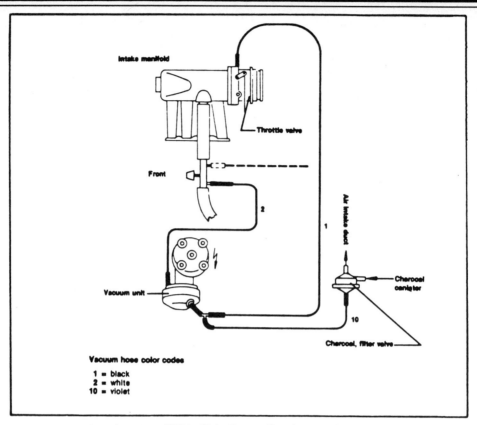

Vacuum hose layout—w/CIS fuel injection—w/4 spd. transmission—California

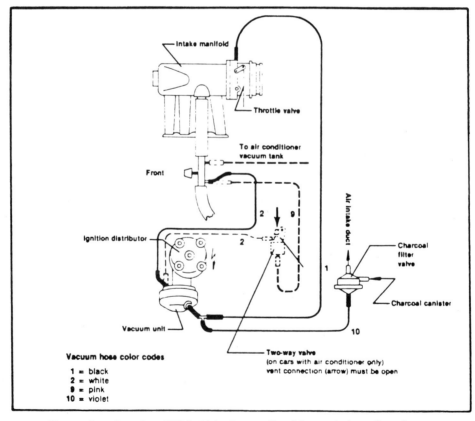

Vacuum hose layout—w/CIS fuel injection—w/4 spd. transmission—Canada

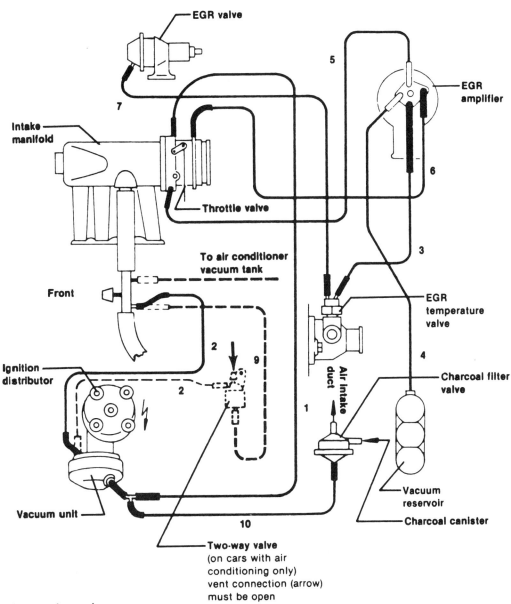

EGR valve

EGR amplifier

5

Intake manifold

7

Throttle valve

6

To air conditioner vacuum tank

3

Front

EGR temperature valve

4

Ignition distributor

2

9

2

Air intake duct

1

Charcoal filter valve

Vacuum unit

10

Vacuum reservoir

Charcoal canister

Two-way valve (on cars with air conditioning only) vent connection (arrow) must be open

**Vacuum hose color codes**

1 = black
2 = white
3 = light blue
4 = light green
5 = gray

6 = red
7 = yellow
9 = pink
10 = violet

Vacuum hose layout—w/CIS fuel injection—w/4 spd. transmission—except California

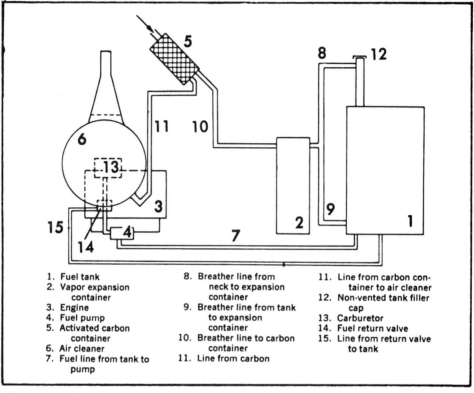

| | | |
|---|---|---|
| 1. Fuel tank | 8. Breather line from neck to expansion container | 11. Line from carbon container to air cleaner |
| 2. Vapor expansion container | 9. Breather line from tank to expansion container | 12. Non-vented tank filler cap |
| 3. Engine | | 13. Carburetor |
| 4. Fuel pump | 10. Breather line to carbon container | 14. Fuel return valve |
| 5. Activated carbon container | 11. Line from carbon | 15. Line from return valve to tank |
| 6. Air cleaner | | |
| 7. Fuel line from tank to pump | | |

Fuel vapor emission control system—typical

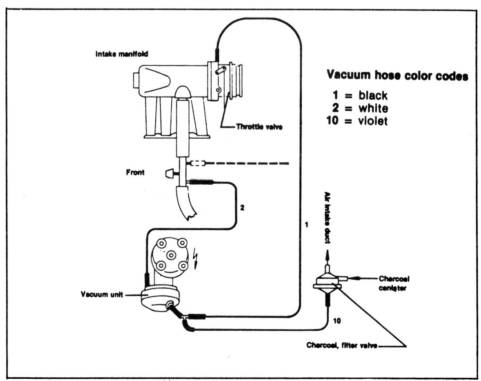

**Vacuum hose color codes**

**1** = black
**2** = white
**10** = violet

AUDI COUPE AND 4000—4 CYL. W/OXYGEN SENSOR

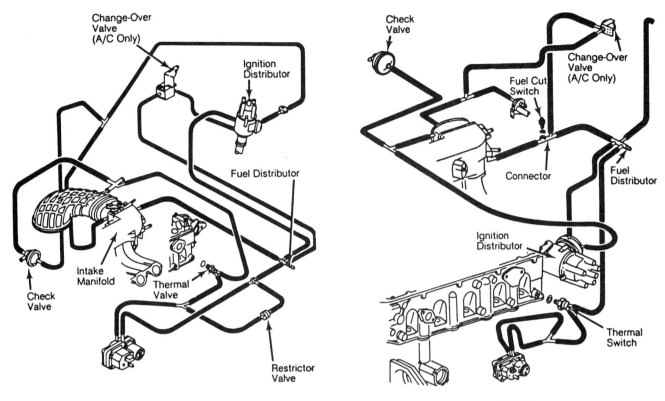

**AUDI 5000 WO/TURBOCHARGER**

**AUDI 5000 W/TURBOCHARGER**

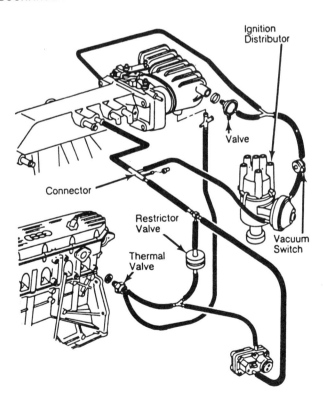

**AUDI 4000—5 CYLINDER MODELS**

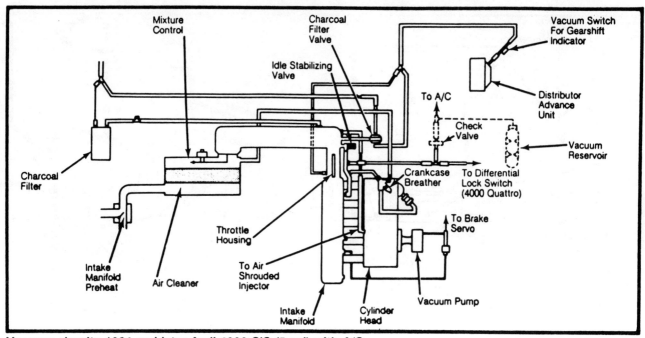

**Vacuum circuits 1984 and later Audi 4000 CIS (5-cyl) with A/C**

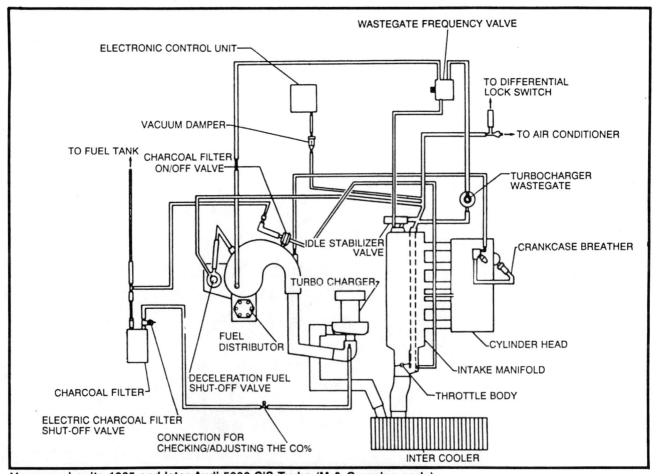

**Vacuum circuits 1985 and later Audi 5000 CIS-Turbo (M & C engine code)**

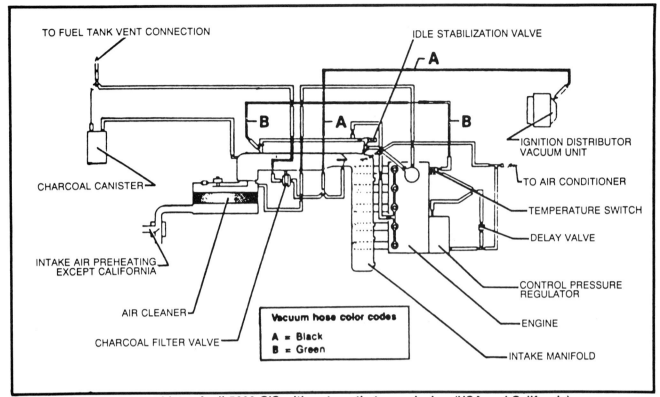

**Vacuum circuits 1984 and later Audi 5000 CIS with automatic transmission (USA and California)**

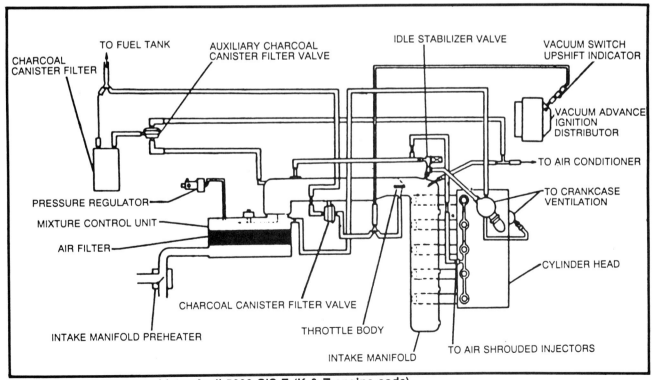

**Vacuum circuits 1984 and later Audi 5000 CIS-E (K & Z engine code)**

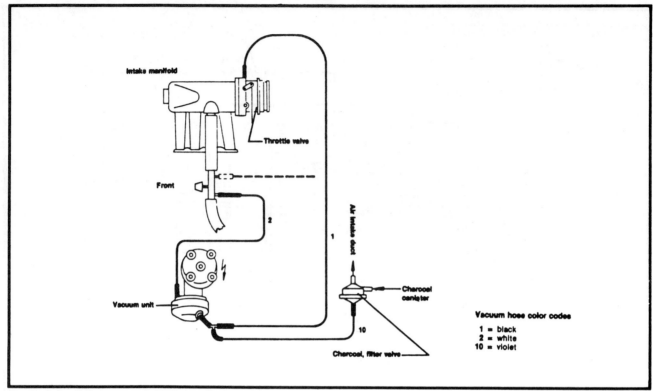

**Typical Audi Coupe and 4000 4 cylinder with oxygen sensor**

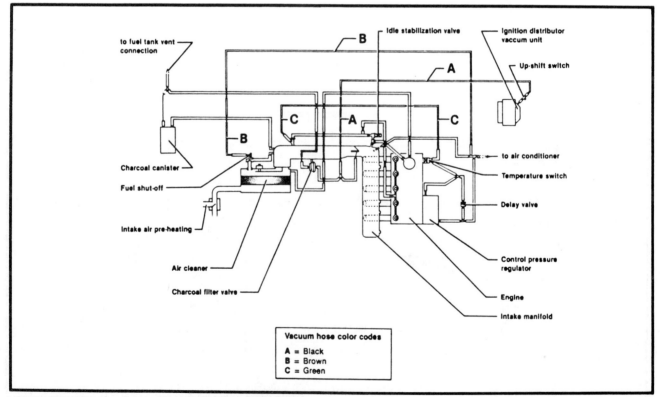

**Audi 5000 USA models with manual transmission**

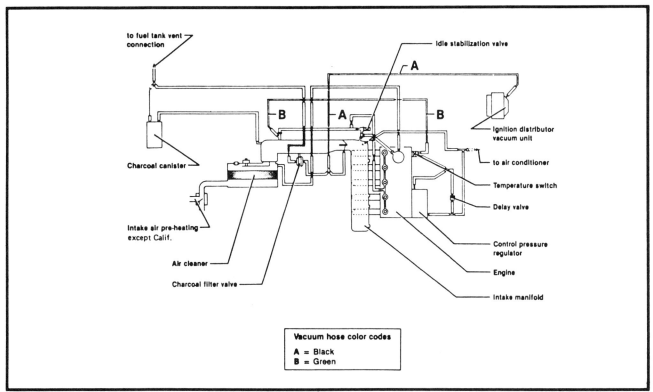

**Audi 5000 USA models with automatic transmission**

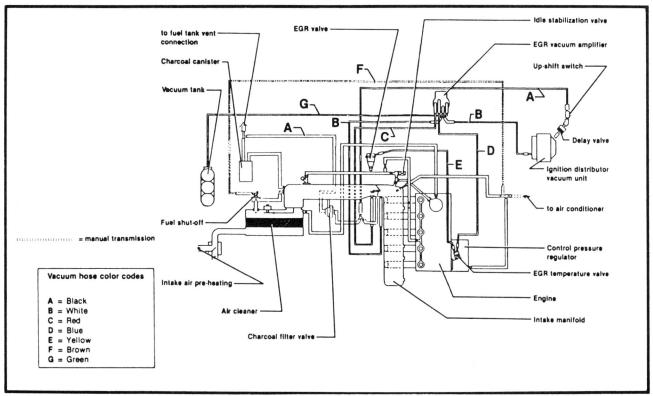

**Audi 5000 Canadian models**

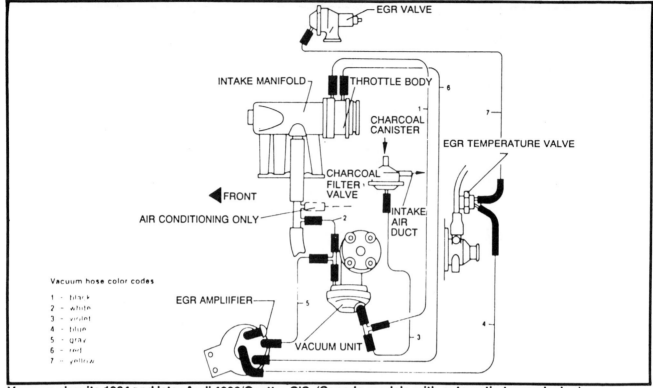

**Vacuum circuits 1984 and later Audi 4000/Quattro CIS (Canada models with automatic transmission)**

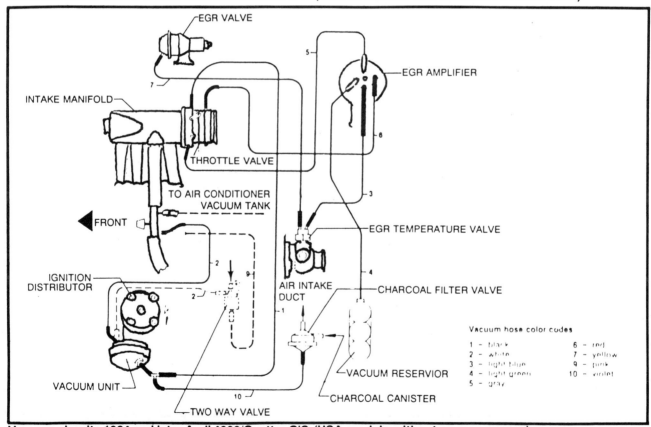

**Vacuum circuits 1984 and later Audi 4000/Quattro CIS (USA models without oxygen sensor)**

# BMW

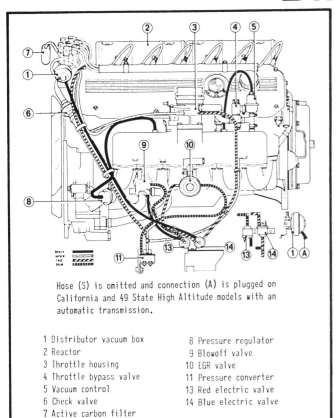

Hose (S) is omitted and connection (A) is plugged on California and 49 State High Altitude models with an automatic transmission.

| | | | |
|---|---|---|---|
| 1 Distributor vacuum box | | 8 Pressure regulator |
| 2 Reactor | | 9 Blowoff valve |
| 3 Throttle housing | | 10 EGR valve |
| 4 Throttle bypass valve | | 11 Pressure converter |
| 5 Vacuum control | | 13 Red electric valve |
| 6 Check valve | | 14 Blue electric valve |
| 7 Active carbon filter | | |

**633CSi vacuum circuits—49 states version**

### Hose Routing Plan
| | | |
|---|---|---|
| 1 Distributor vacuum box | 8 Pressure regulator |
| 2 Reactor | 9 Blowoff valve |
| 3 Throttle housing | 10 EGR valve |
| 4 Throttle bypass valve | 11 Pressure converter |
| 5 Vacuum control | 12 Black electric valve |
| 6 Check valve | 13 Red electric valve |
| 7 Active carbon filter | 14 Blue electric valve |

**733i vacuum circuits—California version**

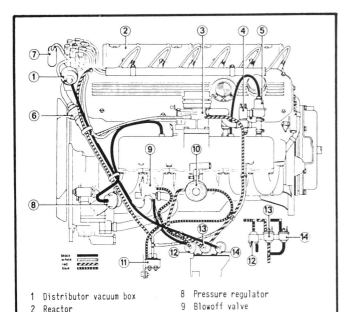

| | | |
|---|---|---|
| 1 Distributor vacuum box | 8 Pressure regulator |
| 2 Reactor | 9 Blowoff valve |
| 3 Throttle housing | 10 EGR valve |
| 4 Throttle bypass valve | 11 Pressure converter |
| 5 Vacuum control | 12 Black electric switching valve |
| 6 Check valve | 13 Red electric switching valve |
| 7 Active carbon filter | 14 Blue electric switching valve |

**633CSi vacuum circuits—California version**

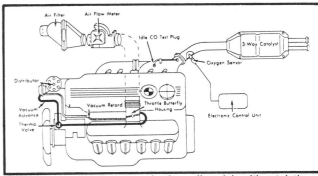

**528i, 633CSi and 733i vacuum circuits—all models with catalytic converter**

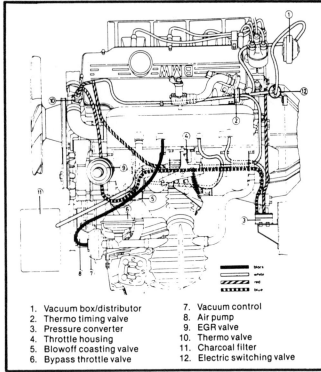

1. Vacuum box/distributor
2. Thermo timing valve
3. Pressure converter
4. Throttle housing
5. Blowoff coasting valve
6. Bypass throttle valve
7. Vacuum control
8. Air pump
9. EGR valve
10. Thermo valve
11. Charcoal filter
12. Electric switching valve

**320i vacuum circuits—all models with manual transmission**

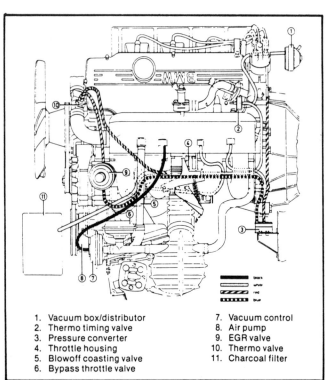

1. Vacuum box/distributor
2. Thermo timing valve
3. Pressure converter
4. Throttle housing
5. Blowoff coasting valve
6. Bypass throttle valve
7. Vacuum control
8. Air pump
9. EGR valve
10. Thermo valve
11. Charcoal filter

**320i vacuum circuits—all models with automatic transmission**

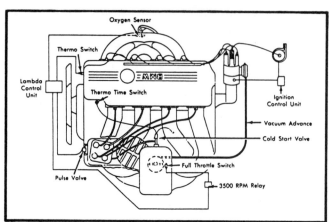

**320i vacuum circuits—all models with catalytic converter**

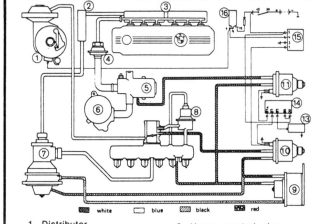

1. Distributor
2. Cyclone exhaust gas filter
3. Reactor
4. Check valve
5. Blow-off valve
6. Air pump
7. EGR valve
8. Vacuum control
9. Vacuum control valve
10. Electric control valve
11. Electric control valve
13. Coolant temperature switch
14. Control relay
15. Speed switch
16. Ignition coil

**528i vacuum circuits—49 states version**

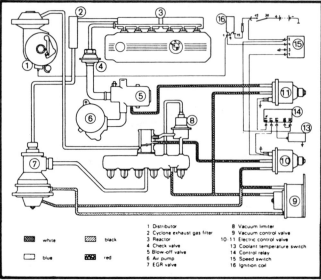

1 Distributor
2 Cyclone exhaust gas filter
3 Reactor
4 Check valve
5 Blow-off valve
6 Air pump
7 EGR valve
8 Vacuum limiter
9 Vacuum control valve
10-11 Electric control valve
13 Coolant temperature switch
14 Control relay
15 Speed switch
16 Ignition coil

**530i vacuum circuits—49 states version**

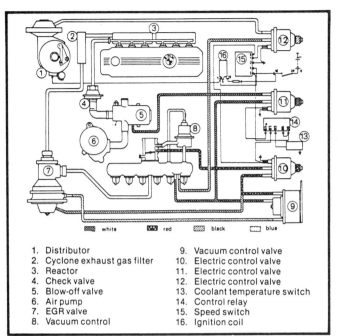

| | |
|---|---|
| 1. Distributor | 9. Vacuum control valve |
| 2. Cyclone exhaust gas filter | 10. Electric control valve |
| 3. Reactor | 11. Electric control valve |
| 4. Check valve | 12. Electric control valve |
| 5. Blow-off valve | 13. Coolant temperature switch |
| 6. Air pump | 14. Control relay |
| 7. EGR valve | 15. Speed switch |
| 8. Vacuum control | 16. Ignition coil |

white   red   black   blue

**528i vacuum circuits—Catalytic converter version**

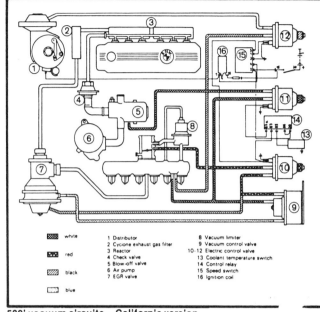

| | |
|---|---|
| 1 Distributor | 8 Vacuum limiter |
| 2 Cyclone exhaust gas filter | 9 Vacuum control valve |
| 3 Reactor | 10-12 Electric control valve |
| 4 Check valve | 13 Coolant temperature switch |
| 5 Blow-off valve | 14 Control relay |
| 6 Air pump | 15 Speed switch |
| 7 EGR valve | 16 Ignition coil |

white   red   black   blue

**530i vacuum circuits—California version**

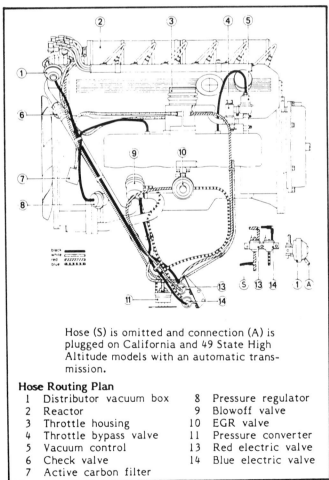

Hose (S) is omitted and connection (A) is plugged on California and 49 State High Altitude models with an automatic transmission.

### Hose Routing Plan

| | | | |
|---|---|---|---|
| 1 | Distributor vacuum box | 8 | Pressure regulator |
| 2 | Reactor | 9 | Blowoff valve |
| 3 | Throttle housing | 10 | EGR valve |
| 4 | Throttle bypass valve | 11 | Pressure converter |
| 5 | Vacuum control | 13 | Red electric valve |
| 6 | Check valve | 14 | Blue electric valve |
| 7 | Active carbon filter | | |

**733i vacuum circuits—49 states version**

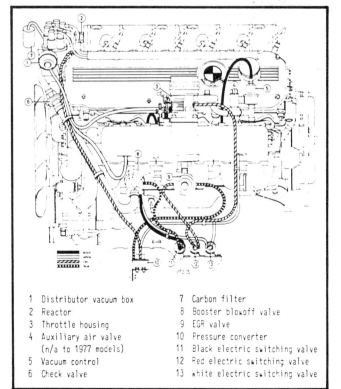

| | | | |
|---|---|---|---|
| 1 | Distributor vacuum box | 7 | Carbon filter |
| 2 | Reactor | 8 | Booster blowoff valve |
| 3 | Throttle housing | 9 | EGR valve |
| 4 | Auxiliary air valve (n/a to 1977 models) | 10 | Pressure converter |
| 5 | Vacuum control | 11 | Black electric switching valve |
| 6 | Check valve | 12 | Red electric switching valve |
| | | 13 | White electric switching valve |

**630CSi vacuum circuits**

**17**

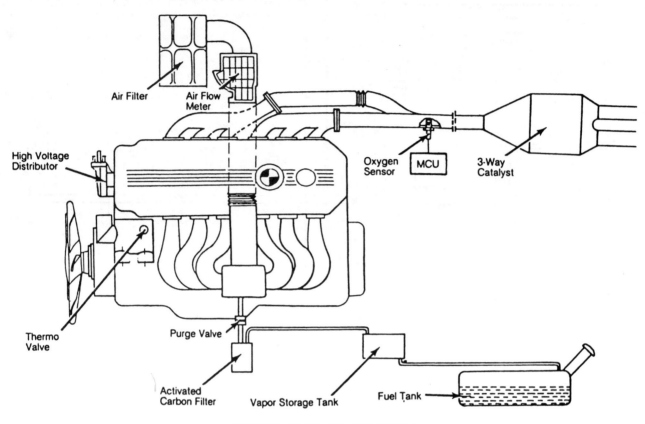

**BMW 533I, 633 CSI AND 733I MODELS**

Air Filter

Air Flow Meter

High Voltage Distributor

Oxygen Sensor

MCU

3-Way Catalyst

Thermo Valve

Purge Valve

Activated Carbon Filter

Vapor Storage Tank

Fuel Tank

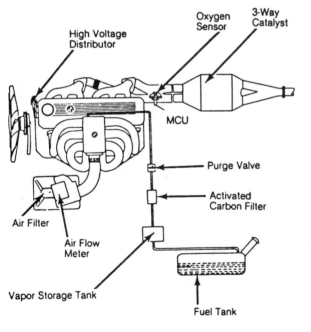

High Voltage Distributor

Oxygen Sensor

3-Way Catalyst

MCU

Purge Valve

Activated Carbon Filter

Air Filter

Air Flow Meter

Vapor Storage Tank

Fuel Tank

**BMW 528e MODELS**

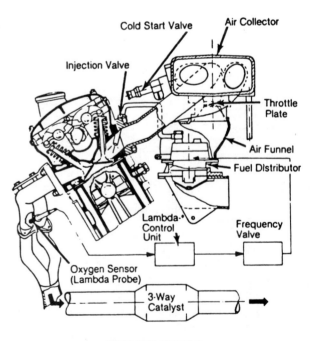

Cold Start Valve

Air Collector

Injection Valve

Throttle Plate

Air Funnel

Fuel Distributor

Lambda-Control Unit

Frequency Valve

Oxygen Sensor (Lambda Probe)

3-Way Catalyst

**BMW 320I MODELS**

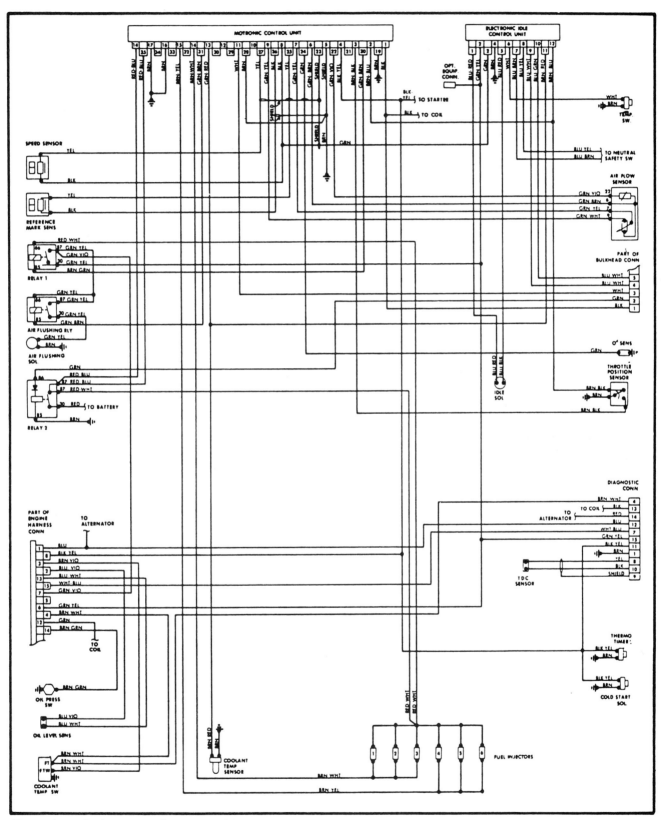

**Motronic emission control system wiring schematic**

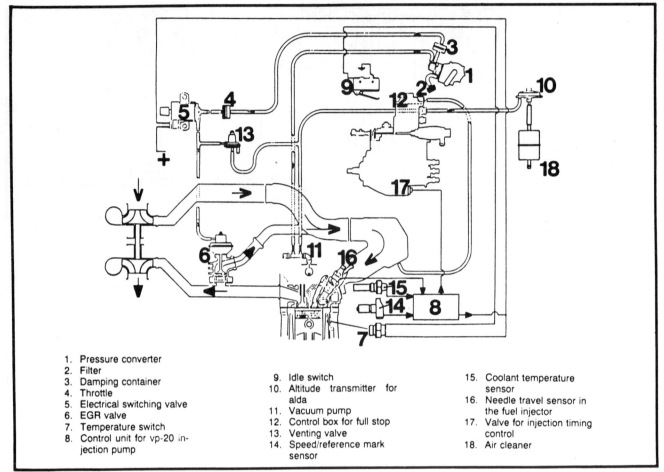

1. Pressure converter
2. Filter
3. Damping container
4. Throttle
5. Electrical switching valve
6. EGR valve
7. Temperature switch
8. Control unit for vp-20 injection pump

9. Idle switch
10. Altitude transmitter for
    alda
11. Vacuum pump
12. Control box for full stop
13. Venting valve
14. Speed/reference mark
    sensor

15. Coolant temperature
    sensor
16. Needle travel sensor in
    the fuel injector
17. Valve for injection timing
    control
18. Air cleaner

**Emission control schematic for the 524 turbo diesel**

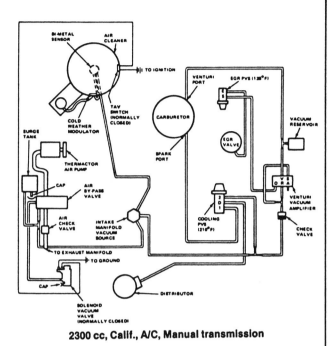

**2300 cc, Calif., A/C, Manual transmission**

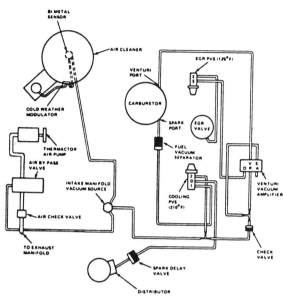

**2300 cc, Federal, Automatic transmission**

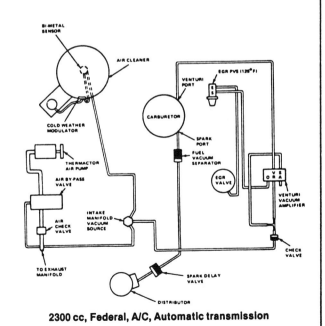

**2300 cc, Federal, A/C, Automatic transmission**

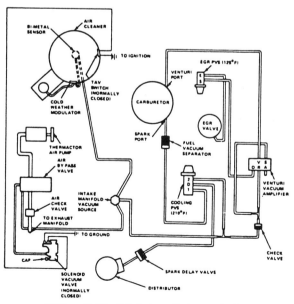

**2300 cc, Calif., A/C, Automatic transmission**

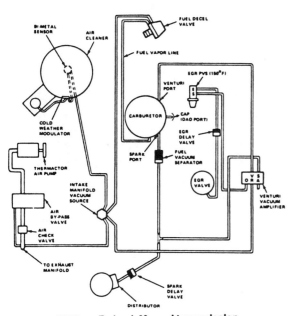

**2300 cc, Federal, Manual transmission**

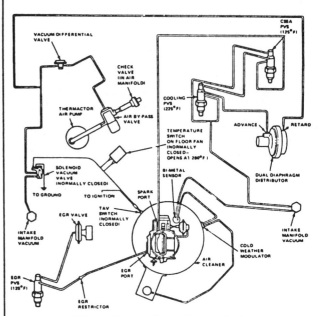

**2800 cc, Federal, Manual transmission**

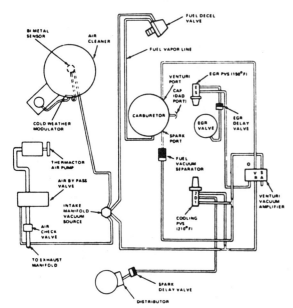

**2300 cc, Federal, A/C, Manual transmission**

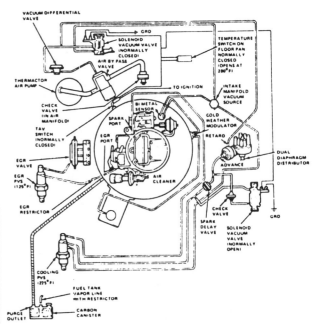

**2800 cc, Calif., Manual transmission**

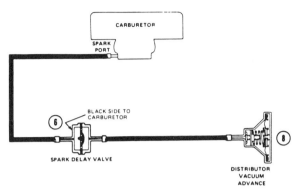

Vacuum circuits—1600 and 2000 engines without A/C

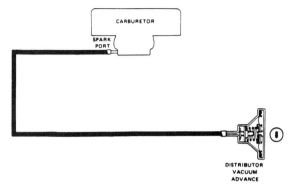

Vacuum circuits—V-6 engine without A/C

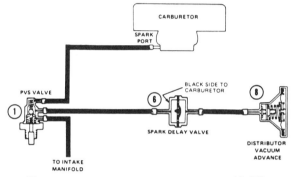

Vacuum circuits—1600 and 2000 engines with A/C

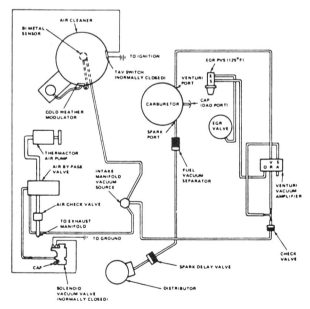

2300 cc, Calif., Automatic transmission

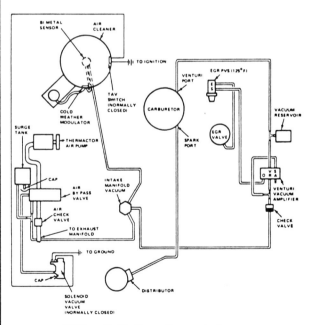

2300 cc, Calif., Manual transmission

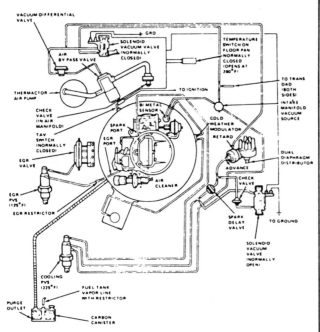

2800 cc, Calif., Automatic transmission

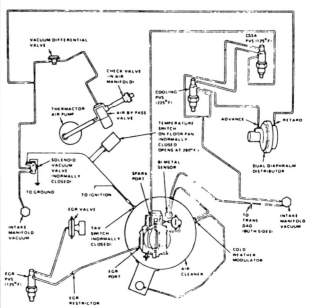

2800 cc, Federal, Automatic transmission

# Chrysler Corp.

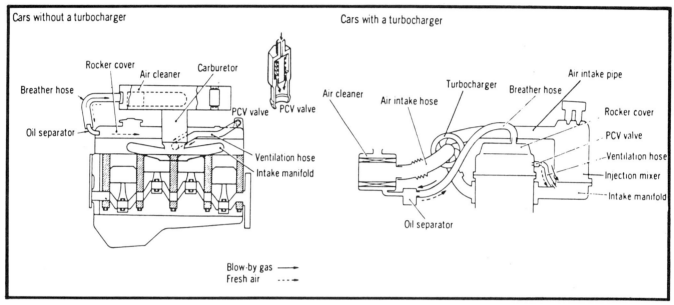

**Crankcase Emission Control system—with and without turbocharger** (© Chrysler Corp.)

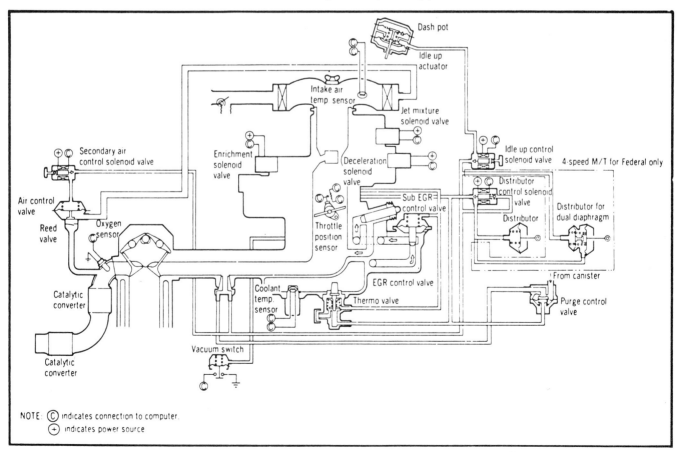

**Schematic of Feedback Carburetor (FBC) system** (© Chrysler Corp.)

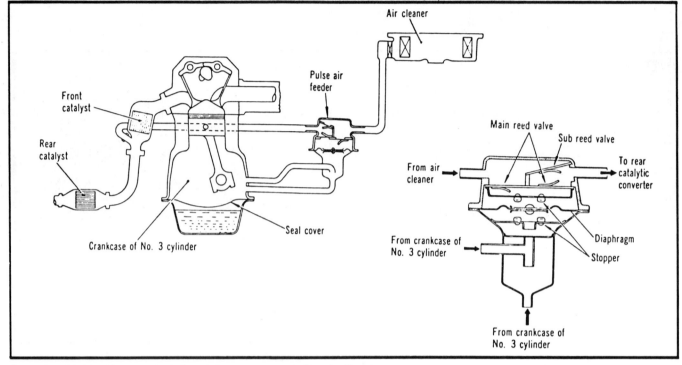

**Secondary Air Supply system for Pulse Air Feeder system** (© Chrysler Corp.)

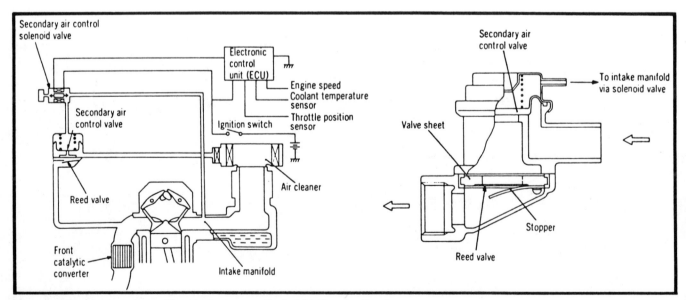

**Secondary Air Supply system without turbocharger—typical** (© Chrysler Corp.)

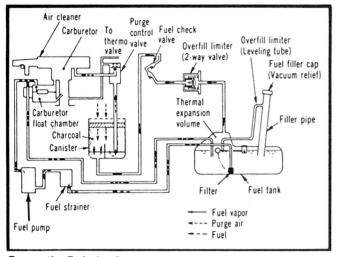

**Evaporative Emission Control system—1984 and later for Canada**
(© Chrysler Corp.)

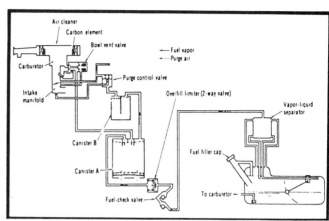

**Evaporative Emission Control system with dual canisters (USA)**

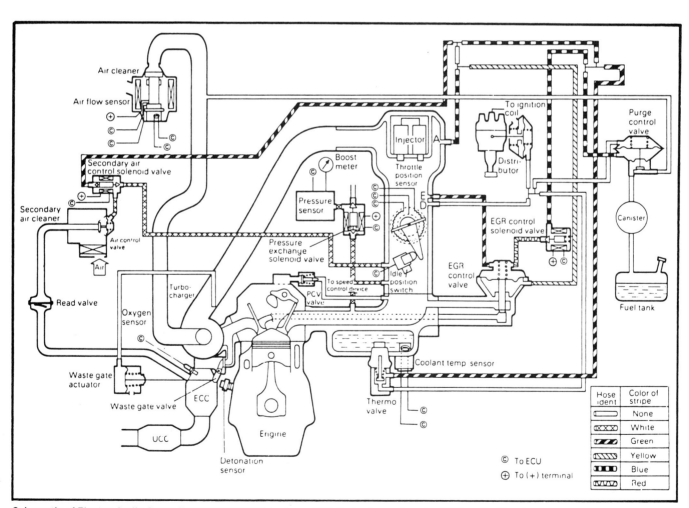

**Schematic of Electronically Controlled Injection (ECI) system—1.6L turbocharged engine** (© Chrysler Corp.)

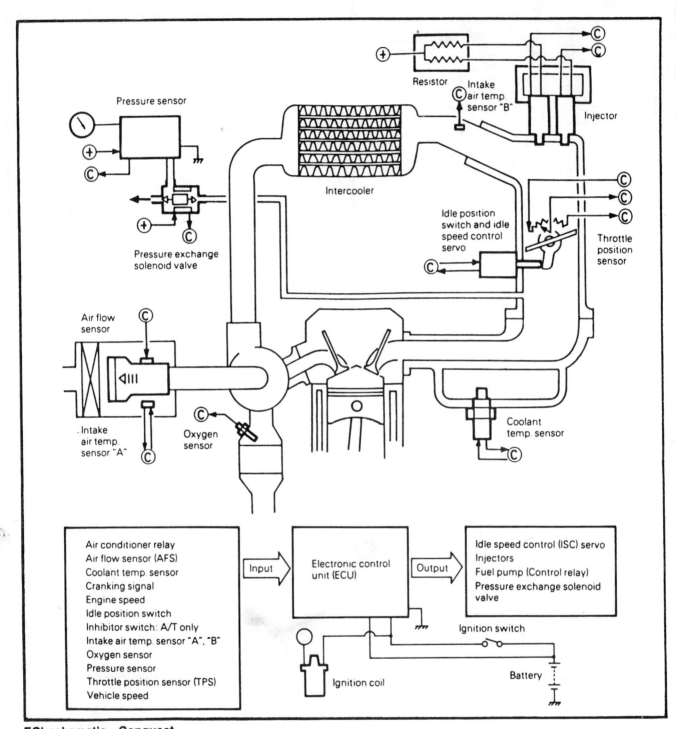

Pressure sensor

Resistor

Intake air temp. sensor "B"

Injector

Intercooler

Idle position switch and idle speed control servo

Throttle position sensor

Pressure exchange solenoid valve

Air flow sensor

Intake air temp. sensor "A"

Oxygen sensor

Coolant temp. sensor

| Air conditioner relay | | | | Idle speed control (ISC) servo |
| Air flow sensor (AFS) | | | | Injectors |
| Coolant temp. sensor | Input | Electronic control unit (ECU) | Output | Fuel pump (Control relay) |
| Cranking signal | | | | Pressure exchange solenoid valve |
| Engine speed | | | | |
| Idle position switch | | | | |
| Inhibitor switch: A/T only | | | | |
| Intake air temp. sensor "A", "B" | | | | |
| Oxygen sensor | | | | |
| Pressure sensor | | | | |
| Throttle position sensor (TPS) | | | | |
| Vehicle speed | | | | |

Ignition switch

Ignition coil

Battery

**ECI schematic — Conquest**

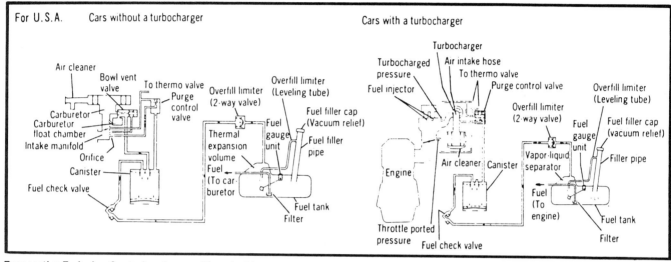

**Evaporative Emission Control system—with and without turbocharger** (© Chrysler Corp.)

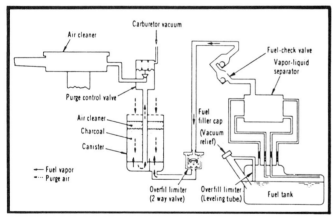

**Evaporative Emission Control system for Canada vehicles— typical 1983** (© Chrysler Corp.)

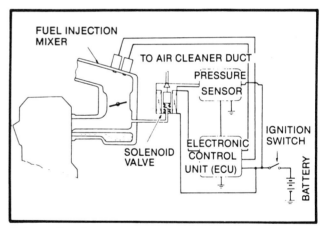

**Schematic of pressure sensor**

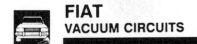

# Fiat

**POWER VALVE**

The power valve is used under certain conditions to supply extra fuel to the main fuel circuit in the primary barrel. With the engine cold, the yellow thermovalve is closed, and no vacuum is applied to the power valve. This allows extra fuel to be supplied to the main fuel circuit in the primary barrel. With the engine hot, the thermovalve is open, and vacuum is applied to the power valve, stopping the extra fuel. To check power valve, disassemble and inspect for damaged diaphragm or sticking ball check valve.

**POWER VALVE**

**VACUUM ACCELERATOR PUMP**

With the engine cold, the green thermovalve is open, and vacuum is applied to the vacuum accelerator pump. During acceleration, there is a vacuum drop in the intake manifold. This allows the vacuum accelerator pump to operate, supplying extra fuel similar to the mechanical accelerator pump. With the engine hot, the thermovalve is closed, and no vacuum is applied to the vacuum accelerator pump. To test vacuum accelerator pump, apply vacuum (10 in. Hg minimum) to vacuum accelerator pump, then check for fuel discharge in primary barrel when vacuum is released.

**VACUUM ACCELERATOR PUMP**

**EGR VALVE**

The EGR valve controls the flow of exhaust gases. With the engine cold, the red thermovalve is closed, and there is no vacuum at the EGR valve. With the engine hot (thermovalve open) and at 3000 RPM, there is vacuum (about 5 in. Hg) at the EGR valve. The 3000 RPM is needed to supply exhaust backpressure to the EGR valve. To test, disconnect vacuum line from EGR valve, then connect a hand vacuum pump to the EGR valve. With engine idling, check that no vacuum can be applied to the EGR valve. With engine at 3000 RPM, check that vacuum (about 5 in. Hg) can be applied.

**EGR VALVE**

**DISTRIBUTOR VACUUM ADVANCE DIAPHRAGM**

To test vacuum advance, apply vacuum to distributor vacuum advance diaphragm. Check that distributor plate advances

**DISTRIBUTOR VACUUM ADVANCE DIAPHRAGM**

**GULP VALVE**

To prevent overrich mixture during deceleration (high manifold vacuum), the gulp valve supplies air directly to the intake manifold. With the engine cold, the electrovalve is closed, and no vacuum is applied to the gulp valve lower chamber. With the engine hot, the electrovalve is open, and vacuum is applied to the gulp valve. To test gulp valve, disconnect vacuum lines to upper and lower chambers. With engine idling, check that engine will not stall when upper chamber hole is blocked, and engine will stall when lower chamber hole is blocked.

**GULP VALVE**

**ELECTROVALVE**

The electrovalve is energized during engine cranking and when the engine is cold (see thermoswitch). This applies vacuum to the gulp valve upper chamber, preventing it from opening. To test, check for correct flow (see diagram) when electrovalve is energized and de-energized.

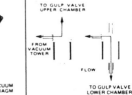

**THERMOSWITCH**

OPENS: >12.2° to 17.8° C (54° to 64° F)

CLOSES: <2.2° to 7.8° C (36° to 46° F)

CONNECTION:

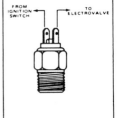

**THERMOVALVE**

COLOR: YELLOW
OPENS: >37° to 43° C (98° to 109° F)
CLOSES: <12° to 18° C (53° to 64° F)

CONNECTION:

**THERMOVALVE**

COLOR: GREEN
OPENS: <12° to 18° C (53° to 64° F)
CLOSES: >37° to 43° C (98° to 109° F)

CONNECTION:

**THERMOVALVE**

COLOR: RED
OPENS: >37° to 43° C (98° to 109° F)
CLOSES: <27° to 33° C (81° to 91° F)

CONNECTION:

**Vacuum controls—128 engine family** (© Fiat Motors of North America)

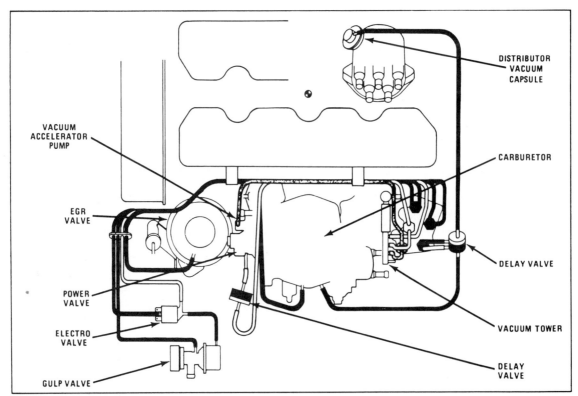

**Vacuum circuits—132 engine family** (© Fiat Motors of North America)

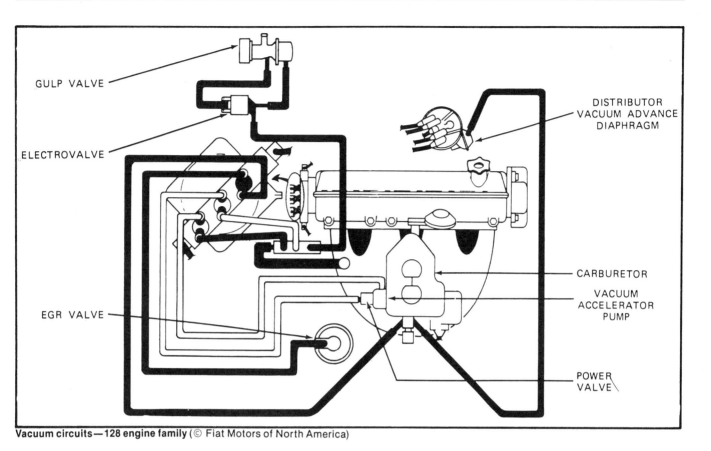

**Vacuum circuits—128 engine family** (© Fiat Motors of North America)

GULP VALVE

ELECTROVALVE

EGR VALVE

DISTRIBUTOR VACUUM ADVANCE DIAPHRAGM

CARBURETOR

VACUUM ACCELERATOR PUMP

POWER VALVE

1. Exhaust gas recirculation intake.
2. EGR valve.
3. EGR valve control thermovalve.
4. EGR valve control vacuum intake.
5. Exhaust gas inlet on intake manifold.

**EGR system—132 engine family** (© Fiat Motors of North America)

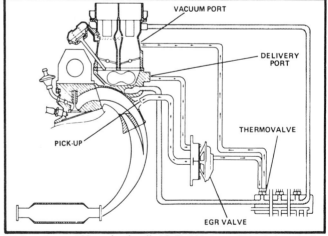

VACUUM PORT

DELIVERY PORT

THERMOVALVE

PICK-UP

EGR VALVE

**EGR system—128 engine family** (© Fiat Motors of North America)

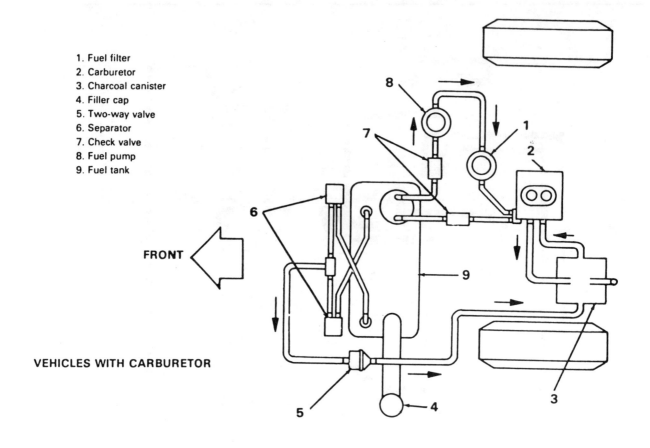

1. Fuel filter
2. Carburetor
3. Charcoal canister
4. Filler cap
5. Two-way valve
6. Separator
7. Check valve
8. Fuel pump
9. Fuel tank

FRONT

**VEHICLES WITH CARBURETOR**

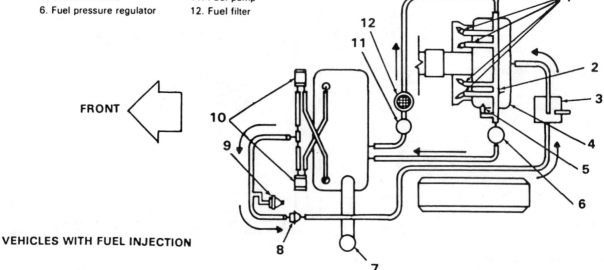

1. Fuel injectors
2. Fuel manifold
3. Charcoal canister
4. Intake manifold
5. Cold start valve
6. Fuel pressure regulator
7. Filler cap
8. Two-way valve
9. Two-way safety relief valve
10. Separator
11. Fuel pump
12. Fuel filter

FRONT

**VEHICLES WITH FUEL INJECTION**

**FIAT X19 MODELS**

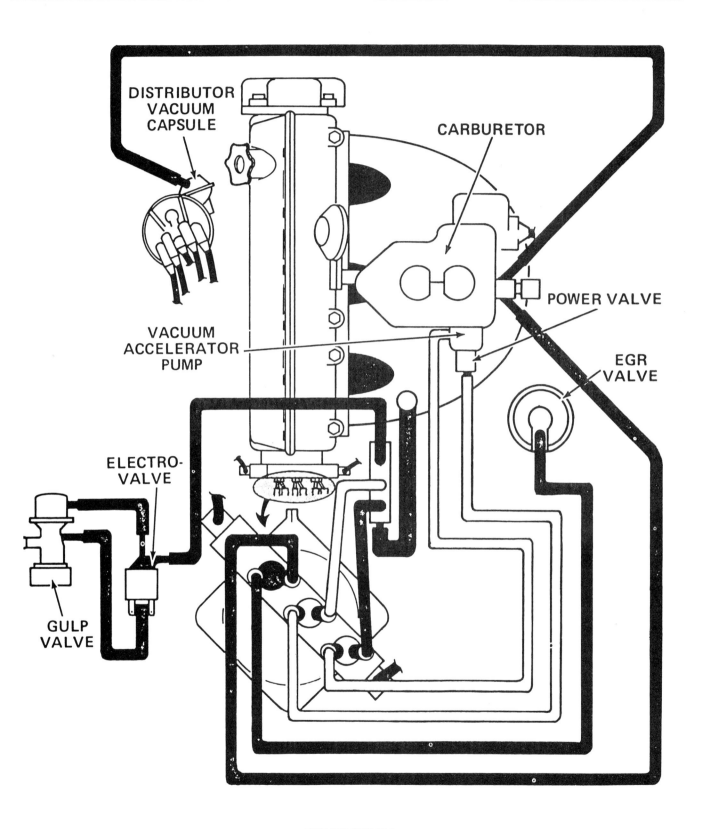

DISTRIBUTOR
VACUUM
CAPSULE

CARBURETOR

POWER VALVE

VACUUM
ACCELERATOR
PUMP

EGR
VALVE

ELECTRO-
VALVE

GULP
VALVE

**FIAT X19 MODELS**

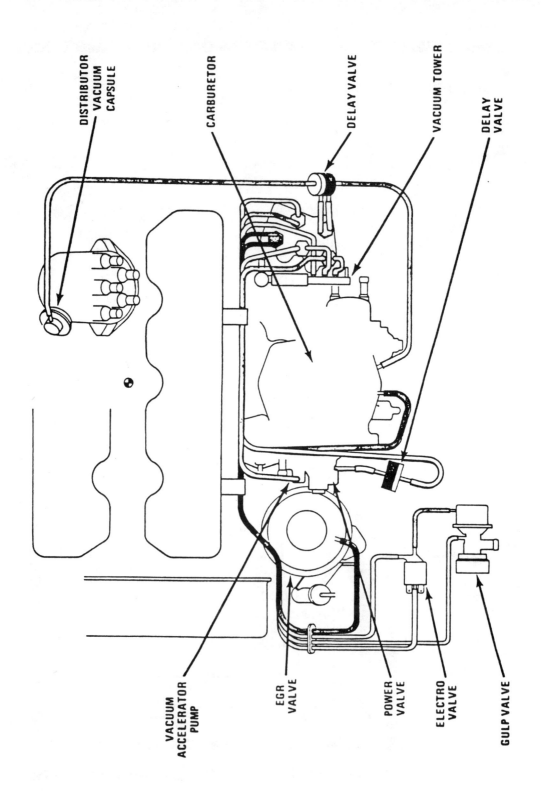

DISTRIBUTOR VACUUM CAPSULE

CARBURETOR

DELAY VALVE

VACUUM TOWER

DELAY VALVE

VACUUM ACCELERATOR PUMP

EGR VALVE

POWER VALVE

ELECTRO VALVE

GULP VALVE

**FIAT SPIDER 2000—CARBURETED ENGINE**

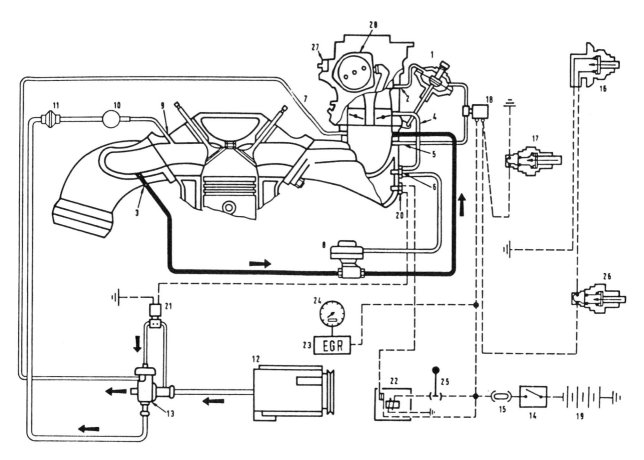

1. Fast idle capsule
2. Continuity hole
3. Exhaust gas recirculation intake
4. EGR valve control vacuum intake
5. Fast idle valve control vacuum intake
6. EGR valve control thermovalve
7. Diverter valve control vacuum intake
8. EGR valve
9. Air injector
10. Air injection manifold
11. Check valve
12. Air pump
13. Diverter valve
14. Ignition contact matched switch

15. Fuse
16. Switch contacts closed by transmission on 3rd-4th gear
17. Fast idle control switch
18. Electrovalve
19. Battery
20. Thermocouple
21. Electrovalve (to 1977 only)
22. Magnetic reversing switch
23. EGR system maintenance warning device*
24. Odometer*
25. Gearshift lever (switch open with transmission in neutral)
26. Switch closed when clutch is engaged
27. Idle stop solenoid
28. Automatic choke system

**FIAT SPIDER 2000—WO/CATALYTIC CONVERTER**

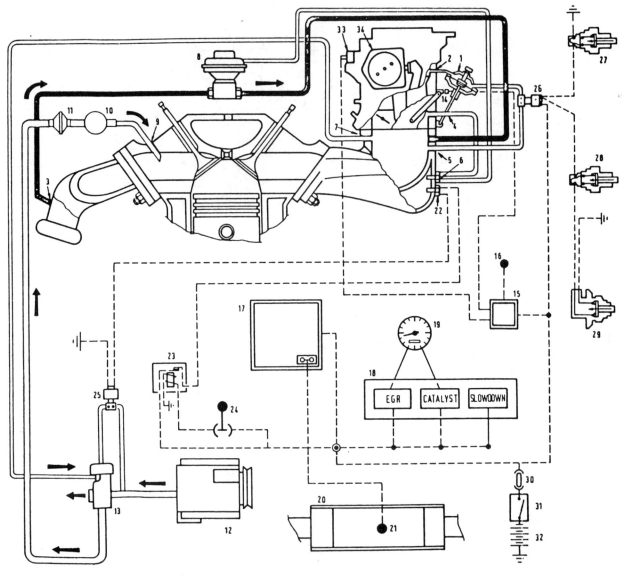

1. Fast idle capsule
2. Continuity hole
3. Exhaust gas recirculation intake
4. EGR valve control vacuum intake
5. Fast idle valve control vacuum intake
6. EGR valve control thermovalve
7. Diverter valve control vacuum intake
8. EGR valve
9. Air injector
10. Air injection manifold

11. Check valve
12. Air injection pump
13. Diverter valve
14. Inhibitor switch
15. Tachymetric switch (operates at 2650 ± 50 rpm)
16. From ignition coil
17. Control unit
18. Warning device panel*

19. Odometer*
20. Catalytic converter
21. Thermocouple
22. Thermoswitch
23. Magnetic reversing switch
24. Gearshift lever (switch open with transmission in neutral)
25. Electrovalve (normally closed)
26. Electrovalve

27. Fast idle control switch
28. Switch closed when clutch is engaged
29. Switch contacts closed by transmission on 3rd-4th gear
30. Fuse
31. Ignition contact matched switch
32. Battery
33. Idle stop solenoid
34. Automatic choke system

*The maintenance reminder system is no longer necessary. If servicing is required, the system should be eliminated.

**FIAT SPIDER 2000—W/CATALYTIC CONVERTER**

# FIESTA

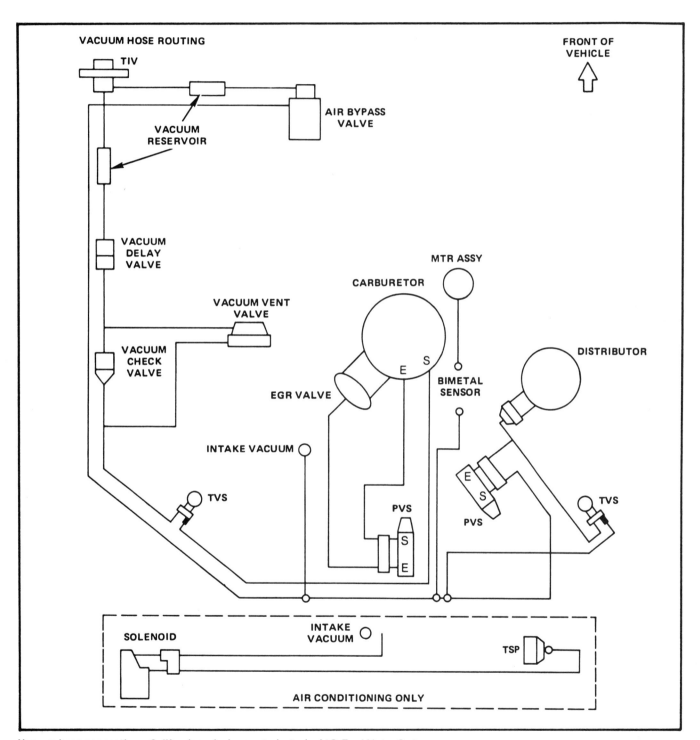

Vacuum hose connections, California emission controls, typical (© Ford Motor Co.)

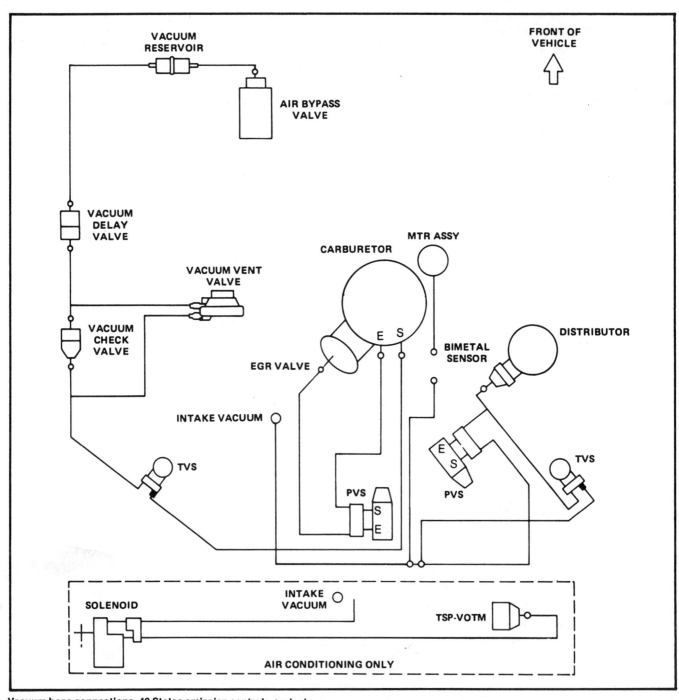

FRONT OF VEHICLE

VACUUM RESERVOIR

AIR BYPASS VALVE

VACUUM DELAY VALVE

VACUUM VENT VALVE

VACUUM CHECK VALVE

CARBURETOR

MTR ASSY

E S

BIMETAL SENSOR

DISTRIBUTOR

EGR VALVE

INTAKE VACUUM

TVS

PVS

S
E

E
S

PVS

TVS

SOLENOID

INTAKE VACUUM

TSP-VOTM

AIR CONDITIONING ONLY

**Vacuum hose connections, 49 States emission controls, typical**
(© Ford Motor Co.)

# Honda

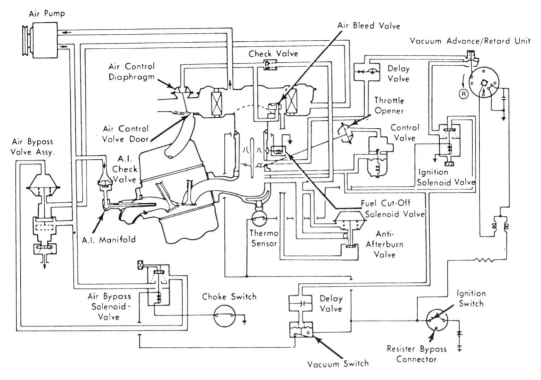

Civic 1200 with manual transmission—1979 model shown

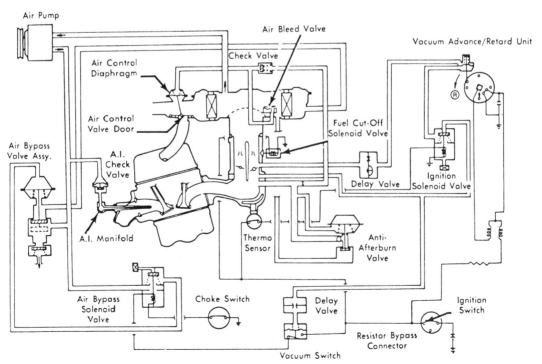

Civic 1200 with automatic transmission—1979 model shown

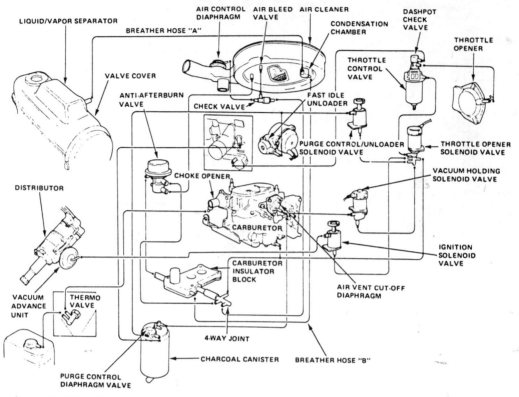

Civic 1300 CVCC 49 states—typical

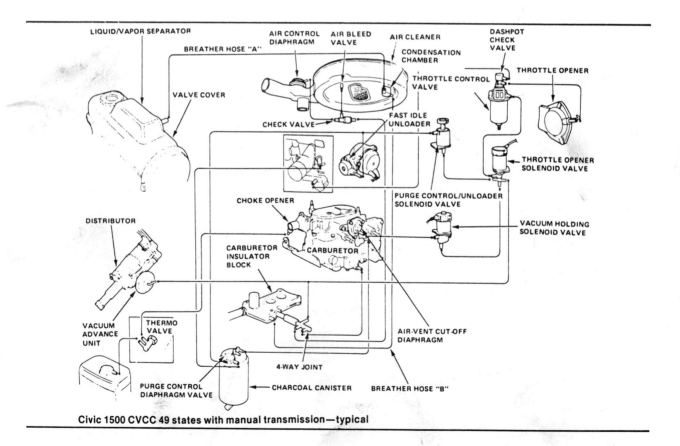

Civic 1500 CVCC 49 states with manual transmission—typical

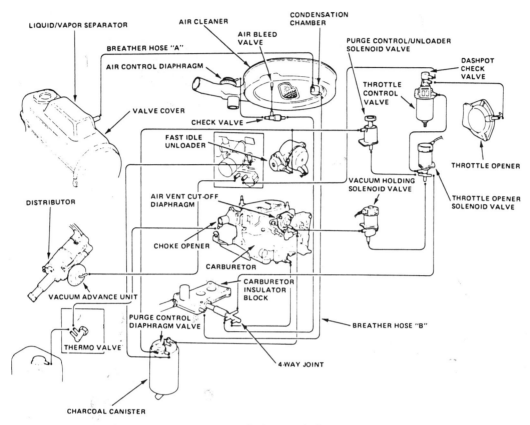

**Civic 1500 CVCC 49 states with automatic transmission—typical**

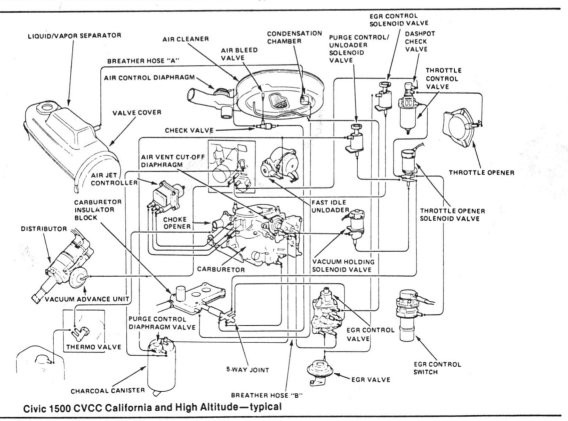

**Civic 1500 CVCC California and High Altitude—typical**

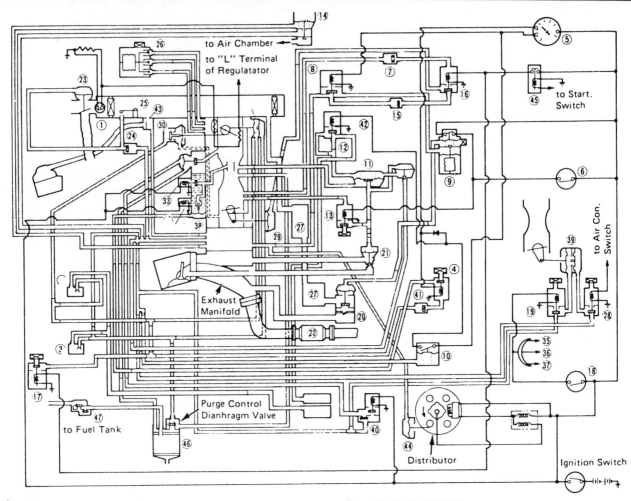

to Air Chamber
to "L" Terminal of Regulatator

to Start. Switch

to Air Con. Switch

Exhaust Manifold

Purge Control Dianhragm Valve

to Fuel Tank

Distributor

Ignition Switch

| | | | |
|---|---|---|---|
| ① | INTAKE AIR TEMP. SENSOR | ㉕ | AIR BLEED VALVE |
| ② | THERMOVALVE A | ㉖ | AIR JET CONTROLLER (CAL AND HI ALT ONLY) |
| ③ | THERMOVALVE B | ㉗ | AIR CHAMBERS A AND B |
| ④ | PJ CUT SOLENOID VALVE | ㉘ | IDLE CONTROL SOLENOID VALVE B |
| ⑤ | SPEED SENSOR | | (CAR WITH AIR CONDITIONER ONLY) |
| ⑥ | THERMOSENSOR A | ㉙ | THROTTLE CONTROLLER |
| ⑦ | DASHPOT CHECK VALVE | ㉚ | CHOKE OPENER |
| | (EXCEPT 1300 49 ST 5-SPEED) | ㉛ | FAST IDLE UNLOADER |
| ⑧ | CONTROL SWITCH SOLENOID VALVE | ㉜ | AIR VENT CUT-OFF DIAPHRAGM |
| ⑨ | CONTROL SWITCH | ㉝ | PRIMARY MAIN FUEL CUT-OFF SOLENOID VALVE |
| ⑩ | VACUUM SWITCH | ㉞ | PRIMARY SLOW MIXTURE CUT-OFF SOLENOID |
| ⑪ | EGR CONTROL VALVE A AND B | | VALVE |
| ⑫ | EGR CONTROL SOLENOID VALVE B | ㉟ | REAR WINDOW DEFROSTER SWITCH |
| ⑬ | EGR CONTROL SOLENOID VALVE A | | (MANUAL TRANSMISSION ONLY) |
| ⑭ | ANTI-AFTERBURN VALVE | ㊱ | HEATER BLOWER SWITCH |
| ⑮ | THROTTLE CONTROLLER CHECK VALVE | | (MANUAL TRANSMISSION ONLY) |
| ⑯ | CRANKING SOLENOID VALVE | ㊲ | HEADLIGHT SWITCH (MANUAL TRANSMISSION |
| ⑰ | CRANKING LEAK SOLENOID VALVE | | ONLY) |
| ⑱ | THERMOSENSOR B | ㊳ | POWER VALVE |
| | (MANUAL TRANSMISSION ONLY) | ㊴ | IDLE CONTROLLER |
| ⑲ | IDLE CONTROL SOLENOID VALVE A | ㊵ | VACUUM HOLDING SOLENOID VALVE |
| | (MANUAL TRANSMISSION ONLY) | ㊶ | POWER VALVE CHECK VALVE |
| ⑳ | AIR SUCTION VALVE AND AIR SUCTION | ㊷ | EGR AIR FILTER |
| | CUT-OFF DIAPHRAGM VALVE | ㊸ | CONDENSATION CHAMBER |
| ㉑ | EGR VALVE | ㊹ | DISTRIBUTOR VACUUM ADVANCE |
| ㉒ | CATALYTIC CONVERTER | ㊺ | STARTER RELAY |
| ㉓ | INTAKE AIR CONTROL DIAPHRAGM | ㊻ | CANISTER |
| ㉔ | CHECK VALVE FOR INTAKE AIR TEMPERATURE | ㊼ | TWO-WAY VALVE |
| | CONTROL | | |

1982 Civic—all models

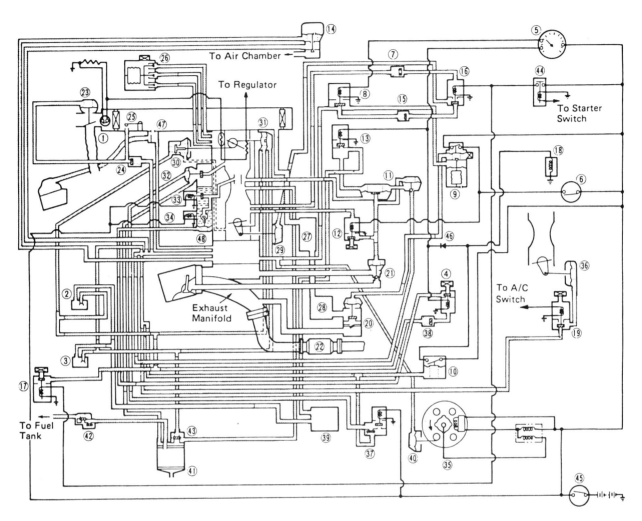

To Air Chamber

To Regulator

To Starter
Switch

To A/C
Switch

Exhaust
Manifold

To Fuel
Tank

| | | | |
|---|---|---|---|
| ① | INTAKE AIR TEMPERATURE SENSOR | ㉕ | AIR BLEED VALVE |
| ② | THERMOVALVE A | ㉖ | AIR JET CONTROLLER (CAL AND HI ALT ONLY) |
| ③ | THERMOVALVE B | ㉗ | AIR CHAMBERS A |
| ④ | POWER VALVE CONTROL SOLENOID VALVE | ㉘ | AIR CHAMBER B |
| ⑤ | SPEED SENSOR | ㉙ | THROTTLE CONTROLLER |
| ⑥ | THERMOSENSOR | ㉚ | CHOKE OPENER |
| ⑦ | DASHPOT CHECK VALVE | ㉛ | FAST IDLE UNLOADER |
| ⑧ | CONTROL SWITCH SOLENOID VALVE | ㉜ | AIR VENT CUT-OFF DIAPHRAGM |
| ⑨ | CONTROL SWITCH | ㉝ | PRIMARY MAIN FUEL CUT-OFF SOLENOID VALVE |
| ⑩ | VACUUM SWITCH | ㉞ | PRIMARY SLOW MIXTURE CUT-OFF SOLENOID VALVE |
| ⑪ | EGR CONTROL VALVE A AND B | | |
| ⑫ | EGR CONTROL SOLENOID VALVE A | ㉟ | DISTRIBUTER |
| ⑬ | EGR CONTROL SOLENOID VALVE B | ㊱ | IDLE CONTROLLER (A/C) |
| ⑭ | ANTI-AFTERBURN VALVE | ㊲ | VACUUM HOLDING SOLENOID VALVE |
| ⑮ | THROTTLE CONTROLLER CHECK VALVE | ㊳ | POWER VALVE CHECK VALVE |
| ⑯ | CRANKING SOLENOID VALVE | ㊴ | AIR FILTER |
| ⑰ | CRANKING LEAK SOLENOID VALVE | ㊵ | DISTRIBUTOR VACUUM ADVANCE |
| ⑱ | AUXILIARY COIL | ㊶ | CANISTER |
| ⑲ | IDLE CONTROL SOLENOID VALVE (A/C) | ㊷ | TWO-WAY VALVE |
| ⑳ | AIR SUCTION VALVE AND AIR SUCTION CUT-OFF DIAPHRAGM VALVE | ㊸ | PURGE CONTROL DIAPHRAGM VALVE |
| | | ㊹ | STARTER RELAY |
| ㉑ | EGR VALVE | ㊺ | IGNITION SWITCH |
| ㉒ | CATALYTIC CONVERTER | ㊻ | DIODE |
| ㉓ | INTAKE AIR CONTROL DIAPHRAGM | ㊼ | CONDENSATION CHAMBER |
| ㉔ | CHECK VALVE FOR INTAKE AIR TEMPERATURE CONTROL | ㊽ | POWER VALVE |

**1982 Accord and Prelude—typical**

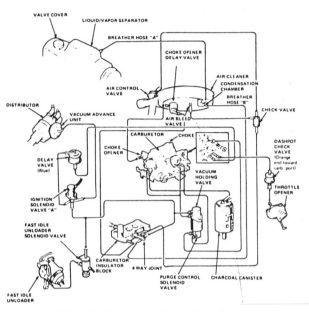

**Accord and Prelude 49 state versions—typical**

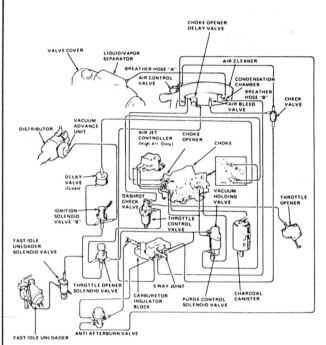

**Accord and Prelude California and High Altitude versions with manual transmission—typical**

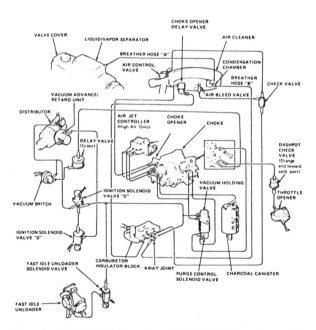

**Accord and Prelude California and High Altitude versions with automatic transmission—typical**

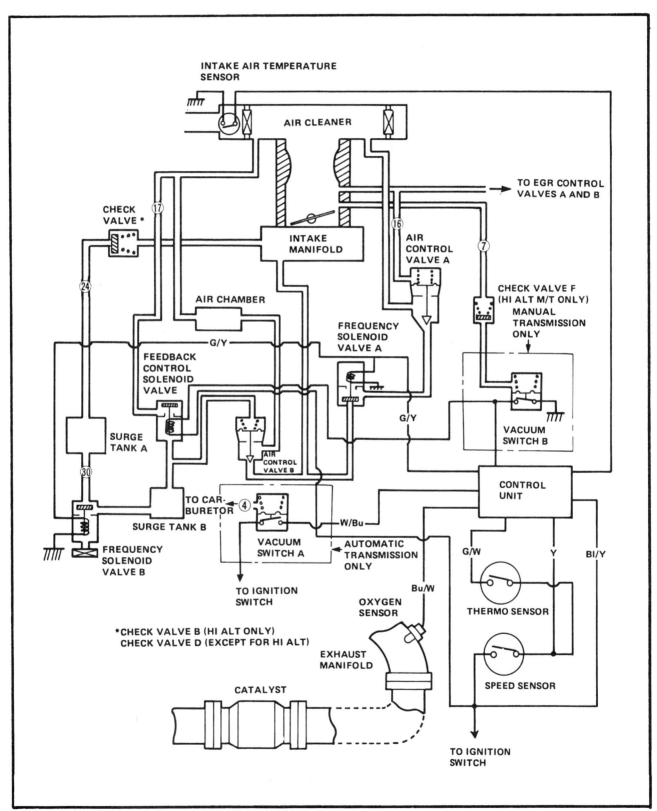

**Feedback control system schematic**

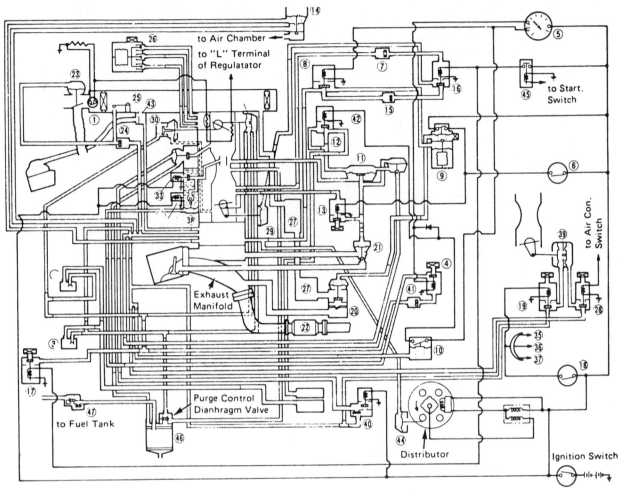

to Air Chamber

to "L" Terminal of Regulatator

to Start. Switch

to Air Con. Switch

Exhaust Manifold

Purge Control Dianhragm Valve

to Fuel Tank

Distributor

Ignition Switch

| | | |
|---|---|---|
| ① | INTAKE AIR TEMP. SENSOR | |
| ② | THERMOVALVE A | |
| ③ | THERMOVALVE B | |
| ④ | PJ CUT SOLENOID VALVE | |
| ⑤ | SPEED SENSOR | |
| ⑥ | THERMOSENSOR A | |
| ⑦ | DASHPOT CHECK VALVE (EXCEPT 1300 49 ST 5-SPEED) | |
| ⑧ | CONTROL SWITCH SOLENOID VALVE | |
| ⑨ | CONTROL SWITCH | |
| ⑩ | VACUUM SWITCH | |
| ⑪ | EGR CONTROL VALVE A AND B | |
| ⑫ | EGR CONTROL SOLENOID VALVE B | |
| ⑬ | EGR CONTROL SOLENOID VALVE A | |
| ⑭ | ANTI-AFTERBURN VALVE | |
| ⑮ | THROTTLE CONTROLLER CHECK VALVE | |
| ⑯ | CRANKING SOLENOID VALVE | |
| ⑰ | CRANKING LEAK SOLENOID VALVE | |
| ⑱ | THERMOSENSOR B (MANUAL TRANSMISSION ONLY) | |
| ⑲ | IDLE CONTROL SOLENOID VALVE A (MANUAL TRANSMISSION ONLY) | |
| ⑳ | AIR SUCTION VALVE AND AIR SUCTION CUT-OFF DIAPHRAGM VALVE | |
| ㉑ | EGR VALVE | |
| ㉒ | CATALYTIC CONVERTER | |
| ㉓ | INTAKE AIR CONTROL DIAPHRAGM | |
| ㉔ | CHECK VALVE FOR INTAKE AIR TEMPERATURE CONTROL | |

| | | |
|---|---|---|
| ㉕ | AIR BLEED VALVE | |
| ㉖ | AIR JET CONTROLLER (CAL AND HI ALT ONLY) | |
| ㉗ | AIR CHAMBERS A AND B | |
| ㉘ | IDLE CONTROL SOLENOID VALVE B (CAR WITH AIR CONDITIONER ONLY) | |
| ㉙ | THROTTLE CONTROLLER | |
| ㉚ | CHOKE OPENER | |
| ㉛ | FAST IDLE UNLOADER | |
| ㉜ | AIR VENT CUT-OFF DIAPHRAGM | |
| ㉝ | PRIMARY MAIN FUEL CUT-OFF SOLENOID VALVE | |
| ㉞ | PRIMARY SLOW MIXTURE CUT-OFF SOLENOID VALVE | |
| ㉟ | REAR WINDOW DEFROSTER SWITCH (MANUAL TRANSMISSION ONLY) | |
| ㊱ | HEATER BLOWER SWITCH (MANUAL TRANSMISSION ONLY) | |
| ㊲ | HEADLIGHT SWITCH (MANUAL TRANSMISSION ONLY) | |
| ㊳ | POWER VALVE | |
| ㊴ | IDLE CONTROLLER | |
| ㊵ | VACUUM HOLDING SOLENOID VALVE | |
| ㊶ | POWER VALVE CHECK VALVE | |
| ㊷ | EGR AIR FILTER | |
| ㊸ | CONDENSATION CHAMBER | |
| ㊹ | DISTRIBUTOR VACUUM ADVANCE | |
| ㊺ | STARTER RELAY | |
| ㊻ | CANISTER | |
| ㊼ | TWO-WAY VALVE | |

**1982 HONDA CIVIC**

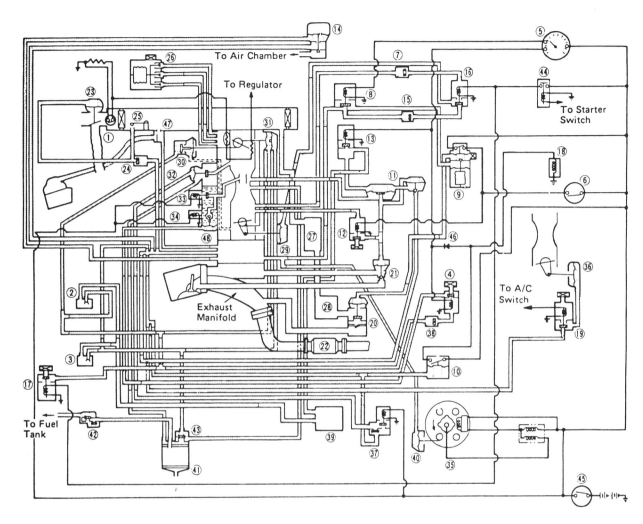

To Air Chamber

To Regulator

To Starter Switch

To A/C Switch

Exhaust Manifold

To Fuel Tank

| | | | |
|---|---|---|---|
| ① | INTAKE AIR TEMPERATURE SENSOR | ㉕ | AIR BLEED VALVE |
| ② | THERMOVALVE A | ㉖ | AIR JET CONTROLLER (CAL AND HI ALT ONLY) |
| ③ | THERMOVALVE B | ㉗ | AIR CHAMBERS A |
| ④ | POWER VALVE CONTROL SOLENOID VALVE | ㉘ | AIR CHAMBER B |
| ⑤ | SPEED SENSOR | ㉙ | THROTTLE CONTROLLER |
| ⑥ | THERMOSENSOR | ㉚ | CHOKE OPENER |
| ⑦ | DASHPOT CHECK VALVE | ㉛ | FAST IDLE UNLOADER |
| ⑧ | CONTROL SWITCH SOLENOID VALVE | ㉜ | AIR VENT CUT-OFF DIAPHRAGM |
| ⑨ | CONTROL SWITCH | ㉝ | PRIMARY MAIN FUEL CUT-OFF SOLENOID VALVE |
| ⑩ | VACUUM SWITCH | ㉞ | PRIMARY SLOW MIXTURE CUT-OFF SOLENOID |
| ⑪ | EGR CONTROL VALVE A AND B | | VALVE |
| ⑫ | EGR CONTROL SOLENOID VALVE A | ㉟ | DISTRIBUTER |
| ⑬ | EGR CONTROL SOLENOID VALVE B | ㊱ | IDLE CONTROLLER (A/C) |
| ⑭ | ANTI-AFTERBURN VALVE | ㊲ | VACUUM HOLDING SOLENOID VALVE |
| ⑮ | THROTTLE CONTROLLER CHECK VALVE | ㊳ | POWER VALVE CHECK VALVE |
| ⑯ | CRANKING SOLENOID VALVE | ㊴ | AIR FILTER |
| ⑰ | CRANKING LEAK SOLENOID VALVE | ㊵ | DISTRIBUTOR VACUUM ADVANCE |
| ⑱ | AUXILIARY COIL | ㊶ | CANISTER |
| ⑲ | IDLE CONTROL SOLENOID VALVE (A/C) | ㊷ | TWO-WAY VALVE |
| ⑳ | AIR SUCTION VALVE AND AIR SUCTION | ㊸ | PURGE CONTROL DIAPHRAGM VALVE |
| | CUT-OFF DIAPHRAGM VALVE | ㊹ | STARTER RELAY |
| ㉑ | EGR VALVE | ㊺ | IGNITION SWITCH |
| ㉒ | CATALYTIC CONVERTER | ㊻ | DIODE |
| ㉓ | INTAKE AIR CONTROL DIAPHRAGM | ㊼ | CONDENSATION CHAMBER |
| ㉔ | CHECK VALVE FOR INTAKE AIR TEMPERATURE | ㊽ | POWER VALVE |
| | CONTROL | | |

**1983 HONDA ACCORD**

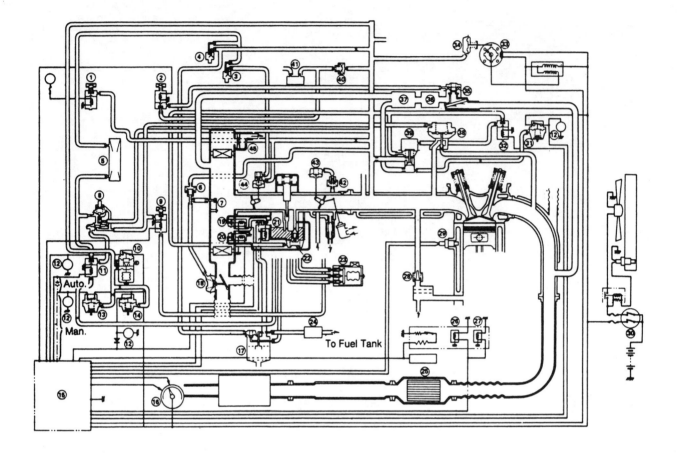

To Fuel Tank

Auto.

Man.

| | |
|---|---|
| 1. Cranking Leak Solenoid Valve | 24. 2-Way Valve |
| 2. Air Suction Control Solenoid Valve | 25. Catalytic Converter |
| 3. Thermovalve A | 26. Auxiliary Slow Mixture |
| 4. Thermovalve B | Cut-Off Solenoid Valve |
| 5. Air Filter | 27. Primary Slow Mixture |
| 6. Check Valve | Cut-Off Solenoid Valve |
| (Intake Air Control) | 28. PCV Valve |
| 7. Air Bleed Valve | 29. Thermister |
| 8. EGR Control Valves A & B | 30. Ignition Switch |
| 9. EGR Control Solenoid Valve A | 31. Vacuum Switch (Air Suction) |
| 10. Control Switch | 32. Anti-Afterburn Control |
| 11. EGR Control Solenoid Valve B | Solenoid Valve |
| 12. Auxiliary Coil | 33. Distributor |
| 13. Vacuum Switch A | 34. Distributor Vacuum Advance |
| (Manual: Main Air Jet) | 35. Air Suction Valve & Air |
| (Automatic: EGR) | Suction Cut-Off Diaphragm Valve |
| 14. Vacuum Switch B (Main Air Jet) | 36. Air Chamber "A" |
| (Federal & High Altitude) | 37. Air Chamber "B" |
| 15. Control Unit | 38. EGR Valve |
| 16. Speed Sensor | 39. Anti-Afterburn Valve |
| 17. Canister | 40. Check Valve |
| 18. Intake Air Control Diaphragm | 41. Vacuum Tank |
| 19. Inner Vent Solenoid Valve | 42. Dashpot Check Valve |
| 20. Main Air Jet Solenoid Valve | 43. Throttle Opener |
| 21. Air Vent Cut-Off Solenoid Valve | 44. Choke Opener |
| 22. Power Valve | 45. Blow-By Filter |
| 23. Air Jet Controller | |
| (Calif. & High Altitude) | |

**1983 HONDA PRELUDE**

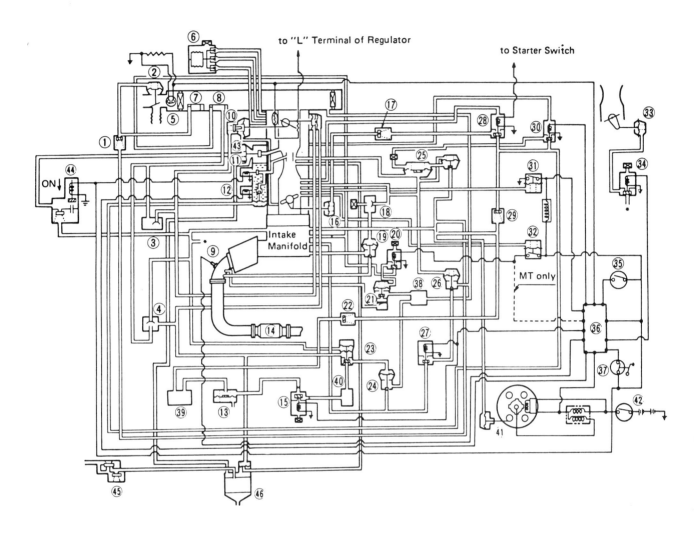

to "L" Terminal of Regulator

to Starter Switch

Intake Manifold

ON

MT only

① CHECK VALVE (INTAKE AIR TEMP.)
② AIR CONTROL DIAPHRAGM
③ THERMOVALVE B
④ THERMOVALVE A
⑤ INTAKE AIR TEMPERATURE SENSOR
⑥ AIR JET CONTROLLER (CAL AND HI ALT ONLY)
⑦ AIR BLEED VALVE
⑧ AIR BLEED VALVE A
⑨ OXYGEN SENSOR
⑩ CHOKE OPENER
⑪ PRIMARY MAIN FUEL CUT-OFF SOLENOID VALVE
⑫ PRIMARY SLOW MIXTURE CUT-OFF SOLENOID VALVE
⑬ CONSTANT VACUUM VALVE
⑭ CATALYTIC CONVERTER
⑮ FREQUENCY SOLENOID VALVE B
⑯ THROTTLE CONTROLLER
⑰ DASHPOT CHECK VALVE
⑱ THERMOVALVE C
⑲ EGR VALVE
⑳ AIR SUCTION CONTROL SOLENOID VALVE
㉑ AIR SUCTION VALVE
㉒ CHECK VALVE B
㉓ VACUUM CONTROL VALVE

㉔ AIR CONTROL VALVE B
㉕ EGR CONTROL VALVES A AND B
㉖ AIR CONTROL VALVE A
㉗ FREQUENCY SOLENOID VALVE A
㉘ CRANKING OPENER SOLENOID VALVE
㉙ CHECK VALVE A
㉚ POWER VALVE CONTROL SOLENOID VALVE
㉛ VACUUM SWITCH A
㉜ VACUUM SWITCH B
㉝ IDLE CONTROLLER
㉞ IDLE CONTROL SOLENOID VALVE
㉟ SPEED SENSOR
㊱ CONTROL UNIT
㊲ CLUTCH SWITCH FOR MANUAL NEUTRAL SWITCH FOR AUTOMATIC
㊳ AIR CHAMBER
㊴ SURGE TANK A
㊵ SURGE TANK B
㊶ DISTRIBUTOR
㊷ IGNITION SWITCH
㊸ AIR VENT CUT OFF DIAPHRAGM
㊹ VACUUM HOLDING SOLENOID VALVE
㊺ TWO-WAY VALVE
㊻ CHARCOAL CANISTER

**1984 HONDA ACCORD**

## 1300 4-SPEED

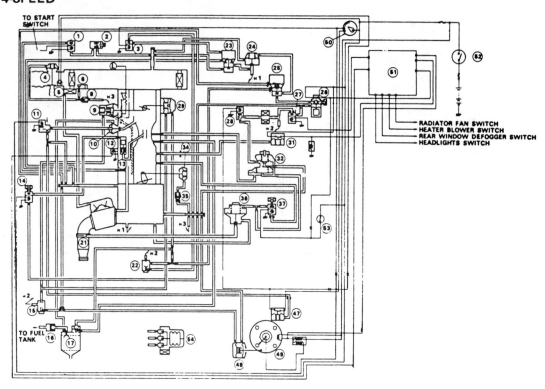

RADIATOR FAN SWITCH
HEATER BLOWER SWITCH
REAR WINDOW DEFOGGER SWITCH
HEADLIGHTS SWITCH

## 1300 5-SPEED

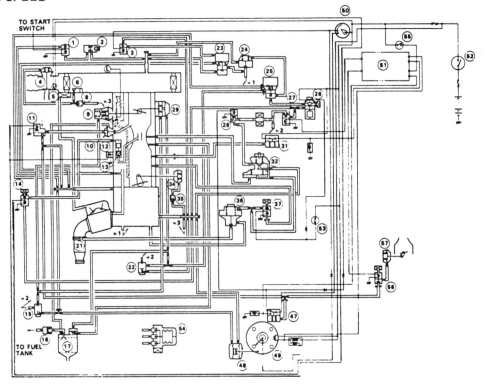

**1984 HONDA CIVIC**

## 1500

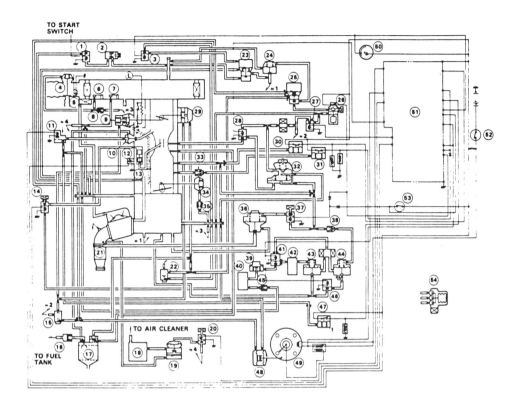

| | | | |
|---|---|---|---|
| ① | CRANKING SOLENOID VALVE | ㉘ | EGR CONTROL SOLENOID VALVE B |
| ② | THERMOVALVE C | ㉙ | FAST IDLE UNLOADER |
| ③ | ANTI-AFTERBURN CONTROL SOLENOID VALVE | ㉚ | VACUUM SWITCH C (1500 ONLY) |
| ④ | INTAKE AIR CONTROL DIAPHRAGM | ㉛ | VACUUM SWITCH B |
| ⑤ | INTAKE AIR TEMP. SENSOR | ㉜ | EGR CONTROL VALVE A & B |
| ⑥ | AIR BLEED VALVE A | ㉝ | CHECK VALVE C (1500 ONLY) |
| ⑦ | AIR BLEED VALVE B (1500 ONLY) | ㉞ | THROTTLE CONTROLLER |
| ⑧ | CHECK VALVE (INTAKE AIR TEMP. CONTROL) | ㉟ | DASHPOT CHECK VALVE |
| ⑨ | CHOKE OPENER | ㊱ | EGR VALVE |
| ⑩ | AIR CUT-OFF DIAPHRAGM | ㊲ | EGR CONTROL SOLENOID VALVE A |
| ⑪ | VACUUM HOLDING SOLENOID VALVE | ㊳ | CHECK VALVE A (1500 ONLY) |
| ⑫ | PRIMARY SLOW MIXTURE CUT-OFF SOLENOID | ㊴ | CONSTANT VACUUM VALVE (1500 ONLY) |
| ⑬ | POWER VALVE | ㊵ | SURGE TANK A (1500 ONLY) |
| ⑭ | POWER VALVE CONTROL SOLENOID VALVE | ㊶ | FREQUENCY SOLENOID VALVE B (1500 ONLY) |
| ⑮ | THERMOVALVE B | ㊷ | SURGE TANK B (1500 ONLY) |
| ⑯ | TWO—WAY VALVE | ㊸ | AIR CONTROL VALVE B (1500 ONLY) |
| ⑰ | CANISTER | ㊹ | AIR CONTROL VALVE A (1500 ONLY) |
| ⑱ | AIR CHAMBER (1500 ONLY) | ㊺ | CHECK VALVE B (1500 ONLY) |
| ⑲ | AIR SUCTION VALVE (1500 ONLY) | ㊻ | FREQUENCY SOLENOID VALVE A (1500 ONLY) |
| ⑳ | AIR SUCTION CONTROL SOLENOID VALVE (1500 ONLY) | ㊼ | VACUUM SWITCH A |
| ㉑ | CATALYTIC CONVERTER | ㊽ | DISTRIBUTOR VACUUM ADVANCE |
| ㉒ | THERMOVALVE A (except for HIALT and CAL 1500 automatic) THERMOVALVE D (HI ALT and CAL 1500 automatic) | ㊾ | DISTRIBUTOR |
| | | ㊿ | SPEED SENSOR |
| | | (51) | CONTROL UNIT |
| ㉓ | ANTI-AFTERBURN VALVE | �52 | IGNITION SWITCH |
| ㉔ | AIR VALVE | �53 | THERMO SENSOR |
| ㉕ | VACUUM CONTROL VALVE (HI ALT and CAL 1500 automatic) | �54 | AIR JET CONTROLLER (CAL and HI ALT) |
| | | �55 | CLUTCH SWITCH (1300 5-SPEED ONLY) |
| ㉖ | CONTROL SWITCH | �56 | THROTTLE CONTROL SOLENOID VALVE (1300 5-SPEED ONLY) |
| ㉗ | AIR CONTROL SOLENOID VALVE (MANUAL TRANSMISSION ONLY) | �57 | THROTTLE CLOSER (1300 5-SPEED ONLY) |

**1984 HONDA CIVIC**

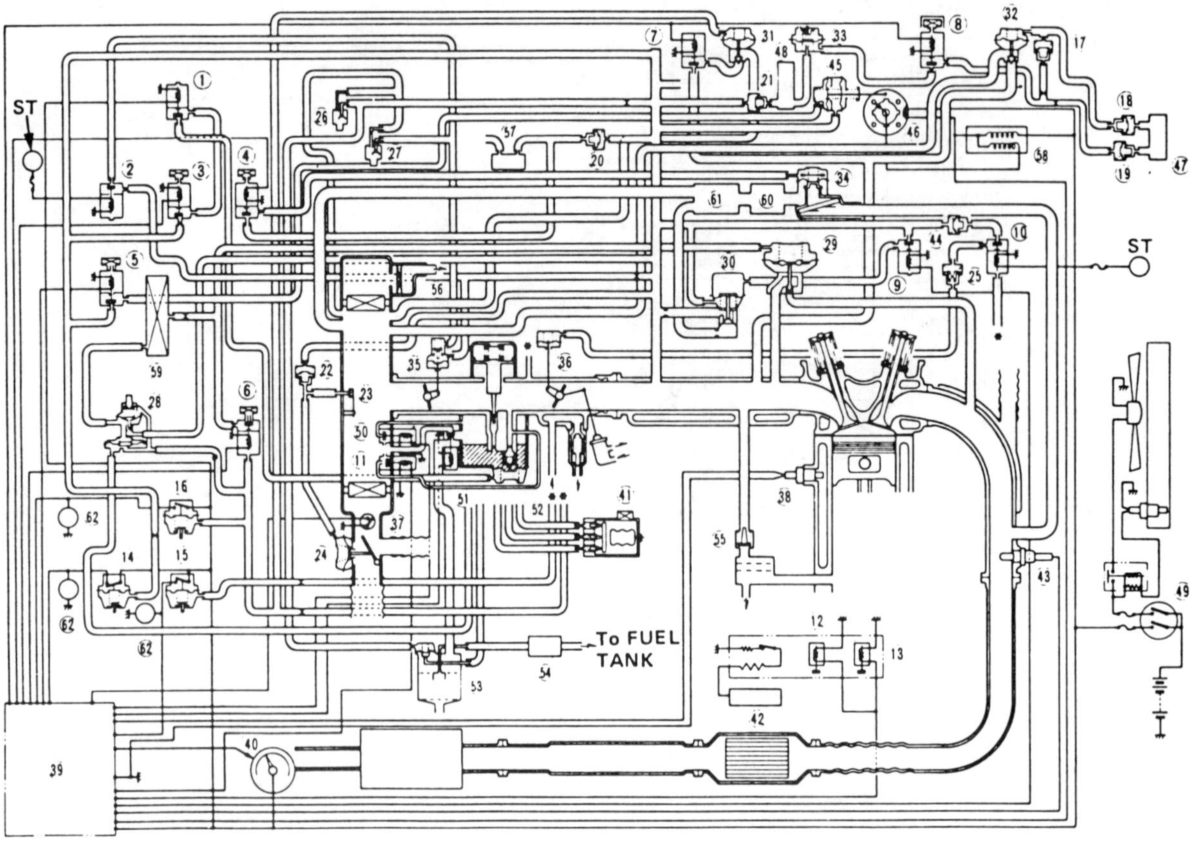
ST
ST
To FUEL
TANK

① POWER VALVE LOCK SOLENOID VALVE
② CRANKING LEAK SOLENOID VALVE
③ POWER VALVE CONTROL SOLENOID VALVE
④ AIR SUCTION CONTROL SOLENOID VALVE
⑤ VACUUM CONTROL SOLENOID VALVE
⑥ EGR CONTROL SOLENOID VALVE A
⑦ FREQUENCY SOLENOID VALVE A
⑧ FREQUENCY SOLENOID VALVE B
⑨ ANTI-AFTERBURN CONTROL SOLENOID VALVE
⑩ CRANKING OPENER SOLENOID VALVE
⑪ MAIN AIR JET CONTROL SOLENOID VALVE
⑫ RIGHT PRIMARY SLOW MIXTURE CUT-OFF SOLENOID VALVE
⑬ LEFT PRIMARY SLOW MIXTURE CUT-OFF SOLENOID VALVE
⑭ VACUUM SWITCH A
⑮ VACUUM SWITCH B
⑯ VACUUM SWITCH C
⑰ CHECK VALVE A
⑱ CHECK VALVE B
⑲ CHECK VALVE C
⑳ CHECK VALVE F
㉑ CHECK VALVE E
㉒ CHECK VALVE (INTAKE AIR TEMP.)
㉓ AIR BLEED VALVE
㉔ INTAKE AIR CONTROL DIAPHRAGM
㉕ DASHPOT CHECK VALVE
㉖ THERMOVALVE B
㉗ THERMOVALVE A
㉘ EGR CONTROL VALVES A & B
㉙ EGR VALVE
㉚ ANTI-AFTERBURN VALVE
㉛ AIR CONTROL VALVE A
㉜ AIR CONTROL VALVE B
㉝ CONSTANT VACUUM VALVE
㉞ AIR SUCTION VALVE
㉟ CHOKE OPENER
㊱ THROTTLE CONTROLLER
㊲ INTAKE AIR TEMPERATURE SWITCH
㊳ THERMOSENSOR
㊴ CONTROL UNIT
㊵ SPEED SENSOR
㊶ AIR JET CONTROLLER
㊷ CATALYTIC CONVERTER
㊸ OXYGEN SENSOR
㊹ CHECK VALVE D
㊺ DISTRIBUTOR VACUUM ADVANCE
㊻ DISTRIBUTOR
㊼ SURGE TANK A
㊽ SURGE TANK B
㊾ IGNITION SWITCH
㊿ INNER VENT SOLENOID VALVE
(51) AIR VENT CUT-OFF SOLENOID VALVE
(52) POWER VALVE
(53) CANISTER
(54) TWO-WAY VALVE
(55) PCV VALVE
(56) BLOW-BY FILTER
(57) VACUUM TANK
(58) IGNITION COIL
(59) AIR FILTER
(60) AIR CHAMBER A
(61) AIR CHAMBER B
(62) AUXILIARY COIL

1984 HONDA PRELUDE

## 1300

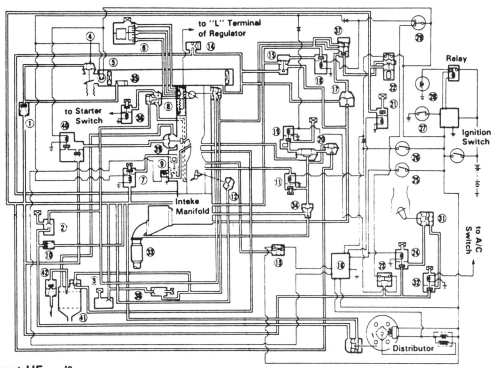

## 1500 except HF

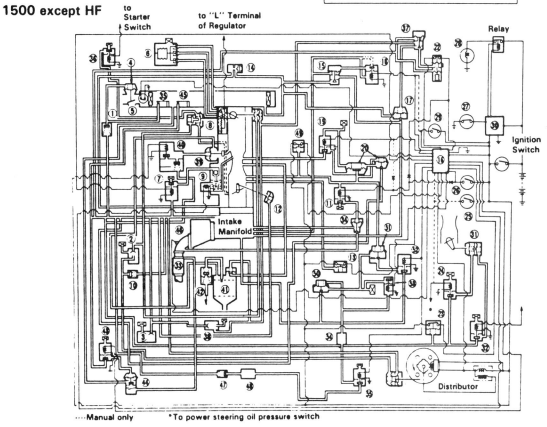

·····Manual only    *To power steering oil pressure switch

**Vacuum and electrical connections–1985 Civic**

**49 ST 1500HF**

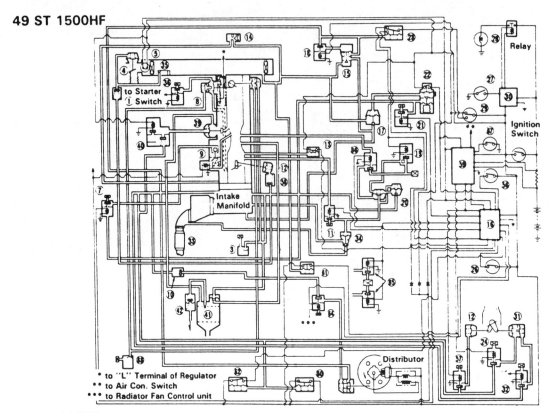

to Starter
Switch

Intake
Manifold

Relay

Ignition
Switch

Distributor

\* to "L" Terminal of Regulator
\*\* to Air Con. Switch
\*\*\* to Radiator Fan Control unit

**CAL 1500HF**

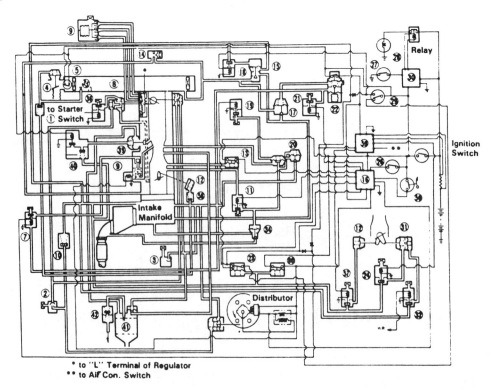

to Starter
Switch

Intake
Manifold

Relay

Ignition
Switch

Distributor

\* to "L" Terminal of Regulator
\*\* to Air Con. Switch

**Vacuum and electrical connections — 1985 Civic**

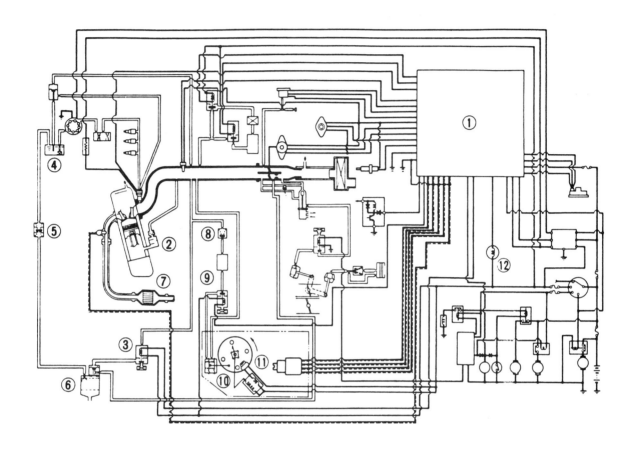

① ELECTRONIC CONTROL UNIT
② PCV VALVE
③ PURGE CUT-OFF SOLENOID VALVE
④ FUEL TANK
⑤ TWO-WAY VALVE
⑥ CHARCOAL CANISTER
⑦ CATALYTIC CONVERTER
⑧ CHECK VALVE
⑨ COLD ADVANCE SOLENOID VALVE
⑩ VACUUM CONTROLLER
⑪ DISTRIBUTOR
⑫ PGM-FI WARNING LIGHT

**Vacuum and electrical connections – 1985 Civic CRX Si**

### HI ALT 1500HF

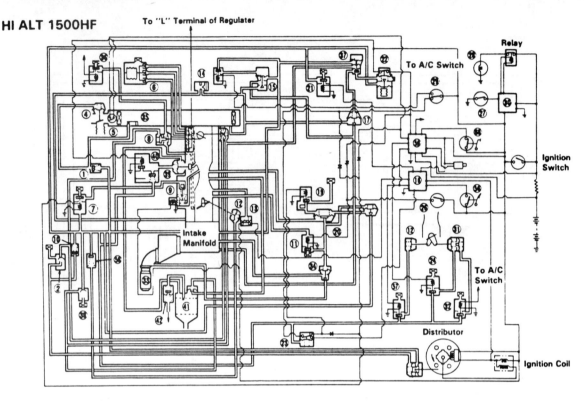

To "L" Terminal of Regulator

Relay

To A/C Switch

Ignition Switch

Intake Manifold

To A/C Switch

Distributor

Ignition Coil

| | | | | |
|---|---|---|---|---|
| ① | CHECK VALVE (INTAKE AIR TEMP. CONTROL) | ㉟ | AIR BLEED VALVE A |
| ② | THERMOVALVE B (Except 49 ST 1500HF) | ㊱ | CRANKING LEAK SOLENOID VALVE |
| ③ | THERMOVALVE A (Except HI ALT 1300/1500HF and 49 ST/HI ALT 1500 Manual except HF) | ㊲ | VACUUM CONTROL VALVE (HT ALT 1300/1500HF and 49 ST/HI ALT 1500 Manual except HF) |
| ④ | AIR CONTROL DIAPHRAGM | ㊳ | THERMOVALVE D (HT ALT 1300/1500HF and 49 ST/ HI ALT 1500 Manual except HF) |
| ⑤ | INTAKE AIR TEMP. SENSOR | ㊴ | AIR VENT CUT-OFF DIAPHRAGM |
| ⑥ | AIR JET CONTROLLER (Except 49 ST 1300/1500HF) | ㊵ | VACUUM HOLDING SOLENOID VALVE |
| ⑦ | POWER VALVE CONTROL SOLENOID VALVE | ㊶ | CHARCOAL CANISTER |
| ⑧ | CHOKE OPENER | ㊷ | TWO-WAY VALVE |
| ⑨ | PRIMARY SLOW MIXTURE CUT-OFF SOLENOID VALVE | ㊸ | *AIR SUCTION CONTROL SOLENOID VALVE |
| ⑩ | CHECK VALVE E | ㊹ | *AIR CONTROL VALVE |
| 11 | EGR CONTROL SOLENOID VALVE A | ㊺ | *AIR BLEED VALVE B |
| 12 | THROTTLE CONTROLLER | ㊻ | *OXYGEN SENSOR |
| 13 | VACUUM SWITCH A | ㊼ | *CHECK VALVE B |
| 14 | THERMOVALVE C | ㊽ | *SURGE TANK A |
| 15 | ANTI-AFTERBURN VALVE | ㊾ | *VACUUM SWITCH C |
| 16 | CONTROL UNIT | ㊿ | *AIR CONTROL VALVE B |
| 17 | AIR VALVE | ⑤ | *AIR CONTROL VALVE A |
| 18 | ANTI-AFTERBURN CONTROL SOLENOID VALVE | ⑤ | *FREQUENCY SOLENOID VALVE A |
| 19 | EGR CONTROL SOLENOID VALVE B (Except 1500 Manual except HF) | ⑤ | *FEEDBACK CONTROL SOLENOID VALVE |
| 20 | EGR CONTROL VALVES A & B | ⑤ | *SURGE TANK B |
| 21 | AIR CONTROL SOLENOID VALVE (1300 and 1500HF) | ⑤ | *FREQUENCY SOLENOID VALVE B |
| 22 | CONTROL SWITCH | ⑤ | CLUTCH SWITCH (1500HF) |
| 23 | VACUUM SWITCH B | ⑤ | THROTTLE CONTROL SOLENOID VALVE (1500HF) |
| 24 | IDLE BOOST SOLENOID VALVE (Except 1500 Automatic without power steering) | ⑤ | DASHPOT CHECK VALVE (1500HF) |
| 25 | THERMOSENSOR A (Except 1500HF and Automatic) | ⑤ | ALTERNATOR CONTROL UNIT (1500HF) |
| 26 | THERMOSENSOR B | ⑥ | VACUUM SWITCH D (49 ST/CAL 1500HF) |
| 27 | AIR TEMP. SENSOR | ⑥ | VACUUM SWITCH E (49 ST 1500HF) |
| 28 | RADIATOR FAN | ⑥ | VACUUM SWITCH F (49 ST 1500HF) |
| 29 | SPEED SENSOR | ⑥ | THERMOVALVE E (49 ST 1500HF) |
| 30 | RADIATOR FAN TIMER | ⑥ | COLD ADVANCE SOLENOID VALVE (49 ST 1500HF) |
| 31 | IDLE CONTROLLER | ⑥ | PRIMARY AIR CUT-OFF SOLENOID VALVE (49 ST 1500HF) |
| 32 | IDLE CONTROL SOLENOID VALVE | ⑥ | EGR CONTROL SOLENOID VALVE C (49 ST 1500HF) |
| 33 | CATALYTIC CONVERTER | ⑥ | STEERING SWITCH (49 ST 1500HF) |
| 34 | EGR VALVE | ⑥ | BRAKE SWITCH (HI ALT 1500HF) |
| | | | *1500 except HF |

**Vacuum and electrical connections–1985 Civic**

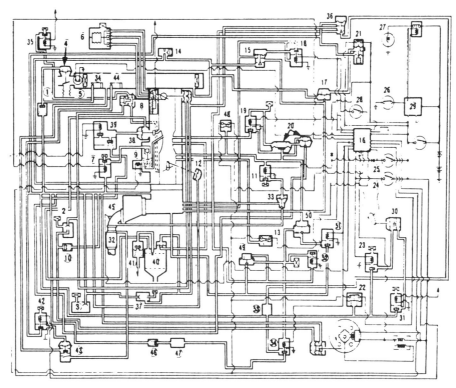

| | | | |
|---|---|---|---|
| ① | CHECK VALVE (INTAKE AIR TEMP. CONTROL) | ㉘ | SPEED SENSOR |
| ② | THERMOVALVE B | ㉙ | RADIATOR FAN TIMER |
| ③ | THERMOVALVE A | ㉚ | IDLE CONTROLLER |
| ④ | AIR CONTROL DIAPHRAGM | ㉛ | IDLE CONTROL SOLENOID VALVE |
| ⑤ | INTAKE AIR TEMP. SENSOR | ㉜ | CATALYTIC CONVERTER |
| ⑥ | AIR JET CONTROLLER | ㉝ | EGR VALVE |
| ⑦ | POWER VALVE CONTROL SOLENOID VALVE | ㉞ | AIR BLEED VALVE A |
| ⑧ | CHOKE OPENER | ㉟ | CRANKING LEAK SOLENOID VALVE |
| ⑨ | PRIMARY SLOW MIXTURE CUT-OFF SOLENOID VALVE | ㊱ | VACUUM CONTROL VALVE (49ST/HI ALT) |
| ⑩ | CHECK VALVE E | ㊲ | THERMOVALVE D (49ST/HI ALT) |
| ⑪ | EGR CONTROL SOLENOID VALVE A | ㊳ | AIR VENT CUT-OFF DIAPHRAGM |
| ⑫ | THROTTLE CONTROLLER | ㊴ | VACUUM HOLDING SOLENOID VALVE |
| ⑬ | VACUUM SWITCH A | ㊵ | CHARCOAL CANISTER |
| ⑭ | THERMOVALVE C | ㊶ | TWO-WAY VALVE |
| ⑮ | ANTI-AFTERBURN VALVE | ㊷ | AIR SUCTION CONTROL SOLENOID VALVE |
| ⑯ | CONTROL UNIT | ㊸ | AIR CONTROL VALVE |
| ⑰ | AIR VALVE | ㊹ | AIR BLEED VALVE B |
| ⑱ | ANTI-AFTERBURN CONTROL SOLENOID VALVE | ㊺ | OXYGEN SENSOR |
| ⑲ | EGR CONTROL SOLENOID VALVE C | ㊻ | CHECK VALVE B |
| ⑳ | EGR CONTROL VALVES A & B | ㊼ | SURGE TANK A |
| ㉑ | CONTROL SWITCH | ㊽ | VACUUM SWITCH C |
| ㉒ | VACUUM SWITCH B | ㊾ | AIR CONTROL VALVE B |
| ㉓ | IDLE BOOST SOLENOID VALVE | ㊿ | AIR CONTROL VALVE A |
| ㉔ | THERMOSENSOR A | ⑤① | FREQUENCY SOLENOID VALVE A |
| ㉕ | THERMOSENSOR B | ⑤② | FEEDBACK CONTROL SOLENOID VALVE |
| ㉖ | AIR TEMP. SENSOR | ⑤③ | SURGE TANK B |
| ㉗ | RADIATOR FAN | ⑤④ | FREQUENCY SOLENOID VALVE B |

**Vacuum and electrical connections – 1985 Civic Wagon 4WD**

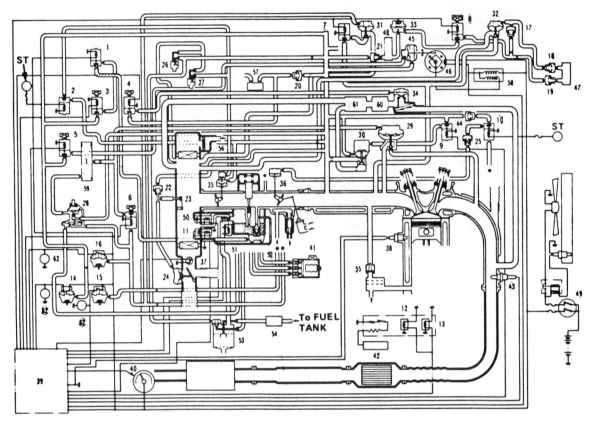

| | | | | |
|---|---|---|---|---|
| ① | POWER VALVE LOCK SOLENOID VALVE | ㉜ | AIR CONTROL VALVE B | |
| ② | CRANKING LEAK SOLENOID VALVE | ㉝ | CONSTANT VACUUM VALVE | |
| ③ | POWER VALVE CONTROL SOLENOID VALVE | ㉞ | AIR SUCTION VALVE | |
| ④ | AIR SUCTION SOLENOID VALVE | ㉟ | CHOKE OPENER | |
| ⑤ | VACUUM CONTROL SOLENOID VALVE | ㊱ | THROTTLE CONTROLLER | |
| ⑥ | EGR CONTROL SOLENOID VALVE A | ㊲ | INTAKE AIR TEMPERATURE SWITCH | |
| ⑦ | FREQUENCY SOLENOID VALVE A | ㊳ | THERMOSENSOR | |
| ⑧ | FREQUENCY SOLENOID VALVE B | ㊴ | CONTROL UNIT | |
| ⑨ | ANTI-AFTERBURN CONTROL SOLENOID VALVE | ㊵ | SPEED SENSOR | |
| ⑩ | CRANKING OPENER SOLENOID VALVE | ㊶ | AIR JET CONTROLLER | |
| ⑪ | MAIN AIR JET CONTROL SOLENOID VALVE | ㊷ | CATALYTIC CONVERTER | |
| ⑫ | RIGHT PRIMARY SLOW MIXTURE CUT-OFF | ㊸ | OXYGEN SENSOR | |
| | SOLENOID VALVE | ㊹ | CHECK VALVE D | |
| ⑬ | LEFT PRIMARY SLOW MIXTURE CUT-OFF | ㊺ | DISTRIBUTOR VACUUM ADVANCE | |
| | SOLENOID VALVE | ㊻ | DISTRIBUTOR | |
| ⑭ | VACUUM SWITCH A | ㊼ | SURGE TANK A | |
| ⑮ | VACUUM SWITCH B | ㊽ | SURGE TANK B | |
| ⑯ | VACUUM SWITCH C | ㊾ | IGNITION SWITCH | |
| ⑰ | CHECK VALVE A | ㊿ | INNER VENT SOLENOID VALVE | |
| ⑱ | CHECK VALVE B | 51 | AIR VENT CUT-OFF SOLENOID VALVE | |
| ⑲ | CHECK VALVE C | 52 | POWER VALVE | |
| ⑳ | CHECK VALVE F | 53 | CANISTER | |
| ㉑ | CHECK VALVE E | 54 | TWO-WAY VALVE | |
| ㉒ | CHECK VALVE (INTAKE AIR TEMP.) | 55 | PCV VALVE | |
| ㉓ | AIR BLEED VALVE | 56 | BLOW-BY FILTER | |
| ㉔ | INTAKE AIR CONTROL DIAPHRAGM | 57 | VACUUM TANK | |
| ㉕ | DASHPOT CHECK VALVE | 58 | IGNITION COIL | |
| ㉖ | THERMOVALVE B | 59 | AIR FILTER | |
| ㉗ | THERMOVALVE A | 60 | AIR CHAMBER A | |
| ㉘ | EGR CONTROL VALVES A & B | 61 | AIR CHAMBER B | |
| ㉙ | EGR VALVE | 62 | AUXILIARY COIL | |
| ㉚ | ANTI-AFTERBURN VALVE | | | |
| ㉛ | AIR CONTROL VALVE A | | | |

**Vacuum and electrical connections—1985 Prelude**

## 1300 (49ST and CAL)

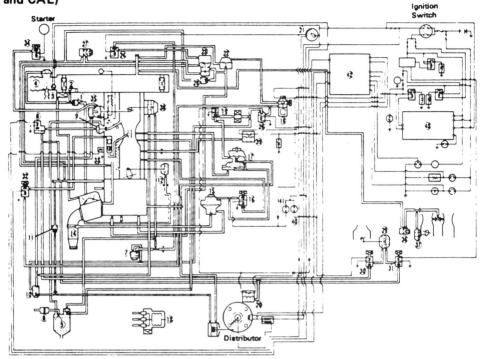

| | | | |
|---|---|---|---|
| ① | CHECK VALVE (INTAKE AIR TEMP.) | ㉓ | ANTI-AFTERBURN VALVE |
| ② | AIR BLEED VALVE | ㉔ | ANTI-AFTERBURN CONTROL SOLENOID VALVE |
| ③ | INTAKE AIR TEMP. SENSOR | ㉕ | VACUUM CONTROL VALVE (HI ALT) |
| ④ | AIR CONTROL DIAPHRAGM | ㉖ | AIR CONTROL SOLENOID VALVE |
| ⑤ | CHARCOAL CANISTER | ㉗ | THERMOVALVE C |
| ⑥ | TWO-WAY VALVE | ㉘ | CHECK VALVE G |
| ⑦ | THERMOVALVE A | ㉙ | IDLE CONTROLLER |
| ⑧ | VACUUM HOLDING SOLENOID VALVE | ㉚ | IDLE BOOST SOLENOID VALVE |
| ⑨ | AIR VENT CUT-OFF DIAPHRAGM | ㉛ | A/C IDLE BOOST SOLENOID VALVE |
| ⑩ | THERMOVALVE B | ㉜ | POWER VALVE CONTROL SOLENOID VALVE |
| ⑪ | CHECK VALVE E | ㉝ | PRIMARY SLOW MIXTURE CUT-OFF SOLENOID VALVE |
| ⑫ | THROTTLE CONTROLLER | ㉞ | CRANKING LEAK SOLENOID VALVE |
| ⑬ | AIR JET CONTROLLER (Except CAL) | ㉟ | CHOKE OPENER |
| ⑭ | CATALYTIC CONVERTER | ㊱ | THERMOVALVE D |
| ⑮ | EGR VALVE | ㊲ | SECONDARY DIAPHRAGM |
| ⑯ | EGR CONTROL SOLENOID VALVE A | ㊳ | FAST IDLE UNLOADER |
| ⑰ | EGR CONTROL VALVE A & B | ㊴ | VACUUM SWITCH A |
| ⑱ | CONTROL SWITCH | ㊵ | THERMOSENSOR A |
| ⑲ | EGR CONTROL SOLENOID VALVE B | ㊶ | THERMOSENSOR B |
| ⑳ | VACUUM SWITCH B | ㊷ | DEVICE CONTROL UNIT A |
| ㉑ | SPEED SENSOR | ㊸ | RADIATOR FAN TIMER |
| ㉒ | AIR VALVE | | |

**Vacuum and electrical connections – 1986 Civic**

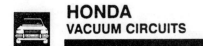

### 1500 M/T (49 ST / HI ALT)

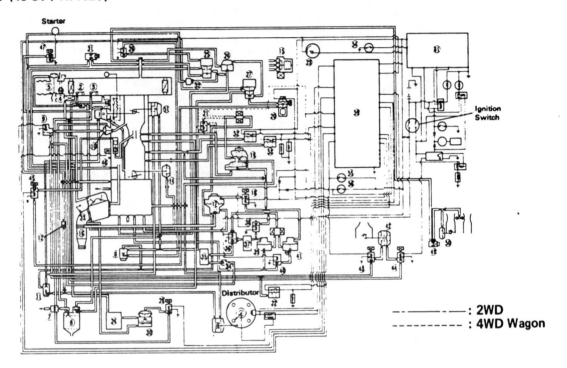

```
:2WD
:4WD Wagon
```

### 1500 M/T (CAL)

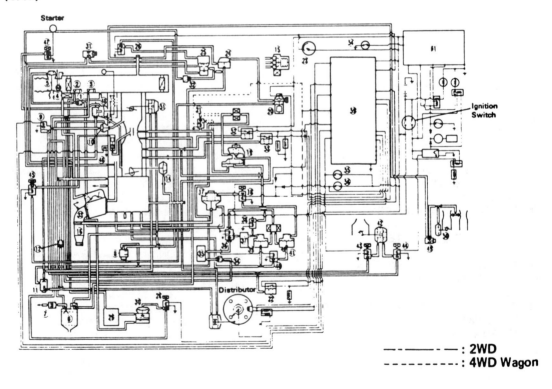

```
:2WD
:4WD Wagon
```

**Vacuum and electrical connections – 1986 Civic**

## 1500 A/T

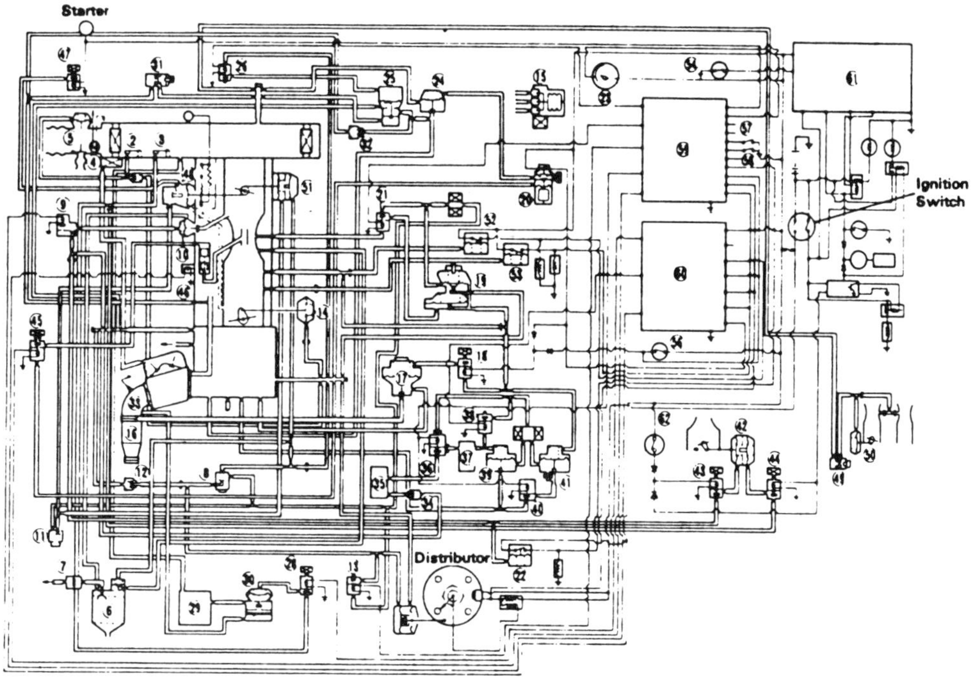


① CHECK VALVE (INTAKE AIR TEMP.)
② AIR BLEED VALVE A
③ AIR BLEED VALVE B
④ INTAKE AIR TEMP. SENSOR
⑤ AIR CONTROL DIAPHRAGM
⑥ CHARCOAL CANISTER
⑦ TWO-WAY VALVE
⑧ THERMOVALVE A
⑨ VACUUM HOLDING SOLENOID VALVE
⑩ AIR VENT CUT-OFF DIAPHRAGM
⑪ THERMOVALVE B
⑫ CHECK VALVE E
⑬ COLD ADVANCE SOLENOID VALVE (A/T)
⑭ THROTTLE CONTROLLER
⑮ AIR JET CONTROLLER
⑯ CATALYTIC CONVERTER
⑰ EGR VALVE
⑱ EGR CONTROL SOLENOID VALVE A
⑲ EGR CONTROL VALVE A & B
⑳ CONTROL SWITCH
㉑ EGR CONTROL SOLENOID VALVE C (A/T & 4WD)
㉒ VACUUM SWITCH B
㉓ SPEED SENSOR
㉔ AIR VALVE
㉕ ANTI-AFTERBURN VALVE
㉖ ANTI-AFTERBURN CONTROL SOLENOID VALVE
㉗ VACUUM CONTROL VALVE (49 ST-M/T)
㉘ AIR SUCTION CONTROL SOLENOID VALVE
㉙ SILENCER
㉚ AIR SUCTION VALVE
㉛ THERMOVALVE C
㉜ CHECK VALVE G
㉝ OXYGEN SENSOR
㉞ CHECK VALVE A
㉟ ACCUMULATOR
㊱ FREQUENCY SOLENOID VALVE B
㊲ PULSE RECTIFIER
㊳ FEEDBACK CONTROL SOLENOID VALVE
㊴ AIR CONTROL VALVE
㊵ FREQUENCY SOLENOID VALVE A
㊶ AIR CONTROL VALVE A
㊷ IDLE CONTROLLER
㊸ IDLE BOOST SOLENOID VALVE (M/T and A/T with power steering)
㊹ A/C IDLE BOOST SOLENOID VALVE
㊺ POWER VALVE CONTROL SOLENOID VALVE
㊻ PRIMARY SLOW MIXTURE CUT-OFF SOLENOID VALVE
㊼ CRANKING LEAK SOLENOID VALVE
㊽ CHOKE OPENER
㊾ THERMOVALVE D
㊿ SECONDARY DIAPHRAGM
(51) FAST IDLE UNLOADER
(52) VACUUM SWITCH C
(53) VACUUM SWITCH A
(54) AIR TEMP. SENSOR
(55) THERMOSNESOR A
(56) THERMOSENSOR B
(57) NEUTRAL SWITCH (A/T)
(58) PARKING SWITCH (A/T)
(59) DEVICE CONTROL UNIT A
(60) DEVICE CONTROL UNIT B (A/T)
(61) RADIATOR FAN TIMER
(62) POWER STEERING OIL PRESSURE SWITCH

Vacuum and electrical connections—1986 Civic

**HF (49 ST)**

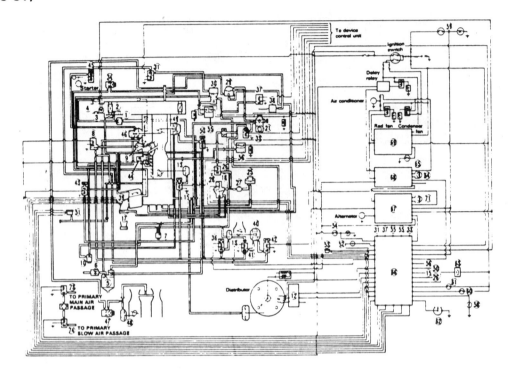

**HF (CAL)**

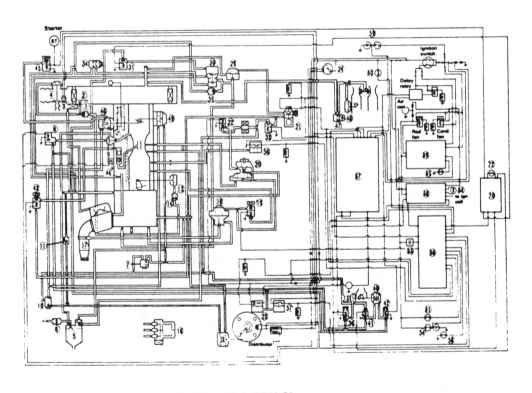

**Vacuum and electrical connections — 1986 Civic Si & CRX Si**

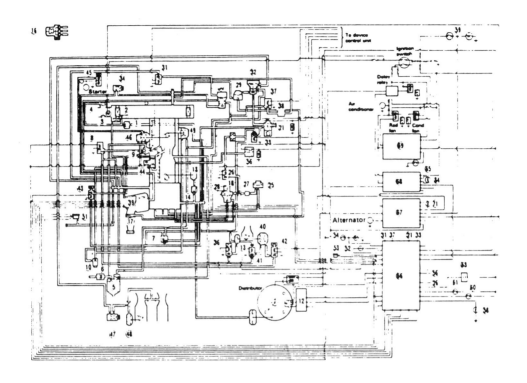

1. CHECK VALVE (INTAKE AIR TEMP.)
2. AIR BLEED VALVE
3. INTAKE AIR TEMP. SENSOR A
4. AIR CONTROL DIAPHRAGM
5. CHARCOAL CANISTER
6. TWO-WAY VALVE
7. THERMOVALVE A
8. VACUUM HOLDING SOLENOID VALVE
9. AIR VENT CUT-OFF DIAPHRAGM
10. THERMOVALVE B
11. CHECK VALVE E
12. IGNITION TIMING CONTROL UNIT (EXCEPT CAL)
13. THROTTLE CONTROLLER
14. DASHPOT CHECK VALVE (EXCEPT 49 ST)
15. DASHPOT CONTROL SOLENOID VALVE (49 ST)
16. AIR JET CONTROLLER (EXCEPT 49 ST)
17. CATALYTIC CONVERTER
18. EGR VALVE
19. EGR CONTROL SOLENOID VALVE A (CAL)
20. EGR CONTROL VALVES A & B (CAL)
21. CONTROL SWITCH
22. EGR CONTROL SOLENOID VALVE B (CAL)
23. VACUUM SWITCH F (CAL)
24. SPEED SENSOR (CAL)
25. CONSTANT VACUUM GENERATOR (EXCEPT CAL)
26. FREQUENCY SOLENOID VALVE B (EXCEPT CAL)
27. ACCUMULATOR (EXCEPT CAL)
28. EGR VALVE LIFT SENSOR (EXCEPT CAL)
29. AIR VALVE
30. ANTI-AFTERBURN VALVE
31. ANTI-AFTERBURN CONTROL SOLENOID VALVE
32. VACUUM CONTROL VALVE (HI ALT)
33. AIR CONTROL SOLENOID VALVE
34. THERMOVALVE C
35. CHECK VALVE G (CAL)
36. THROTTLE CONTROL SOLENOID VALVE
37. FREQUENCY SOLENOID VALVE A (EXCEPT CAL)
38. AIR CHAMBER (EXCEPT CAL)
39. OXYGEN SENSOR (EXCEPT CAL)
40. IDLE CONTROLLER
41. IDLE BOOST SOLENOID VALVE
42. A/C IDLE BOOST SOLENOID VALVE
43. POWER VALVE CONTROL SOLENOID VALVE
44. PRIMARY SLOW MIXTURE CUT-OFF SOLENOID VALVE
45. CRANKING LEAK SOLENOID VALVE
46. CHOKE OPENER
47. THERMOVALVE D
48. SECONDARY DIAPHRAGM
49. FAST IDLE UNLOADER
50. UNLOADER SOLENOID VALVE (49 ST)
51. MANIFOLD ABSOLUTE PRESSURE SENSOR (EXCEPT CAL)
52. COOLANT TEMPERATURE SENSOR A (EXCEPT CAL)
53. ATMOSPHERIC PRESSURE SENSOR (EXCEPT CAL)
54. BACK-UP LIGHT SWITCH
55. VACUUM SWITCH D (49 ST)
56. VACUUM SWITCH A
57. VACUUM SWITCH E (CAL)
58. SPEED PULSER
59. BRAKE LIGHT SWITCH
60. CLUTCH SWITCH
61. NEUTRAL SWITCH
62. STEERING SWITCH (49 ST)
63. SHIFT UP INDICATOR LIGHT
64. COOLANT TEMPERATURE SENSOR B
65. INTAKE AIR TEMP. SENSOR B
66. DEVICE CONTROL UNIT
67. ALTERNATOR CONTROL UNIT
68. RADIATOR FAN CONTROL UNIT
69. RADIATOR FAN TIMER
70. THERMO CONTROL UNIT (CAL)
71. RESISTOR
72. COOLANT TEMPERATURE SENSOR C (CAL)
73. PRIMARY MAIN AIR CUT-OFF SOLENOID VALVE (49 ST)
74. PRIMARY SLOW AIR CUT-OFF SOLENOID VALVE (49 ST)

**Vacuum and electrical connections – 1986 Civic Si & CRX Si**

### Std. M/T (49 ST/HI ALT)

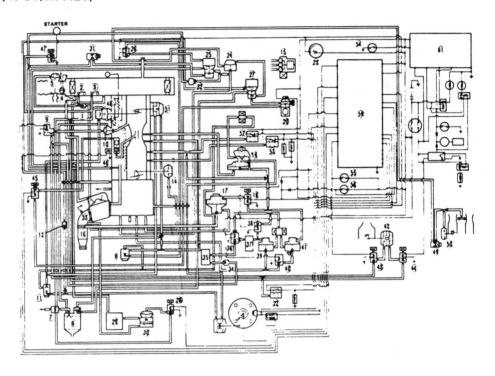

### Std. M/T (CAL)

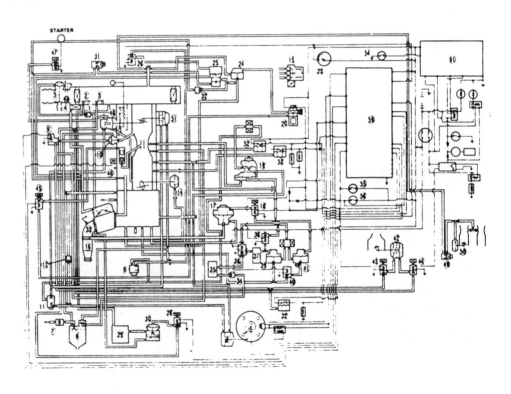

**Vacuum and electrical connections — 1986 Civic Si & CRX Si**

**Std. A/T**

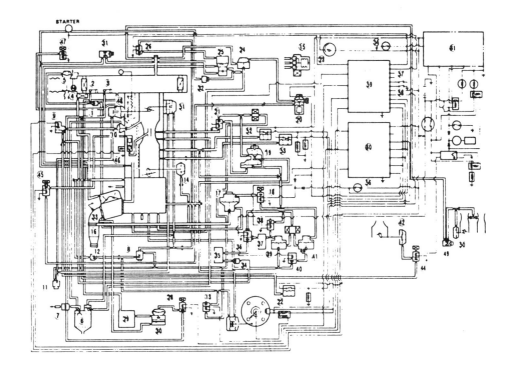

| | | | |
|---|---|---|---|
| ① | CHECK VALVE (INTAKE AIR TEMP.) | ㊱ | FREQUENCY SOLENOID VALVE B |
| ② | AIR BLEED VALVE A | ㊲ | PULSE RECTIFIER |
| ③ | AIR BLEED VALVE B | ㊳ | FEEDBACK CONTROL SOLENOID VALVE |
| ④ | INTAKE AIR TEMP. SENSOR A | ㊴ | AIR CONTROL VALVE B |
| ⑤ | AIR CONTROL DIAPHRAGM | ㊵ | FREQUENCY SOLENOID VALVE A |
| ⑥ | CHARCOAL CANISTER | ㊶ | AIR CONTROL VALVE A |
| ⑦ | TWO-WAY VALVE | ㊷ | IDLE CONTROLLER |
| ⑧ | THERMOVALVE A | ㊸ | IDLE BOOST SOLENOID VALVE (M/T) |
| ⑨ | VACUUM HOLDING SOLENOID VALVE | ㊹ | A/C IDLE BOOST SOLENOID VALVE |
| ⑩ | AIR VENT CUT-OFF DIAPHRAGM | ㊺ | POWER VALVE CONTROL SOLENOID VALVE |
| ⑪ | THERMOVALVE B | ㊻ | PRIMARY SLOW MIXTURE CUT-OFF SOLENOID VALVE |
| ⑫ | CHECK VALVE E | ㊼ | CRANKING LEAK SOLENOID VALVE |
| ⑬ | COLD ADVANCE SOLENOID VALVE (A/T) | ㊽ | CHOKE OPENER |
| ⑭ | THROTTLE CONTROLLER | ㊾ | THERMOVALVE D |
| ⑮ | AIR JET CONTROLLER | ㊿ | SECONDARY DIAPHRAGM |
| ⑯ | CATALYTIC CONVERTER | 51 | FAST IDLE UNLOADER |
| ⑰ | EGR VALVE | 52 | VACUUM SWITCH C |
| ⑱ | EGR CONTROL SOLENOID VALVE A | 53 | VACUUM SWITCH A |
| ⑲ | EGR CONTROL VALVES A & B | 54 | INTAKE AIR TEMP. SENSOR B |
| ⑳ | CONTROL SWITCH | 55 | THERMOSENSOR A |
| 21 | EGR CONTROL SOLENOID VALVE C (A/T) | 56 | THERMOSENSOR B (M/T) |
| 22 | VACUUM SWITCH B | 57 | SHIFT POSITION SWITCH "N" (A/T) |
| 23 | SPEED SENSOR | 58 | SHIFT POSITION SWITCH "P" (A/T) |
| 24 | AIR VALVE | 59 | DEVICE CONTROL UNIT A |
| 25 | ANTI-AFTERBURN VALVE | 60 | DEVICE CONTROL UNIT B (A/T) |
| 26 | ANTI-AFTERBURN CONTROL SOLENOID VALVE | 61 | RADIATOR FAN TIMER |
| 27 | VACUUM CONTROL VALVE (M/T 49ST) | | |
| 28 | AIR SUCTION CONTROL SOLENOID VALVE | | |
| 29 | SILENCER | | |
| 30 | AIR SUCTION VALVE | | |
| 31 | THERMOVALVE C | | |
| 32 | CHECK VALVE G | | |
| 33 | OXYGEN SENSOR | | |
| 34 | CHECK VALVE A | | |
| 35 | ACCUMULATOR | | |

**Vacuum and electrical connections – 1986 Civic Si & CRX Si**

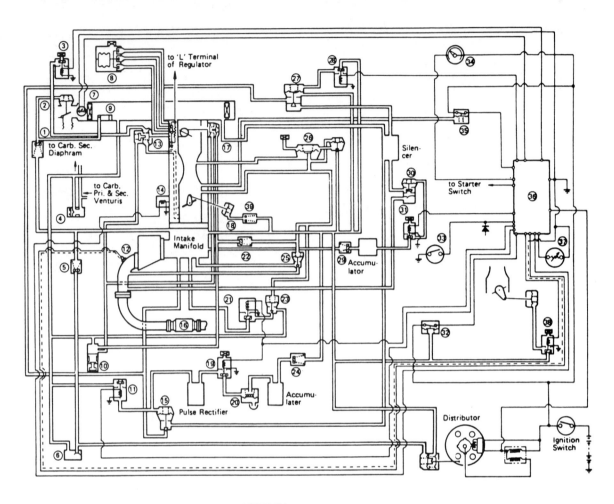

to 'L' Terminal
of Regulator

to Carb. Sec.
Diaphram

to Carb.
Pri. & Sec.
Venturis

Intake
Manifold

Silen-
cer

to Starter
Switch

Accumu-
lator

Accumu-
lator

Pulse Rectifier

Distributor

Ignition
Switch

① CHECK VALVE (INTAKE AIR TEMP. CONTROL)
② AIR CONTROL DIAPHRAGM
③ CRANKING LEAK SOLENOID VALVE
④ THERMOVALVE C
⑤ CHECK VALVE E
⑥ THERMOVALVE B
⑦ INTAKE AIR TEMP. SENSOR
⑧ AIR JET CONTROLLER
⑨ AIR BLEED VALVE
⑩ THERMOVALVE A
⑪ FEEDBACK CONTROL SOLENOID VALVE
⑫ OXYGEN SENSOR
⑬ CHOKE OPENER
⑭ PRIMARY SLOW MIXTURE CUT-OFF
   SOLENOID VALVE
⑮ AIR CONTROL VALVE B
⑯ CONVERTER ASSY
⑰ FAST IDLE UNLOADER
⑱ THROTTLE CONTROLLER
⑲ FREQUENCY SOLENOID VALVE B
⑳ CV GENERATOR

㉑ FREQUENCY SOLENOID VALVE A
㉒ CHECK VALVE A
㉓ AIR CONTROL VALVE A
㉔ CHECK VALVE B
㉕ EGR VALVE
㉖ EGR CONTROL VALVE A&B
㉗ ANTI-AFTERBURN VALVE
㉘ ANTI-AFTERBURN CONTROL SOLENOID VALVE
㉙ CHECK VALVE C
㉚ AIR SUCTION VALVE
㉛ AIR SUCTION CONTROL SOLENOID VALVE
㉜ VACUUM SWITCH A
㉝ CLUTCH SWITCH
㉞ SPEED SENSOR
㉟ VACUUM SWITCH B
㊱ CONTROL UNIT
㊲ THERMOSENSOR
㊳ A/C IDLE BOOST SOLENOID VALVE
㊴ DASHPOT CHECK VALVE

**Vacuum and electrical connections – 1986 Accord w/man. trans.**

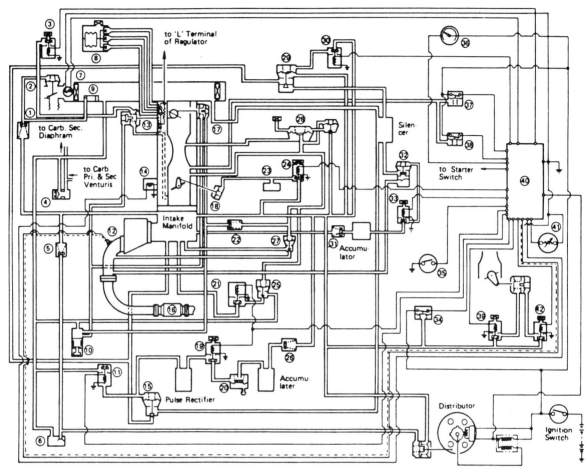

1. CHECK VALVE (INTAKE AIR TEMP. CONTROL)
2. AIR CONTROL DIAPHRAGM
3. CRANKING LEAK SOLENOID VALVE
4. THERMOVALVE C
5. CHECK VALVE E
6. THERMOVALVE B
7. INTAKE AIR TEMP. SENSOR
8. AIR JET CONTROLLER
9. AIR BLEED VALVE
10. THERMOVALVE A
11. FEEDBACK CONTROL SOLENOID VALVE
12. OXYGEN SENSOR
13. CHOKE OPENER
14. PRIMARY SLOW MIXTURE CUT-OFF
    SOLENOID VALVE
15. AIR CONTROL VALVE B
16. CONVERTER ASSY
17. FAST IDLE UNLOADER
18. THROTTLE CONTROLLER
19. FREQUENCY SOLENOID VALVE B
20. CV GENERATOR

21. FREQUENCY SOLENOID VALVE A
22. CHECK VALVE A
23. PULSE RECTIFIER
24. FREQUENCY SOLENOID VALVE C
25. AIR CONTROL VALVE A
26. CHECK VALVE B
27. EGR VALVE
28. EGR CONTROL VALVE A&B
29. ANTI-AFTERBURN VALVE
30. ANTI-AFTERBURN CONTROL SOLENOID VALVE
31. CHECK VALVE C
32. AIR SUCTION VALVE
33. AIR SUCTION CONTROL SOLENOID VALVE
34. VACUUM SWITCH A
35. SHIFT LEVER POSITION SWITCH
36. SPEED SENSOR
37. VACUUM SWITCH B
38. VACUUM SWITCH C (49 ST and HI ALT only)
39. IDLE BOOST SOLENOID VALVE
40. CONTROL UNIT
41. THERMOSENSOR
42. A/C IDLE BOOST SOLENOID VALVE

Vacuum and electrical connections – 1986 Accord w/auto. trans.

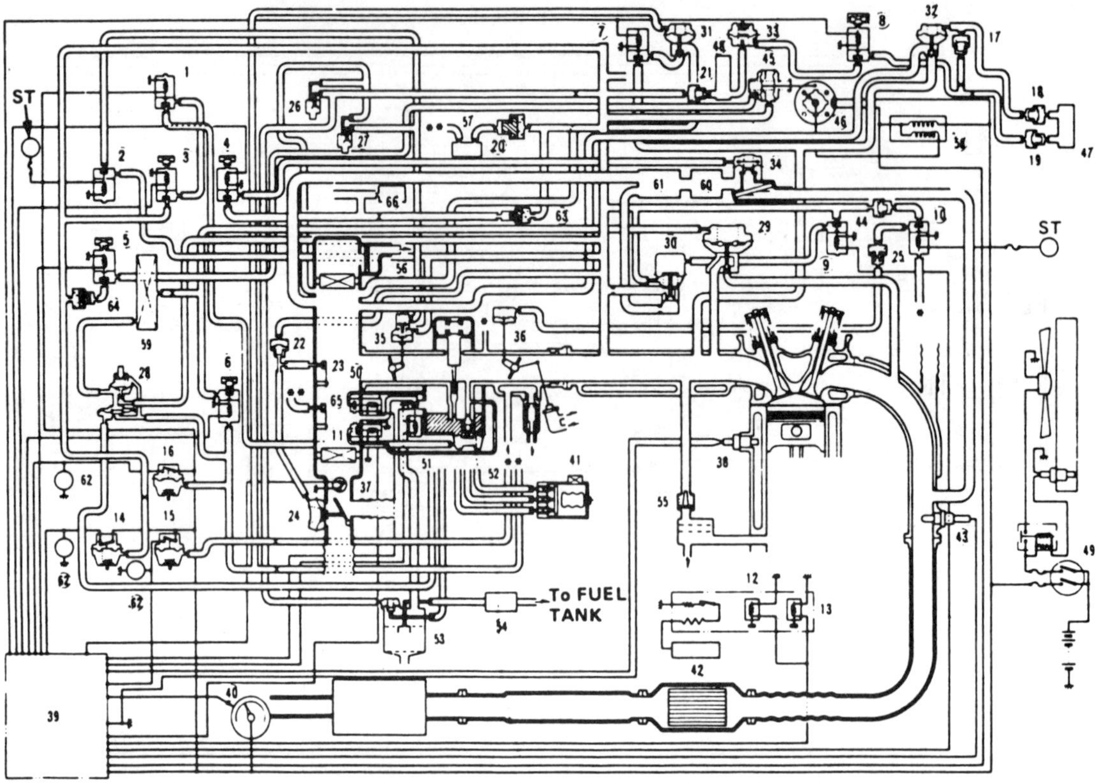


① POWER VALVE LOCK SOLENOID VALVE
② CRANKING LEAK SOLENOID VALVE
③ POWER VALVE CONTROL SOLENOID VALVE
④ AIR SUCTION CONTROL SOLENOID VALVE
⑤ VACUUM CONTROL SOLENOID VALVE
⑥ EGR CONTROL SOLENOID VALVE A
⑦ FREQUENCY SOLENOID VALVE A
⑧ FREQUENCY SOLENOID VALVE B
⑨ ANTI-AFTERBURN CONTROL SOLENOID VALVE
⑩ CRANKING OPENER SOLENOID VALVE
⑪ MAIN AIR JET CONTROL SOLENOID VALVE
⑫ RIGHT PRIMARY SLOW MIXTURE CUT-OFF SOLENOID VALVE
⑬ LEFT PRIMARY SLOW MIXTURE CUT-OFF SOLENOID VALVE
⑭ VACUUM SWITCH A
⑮ VACUUM SWITCH B
⑯ VACUUM SWITCH C
⑰ CHECK VALVE A
⑱ CHECK VALVE B
⑲ CHECK VALVE C
⑳ CHECK VALVE F
㉑ CHECK VALVE E
㉒ CHECK VALVE (INTAKE AIR TEMP.)
㉓ AIR BLEED VALVE A
㉔ INTAKE AIR CONTROL DIAPHRAGM
㉕ DASHPOT CHECK VALVE
㉖ THERMOVALVE B
㉗ THERMOVALVE A
㉘ EGR CONTROL VALVES A & B
㉙ EGR VALVE
㉚ ANTI-AFTERBURN VALVE
㉛ AIR CONTROL VALVE A
32 AIR CONTROL VALVE B
33 CONSTANT VACUUM VALVE
㉞ AIR SUCTION VALVE
㉟ CHOKE OPENER
㊱ THROTTLE CONTROLLER
㊲ INTAKE AIR TEMPERATURE SWITCH
㊳ THERMOSENSOR
㊴ CONTROL UNIT
㊵ SPEED SENSOR
㊶ AIR JET CONTROLLER
㊷ CATALYTIC CONVERTER
㊸ OXYGEN SENSOR
㊹ CHECK VALVE D
㊺ DISTRIBUTOR VACUUM ADVANCE
㊻ DISTRIBUTOR
㊼ SURGE TANK A
㊽ SURGE TANK B
㊾ IGNITION SWITCH
㊿ INNER VENT SOLENOID VALVE
(51) AIR VENT CUT-OFF SOLENOID VALVE
(52) POWER VALVE
(53) CANISTER
(54) TWO-WAY VALVE
(55) PCV VALVE
(56) BLOW-BY FILTER
(57) VACUUM TANK A
(58) IGNITION COIL
(59) AIR FILTER
(60) AIR CHAMBER A
(61) AIR CHAMBER B
(62) AUXILIARY COIL
(63) CHECK VALVE G
(64) CHECK VALVE H
(65) AIR BLEED VALVE B
(66) VACUUM TANK B

Vacuum and electrical connections—1986 Prelude

# Hyundai

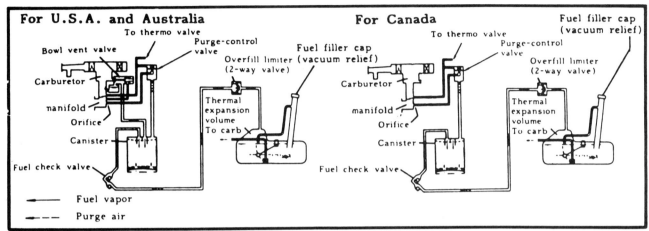

**For U.S.A. and Australia**

Bowl vent valve
To thermo valve
Purge-control valve
Carburetor
Fuel filler cap (vacuum relief)
Overfill limiter (2-way valve)
manifold
Orifice
Thermal expansion volume
To carb
Canister
Fuel check valve

→ Fuel vapor
--→ Purge air

**For Canada**

To thermo valve
Purge-control valve
Fuel filler cap (vacuum relief)
Carburetor
Overfill limiter (2-way valve)
manifold
Orifice
Thermal expansion volume
To carb
Canister
Fuel check valve

**Evaporative emission control system — Excel**

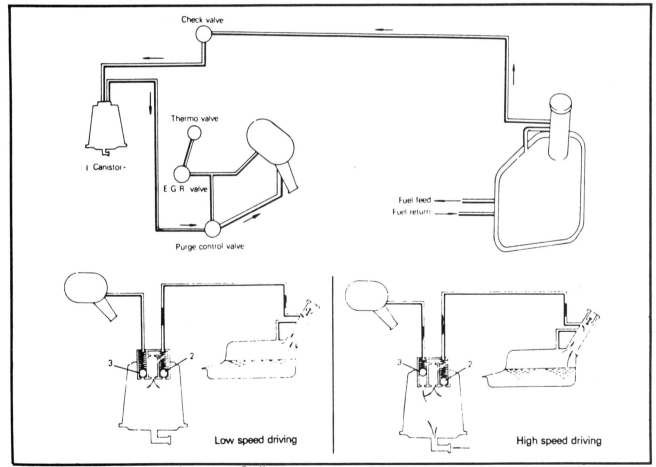

Check valve

Thermo valve

Canistor

E G R valve

Fuel feed
Fuel return

Purge control valve

3    2    Low speed driving

3    2    High speed driving

**Evaporative emission control system — Stellar**

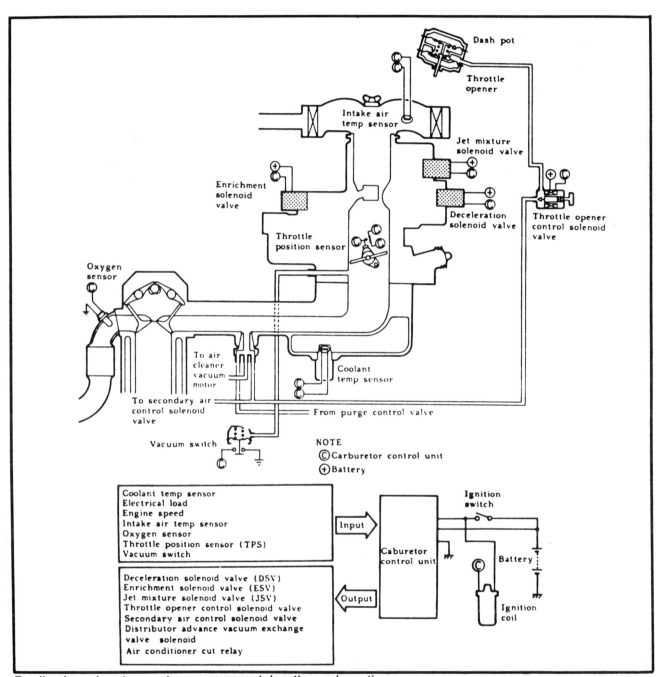

Feedback carburetor system—component location schematic

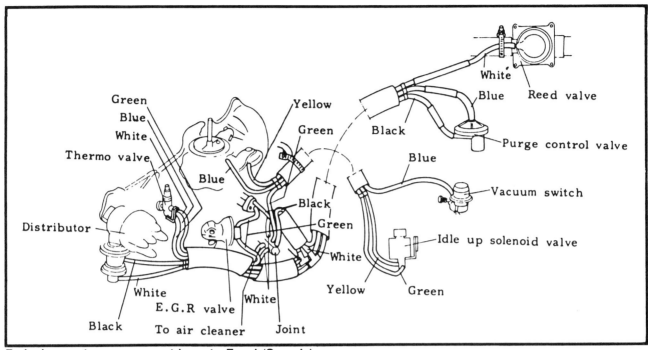

**Emission system component layout – Excel (Canada)**

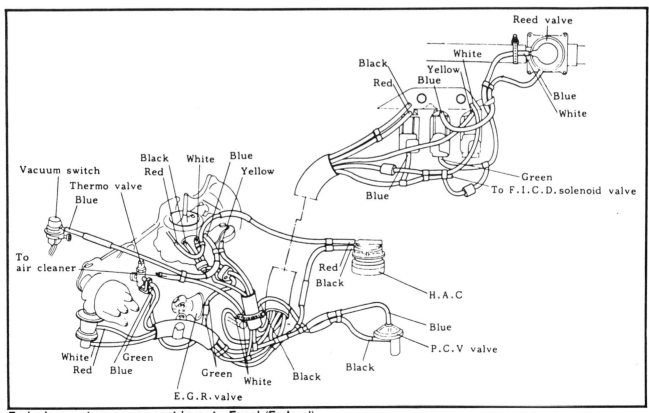

**Emission system component layout – Excel (Federal)**

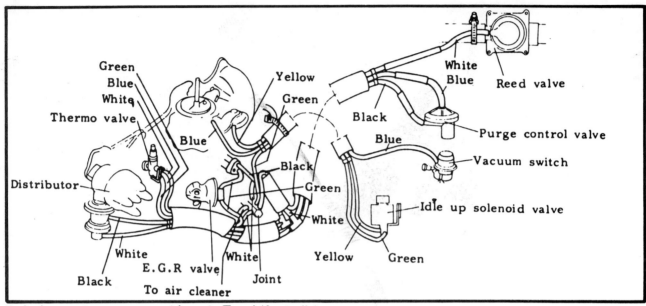

**Emission system component layout – Excel (Australia)**

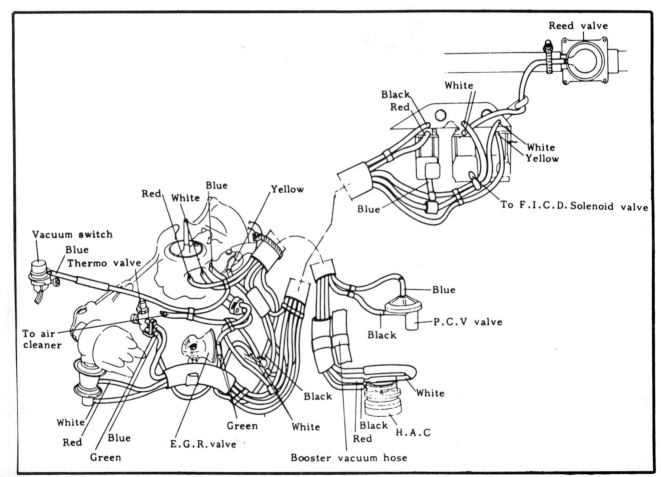

**Emission system component layout – Excel (California)**

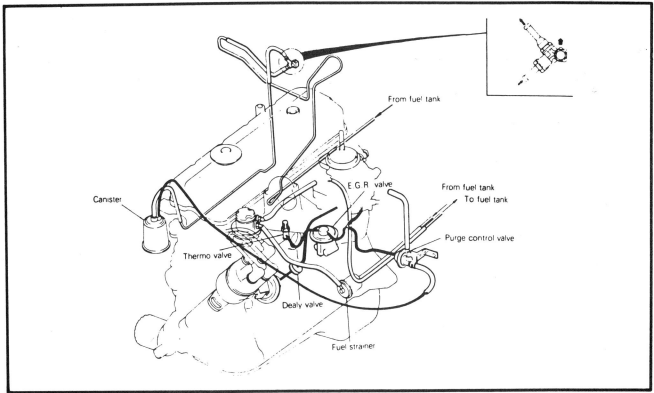

**Emission system component layout – Pony**

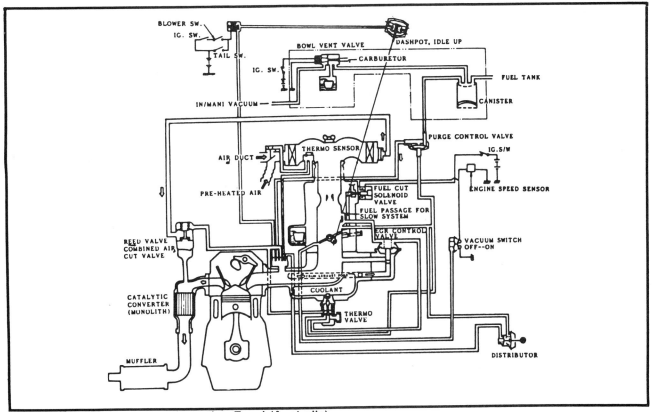

**Emission system vacuum schematic – Excel (Australia)**

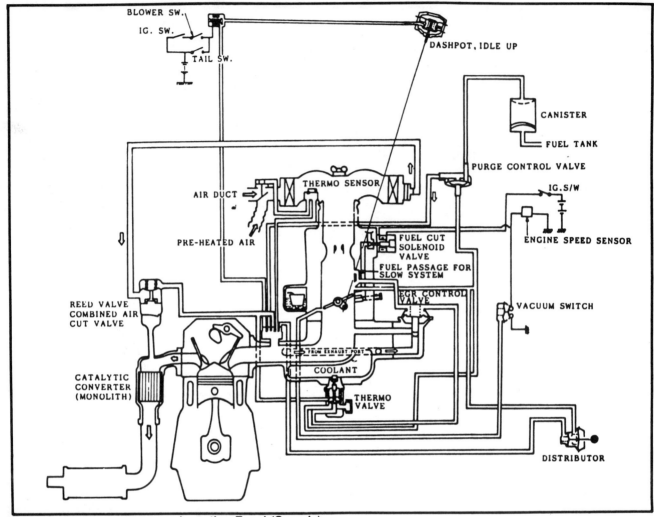

**Emission system vacuum schematic – Excel (Canada)**

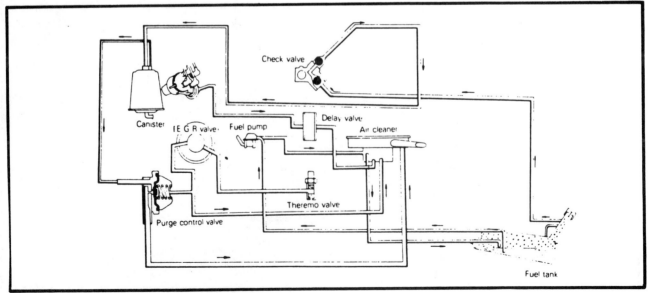

**Emission system vacuum schematic – Pony**

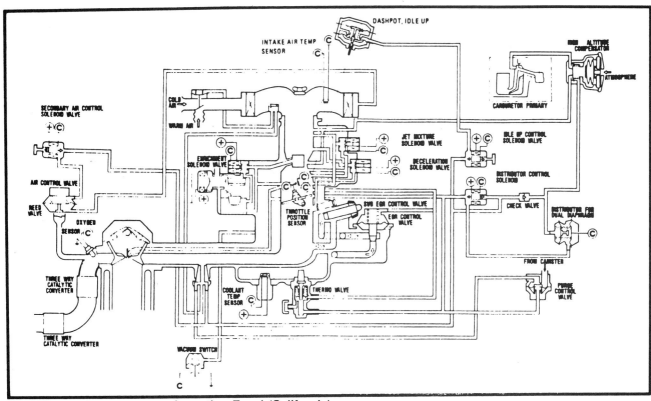

**Emission system vacuum schematic—Excel (California)**

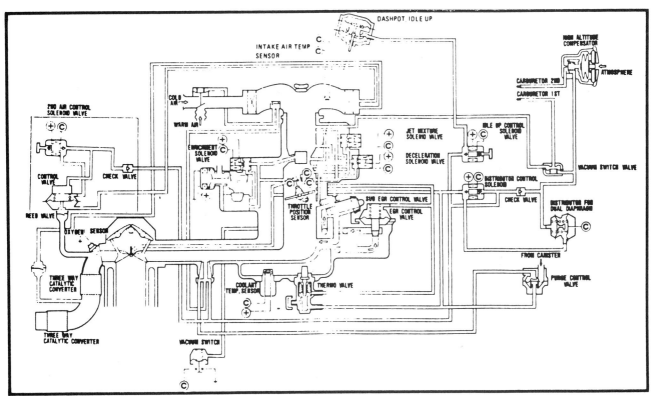

**Emission system vacuum schematic—Excel (Federal)**

# Isuzu

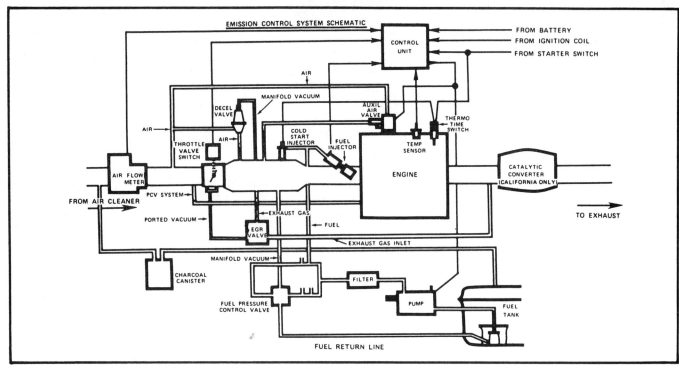

EMISSION CONTROL SYSTEM SCHEMATIC

**1975 fuel injection models**

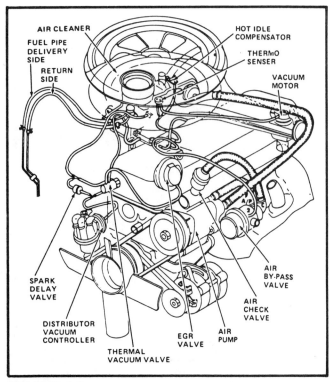

**1976-79 49 states**

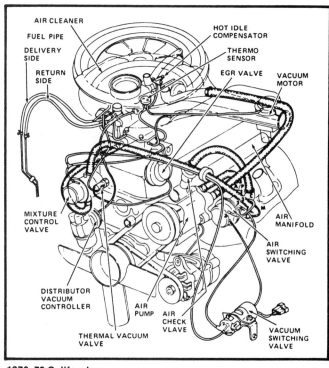

**1976-79 California**

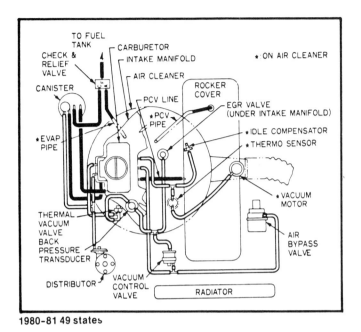

**1980-81 49 states**

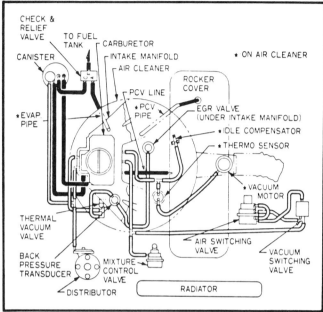

**1980-81 California**

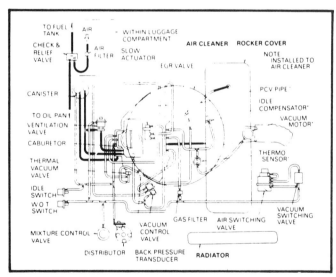

**1982-83 All models**

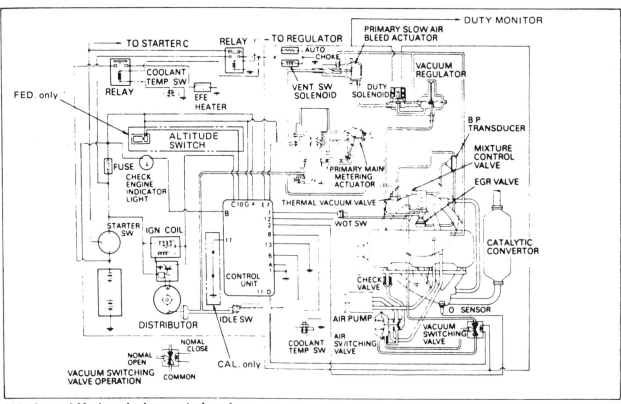

1984 Isuzu I-Mark emission control system

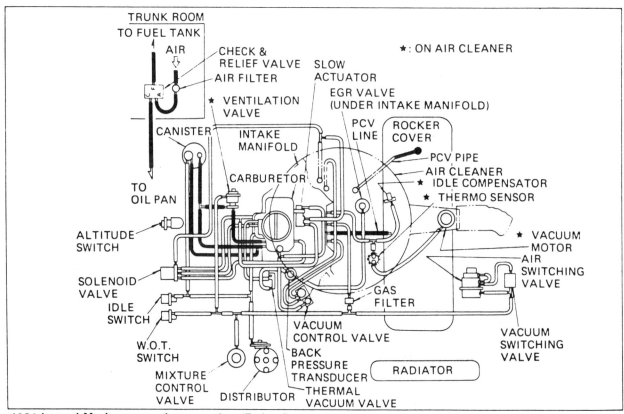

1984 Isuzu I-Mark vacuum hose routing (Federal)

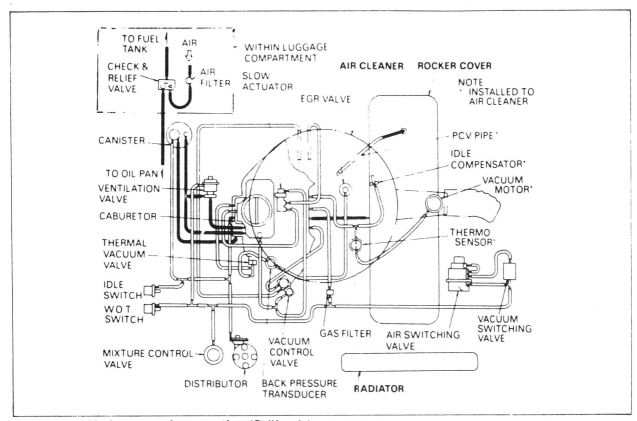

**1984 Isuzu I-Mark vacuum hose routing (California)**

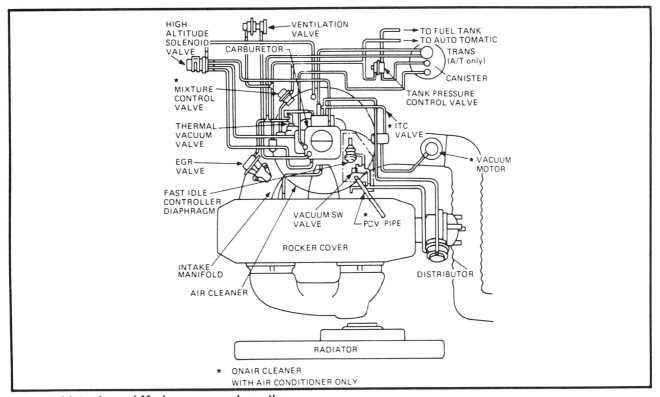

**1985 and later Isuzu I-Mark vacuum schematic**

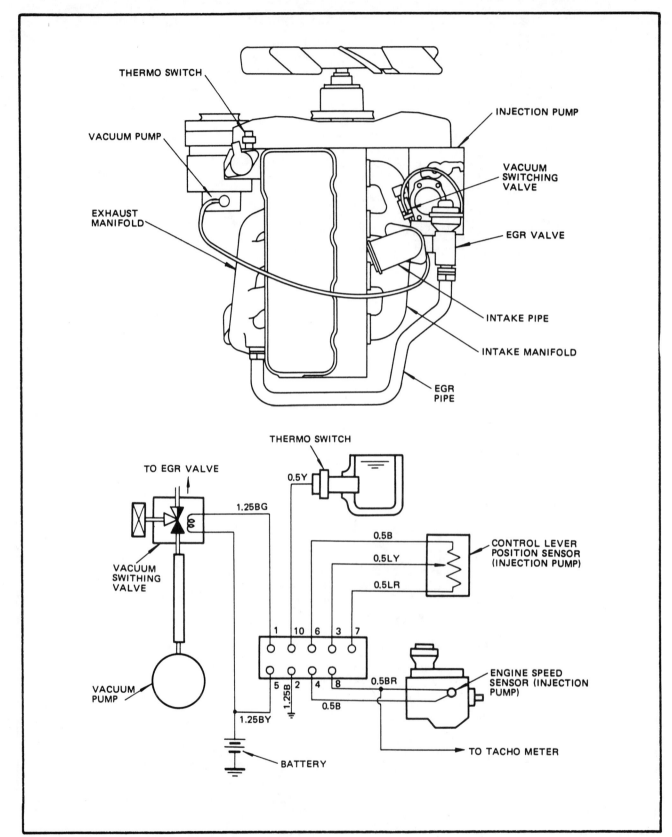

**Diesel engine EGR system—California vehicles**

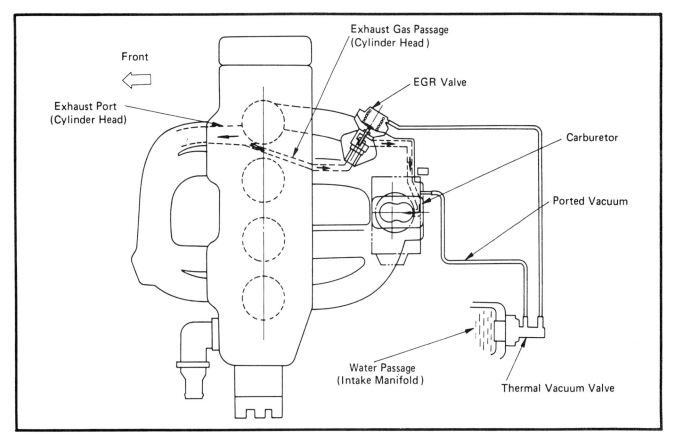

**EGR system and related components – 1985 and later**

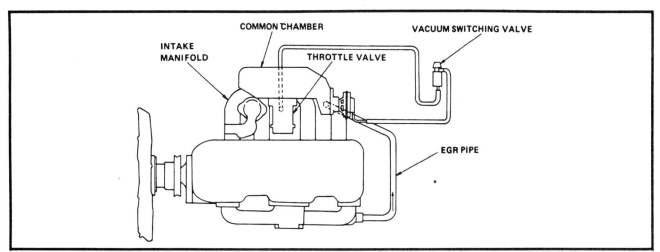

**Impulse EGR system**

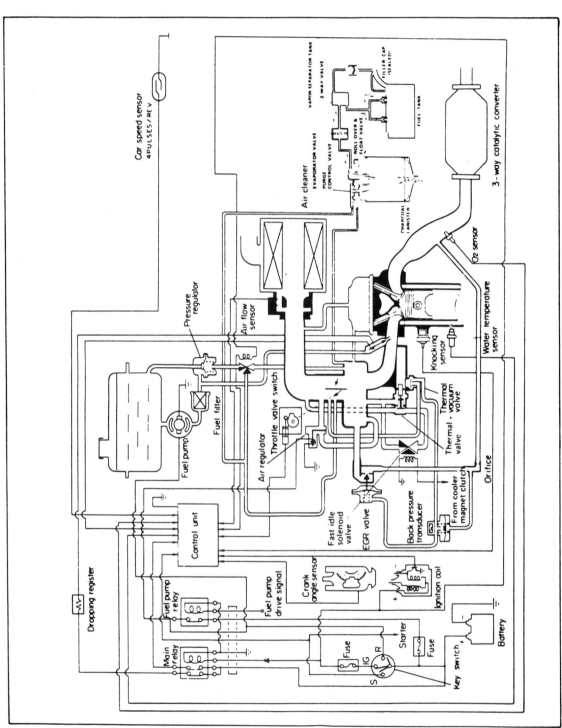

**Isuzu Impulse (JR) Emission Control System**

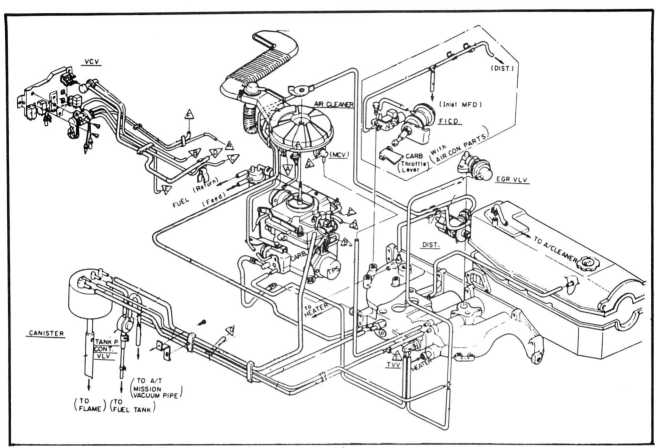

**1985 and later Isuzu I-Mark emission system component layout**

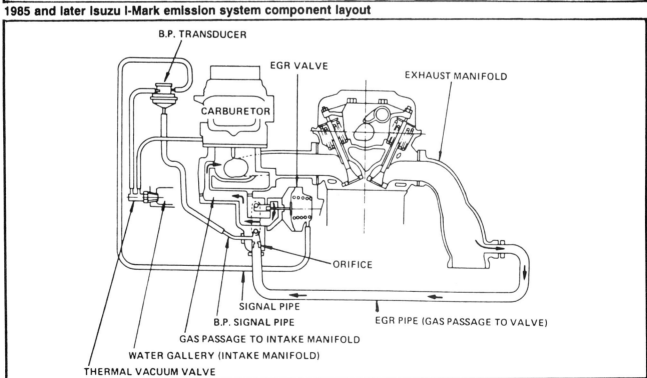

**1984 Isuzu I-Mark EGR system**

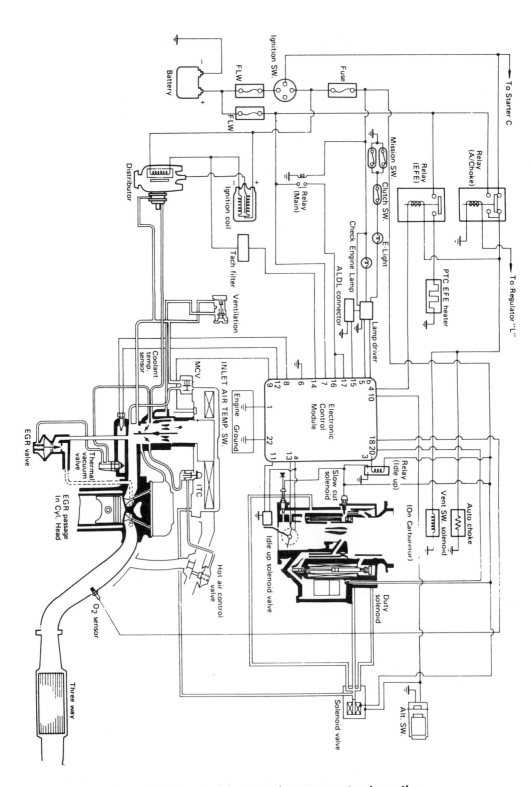

**1985 and later Isuzu I-Mark emission control component schematic**

# Mazda

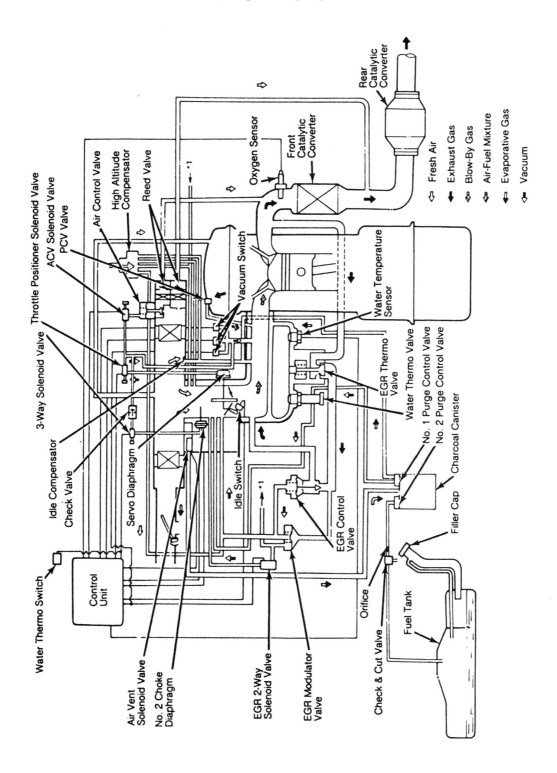

Rear Catalytic Converter

Front Catalytic Converter

Oxygen Sensor

Water Temperature Sensor

Water Thermo Valve

EGR Thermo Valve

No. 1 Purge Control Valve
No. 2 Purge Control Valve

Charcoal Canister

Filler Cap

Fuel Tank

Check & Cut Valve

Orifice

EGR Control Valve

EGR Modulator Valve

EGR 2-Way Solenoid Valve

No. 2 Choke Diaphragm

Air Vent Solenoid Valve

Water Thermo Switch

Control Unit

Idle Compensator

Check Valve

3-Way Solenoid Valve

Servo Diaphragm

Idle Switch

Throttle Positioner Solenoid Valve
ACV Solenoid Valve
PCV Valve

Air Control Valve

High Altitude Compensator

Reed Valve

Vacuum Switch

⇨ Fresh Air
⬇ Exhaust Gas
⬇ Blow-By Gas
⬆ Air-Fuel Mixture
⬆ Evaporative Gas
⬇ Vacuum

**MAZDA GLC MODELS—FEDERAL**

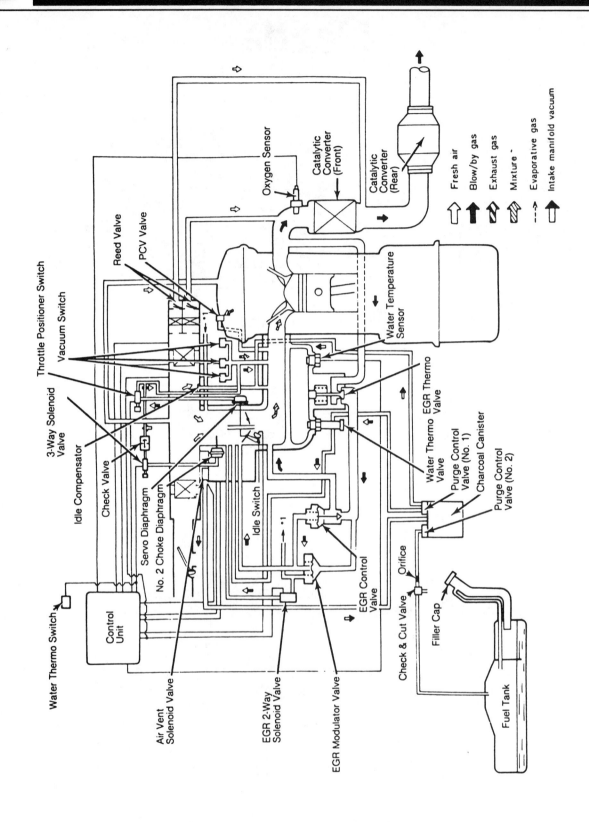

Fresh air

Blow/by gas

Exhaust gas

Mixture

Evaporative gas

Intake manifold vacuum

Oxygen Sensor

Catalytic Converter (Front)

Catalytic Converter (Rear)

Water Temperature Sensor

Reed Valve

PCV Valve

Throttle Positioner Switch

Vacuum Switch

Water Thermo EGR Thermo Valve

3-Way Solenoid Valve

Idle Compensator

Check Valve

Servo Diaphragm

No. 2 Choke Diaphragm

Idle Switch

Water Thermo Valve

Purge Control Valve (No. 1)

Charcoal Canister

Purge Control Valve (No. 2)

Water Thermo Switch

Control Unit

Air Vent Solenoid Valve

EGR 2-Way Solenoid Valve

EGR Modulator Valve

EGR Control Valve

Check & Cut Valve

Orifice

Filler Cap

Fuel Tank

**MAZDA GLC MODELS—CALIFORNIA**

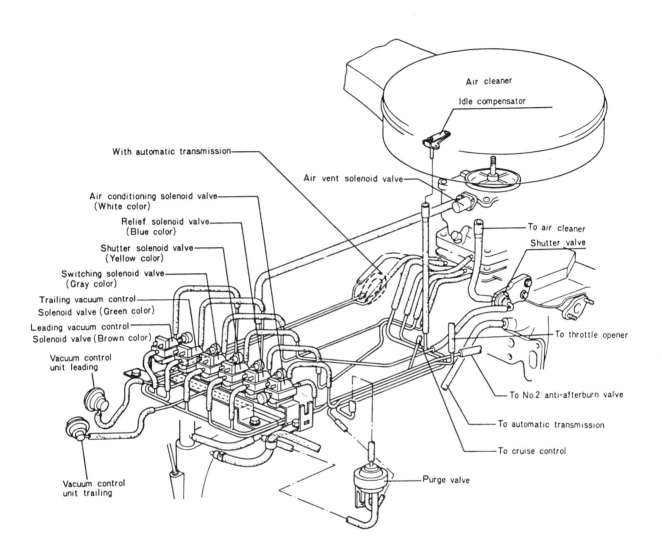

Air cleaner

Idle compensator

With automatic transmission

Air vent solenoid valve

Air conditioning solenoid valve
(White color)

Relief solenoid valve
(Blue color)

Shutter solenoid valve
(Yellow color)

Switching solenoid valve
(Gray color)

Trailing vacuum control
Solenoid valve (Green color)

Leading vacuum control
Solenoid valve (Brown color)

Vacuum control
unit leading

Vacuum control
unit trailing

To air cleaner

Shutter valve

To throttle opener

To No.2 anti-afterburn valve

To automatic transmission

To cruise control

Purge valve

**1983 MAZDA RX7—FEDERAL & CALIF.**

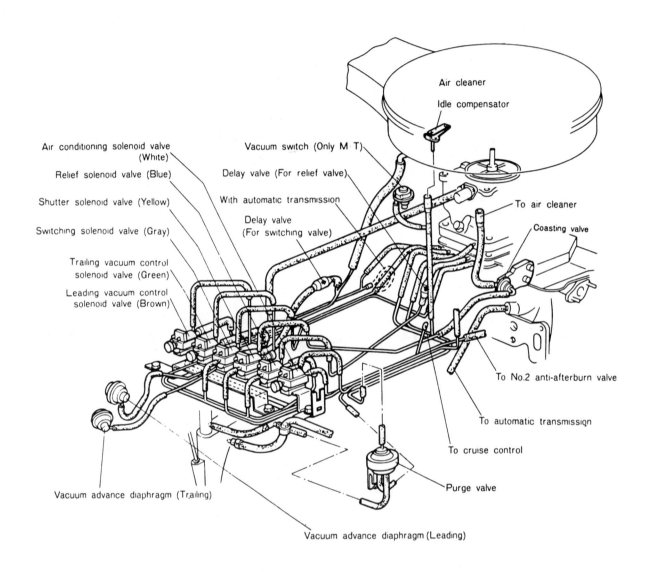

Air cleaner

Idle compensator

Air conditioning solenoid valve (White)

Relief solenoid valve (Blue)

Shutter solenoid valve (Yellow)

Switching solenoid valve (Gray)

Trailing vacuum control solenoid valve (Green)

Leading vacuum control solenoid valve (Brown)

Vacuum switch (Only M T)

Delay valve (For relief valve)

With automatic transmission

Delay valve (For switching valve)

To air cleaner

Coasting valve

To No.2 anti-afterburn valve

To automatic transmission

To cruise control

Purge valve

Vacuum advance diaphragm (Trailing)

Vacuum advance diaphragm (Leading)

**1984 MAZDA RX7—12A ENG.—FEDERAL & CALIF.**

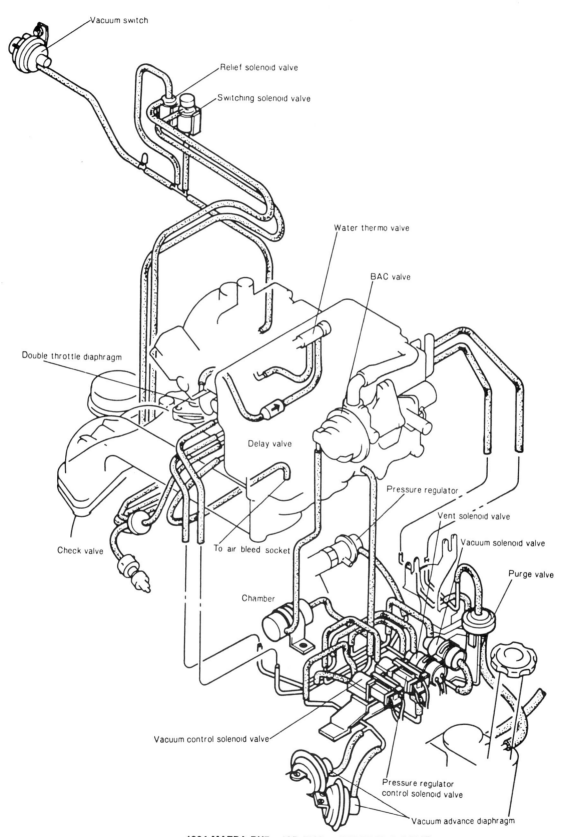

Vacuum switch

Relief solenoid valve

Switching solenoid valve

Water thermo valve

BAC valve

Double throttle diaphragm

Delay valve

Pressure regulator

Vent solenoid valve

Vacuum solenoid valve

Purge valve

Check valve

To air bleed socket

Chamber

Vacuum control solenoid valve

Pressure regulator
control solenoid valve

Vacuum advance diaphragm

**1984 MAZDA RX7—13B ENG.—FEDERAL & CALIF.**

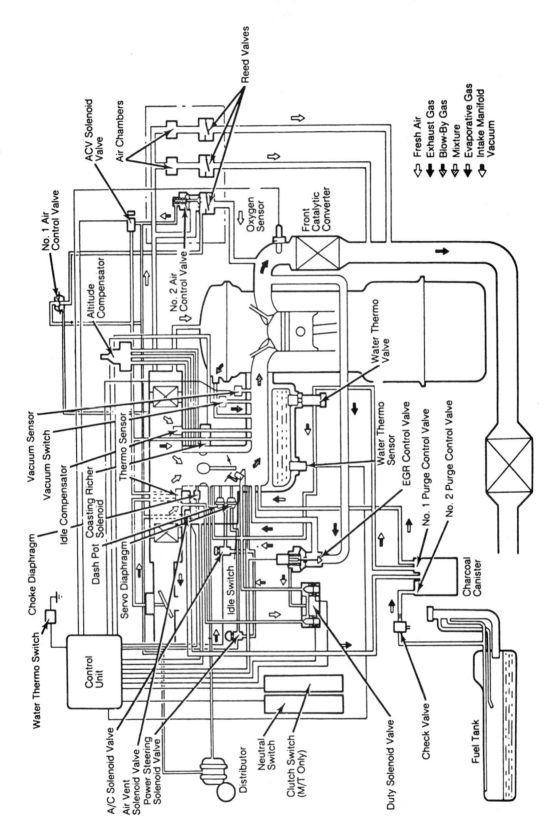

MAZDA 626 MODELS—FEDERAL

Reed Valves

ACV Solenoid Valve
Air Chambers

No. 1 Air Control Valve
Altitude Compensator
No. 2 Air Control Valve
Oxygen Sensor
Front Catalytic Converter
Water Thermo Valve

Fresh Air
Exhaust Gas
Blow-By Gas
Mixture
Evaporative Gas
Intake Manifold Vacuum

Vacuum Sensor
Vacuum Switch
Idle Compensator
Thermo Sensor
Dash Pot
Coasting Richer Solenoid
Servo Diaphragm
Idle Switch
Water Thermo Sensor
EGR Control Valve
No. 1 Purge Control Valve
No. 2 Purge Control Valve
Charcoal Canister

Choke Diaphragm
Water Thermo Switch
Control Unit
A/C Solenoid Valve
Air Vent Solenoid Valve
Power Steering Solenoid Valve
Distributor
Neutral Switch
Clutch Switch (M/T Only)
Duty Solenoid Valve
Check Valve
Fuel Tank

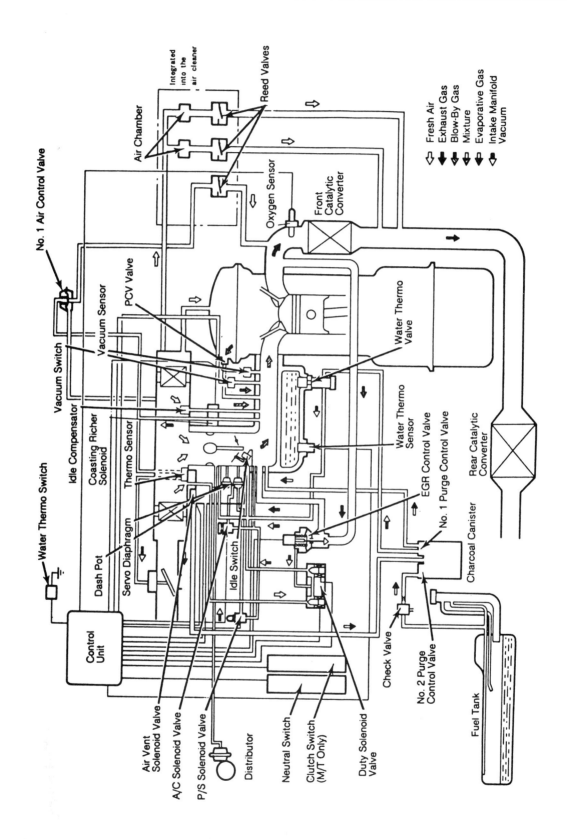

MAZDA 626 MODELS—CALIFORNIA

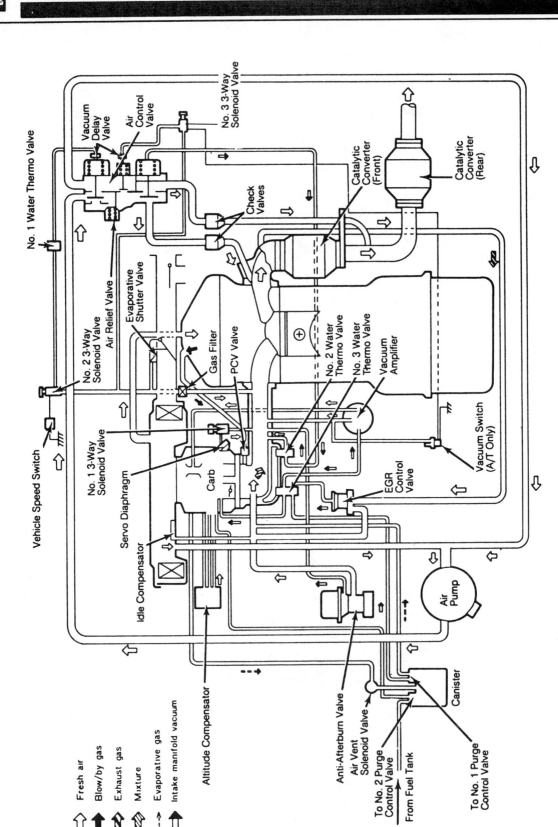

No. 3 3-Way Solenoid Valve

Vacuum Delay Valve

Air Control Valve

No. 1 Water Thermo Valve

Catalytic Converter (Front)

Catalytic Converter (Rear)

Check Valves

Air Relief Valve

Evaporative Shutter Valve

No. 2 3-Way Solenoid Valve

Gas Filter

PCV Valve

No. 2 Water Thermo Valve

No. 3 Water Thermo Valve

Vacuum Amplifier

Vehicle Speed Switch

No. 1 3-Way Solenoid Valve

Servo Diaphragm

Carb

Vacuum Switch (A/T Only)

EGR Control Valve

Idle Compensator

Altitude Compensator

Air Pump

Anti-Afterburn Valve

Air Vent Solenoid Valve

To No. 2 Purge Control Valve

From Fuel Tank

Canister

To No. 1 Purge Control Valve

Fresh air
Blow/by gas
Exhaust gas
Mixture
Evaporative gas
Intake manifold vacuum

**MAZDA GLC WAGON**

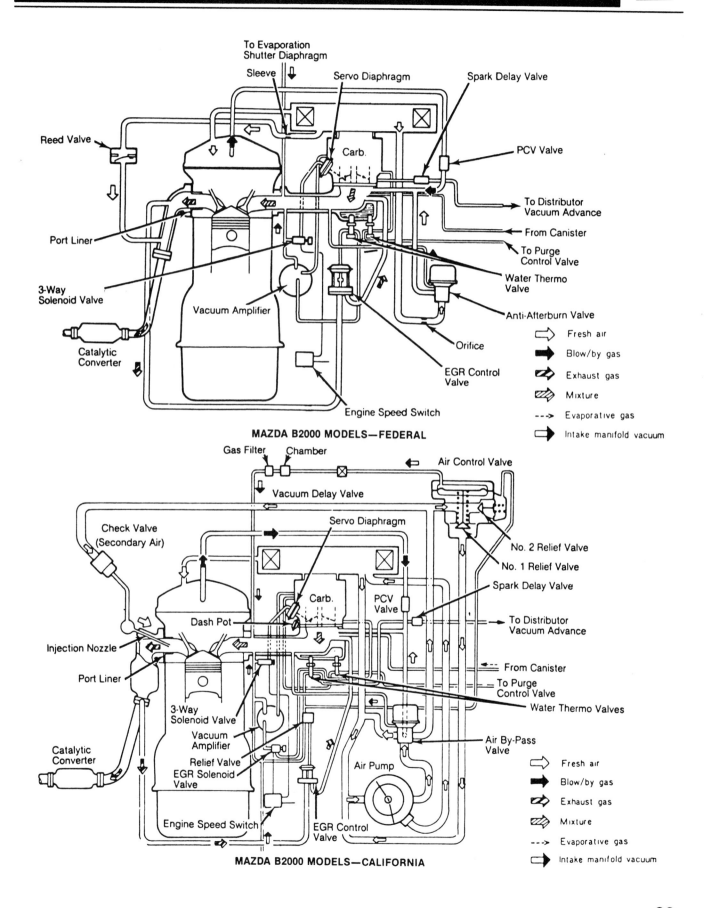

To Evaporation
Shutter Diaphragm

Sleeve

Servo Diaphragm

Spark Delay Valve

Reed Valve

Carb.

PCV Valve

Port Liner

To Distributor
Vacuum Advance

From Canister

To Purge
Control Valve

Water Thermo
Valve

3-Way
Solenoid Valve

Vacuum Amplifier

Anti-Afterburn Valve

Catalytic
Converter

Orifice

EGR Control
Valve

Engine Speed Switch

⟹ Fresh air

⟹ Blow/by gas

⟹ Exhaust gas

⟹ Mixture

--→ Evaporative gas

⟹ Intake manifold vacuum

**MAZDA B2000 MODELS—FEDERAL**

Gas Filter

Chamber

Air Control Valve

Vacuum Delay Valve

Check Valve
(Secondary Air)

Servo Diaphragm

No. 2 Relief Valve

No. 1 Relief Valve

Carb.

PCV
Valve

Spark Delay Valve

Dash Pot

To Distributor
Vacuum Advance

Injection Nozzle

Port Liner

From Canister

To Purge
Control Valve

Water Thermo Valves

3-Way
Solenoid Valve

Vacuum
Amplifier

Relief Valve
EGR Solenoid
Valve

Air By-Pass
Valve

Catalytic
Converter

Air Pump

Engine Speed Switch

EGR Control
Valve

⟹ Fresh air

⟹ Blow/by gas

⟹ Exhaust gas

⟹ Mixture

--→ Evaporative gas

⟹ Intake manifold vacuum

**MAZDA B2000 MODELS—CALIFORNIA**

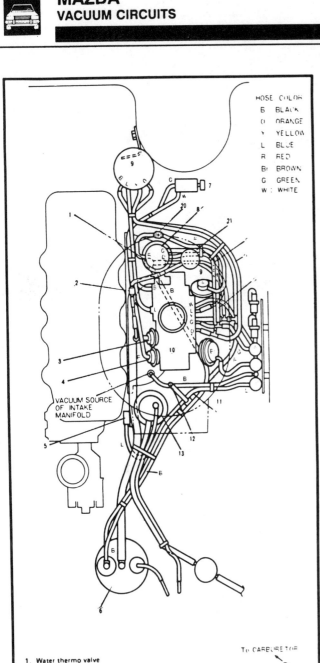

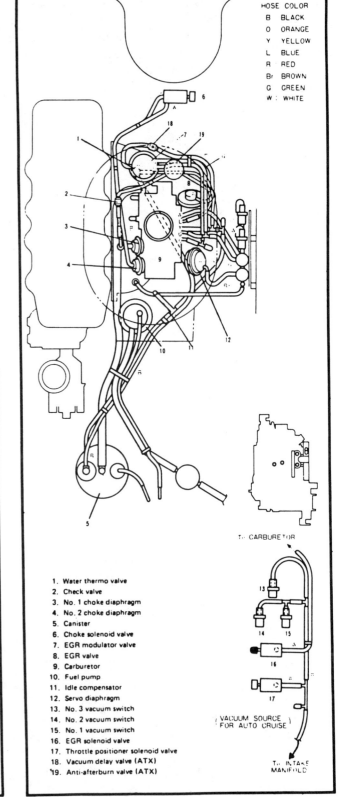

HOSE COLOR
B  BLACK
O  ORANGE
Y  YELLOW
L  BLUE
R  RED
Br  BROWN
G  GREEN
W : WHITE

VACUUM SOURCE
OF INTAKE
MANIFOLD

To CARBURETOR

1.  Water thermo valve
2.  Check valve
3.  No. 1 choke diaphragm
4.  No. 2 choke diaphragm
5.  Air control valve
6.  Canister
7.  Choke solenoid valve
8.  EGR modulator valve
9.  EGR valve
10.  Carburetor
11.  Servo diaphragm
12.  Idle compensator
13.  Fuel pump
14.  No. 3 vacuum switch
15.  No. 2 vacuum switch
16.  No. 1 vacuum switch
17.  EGR solenoid valve
18.  Throttle positioner solenoid valve
19.  ACV solenoid valve
20.  Vacuum delay valve (ATX)
21.  Anti-afterburn valve (ATX)

**1984-85 GLC models (Federal)**

HOSE COLOR
B  BLACK
O  ORANGE
Y  YELLOW
L  BLUE
R  RED
Br  BROWN
G  GREEN
W : WHITE

To CARBURETOR

1.  Water thermo valve
2.  Check valve
3.  No. 1 choke diaphragm
4.  No. 2 choke diaphragm
5.  Canister
6.  Choke solenoid valve
7.  EGR modulator valve
8.  EGR valve
9.  Carburetor
10.  Fuel pump
11.  Idle compensator
12.  Servo diaphragm
13.  No. 3 vacuum switch
14.  No. 2 vacuum switch
15.  No. 1 vacuum switch
16.  EGR solenoid valve
17.  Throttle positioner solenoid valve
18.  Vacuum delay valve (ATX)
'19.  Anti-afterburn valve (ATX)

VACUUM SOURCE
FOR AUTO CRUISE

To INTAKE
MANIFOLD

**1984-85 GLC models (California and Canada)**

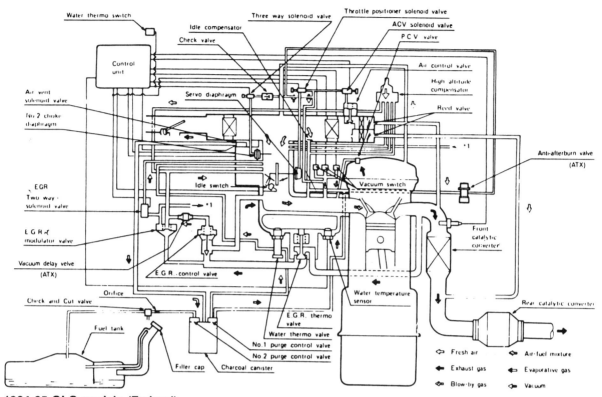

**1984-85 GLC models (Federal)**

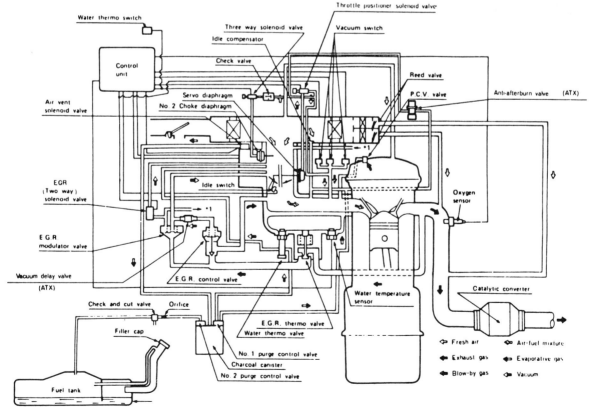

**1984-85 GLC models (Canada)**

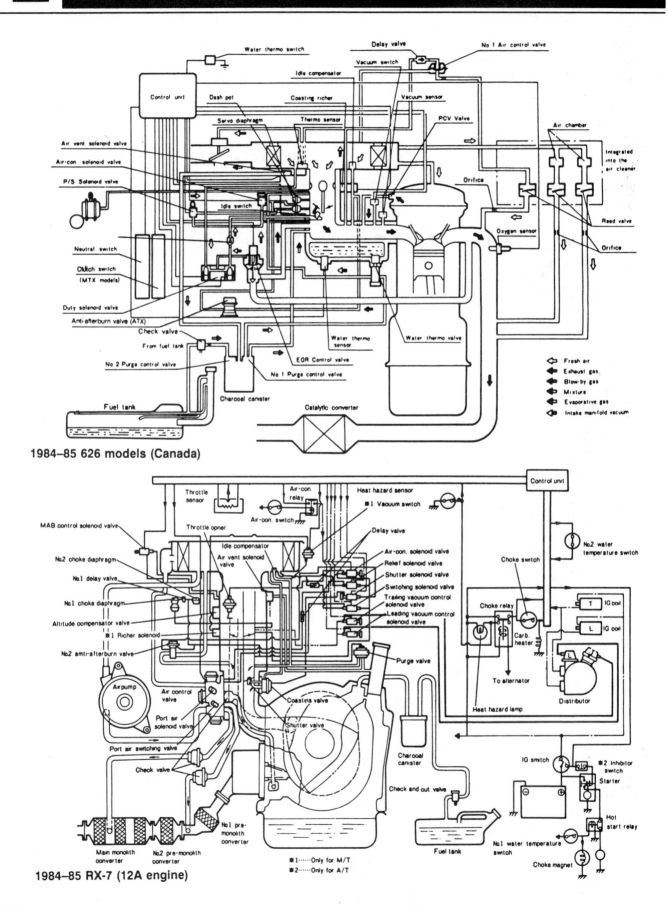

1984–85 626 models (Canada)

1984–85 RX-7 (12A engine)

※1......Only for M/T
※2......Only for A/T

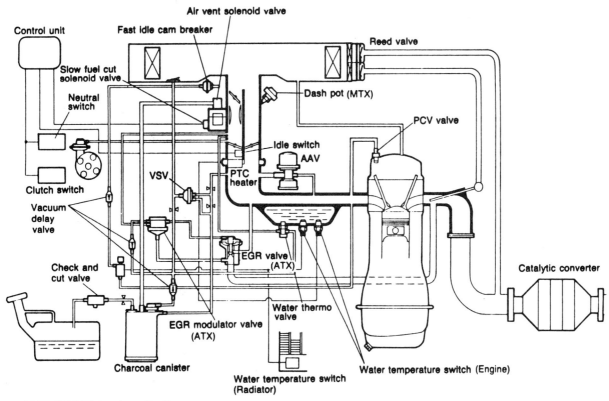

1986–87 323 (carburetted)

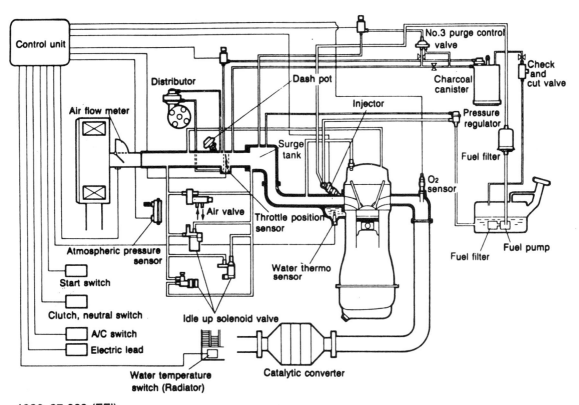

1986–87 323 (EFI)

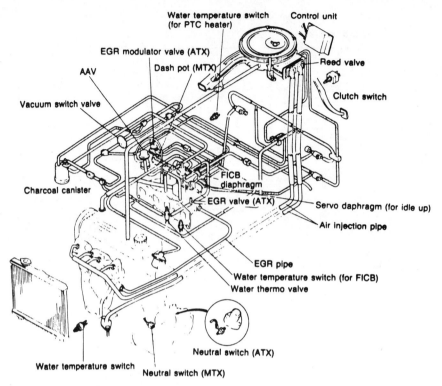

Water temperature switch (for PTC heater)

Control unit

EGR modulator valve (ATX)

Dash pot (MTX)

Reed valve

AAV

Clutch switch

Vacuum switch valve

Charcoal canister

FICB diaphragm

EGR valve (ATX)

Servo daphragm (for idle up)

Air injection pipe

EGR pipe

Water temperature switch (for FICB)

Water thermo valve

Water temperature switch

Neutral switch (MTX)

Neutral switch (ATX)

**Vacuum hose routing 1986–87 323 (carburetted)**

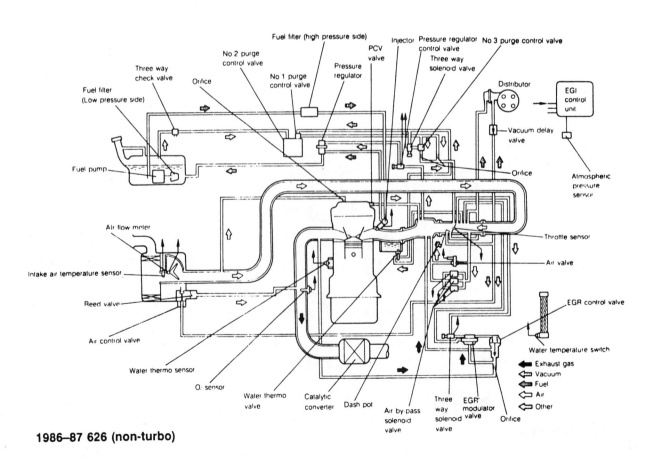

Fuel filter (high pressure side)

Injector

Pressure regulator control valve

No 3 purge control valve

No 2 purge control valve

PCV valve

Three way solenoid valve

Three way check valve

Orifice

No 1 purge control valve

Pressure regulator

Distributor

EGI control unit

Fuel filter (Low pressure side)

Vacuum delay valve

Fuel pump

Orifice

Atmospheric pressure sensor

Air flow meter

Throttle sensor

Intake air temperature sensor

Air valve

Reed valve

EGR control valve

Air control valve

Water temperature switch

Water thermo sensor

O₂ sensor

Exhaust gas

Vacuum

Fuel

Water thermo valve

Catalytic converter

Dash pot

Air by pass solenoid valve

Three way solenoid valve

EGR modulator valve

Orifice

Air

Other

**1986–87 626 (non-turbo)**

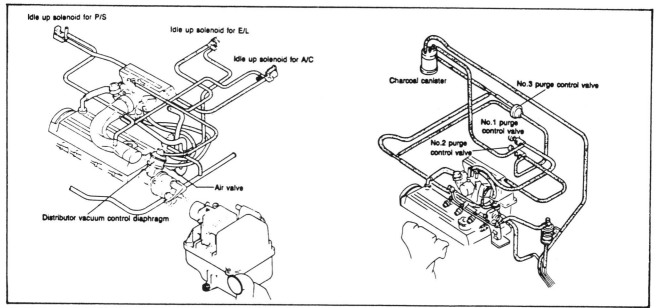

**1986–87 323 (EFI)**

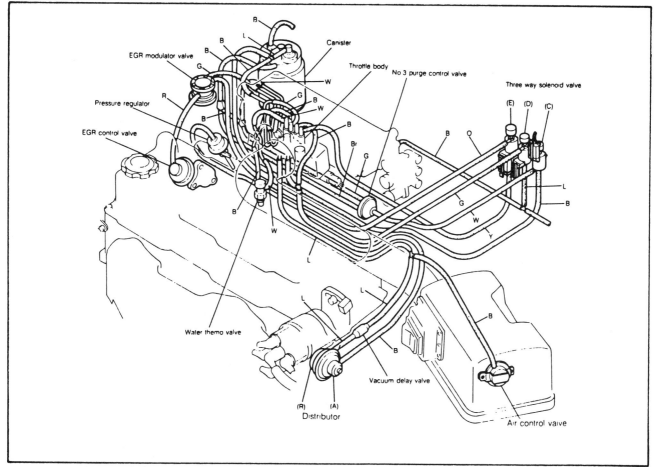

**1986–87 626 (non-turbo)**

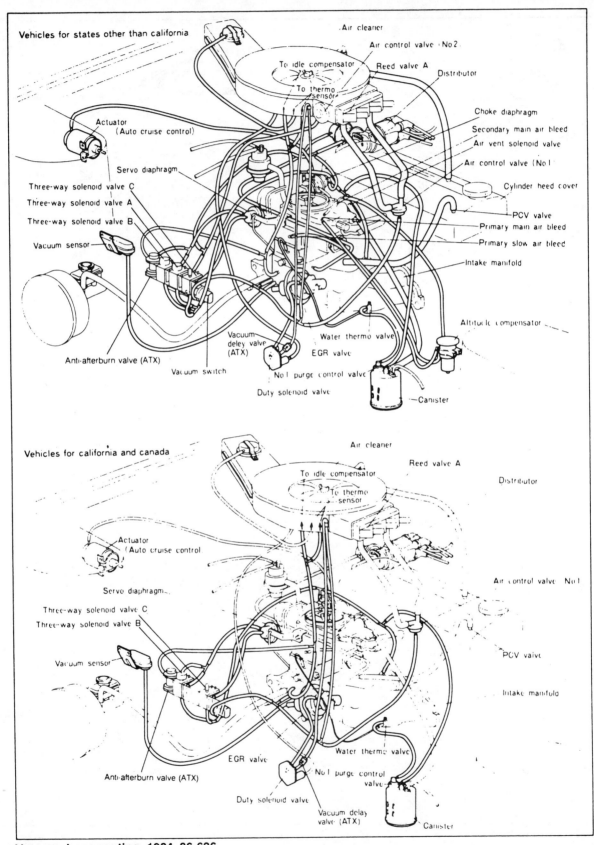

**Vehicles for states other than california**

Air cleaner

Air control valve (No 2)

To idle compensator

Reed valve A

Distributor

To thermo sensor

Choke diaphragm

Secondary main air bleed

Air vent solenoid valve

Air control valve (No 1)

Actuator (Auto cruise control)

Cylinder heed cover

Servo diaphragm

PCV valve

Three-way solenoid valve C

Primary main air bleed

Three-way solenoid valve A

Primary slow air bleed

Three-way solenoid valve B

Vacuum sensor

Intake manifold

Altitude compensator

Vacuum delay valve (ATX)

Water thermo valve

Anti-afterburn valve (ATX)

EGR valve

Vacuum switch

No 1 purge control valve

Duty solenoid valve

Canister

**Vehicles for california and canada**

Air cleaner

To idle compensator

Reed valve A

Distributor

To thermo sensor

Actuator (Auto cruise control)

Air control valve No 1

Servo diaphragm

Three-way solenoid valve C

Three-way solenoid valve B

PCV valve

Vacuum sensor

Intake manifold

EGR valve

Water thermo valve

Anti-afterburn valve (ATX)

No 1 purge control valve

Duty solenoid valve

Vacuum delay valve (ATX)

Canister

**Vacuum hose routing, 1984–86 626**

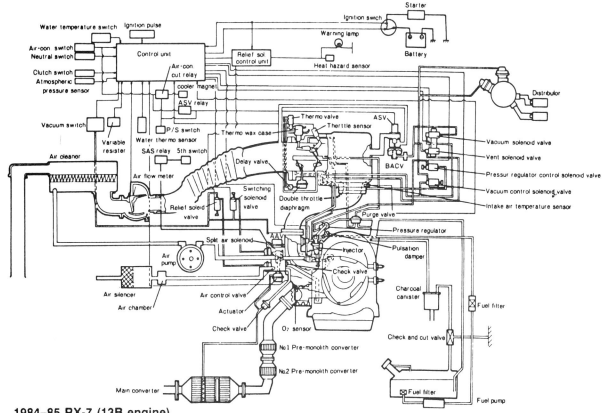

**1984–85 RX-7 (13B engine)**

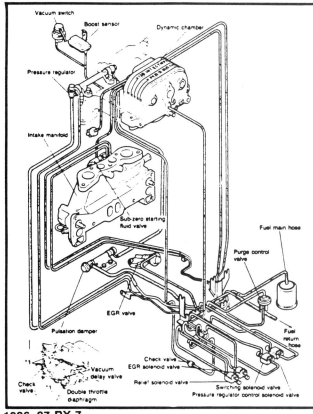

**1986–87 RX-7**

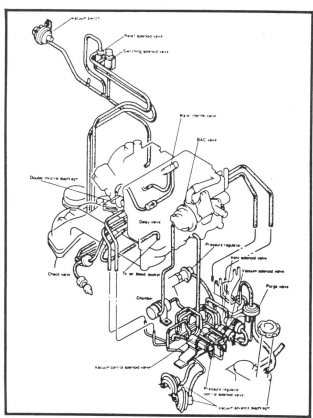

**Vacuum hose routing, 1984–85 RX-7 (13B engine)**

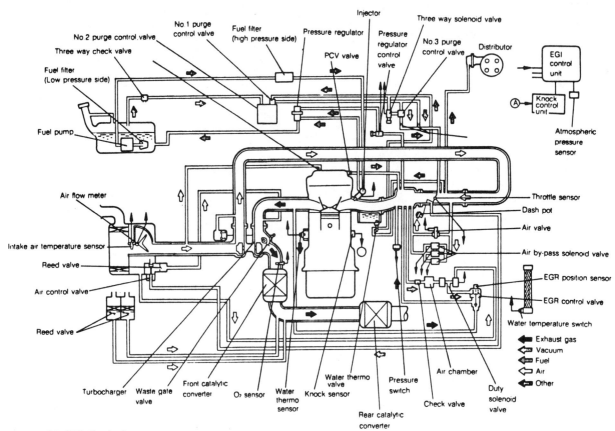

No 2 purge control valve
No.1 purge control valve
Fuel filter (high pressure side)
Pressure regulator
Injector
Three way solenoid valve
Three way check valve
Pressure regulator control valve
No.3 purge control valve
Distributor
Fuel filter (Low pressure side)
PCV valve
EGI control unit
Knock control unit
Atmospheric pressure sensor
Fuel pump
Air flow meter
Throttle sensor
Dash pot
Air valve
Intake air temperature sensor
Air by-pass solenoid valve
Reed valve
EGR position sensor
Air control valve
EGR control valve
Water temperature switch
Reed valve

Exhaust gas
Vacuum
Fuel
Air
Other

Turbocharger
Waste gate valve
Front catalytic converter
O₂ sensor
Water thermo sensor
Knock sensor
Water thermo valve
Pressure switch
Air chamber
Check valve
Duty solenoid valve
Rear catalytic converter

**1986–87 626 (turbo)**

| Component | Color | Connected to: |
|---|---|---|
| Air control valve | Black | Vacuum delay valve |
| | Blue | Throttle body |
| Three way solenoid valve (D) | Black | Auto cruise control actuator |
| | Blue & black | Surge tank |
| | Green | Pressure regulator |
| Three way solenoid valve (C) | Blue | No. 1 purge control valve and water thermo valve |
| | Black | |
| | White | No. 3 purge control valve |
| No. 3 purge control valve | Black | Vacuum hose between canister and throttle body (canister side) |
| | Green | Vacuum hose between canister and throttle body (throttle body side) |
| | White | Three way solenoid valve (C) |
| Three way solenoid valve (E) | Yellow | Throttle body |
| | Orahge | EGR modulator valve |
| EGR modulator valve | Green | Throttle body |
| | Orange | Three way solenoid valve (E) |
| | Red | EGR control valve |
| Water thermo valve | Black | No. 1 purge control valve |
| | White | Throttle body |
| Vacuum delay valve | Blue | Throttle body |
| | Blue | Distributor, diaphragm (R) |
| | Black | Air control valve |
| Distributor diaphragm (A) | Black | Throttle body |
| Canister | Black | Water thermo valve |
| | Black | Throttle body |
| | Black | Evaporation pipe |

**1986–87 626 (non-turbo)**

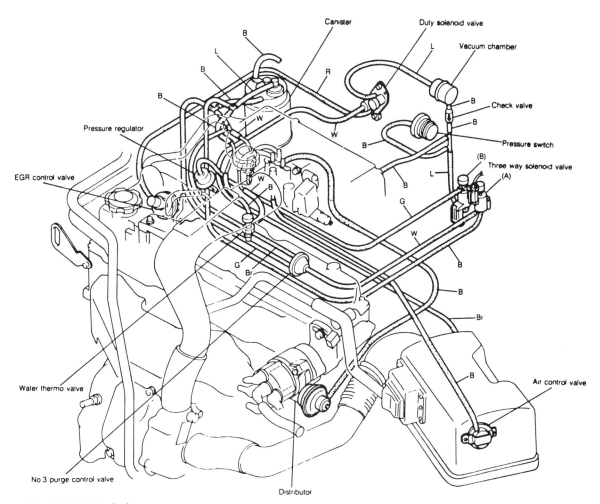

**1986–87 626 (turbo)**

| Component | Color | Connected to: |
|---|---|---|
| Air control valve | Black | Throttle body |
| Distributor diaphragm | Black | Throttle body |
| Three way solenoid valve (A) | Black and blue | No. 1 purge control valve and water thermo valve |
| | White | No. 3 purge control valve |
| Three way solenoid valve (B) | Green | Pressure regulator |
| | Blue and black | Check valve |
| | Blue and black | Pressure switch |
| | Blue and black | Surge tank |
| No. 3 purge control valve | White | Three way solenoid valve (A) |
| | Green | Vacuum hose between canister and throttle body (Canister side) |
| | Brown | Vacuum hose between canister and throttle body (throttle body side) |
| Duty solenoid valve | Blue | Vacuum chamber |
| | White and Brown | Air cleaner |
| | Red | EGR control valve |
| Canister | Black and white | Water Thermo valve |
| | Blue and black | Throttle body |
| | Black | Evaporation pipe |

**1986–87 626 (turbo)**

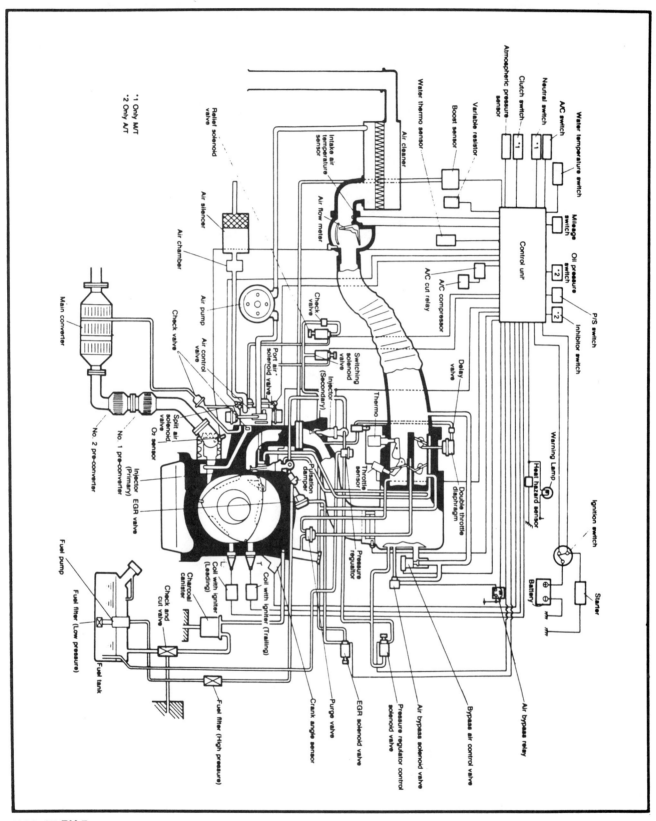

# Mercedes-Benz

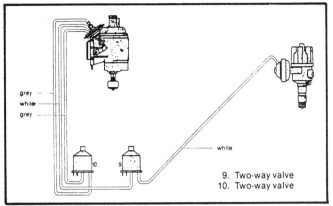

1970–71 220/8

9. Two-way valve
10. Two-way valve

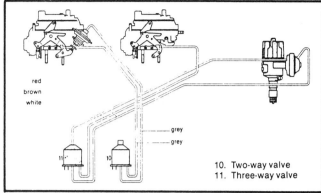

1970–71 250/8 and 280S/8

10. Two-way valve
11. Three-way valve

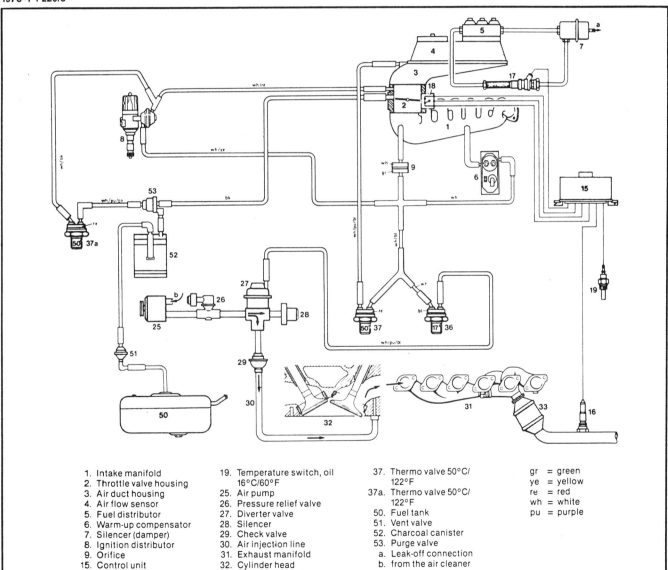

1981 and later 280E and 280CE

| | | | |
|---|---|---|---|
| 1. Intake manifold | 19. Temperature switch, oil 16°C/60°F | 37. Thermo valve 50°C/ 122°F | gr = green |
| 2. Throttle valve housing | 25. Air pump | 37a. Thermo valve 50°C/ 122°F | ye = yellow |
| 3. Air duct housing | 26. Pressure relief valve | | re = red |
| 4. Air flow sensor | 27. Diverter valve | 50. Fuel tank | wh = white |
| 5. Fuel distributor | 28. Silencer | 51. Vent valve | pu = purple |
| 6. Warm-up compensator | 29. Check valve | 52. Charcoal canister | |
| 7. Silencer (damper) | 30. Air injection line | 53. Purge valve | |
| 8. Ignition distributor | 31. Exhaust manifold | a. Leak-off connection | |
| 9. Orifice | 32. Cylinder head | b. from the air cleaner | |
| 15. Control unit | 33. Primary catalyst | Color code | |
| 16. Oxygen sensor | 36. Thermo valve 17°C/ 63°F | bk = black | |
| 17. Frequency valve | | bl = blue | |
| 18. Throttle valve switch | | | |

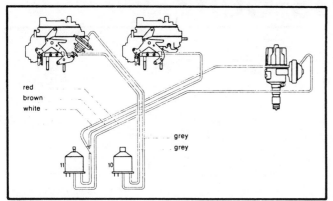

**1972 250 and 250C**

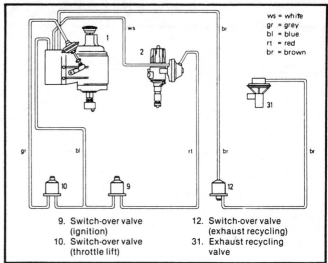

ws = white
gr = grey
bl = blue
rt = red
br = brown

9. Switch-over valve (ignition)
10. Switch-over valve (throttle lift)
12. Switch-over valve (exhaust recycling)
31. Exhaust recycling valve

**1973 220**

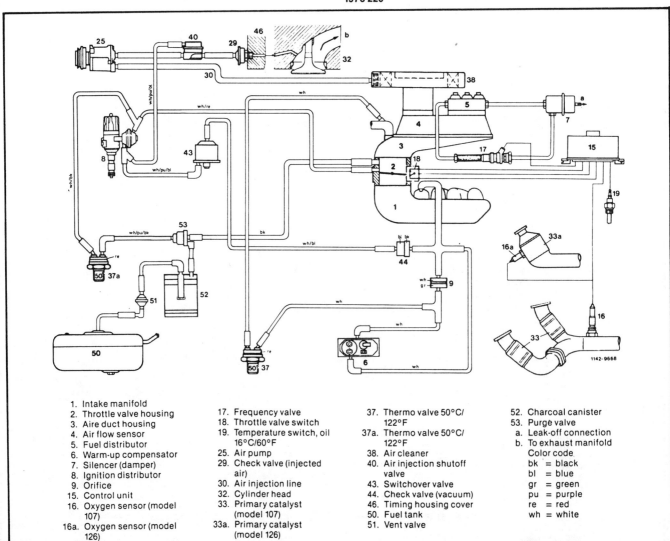

1. Intake manifold
2. Throttle valve housing
3. Aire duct housing
4. Air flow sensor
5. Fuel distributor
6. Warm-up compensator
7. Silencer (damper)
8. Ignition distributor
9. Orifice
15. Control unit
16. Oxygen sensor (model 107)
16a. Oxygen sensor (model 126)

17. Frequency valve
18. Throttle valve switch
19. Temperature switch, oil 16°C/60°F
25. Air pump
29. Check valve (injected air)
30. Air injection line
32. Cylinder head
33. Primary catalyst (model 107)
33a. Primary catalyst (model 126)

37. Thermo valve 50°C/ 122°F
37a. Thermo valve 50°C/ 122°F
38. Air cleaner
40. Air injection shutoff valve
43. Switchover valve
44. Check valve (vacuum)
46. Timing housing cover
50. Fuel tank
51. Vent valve

52. Charcoal canister
53. Purge valve
a. Leak-off connection
b. To exhaust manifold
Color code
bk = black
bl = blue
gr = green
pu = purple
re = red
wh = white

**1980 and later 380SEL, 380SL and 380SLC**

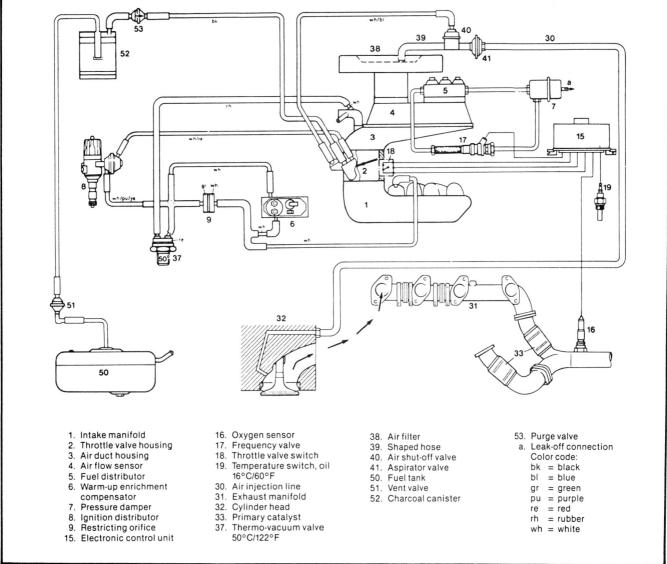

1. Intake manifold
2. Throttle valve housing
3. Air duct housing
4. Air flow sensor
5. Fuel distributor
6. Warm-up enrichment compensator
7. Pressure damper
8. Ignition distributor
9. Restricting orifice
15. Electronic control unit

16. Oxygen sensor
17. Frequency valve
18. Throttle valve switch
19. Temperature switch, oil 16°C/60°F
30. Air injection line
31. Exhaust manifold
32. Cylinder head
33. Primary catalyst
37. Thermo-vacuum valve 50°C/122°F

38. Air filter
39. Shaped hose
40. Air shut-off valve
41. Aspirator valve
50. Fuel tank
51. Vent valve
52. Charcoal canister

53. Purge valve
a. Leak-off connection
   Color code:
   bk = black
   bl = blue
   gr = green
   pu = purple
   re = red
   rh = rubber
   wh = white

**1980 and later 450SEL, 450SL and 450SLC**

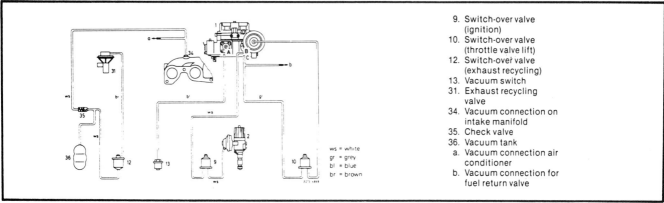

9. Switch-over valve (ignition)
10. Switch-over valve (throttle valve lift)
12. Switch-over valve (exhaust recycling)
13. Vacuum switch
31. Exhaust recycling valve
34. Vacuum connection on intake manifold
35. Check valve
36. Vacuum tank
a. Vacuum connection air conditioner
b. Vacuum connection for fuel return valve

ws = white
gr = grey
bl = blue
br = brown

**1973 280 and 280C**

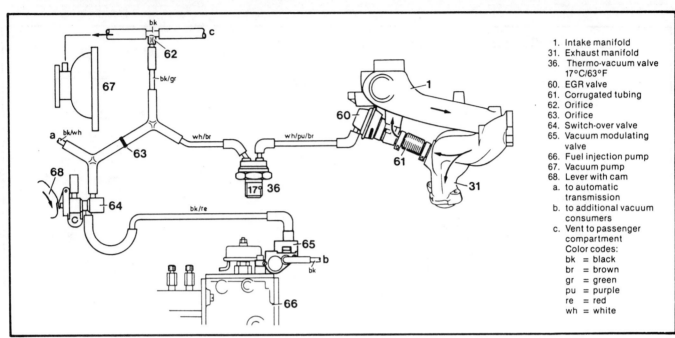

1. Intake manifold
31. Exhaust manifold
36. Thermo-vacuum valve 17°C/63°F
60. EGR valve
61. Corrugated tubing
62. Orifice
63. Orifice
64. Switch-over valve
65. Vacuum modulating valve
66. Fuel injection pump
67. Vacuum pump
68. Lever with cam
a. to automatic transmission
b. to additional vacuum consumers
c. Vent to passenger compartment

Color codes:
bk = black
br = brown
gr = green
pu = purple
re = red
wh = white

**1980 300D, 300CD and 300TD**

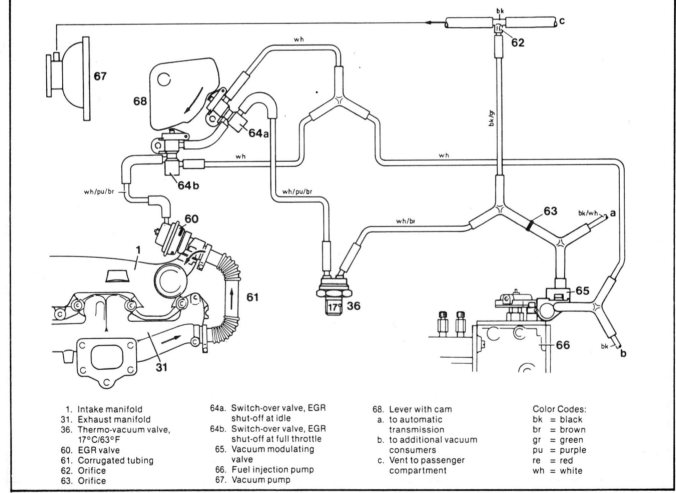

1. Intake manifold
31. Exhaust manifold
36. Thermo-vacuum valve, 17°C/63°F
60. EGR valve
61. Corrugated tubing
62. Orifice
63. Orifice

64a. Switch-over valve, EGR shut-off at idle
64b. Switch-over valve, EGR shut-off at full throttle
65. Vacuum modulating valve
66. Fuel injection pump
67. Vacuum pump

68. Lever with cam
a. to automatic transmission
b. to additional vacuum consumers
c. Vent to passenger compartment

Color Codes:
bk = black
br = brown
gr = green
pu = purple
re = red
wh = white

**1980 and later 300SD**

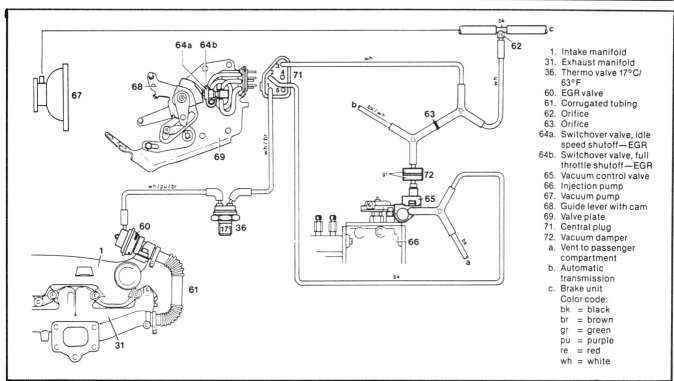

1. Intake manifold
31. Exhaust manifold
36. Thermo valve 17°C/63°F
60. EGR valve
61. Corrugated tubing
62. Orifice
63. Orifice
64a. Switchover valve, idle speed shutoff—EGR
64b. Switchover valve, full throttle shutoff—EGR
65. Vacuum control valve
66. Injection pump
67. Vacuum pump
68. Guide lever with cam
69. Valve plate
71. Central plug
72. Vacuum damper
 a. Vent to passenger compartment
 b. Automatic transmission
 c. Brake unit
 Color code:
 bk = black
 br = brown
 gr = green
 pu = purple
 re = red
 wh = white

**1982-83 300D, 300CD and 300TD**

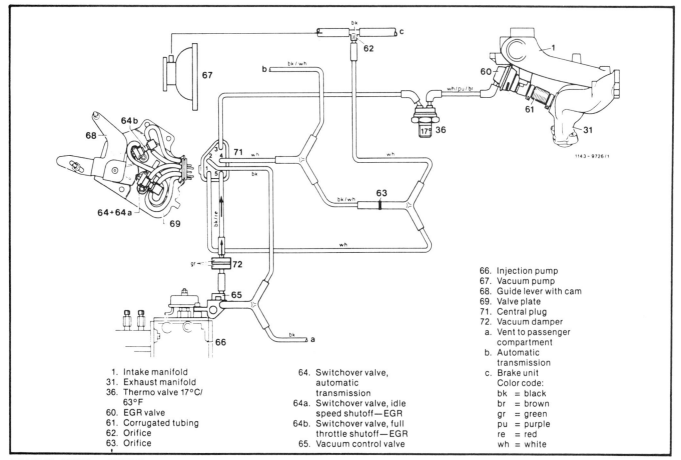

66. Injection pump
67. Vacuum pump
68. Guide lever with cam
69. Valve plate
71. Central plug
72. Vacuum damper
 a. Vent to passenger compartment
 b. Automatic transmission
 c. Brake unit
 Color code:
 bk = black
 br = brown
 gr = green
 pu = purple
 re = red
 wh = white

1. Intake manifold
31. Exhaust manifold
36. Thermo valve 17°C/63°F
60. EGR valve
61. Corrugated tubing
62. Orifice
63. Orifice
64. Switchover valve, automatic transmission
64a. Switchover valve, idle speed shutoff—EGR
64b. Switchover valve, full throttle shutoff—EGR
65. Vacuum control valve

**1981 300D, 300CD and 300TD**

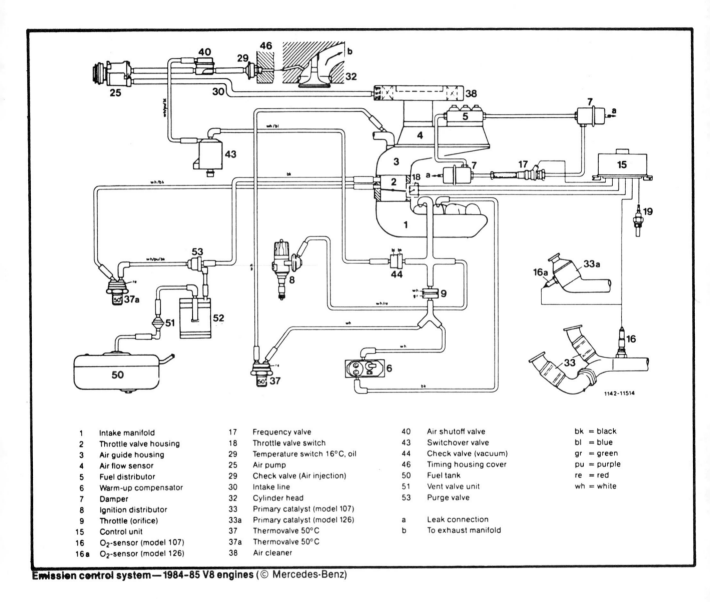

**Emission control system—1984-85 V8 engines** (© Mercedes-Benz)

| | | | | | | |
|---|---|---|---|---|---|---|
| 1 | Intake manifold | 17 | Frequency valve | 40 | Air shutoff valve | bk = black |
| 2 | Throttle valve housing | 18 | Throttle valve switch | 43 | Switchover valve | bl = blue |
| 3 | Air guide housing | 29 | Temperature switch 16°C, oil | 44 | Check valve (vacuum) | gr = green |
| 4 | Air flow sensor | 25 | Air pump | 46 | Timing housing cover | pu = purple |
| 5 | Fuel distributor | 29 | Check valve (Air injection) | 50 | Fuel tank | re = red |
| 6 | Warm-up compensator | 30 | Intake line | 51 | Vent valve unit | wh = white |
| 7 | Damper | 32 | Cylinder head | 53 | Purge valve | |
| 8 | Ignition distributor | 33 | Primary catalyst (model 107) | | | |
| 9 | Throttle (orifice) | 33a | Primary catalyst (model 126) | a | Leak connection | |
| 15 | Control unit | 37 | Thermovalve 50°C | b | To exhaust manifold | |
| 16 | O₂-sensor (model 107) | 37a | Thermovalve 50°C | | | |
| 16a | O₂-sensor (model 126) | 38 | Air cleaner | | | |

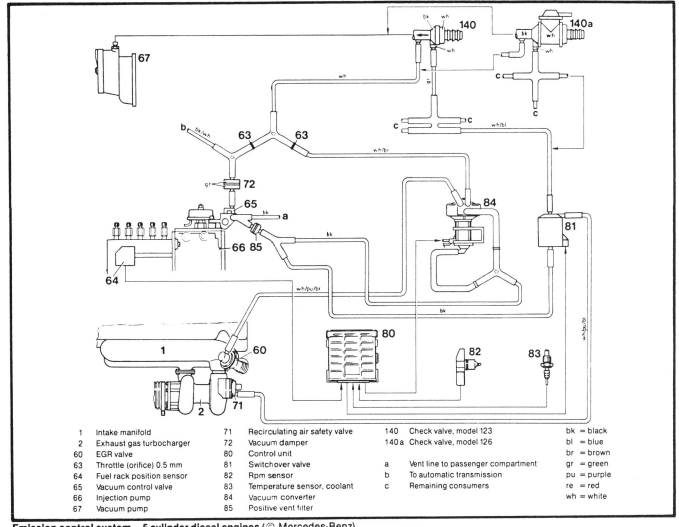

| | | | | | | | |
|---|---|---|---|---|---|---|---|
| 1 | Intake manifold | 71 | Recirculating air safety valve | 140 | Check valve, model 123 | bk | = black |
| 2 | Exhaust gas turbocharger | 72 | Vacuum damper | 140 a | Check valve, model 126 | bl | = blue |
| 60 | EGR valve | 80 | Control unit | | | br | = brown |
| 63 | Throttle (orifice) 0.5 mm | 81 | Switchover valve | a | Vent line to passenger compartment | gr | = green |
| 64 | Fuel rack position sensor | 82 | Rpm sensor | b | To automatic transmission | pu | = purple |
| 65 | Vacuum control valve | 83 | Temperature sensor, coolant | c | Remaining consumers | re | = red |
| 66 | Injection pump | 84 | Vacuum converter | | | wh | = white |
| 67 | Vacuum pump | 85 | Positive vent filter | | | | |

**Emission control system—5 cylinder diesel engines** (© Mercedes-Benz)

111

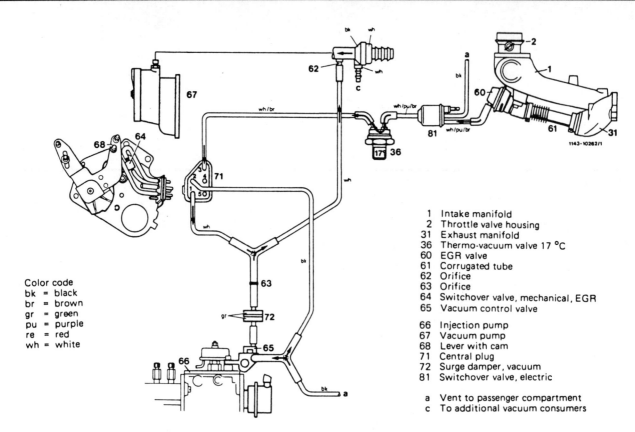

**Color code**
bk = black
br = brown
gr = green
pu = purple
re = red
wh = white

1   Intake manifold
2   Throttle valve housing
31  Exhaust manifold
36  Thermo-vacuum valve 17 °C
60  EGR valve
61  Corrugated tube
62  Orifice
63  Orifice
64  Switchover valve, mechanical, EGR
65  Vacuum control valve
66  Injection pump
67  Vacuum pump
68  Lever with cam
71  Central plug
72  Surge damper, vacuum
81  Switchover valve, electric

a   Vent to passenger compartment
c   To additional vacuum consumers

**MERCEDES-BENZ 240D—DIESEL-MAN. TRANS.**

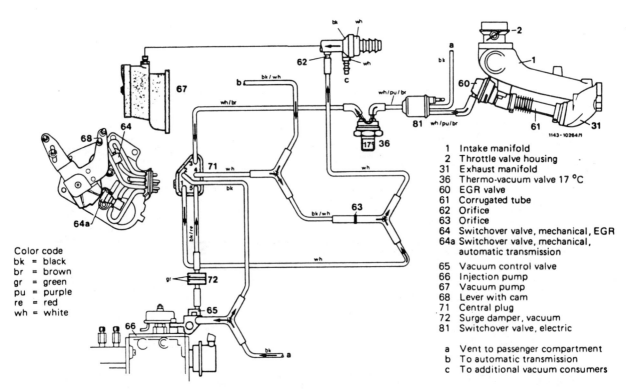

**Color code**
bk = black
br = brown
gr = green
pu = purple
re = red
wh = white

1   Intake manifold
2   Throttle valve housing
31  Exhaust manifold
36  Thermo-vacuum valve 17 °C
60  EGR valve
61  Corrugated tube
62  Orifice
63  Orifice
64  Switchover valve, mechanical, EGR
64a Switchover valve, mechanical,
    automatic transmission
65  Vacuum control valve
66  Injection pump
67  Vacuum pump
68  Lever with cam
71  Central plug
72  Surge damper, vacuum
81  Switchover valve, electric

a   Vent to passenger compartment
b   To automatic transmission
c   To additional vacuum consumers

**MERCEDES-BENZ 240D—DIESEL-AUTO TRANS.**

112

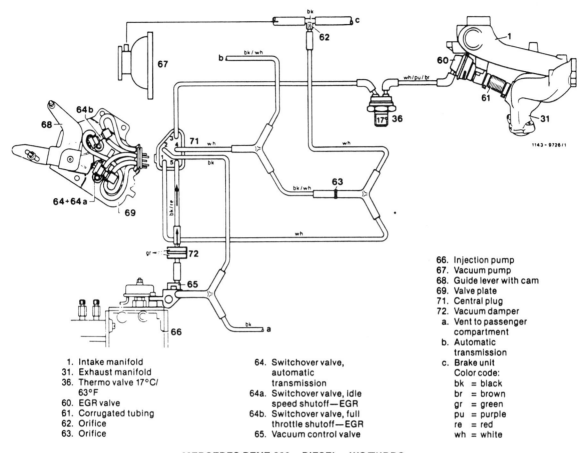

1. Intake manifold
31. Exhaust manifold
36. Thermo valve 17°C/ 63°F
60. EGR valve
61. Corrugated tubing
62. Orifice
63. Orifice

64. Switchover valve, automatic transmission
64a. Switchover valve, idle speed shutoff—EGR
64b. Switchover valve, full throttle shutoff—EGR
65. Vacuum control valve

66. Injection pump
67. Vacuum pump
68. Guide lever with cam
69. Valve plate
71. Central plug
72. Vacuum damper
a. Vent to passenger compartment
b. Automatic transmission
c. Brake unit

Color code:
bk = black
br = brown
gr = green
pu = purple
re = red
wh = white

**MERCEDES-BENZ 300—DIESEL—WO/TURBO**

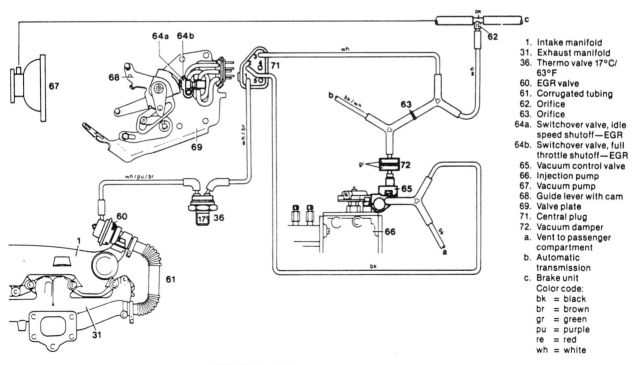

1. Intake manifold
31. Exhaust manifold
36. Thermo valve 17°C/ 63°F
60. EGR valve
61. Corrugated tubing
62. Orifice
63. Orifice
64a. Switchover valve, idle speed shutoff—EGR
64b. Switchover valve, full throttle shutoff—EGR
65. Vacuum control valve
66. Injection pump
67. Vacuum pump
68. Guide lever with cam
69. Valve plate
71. Central plug
72. Vacuum damper
a. Vent to passenger compartment
b. Automatic transmission
c. Brake unit

Color code:
bk = black
br = brown
gr = green
pu = purple
re = red
wh = white

**MERCEDES-BENZ 300—DIESEL—W/TURBO.**

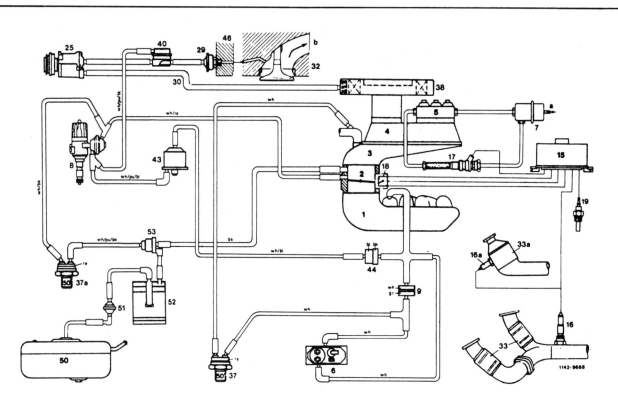

1. Intake manifold
2. Throttle valve housing
3. Aire duct housing
4. Air flow sensor
5. Fuel distributor
6. Warm-up compensator
7. Silencer (damper)
8. Ignition distributor
9. Orifice
15. Control unit
16. Oxygen sensor (model 107)
16a. Oxygen sensor (model 126)

17. Frequency valve
18. Throttle valve switch
19. Temperature switch, oil 16°C/60°F
25. Air pump
29. Check valve (injected air)
30. Air injection line
32. Cylinder head
33. Primary catalyst (model 107)
33a. Primary catalyst (model 126)

37. Thermo valve 50°C/ 122°F
37a. Thermo valve 50°C/ 122°F
38. Air cleaner
40. Air injection shutoff valve
43. Switchover valve
44. Check valve (vacuum)
46. Timing housing cover
50. Fuel tank
51. Vent valve

52. Charcoal canister
53. Purge valve
a. Leak-off connection
b. To exhaust manifold
Color code
bk = black
bl = blue
gr = green
pu = purple
re = red
wh = white

**MERCEDES-BENZ 380 SERIES**

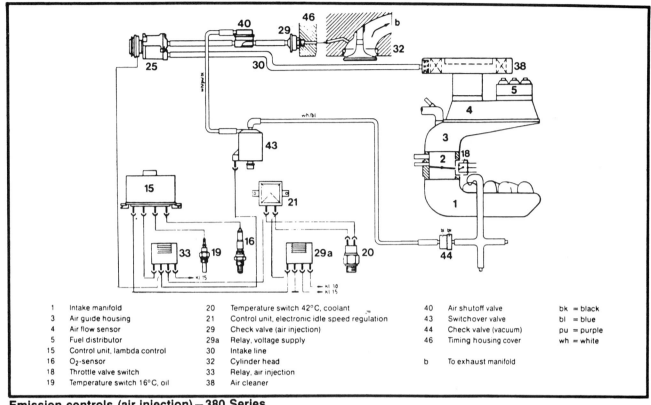

| | | | | | | |
|---|---|---|---|---|---|---|
| 1 | Intake manifold | 20 | Temperature switch 42°C, coolant | 40 | Air shutoff valve | bk = black |
| 3 | Air guide housing | 21 | Control unit, electronic idle speed regulation | 43 | Switchover valve | bl = blue |
| 4 | Air flow sensor | 29 | Check valve (air injection) | 44 | Check valve (vacuum) | pu = purple |
| 5 | Fuel distributor | 29a | Relay, voltage supply | 46 | Timing housing cover | wh = white |
| 15 | Control unit, lambda control | 30 | Intake line | | | |
| 16 | O$_2$-sensor | 32 | Cylinder head | b | To exhaust manifold | |
| 18 | Throttle valve switch | 33 | Relay, air injection | | | |
| 19 | Temperature switch 16°C, oil | 38 | Air cleaner | | | |

**Emission controls (air injection) – 380 Series**

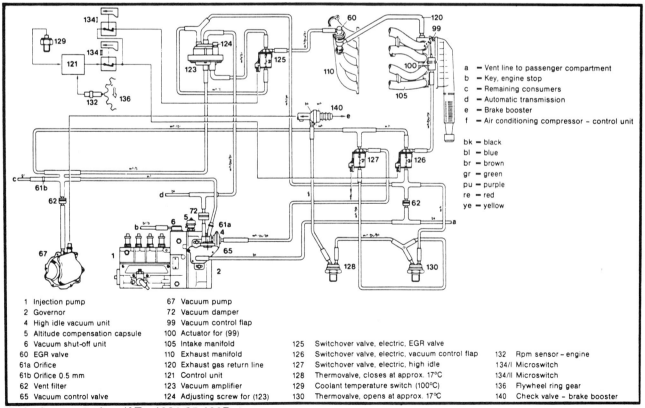

| | | | | | | |
|---|---|---|---|---|---|---|
| | | | | a – Vent line to passenger compartment | | |
| | | | | b – Key, engine stop | | |
| | | | | c – Remaining consumers | | |
| | | | | d – Automatic transmission | | |
| | | | | e – Brake booster | | |
| | | | | f – Air conditioning compressor – control unit | | |
| | | | | | | |
| | | | | bk = black | | |
| | | | | bl = blue | | |
| | | | | br = brown | | |
| | | | | gr = green | | |
| | | | | pu = purple | | |
| | | | | re = red | | |
| | | | | ye = yellow | | |

| | | | | | | | |
|---|---|---|---|---|---|---|---|
| 1 | Injection pump | 67 | Vacuum pump | | | | |
| 2 | Governor | 72 | Vacuum damper | | | | |
| 4 | High idle vacuum unit | 99 | Vacuum control flap | | | | |
| 5 | Altitude compensation capsule | 100 | Actuator for (99) | | | | |
| 6 | Vacuum shut-off unit | 105 | Intake manifold | 125 | Switchover valve, electric, EGR valve | 132 | Rpm sensor – engine |
| 60 | EGR valve | 110 | Exhaust manifold | 126 | Switchover valve, electric, vacuum control flap | 134/I | Microswitch |
| 61a | Orifice | 120 | Exhaust gas return line | 127 | Switchover valve, electric, high idle | 134/II | Microswitch |
| 61b | Orifice 0.5 mm | 121 | Control unit | 128 | Thermovalve, closes at approx. 17°C | 136 | Flywheel ring gear |
| 62 | Vent filter | 123 | Vacuum amplifier | 129 | Coolant temperature switch (100°C) | 140 | Check valve – brake booster |
| 65 | Vacuum control valve | 124 | Adjusting screw for (123) | 130 | Thermovalve, opens at approx. 17°C | | |

**Emission controls w/AT – 1984-85 190D**

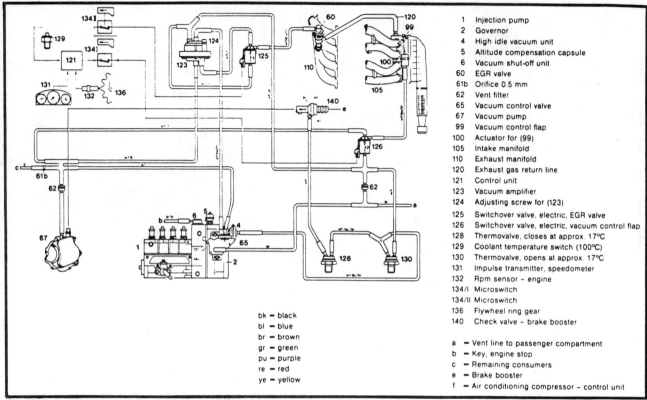

| | | |
|---|---|---|
| 1 | Injection pump |
| 2 | Governor |
| 4 | High idle vacuum unit |
| 5 | Altitude compensation capsule |
| 6 | Vacuum shut-off unit |
| 60 | EGR valve |
| 61b | Orifice 0.5 mm |
| 62 | Vent filter |
| 65 | Vacuum control valve |
| 67 | Vacuum pump |
| 99 | Vacuum control flap |
| 100 | Actuator for (99) |
| 105 | Intake manifold |
| 110 | Exhaust manifold |
| 120 | Exhaust gas return line |
| 121 | Control unit |
| 123 | Vacuum amplifier |
| 124 | Adjusting screw for (123) |
| 125 | Switchover valve, electric, EGR valve |
| 126 | Switchover valve, electric, vacuum control flap |
| 128 | Thermovalve, closes at approx. 17°C |
| 129 | Coolant temperature switch (100°C) |
| 130 | Thermovalve, opens at approx. 17°C |
| 131 | Impulse transmitter, speedometer |
| 132 | Rpm sensor – engine |
| 134/I | Microswitch |
| 134/II | Microswitch |
| 136 | Flywheel ring gear |
| 140 | Check valve – brake booster |

bk = black
bl = blue
br = brown
gr = green
pu = purple
re = red
ye = yellow

a = Vent line to passenger compartment
b = Key, engine stop
c = Remaining consumers
e = Brake booster
f = Air conditioning compressor – control unit

**Emission controls w/MT – 1984-85 190D**

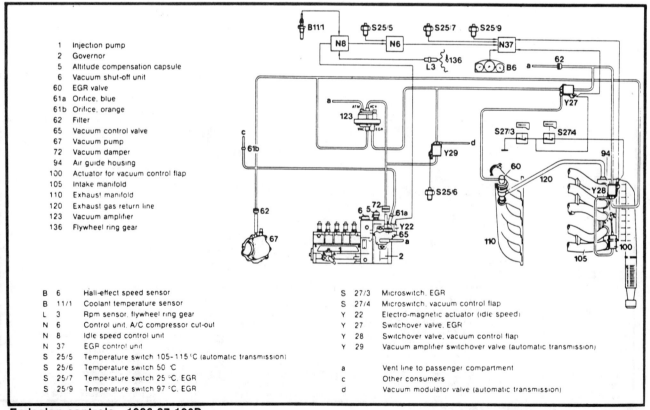

| | | |
|---|---|---|
| 1 | Injection pump |
| 2 | Governor |
| 5 | Altitude compensation capsule |
| 6 | Vacuum shut-off unit |
| 60 | EGR valve |
| 61a | Orifice, blue |
| 61b | Orifice, orange |
| 62 | Filter |
| 65 | Vacuum control valve |
| 67 | Vacuum pump |
| 72 | Vacuum damper |
| 94 | Air guide housing |
| 100 | Actuator for vacuum control flap |
| 105 | Intake manifold |
| 110 | Exhaust manifold |
| 120 | Exhaust gas return line |
| 123 | Vacuum amplifier |
| 136 | Flywheel ring gear |

| | | |
|---|---|---|
| B 6 | Hall-effect speed sensor |
| B 11/1 | Coolant temperature sensor |
| L 3 | Rpm sensor, flywheel ring gear |
| N 6 | Control unit, A/C compressor cut-out |
| N 8 | Idle speed control unit |
| N 37 | EGR control unit |
| S 25/5 | Temperature switch 105-115°C (automatic transmission) |
| S 25/6 | Temperature switch 50°C |
| S 25/7 | Temperature switch 25°C, EGR |
| S 25/9 | Temperature switch 97°C, EGR |
| S 27/3 | Microswitch, EGR |
| S 27/4 | Microswitch, vacuum control flap |
| Y 22 | Electro-magnetic actuator (idle speed) |
| Y 27 | Switchover valve, EGR |
| Y 28 | Switchover valve, vacuum control flap |
| Y 29 | Vacuum amplifier switchover valve (automatic transmission) |
| a | Vent line to passenger compartment |
| c | Other consumers |
| d | Vacuum modulator valve (automatic transmission) |

**Emission controls – 1986-87 190D**

116

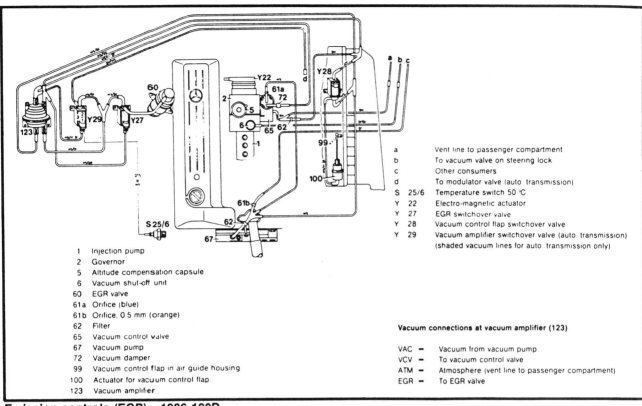

a   Vent line to passenger compartment
b   To vacuum valve on steering lock
c   Other consumers
d   To modulator valve (auto. transmission)
S 25/6   Temperature switch 50 °C
Y 22   Electro-magnetic actuator
Y 27   EGR switchover valve
Y 28   Vacuum control flap switchover valve
Y 29   Vacuum amplifier switchover valve (auto. transmission)
(shaded vacuum lines for auto. transmission only)

1   Injection pump
2   Governor
5   Altitude compensation capsule
6   Vacuum shut-off unit
60   EGR valve
61a   Orifice (blue)
61b   Orifice, 0.5 mm (orange)
62   Filter
65   Vacuum control valve
67   Vacuum pump
72   Vacuum damper
99   Vacuum control flap in air guide housing
100   Actuator for vacuum control flap
123   Vacuum amplifier

**Vacuum connections at vacuum amplifier (123)**

VAC =   Vacuum from vacuum pump
VCV =   To vacuum control valve
ATM =   Atmosphere (vent line to passenger compartment)
EGR =   To EGR valve

**Emission controls (EGR) — 1986 190D**

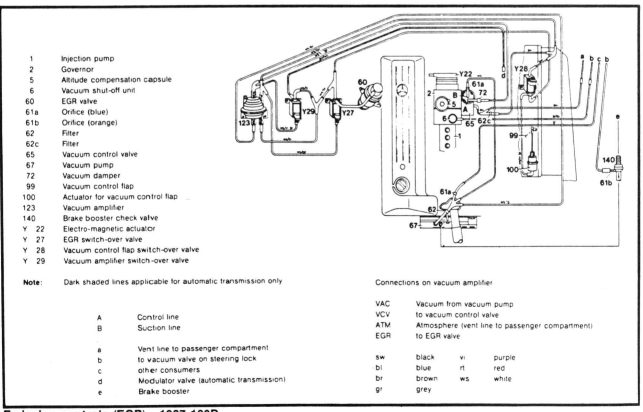

1   Injection pump
2   Governor
5   Altitude compensation capsule
6   Vacuum shut-off unit
60   EGR valve
61a   Orifice (blue)
61b   Orifice (orange)
62   Filter
62c   Filter
65   Vacuum control valve
67   Vacuum pump
72   Vacuum damper
99   Vacuum control flap
100   Actuator for vacuum control flap
123   Vacuum amplifier
140   Brake booster check valve
Y 22   Electro-magnetic actuator
Y 27   EGR switch-over valve
Y 28   Vacuum control flap switch-over valve
Y 29   Vacuum amplifier switch-over valve

**Note:**   Dark shaded lines applicable for automatic transmission only

A   Control line
B   Suction line

a   Vent line to passenger compartment
b   to vacuum valve on steering lock
c   other consumers
d   Modulator valve (automatic transmission)
e   Brake booster

Connections on vacuum amplifier

VAC   Vacuum from vacuum pump
VCV   to vacuum control valve
ATM   Atmosphere (vent line to passenger compartment)
EGR   to EGR valve

| sw | black | vi | purple |
|----|-------|----|--------|
| bl | blue | rt | red |
| br | brown | ws | white |
| gr | grey | | |

**Emission controls (EGR) — 1987 190D**

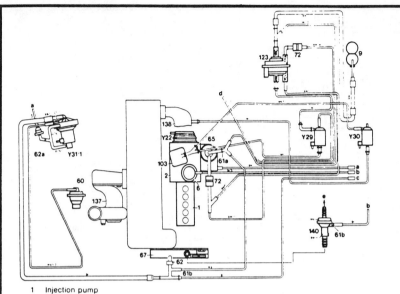

| a | Vent line to passenger compartment |
| b | Key, engine stop |
| c | Other consumers |
| d | Vacuum modulator valve (automatic transmission) |
| e | Brake booster |

**Connections on vacuum amplifier and vacuum transducer**

| PRE | Boost pressure from aneroid compensator (ALDA) |
| TRA | To vacuum modulator valve, automatic transmission |
| VAC | Vacuum from vacuum pump |
| VCV | To vacuum control valve |
| ATM | Vent line to passenger compartment |
| OUT | To EGR valve |

| sw | = black |
| bl | = blue |
| br | = brown |
| gr | = grey |
| vi | = purple |
| rt | = red |
| ws | = white |

| 1 | Injection pump | | 72 | Vacuum damper |
| 2 | Governor | | 103 | Aneroid compensator (ALDA) |
| 6 | Vacuum shut-off unit | | 123 | Vacuum amplifier |
| 9 | Vacuum reservoir (in left front wheel housing behind plastic liner) | | 137 | Turbocharger |
| 60 | EGR valve | | 138 | Intake manifold |
| 61a | Orifice | | 140 | Brake booster check valve |
| 61b | Orifice | | Y22 | Electro-magnetic actuator (idle speed) |
| 62 | Filter | | Y29 | Vacuum amplifier switch-over valve, automatic transmission |
| 62a | Filter | | Y30 | Engine overload protection switch-over valve |
| 65 | Vacuum control valve | | Y31/1 | EGR valve vacuum transducer |
| 67 | Vacuum pump | | | |

**Emission controls – 1987 190D (Turbo)**

| 1 | Injection pump |
| 2 | Governor |
| 60 | EGR valve |
| 61a | Orifice |
| 61b | Orifice |
| 62 | Filter |
| 62a | Filter |
| 65 | Vacuum control valve |
| 67 | Vacuum pump |
| 72 | Vacuum damper |
| 103 | Aneroid compensator (ALDA) |
| 110 | Exhaust manifold |
| 123 | Vacuum amplifier |
| 137 | Turbocharger |
| 138 | Intake manifold |
| B2/1 | Air flow sensor (EDS) |
| B2/1a | Air temperature sensor |
| B11/4 | Coolant temperature sensor (EDS) |
| B18 | Altitude correction capsule |
| L3 | Ring gear speed sensor |
| L7 | Fuel rack position sensor |
| N39 | EDS control unit |

| S25/6 | Temperature switch 50°C |
| S66 | Engine overload protection switch (1.2 bar) |
| Y22 | Electro-magnetic actuator (idle speed) |
| Y29 | Vacuum amplifier, switch-over valve, automatic transmission |
| Y30 | Engine overload protection, switch-over valve |
| Y31/1 | EGR valve, vacuum transducer |

| a | Vent line to passenger compartment |
| c | Remaining consumers |
| A | Intake air |
| B | Exhaust gas |

**Connections on vacuum amplifier and vacuum transducer**

| PRE | Boost pressure from aneroid compensator (ALDA) |
| TRA | to vacuum modulator valve, automatic transmission |
| VAC | Vacuum from vacuum pump |
| VCV | to vacuum control valve |
| ATM | Vent line to passenger compartment |
| OUT | to EGR valve |

**Emission controls (EDS) – 1987 190D (Turbo)**

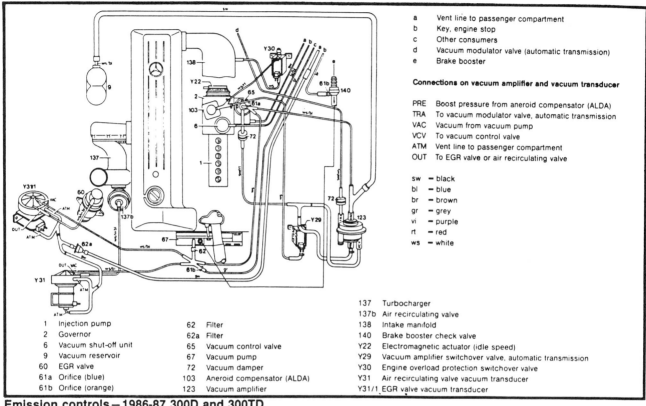

a    Vent line to passenger compartment
b    Key, engine stop
c    Other consumers
d    Vacuum modulator valve (automatic transmission)
e    Brake booster

**Connections on vacuum amplifier and vacuum transducer**

PRE    Boost pressure from aneroid compensator (ALDA)
TRA    To vacuum modulator valve, automatic transmission
VAC    Vacuum from vacuum pump
VCV    To vacuum control valve
ATM    Vent line to passenger compartment
OUT    To EGR valve or air recirculating valve

sw  = black
bl  = blue
br  = brown
gr  = grey
vi  = purple
rt  = red
ws  = white

| | | | | |
|---|---|---|---|---|
| 1 | Injection pump | 62 | Filter | |
| 2 | Governor | 62a | Filter | |
| 6 | Vacuum shut-off unit | 65 | Vacuum control valve | |
| 9 | Vacuum reservoir | 67 | Vacuum pump | |
| 60 | EGR valve | 72 | Vacuum damper | |
| 61a | Orifice (blue) | 103 | Aneroid compensator (ALDA) | |
| 61b | Orifice (orange) | 123 | Vacuum amplifier | |

137    Turbocharger
137b  Air recirculating valve
138   Intake manifold
140   Brake booster check valve
Y22   Electromagnetic actuator (idle speed)
Y29   Vacuum amplifier switchover valve, automatic transmission
Y30   Engine overload protection switchover valve
Y31   Air recirculating valve vacuum transducer
Y31/1 EGR valve vacuum transducer

**Emission controls – 1986-87 300D and 300TD**

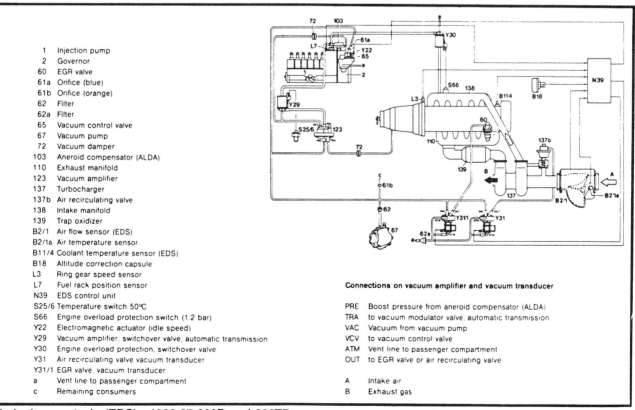

1      Injection pump
2      Governor
60     EGR valve
61a    Orifice (blue)
61b    Orifice (orange)
62     Filter
62a    Filter
65     Vacuum control valve
67     Vacuum pump
72     Vacuum damper
103    Aneroid compensator (ALDA)
110    Exhaust manifold
123    Vacuum amplifier
137    Turbocharger
137b  Air recirculating valve
138   Intake manifold
139   Trap oxidizer
B2/1  Air flow sensor (EDS)
B2/1a Air temperature sensor
B11/4 Coolant temperature sensor (EDS)
B18   Altitude correction capsule
L3    Ring gear speed sensor
L7    Fuel rack position sensor
N39   EDS control unit
S25/6 Temperature switch 50°C
S66   Engine overload protection switch (1.2 bar)
Y22   Electromagnetic actuator (idle speed)
Y29   Vacuum amplifier, switchover valve, automatic transmission
Y30   Engine overload protection, switchover valve
Y31   Air recirculating valve vacuum transducer
Y31/1 EGR valve, vacuum transducer
a     Vent line to passenger compartment
c     Remaining consumers

**Connections on vacuum amplifier and vacuum transducer**

PRE    Boost pressure from aneroid compensator (ALDA)
TRA    to vacuum modulator valve, automatic transmission
VAC    Vacuum from vacuum pump
VCV    to vacuum control valve
ATM    Vent line to passenger compartment
OUT    to EGR valve or air recirculating valve

A    Intake air
B    Exhaust gas

**Emission controls (EDS) – 1986-87 300D and 300TD**

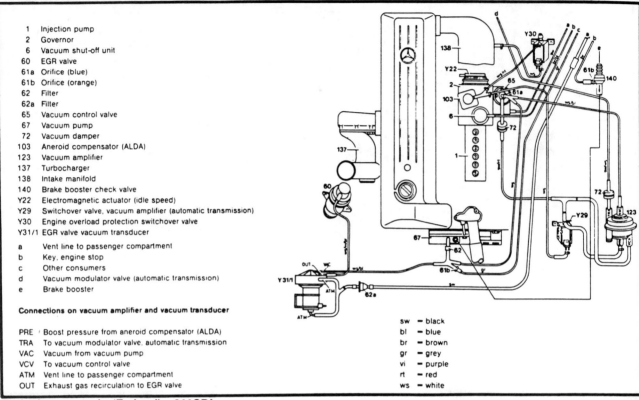

1 Injection pump
2 Governor
6 Vacuum shut-off unit
60 EGR valve
61a Orifice (blue)
61b Orifice (orange)
62 Filter
62a Filter
65 Vacuum control valve
67 Vacuum pump
72 Vacuum damper
103 Aneroid compensator (ALDA)
123 Vacuum amplifier
137 Turbocharger
138 Intake manifold
140 Brake booster check valve
Y22 Electromagnetic actuator (idle speed)
Y29 Switchover valve, vacuum amplifier (automatic transmission)
Y30 Engine overload protection switchover valve
Y31/1 EGR valve vacuum transducer

a Vent line to passenger compartment
b Key, engine stop
c Other consumers
d Vacuum modulator valve (automatic transmission)
e Brake booster

**Connections on vacuum amplifier and vacuum transducer**

PRE   Boost pressure from aneroid compensator (ALDA)
TRA   To vacuum modulator valve, automatic transmission
VAC   Vacuum from vacuum pump
VCV   To vacuum control valve
ATM   Vent line to passenger compartment
OUT   Exhaust gas recirculation to EGR valve

sw = black
bl = blue
br = brown
gr = grey
vi = purple
rt = red
ws = white

**Emission controls (Federal) — 300SDL**

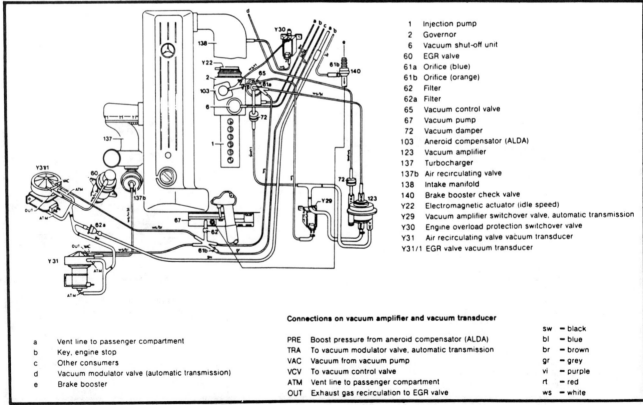

1 Injection pump
2 Governor
6 Vacuum shut-off unit
60 EGR valve
61a Orifice (blue)
61b Orifice (orange)
62 Filter
62a Filter
65 Vacuum control valve
67 Vacuum pump
72 Vacuum damper
103 Aneroid compensator (ALDA)
123 Vacuum amplifier
137 Turbocharger
137b Air recirculating valve
138 Intake manifold
140 Brake booster check valve
Y22 Electromagnetic actuator (idle speed)
Y29 Vacuum amplifier switchover valve, automatic transmission
Y30 Engine overload protection switchover valve
Y31 Air recirculating valve vacuum transducer
Y31/1 EGR valve vacuum transducer

a Vent line to passenger compartment
b Key, engine stop
c Other consumers
d Vacuum modulator valve (automatic transmission)
e Brake booster

**Connections on vacuum amplifier and vacuum transducer**

PRE   Boost pressure from aneroid compensator (ALDA)
TRA   To vacuum modulator valve, automatic transmission
VAC   Vacuum from vacuum pump
VCV   To vacuum control valve
ATM   Vent line to passenger compartment
OUT   Exhaust gas recirculation to EGR valve

sw = black
bl = blue
br = brown
gr = grey
vi = purple
rt = red
ws = white

**Emission controls (California) — 300SDL**

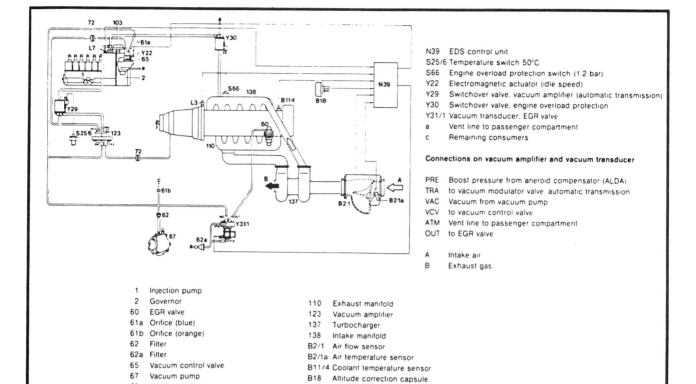

N39   EDS control unit
S25/6 Temperature switch 50°C
S66   Engine overload protection switch (1.2 bar)
Y22   Electromagnetic actuator (idle speed)
Y29   Switchover valve, vacuum amplifier (automatic transmission)
Y30   Switchover valve, engine overload protection
Y31/1 Vacuum transducer, EGR valve
a     Vent line to passenger compartment
c     Remaining consumers

### Connections on vacuum amplifier and vacuum transducer

PRE   Boost pressure from aneroid compensator (ALDA)
TRA   to vacuum modulator valve, automatic transmission
VAC   Vacuum from vacuum pump
VCV   to vacuum control valve
ATM   Vent line to passenger compartment
OUT   to EGR valve

A     Intake air
B     Exhaust gas

| | |
|---|---|
| 1   Injection pump | |
| 2   Governor | 110  Exhaust manifold |
| 60  EGR valve | 123  Vacuum amplifier |
| 61a Orifice (blue) | 137  Turbocharger |
| 61b Orifice (orange) | 138  Intake manifold |
| 62  Filter | B2/1  Air flow sensor |
| 62a Filter | B2/1a Air temperature sensor |
| 65  Vacuum control valve | B11/4 Coolant temperature sensor |
| 67  Vacuum pump | B18  Altitude correction capsule |
| 72  Vacuum damper | L3   Rpm sensor, flywheel ring gear |
| 103 Aneroid compensator (ALDA) | L7   Fuel rack position sensor |

**Emission controls (Federal w/EDS) – 300SDL**

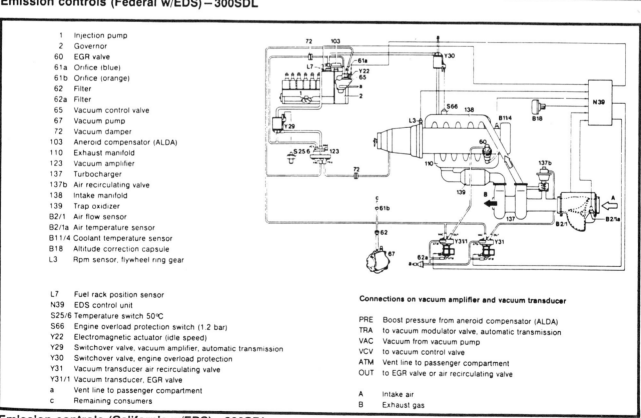

| | |
|---|---|
| 1    Injection pump | |
| 2    Governor | |
| 60   EGR valve | |
| 61a  Orifice (blue) | |
| 61b  Orifice (orange) | |
| 62   Filter | |
| 62a  Filter | |
| 65   Vacuum control valve | |
| 67   Vacuum pump | |
| 72   Vacuum damper | |
| 103  Aneroid compensator (ALDA) | |
| 110  Exhaust manifold | |
| 123  Vacuum amplifier | |
| 137  Turbocharger | |
| 137b Air recirculating valve | |
| 138  Intake manifold | |
| 139  Trap oxidizer | |
| B2/1  Air flow sensor | |
| B2/1a Air temperature sensor | |
| B11/4 Coolant temperature sensor | |
| B18  Altitude correction capsule | |
| L3   Rpm sensor, flywheel ring gear | |

L7    Fuel rack position sensor
N39   EDS control unit
S25/6 Temperature switch 50°C
S66   Engine overload protection switch (1.2 bar)
Y22   Electromagnetic actuator (idle speed)
Y29   Switchover valve, vacuum amplifier, automatic transmission
Y30   Switchover valve, engine overload protection
Y31   Vacuum transducer air recirculating valve
Y31/1 Vacuum transducer, EGR valve
a     Vent line to passenger compartment
c     Remaining consumers

### Connections on vacuum amplifier and vacuum transducer

PRE   Boost pressure from aneroid compensator (ALDA)
TRA   to vacuum modulator valve, automatic transmission
VAC   Vacuum from vacuum pump
VCV   to vacuum control valve
ATM   Vent line to passenger compartment
OUT   to EGR valve or air recirculating valve

A     Intake air
B     Exhaust gas

**Emission controls (California w/EDS) – 300SDL**

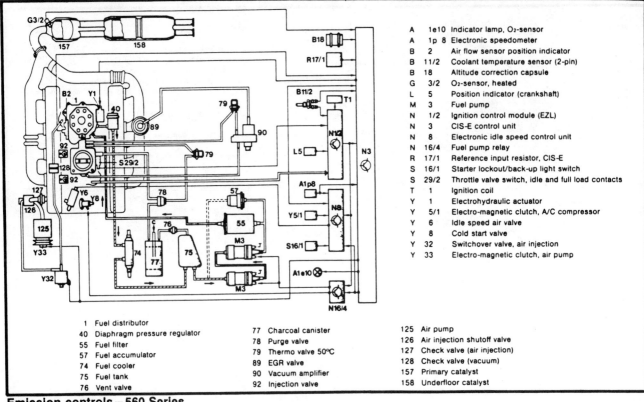

| | | |
|---|---|---|
| A | 1e10 | Indicator lamp, O₂-sensor |
| A | 1p 8 | Electronic speedometer |
| B | 2 | Air flow sensor position indicator |
| B | 11/2 | Coolant temperature sensor (2-pin) |
| B | 18 | Altitude correction capsule |
| G | 3/2 | O₂-sensor, heated |
| L | 5 | Position indicator (crankshaft) |
| M | 3 | Fuel pump |
| N | 1/2 | Ignition control module (EZL) |
| N | 3 | CIS-E control unit |
| N | 8 | Electronic idle speed control unit |
| N | 16/4 | Fuel pump relay |
| R | 17/1 | Reference input resistor, CIS-E |
| S | 16/1 | Starter lockout/back-up light switch |
| S | 29/2 | Throttle valve switch, idle and full load contacts |
| T | 1 | Ignition coil |
| Y | 1 | Electrohydraulic actuator |
| Y | 5/1 | Electro-magnetic clutch, A/C compressor |
| Y | 6 | Idle speed air valve |
| Y | 8 | Cold start valve |
| Y | 32 | Switchover valve, air injection |
| Y | 33 | Electro-magnetic clutch, air pump |

| | | | | | |
|---|---|---|---|---|---|
| 1 | Fuel distributor | 77 | Charcoal canister | 125 | Air pump |
| 40 | Diaphragm pressure regulator | 78 | Purge valve | 126 | Air injection shutoff valve |
| 55 | Fuel filter | 79 | Thermo valve 50°C | 127 | Check valve (air injection) |
| 57 | Fuel accumulator | 89 | EGR valve | 128 | Check valve (vacuum) |
| 74 | Fuel cooler | 90 | Vacuum amplifier | 157 | Primary catalyst |
| 75 | Fuel tank | 92 | Injection valve | 158 | Underfloor catalyst |
| 76 | Vent valve | | | | |

**Emission controls—560 Series**

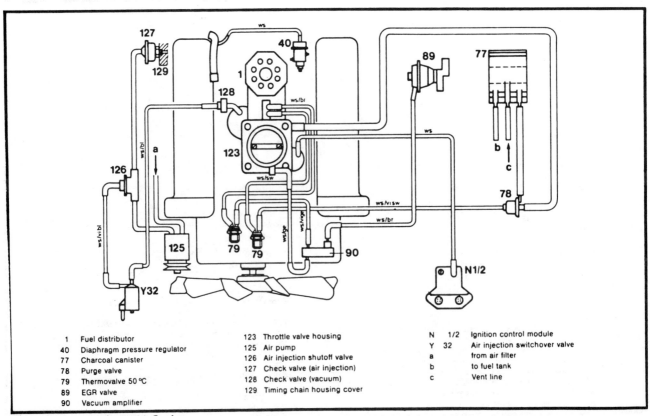

| | | | | | | |
|---|---|---|---|---|---|---|
| 1 | Fuel distributor | 123 | Throttle valve housing | N | 1/2 | Ignition control module |
| 40 | Diaphragm pressure regulator | 125 | Air pump | Y | 32 | Air injection switchover valve |
| 77 | Charcoal canister | 126 | Air injection shutoff valve | a | | from air filter |
| 78 | Purge valve | 127 | Check valve (air injection) | b | | to fuel tank |
| 79 | Thermovalve 50 °C | 128 | Check valve (vacuum) | c | | Vent line |
| 89 | EGR valve | 129 | Timing chain housing cover | | | |
| 90 | Vacuum amplifier | | | | | |

**Emission controls—560 Series**

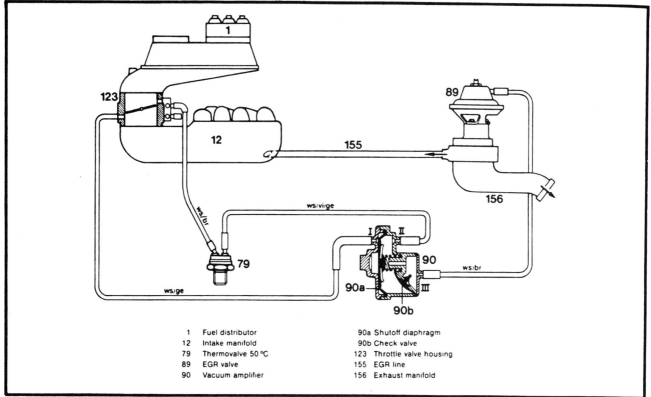

| | | | |
|---|---|---|---|
| 1 | Fuel distributor | 90a | Shutoff diaphragm |
| 12 | Intake manifold | 90b | Check valve |
| 79 | Thermovalve 50 °C | 123 | Throttle valve housing |
| 89 | EGR valve | 155 | EGR line |
| 90 | Vacuum amplifier | 156 | Exhaust manifold |

**Emission controls (EGR) – 560 Series**

# Merkur

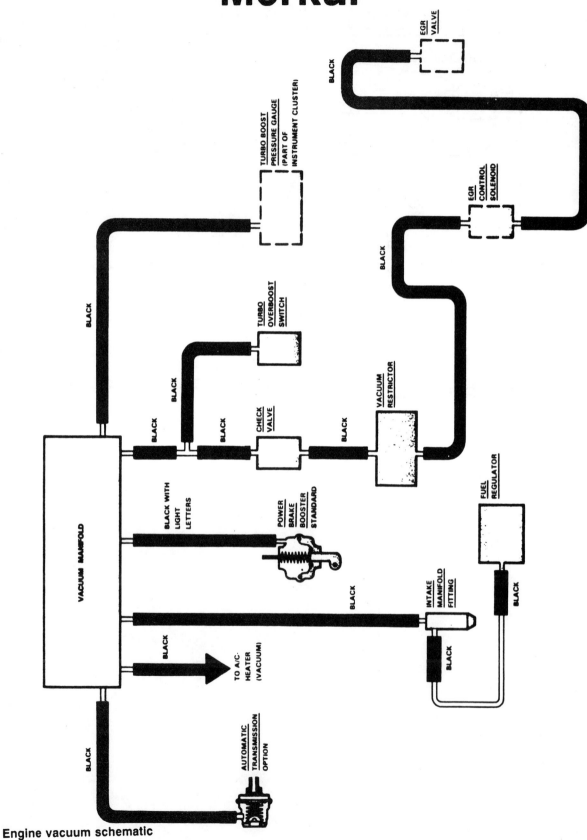

Engine vacuum schematic

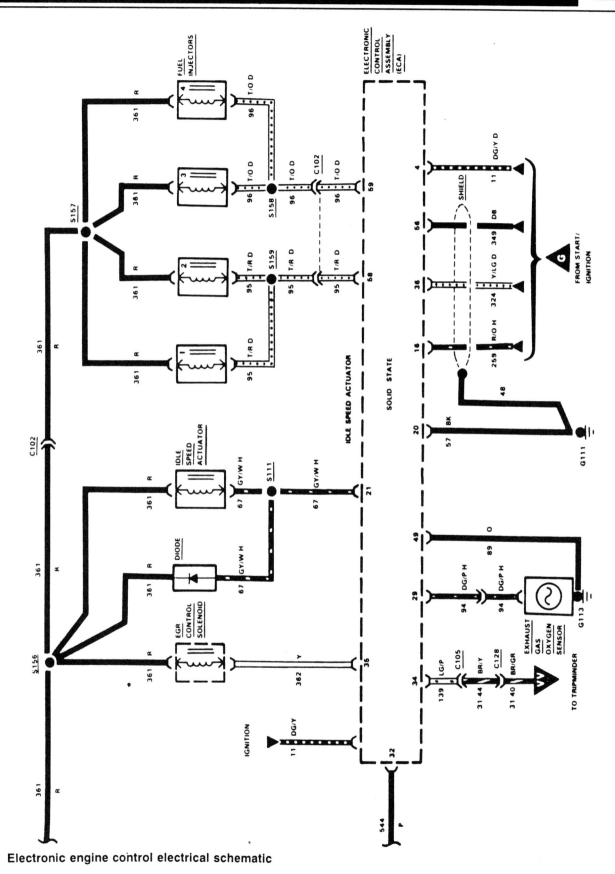

Electronic engine control electrical schematic

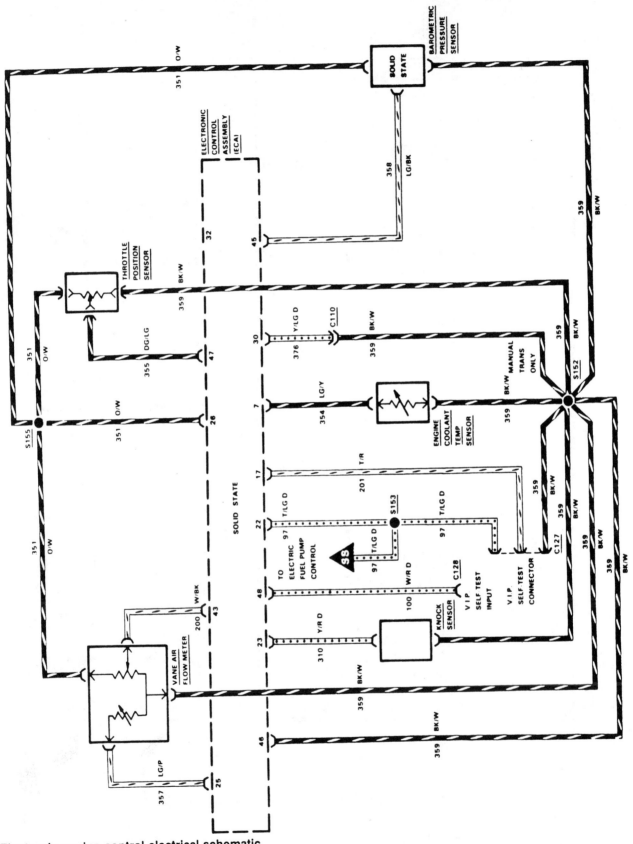

Electronic engine control electrical schematic

# Mitsubishi

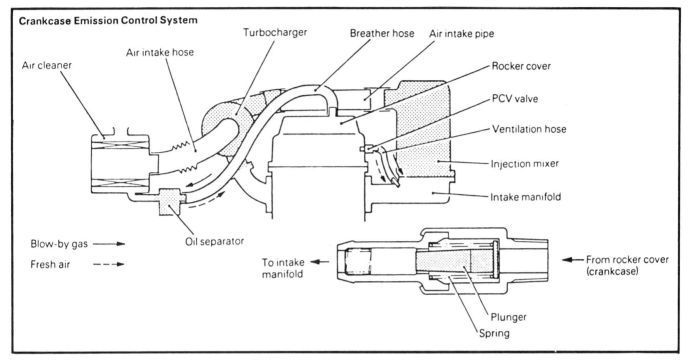

Crankcase Emission Control System—typical of Electronically Controlled Fuel Injected (ECI) Engines
(© Mitsubishi Motor Sales of America, Inc.)

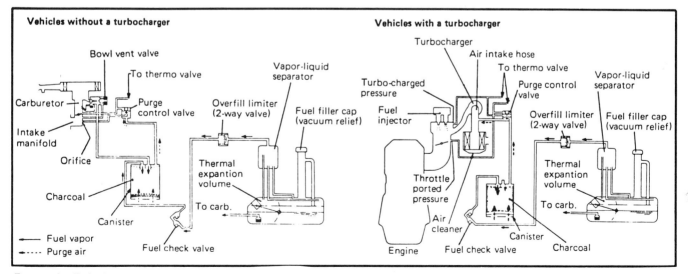

Evaporative Emission Control System used with or without turbocharged systems on the engines
(© Mitsubishi Motor Sales of America, Inc.)

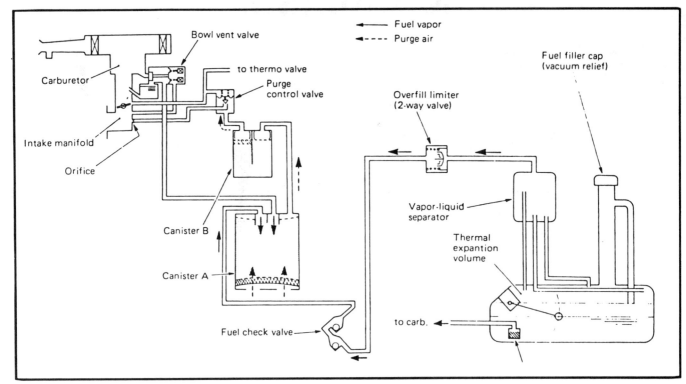

**Evaporative Emission Control System, using large (A) and small (B) storage canisters**
**(© Mitsubishi Motor Sales of America, Inc.)**

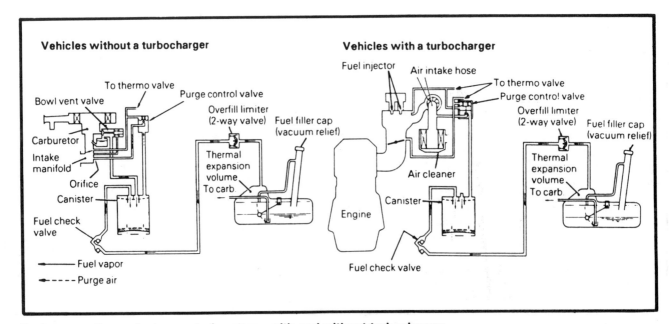

**Fuel evaporative emission control system—with and without turbocharger**

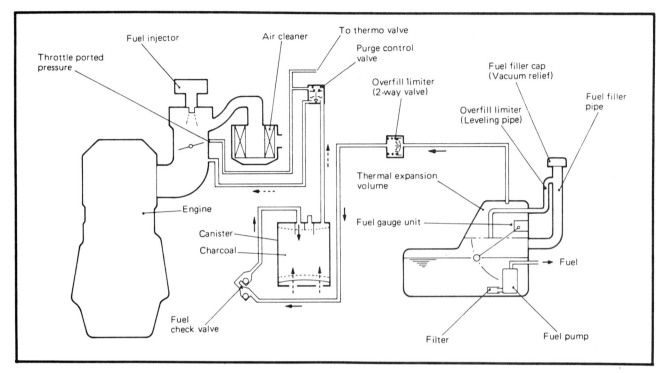

**Fuel evaporative emission control system with fuel injection**

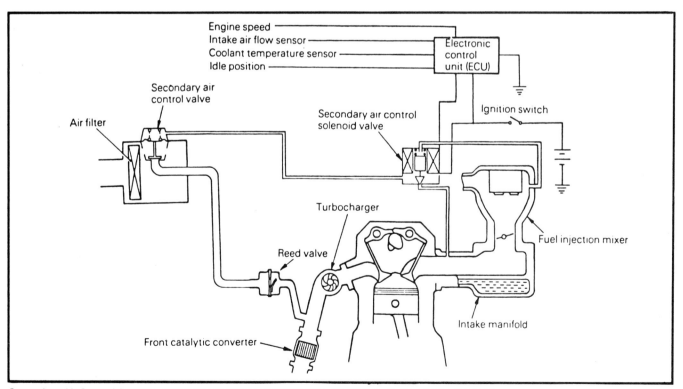

**Secondary Air Control System—with turbocharger system** (© Mitsubishi Motor Sales of America, Inc.)

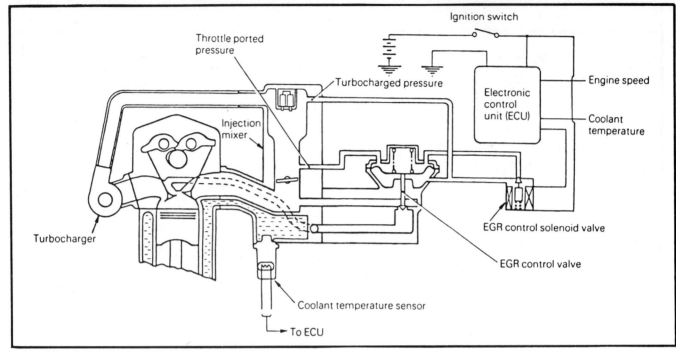

EGR System on Electronic Fuel Injected engines (© Mitsubishi Motor Sales of America, Inc.)

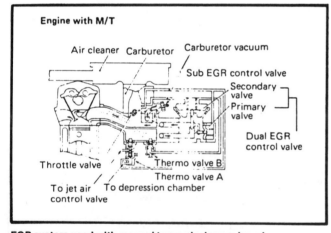

EGR system used with manual transmission equipped engines (© Mitsubishi Motor Sales of America, Inc.)

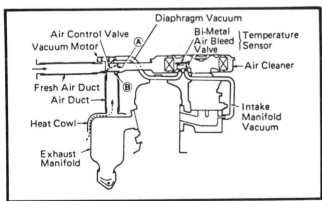

Heated air intake system with carbureted engines—typical (© Mitsubishi Motor Sales of America, Inc.)

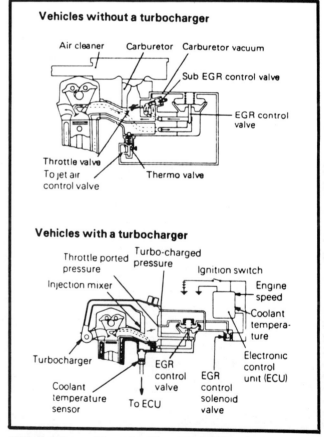

**EGR system with and without turbocharger**

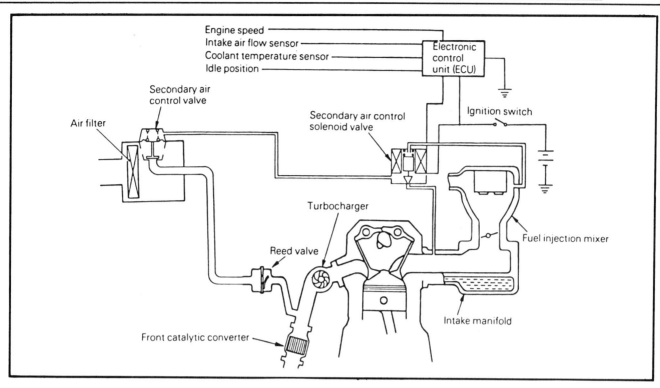

**Secondary air supply system – typical**

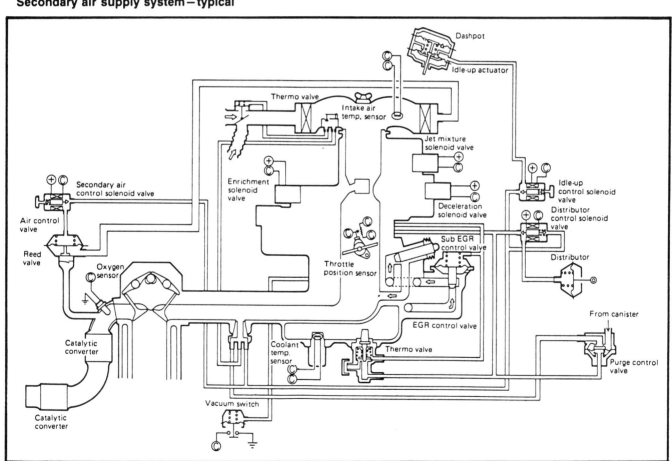

**Schematic of Feedback Carburetor System** (© Mitsubishi Motor Sales of America, Inc.)

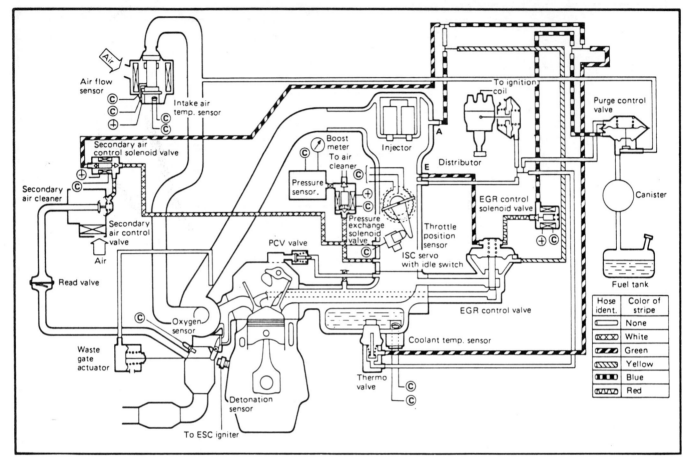

**Schematic of Electronically Controlled Injection System vacuum system** (© Mitsubishi Motor Sales of America, Inc.)

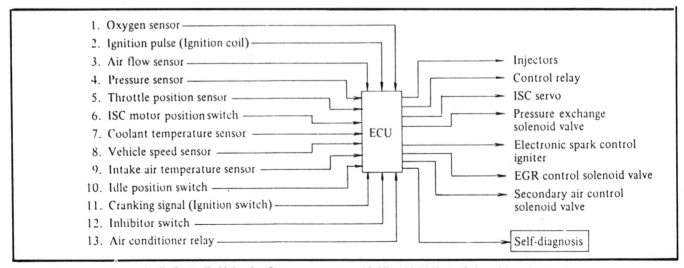

**System diagram of Electronically Controlled Injection System parameters** (© Mitsubishi Motor Sales of America, Inc.)

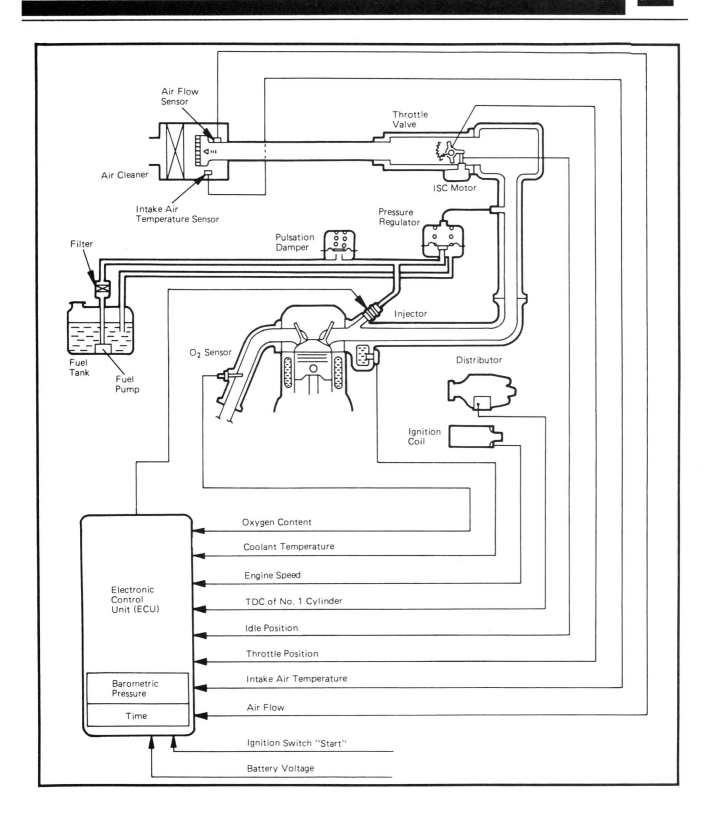

**Multi-point injection system schematic**

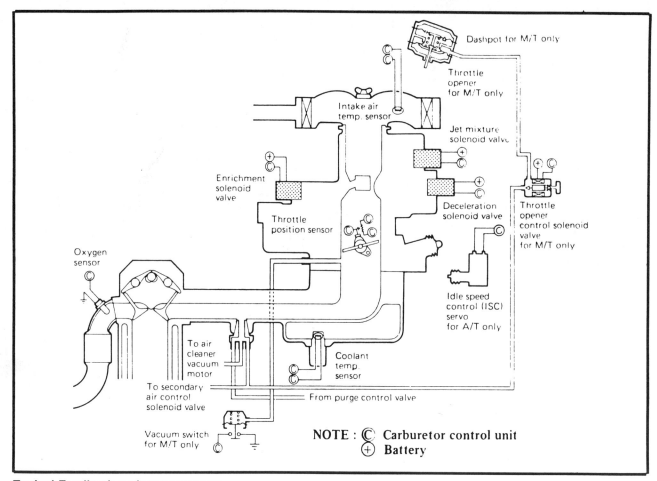

**Typical Feedback carburetor system**

# Nissan/Datsun

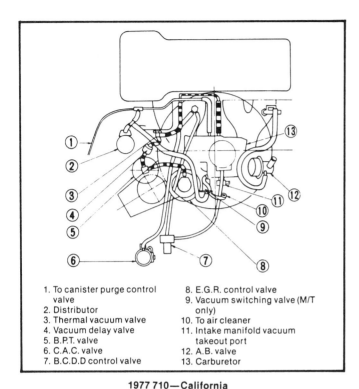

1. To canister purge control valve
2. Distributor
3. Thermal vacuum valve
4. Vacuum delay valve
5. B.P.T. valve
6. C.A.C. valve
7. B.C.D.D control valve
8. E.G.R. control valve
9. Vacuum switching valve (M/T only)
10. To air cleaner
11. Intake manifold vacuum takeout port
12. A.B. valve
13. Carburetor

**1977 710—California**

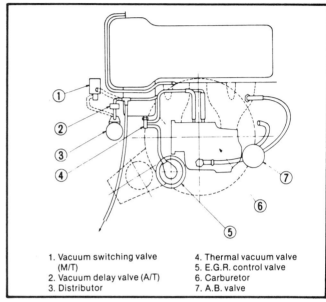

1. Vacuum switching valve (M/T)
2. Vacuum delay valve (A/T)
3. Distributor
4. Thermal vacuum valve
5. E.G.R. control valve
6. Carburetor
7. A.B. valve

**1977 710—Canada**

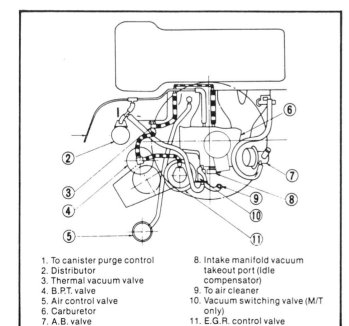

1. To canister purge control
2. Distributor
3. Thermal vacuum valve
4. B.P.T. valve
5. Air control valve
6. Carburetor
7. A.B. valve
8. Intake manifold vacuum takeout port (Idle compensator)
9. To air cleaner
10. Vacuum switching valve (M/T only)
11. E.G.R. control valve

**1977 710—Federal**

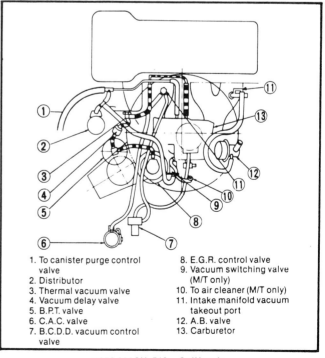

1. To canister purge control valve
2. Distributor
3. Thermal vacuum valve
4. Vacuum delay valve
5. B.P.T. valve
6. C.A.C. valve
7. B.C.D.D. vacuum control valve
8. E.G.R. control valve
9. Vacuum switching valve (M/T only)
10. To air cleaner (M/T only)
11. Intake manifold vacuum takeout port
12. A.B. valve
13. Carburetor

**1979 200SX, 510—California**

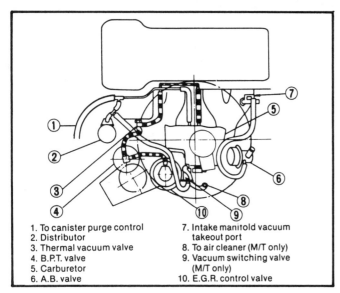

1. To canister purge control
2. Distributor
3. Thermal vacuum valve
4. B.P.T. valve
5. Carburetor
6. A.B. valve
7. Intake manifold vacuum takeout port
8. To air cleaner (M/T only)
9. Vacuum switching valve (M/T only)
10. E.G.R. control valve

**1979 200SX, 510—Federal**

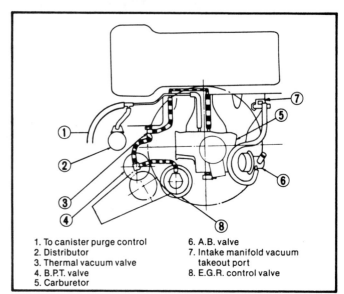

1. To canister purge control
2. Distributor
3. Thermal vacuum valve
4. B.P.T. valve
5. Carburetor
6. A.B. valve
7. Intake manifold vacuum takeout port
8. E.G.R. control valve

**1979 200SX, 510—Canada**

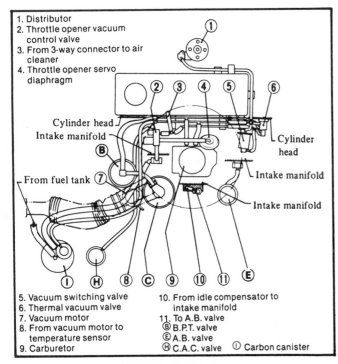

1. Distributor
2. Throttle opener vacuum control valve
3. From 3-way connector to air cleaner
4. Throttle opener servo diaphragm

Cylinder head
Intake manifold
From fuel tank
Cylinder head
Intake manifold
Intake manifold

5. Vacuum switching valve
6. Thermal vacuum valve
7. Vacuum motor
8. From vacuum motor to temperature sensor
9. Carburetor
10. From idle compensator to intake manifold
11. To A.B. valve
Ⓑ B.P.T. valve
Ⓔ A.B. valve
Ⓗ C.A.C. valve
Ⓘ Carbon canister

**1979 210—California**

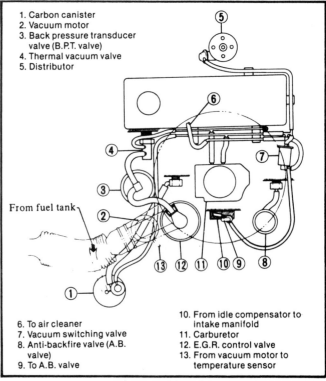

1. Carbon canister
2. Vacuum motor
3. Back pressure transducer valve (B.P.T. valve)
4. Thermal vacuum valve
5. Distributor

From fuel tank

6. To air cleaner
7. Vacuum switching valve
8. Anti-backfire valve (A.B. valve)
9. To A.B. valve
10. From idle compensator to intake manifold
11. Carburetor
12. E.G.R. control valve
13. From vacuum motor to temperature sensor

**1979 210—FU model**

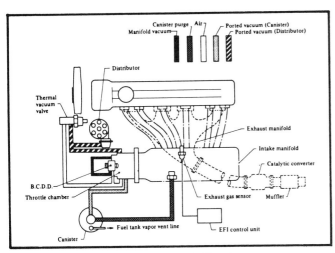

**1980 280ZX, 810—California**

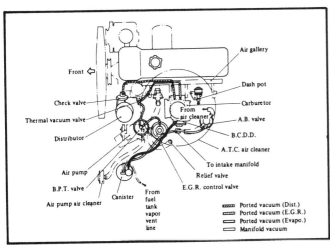

**1980 510—Canada**

Ported vacuum (Dist.)
Ported vacuum (E.G.R.)
Ported vacuum (Evapo.)
Manifold vacuum

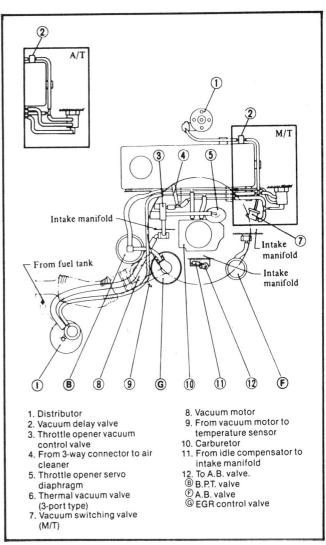

1. Distributor
2. Vacuum delay valve
3. Throttle opener vacuum control valve
4. From 3-way connector to air cleaner
5. Throttle opener servo diaphragm
6. Thermal vacuum valve (3-port type)
7. Vacuum switching valve (M/T)
8. Vacuum motor
9. From vacuum motor to temperature sensor
10. Carburetor
11. From idle compensator to intake manifold
12. To A.B. valve.
B. B.P.T. valve
F. A.B. valve
G. EGR control valve

**1979 210—Federal**

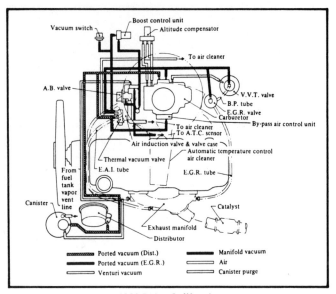

**1980 510—California**

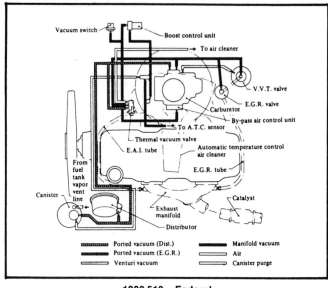

**1980 510—Federal**

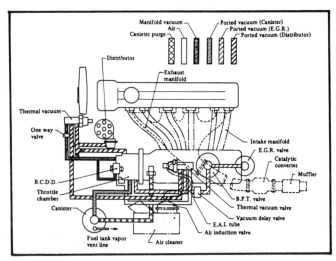

**1980 280ZX, 810—Federal**

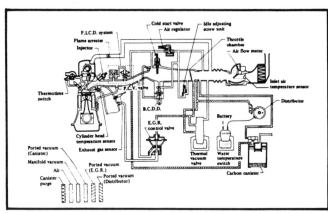

**1982 280ZX, 810 gasoline models**

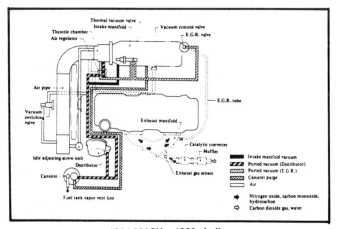

**1981 200SX—1980 similar**

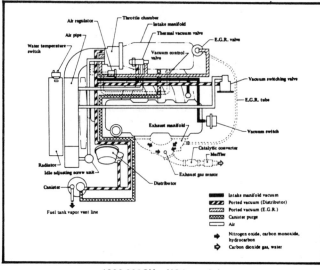

**1982 200SX—USA models**

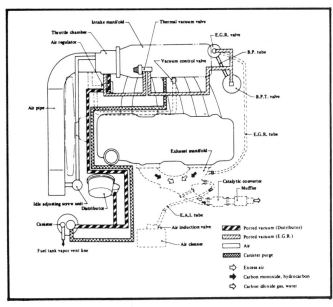

1982 200SX—Canada models

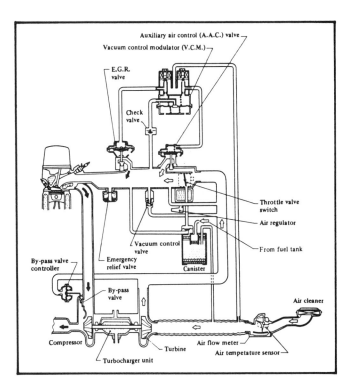

1982 280ZX Turbo models

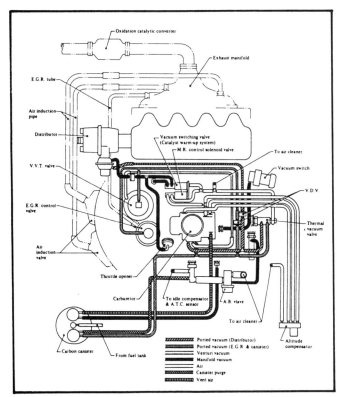

1982 Sentra—California

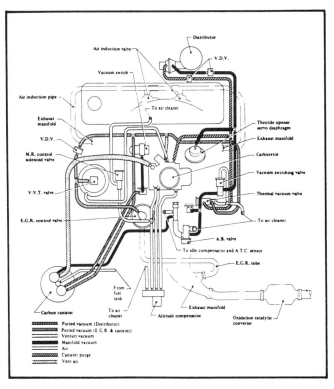

1982 210—California

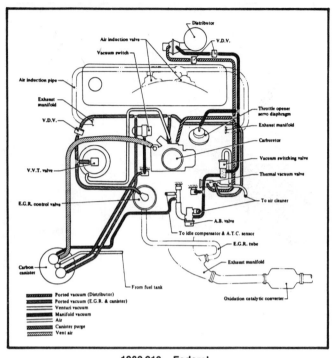

**1982 210—Federal**

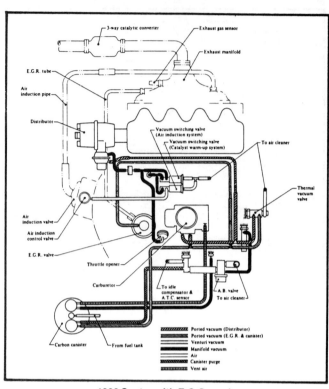

**1982 Sentra with E.C.C. engine**

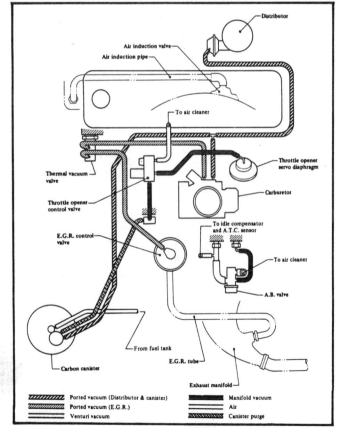

**1982 210—Canada**

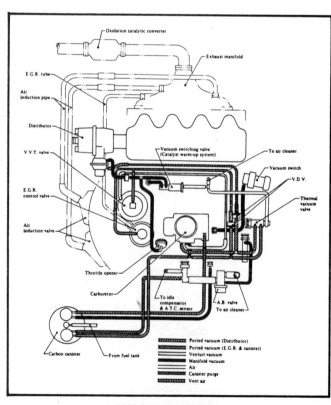

**1982 Sentra—Federal**

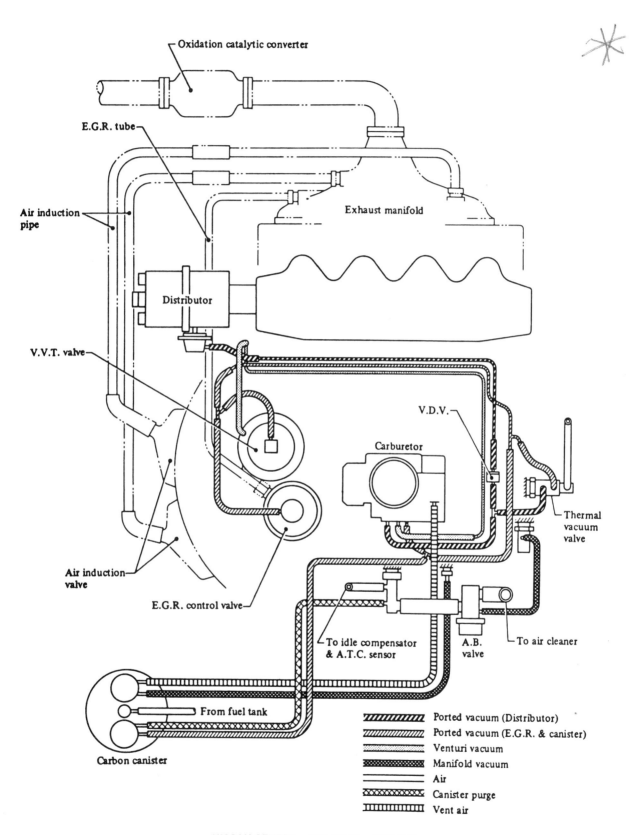

Oxidation catalytic converter

E.G.R. tube

Air induction pipe

Exhaust manifold

Distributor

V.V.T. valve

V.D.V.

Carburetor

Thermal vacuum valve

Air induction valve

E.G.R. control valve

To idle compensator & A.T.C. sensor

A.B. valve

To air cleaner

From fuel tank

Carbon canister

| | |
|---|---|
| //////// | Ported vacuum (Distributor) |
| //////// | Ported vacuum (E.G.R. & canister) |
| | Venturi vacuum |
| | Manifold vacuum |
| | Air |
| XXXXXXXXX | Canister purge |
| IIIIIIIIIII | Vent air |

**NISSAN SENTRA—EXC M.P.G.—FEDERAL**

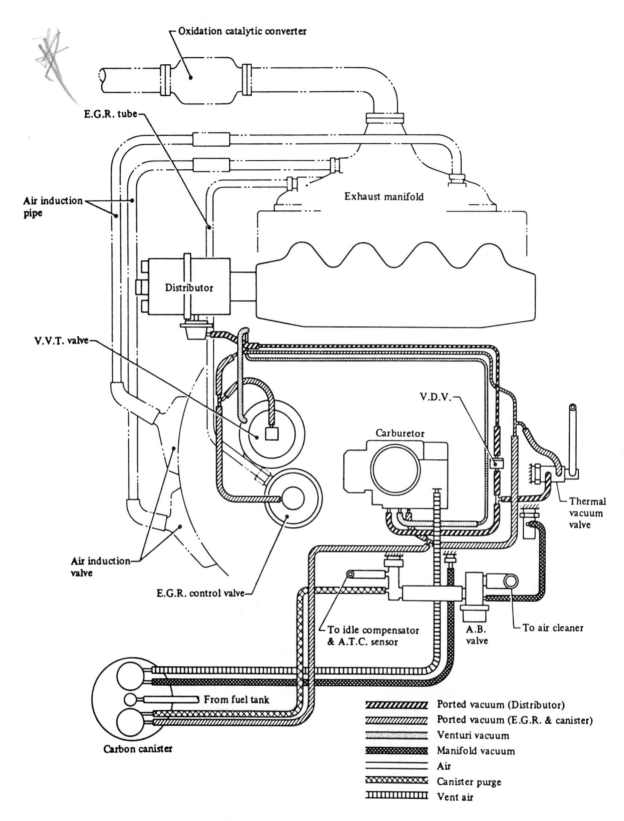

Oxidation catalytic converter

E.G.R. tube

Air induction pipe

Distributor

Exhaust manifold

V.V.T. valve

V.D.V.

Carburetor

Thermal vacuum valve

Air induction valve

E.G.R. control valve

To idle compensator & A.T.C. sensor

A.B. valve

To air cleaner

From fuel tank

Carbon canister

Ported vacuum (Distributor)
Ported vacuum (E.G.R. & canister)
Venturi vacuum
Manifold vacuum
Air
Canister purge
Vent air

**NISSAN SENTRA—EXC M.P.G.—FEDERAL**

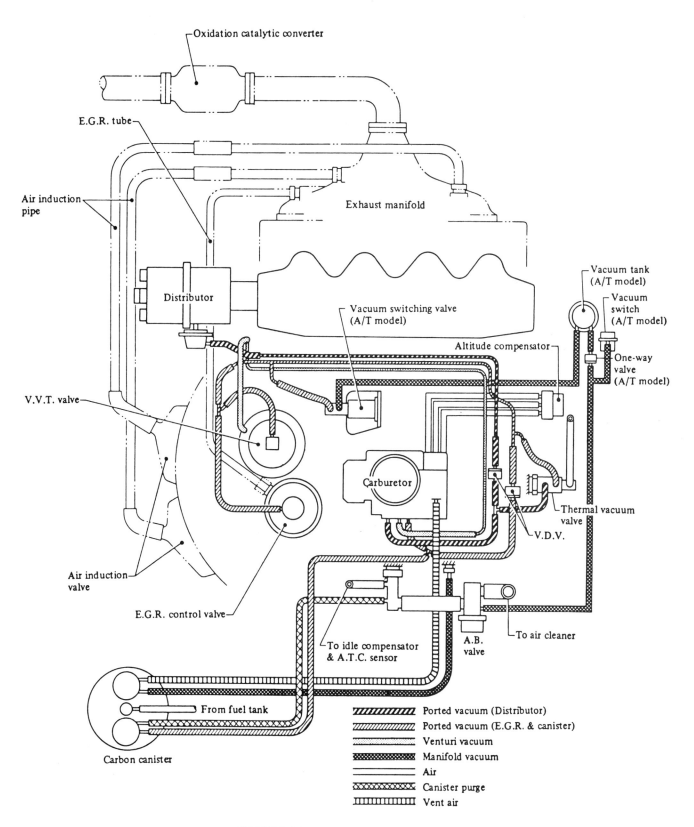

- Oxidation catalytic converter
- E.G.R. tube
- Air induction pipe
- Distributor
- Exhaust manifold
- Vacuum switching valve (A/T model)
- Altitude compensator
- Vacuum tank (A/T model)
- Vacuum switch (A/T model)
- One-way valve (A/T model)
- V.V.T. valve
- Carburetor
- Thermal vacuum valve
- V.D.V.
- Air induction valve
- E.G.R. control valve
- To idle compensator & A.T.C. sensor
- A.B. valve
- To air cleaner
- From fuel tank
- Carbon canister

| | |
|---|---|
| ▨▨▨ | Ported vacuum (Distributor) |
| ▨▨▨ | Ported vacuum (E.G.R. & canister) |
| ▭▭▭ | Venturi vacuum |
| ▨▨▨ | Manifold vacuum |
| ▭▭▭ | Air |
| ▩▩▩ | Canister purge |
| ▥▥▥ | Vent air |

**NISSAN SENTRA—FEDERAL—HIGH ALT.**

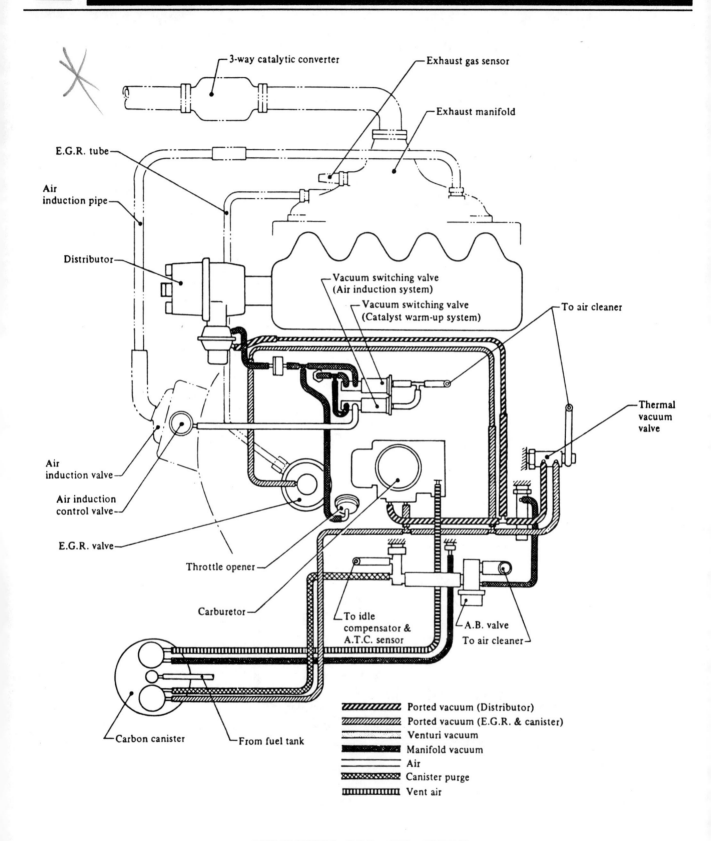

3-way catalytic converter

Exhaust gas sensor

Exhaust manifold

E.G.R. tube

Air induction pipe

Distributor

Vacuum switching valve (Air induction system)

Vacuum switching valve (Catalyst warm-up system)

To air cleaner

Thermal vacuum valve

Air induction valve

Air induction control valve

E.G.R. valve

Throttle opener

Carburetor

To idle compensator & A.T.C. sensor

A.B. valve

To air cleaner

Carbon canister

From fuel tank

| | |
|---|---|
| ///// | Ported vacuum (Distributor) |
| ///// | Ported vacuum (E.G.R. & canister) |
| ===== | Venturi vacuum |
| ▬▬▬ | Manifold vacuum |
| ===== | Air |
| XXXXX | Canister purge |
| IIIIII | Vent air |

**NISSAN SENTRA—E.C.C.—MPG—FEDERAL**

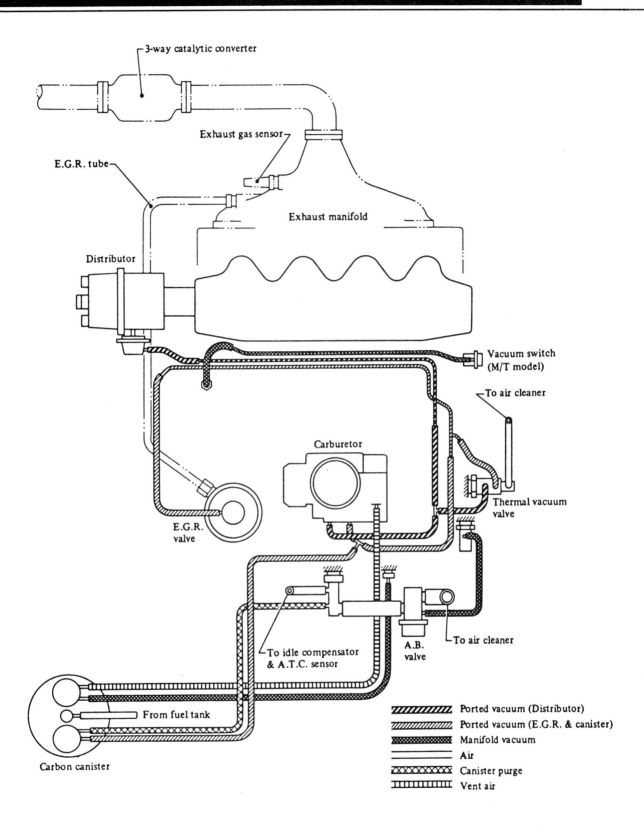

3-way catalytic converter

Exhaust gas sensor

E.G.R. tube

Exhaust manifold

Distributor

Vacuum switch
(M/T model)

To air cleaner

Carburetor

Thermal vacuum
valve

E.G.R.
valve

To idle compensator
& A.T.C. sensor

A.B.
valve

To air cleaner

From fuel tank

Carbon canister

| | |
|---|---|
| ▨▨▨▨▨ | Ported vacuum (Distributor) |
| ▨▨▨▨ | Ported vacuum (E.G.R. & canister) |
| ▨▨▨▨▨ | Manifold vacuum |
| ——— | Air |
| ✕✕✕✕✕ | Canister purge |
| ⅢⅢⅢⅢ | Vent air |

**NISSAN SENTRA—E.C.C.—M.P.G.—CALIFORNIA**

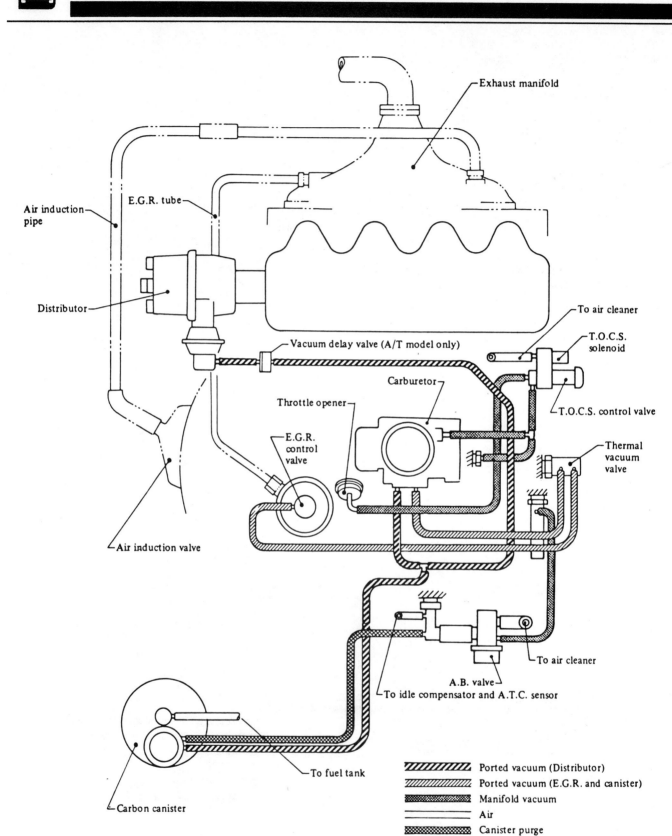

Exhaust manifold

Air induction
pipe

E.G.R. tube

Distributor

To air cleaner

T.O.C.S.
solenoid

T.O.C.S. control valve

Vacuum delay valve (A/T model only)

Carburetor

Throttle opener

Thermal
vacuum
valve

E.G.R.
control
valve

Air induction valve

A.B. valve

To air cleaner

To idle compensator and A.T.C. sensor

To fuel tank

Carbon canister

| | |
|---|---|
| ///////// | Ported vacuum (Distributor) |
| ///////// | Ported vacuum (E.G.R. and canister) |
| ▨▨▨▨▨ | Manifold vacuum |
| ───── | Air |
| ▨▨▨▨▨ | Canister purge |

**NISSAN SENTRA—CANADA**

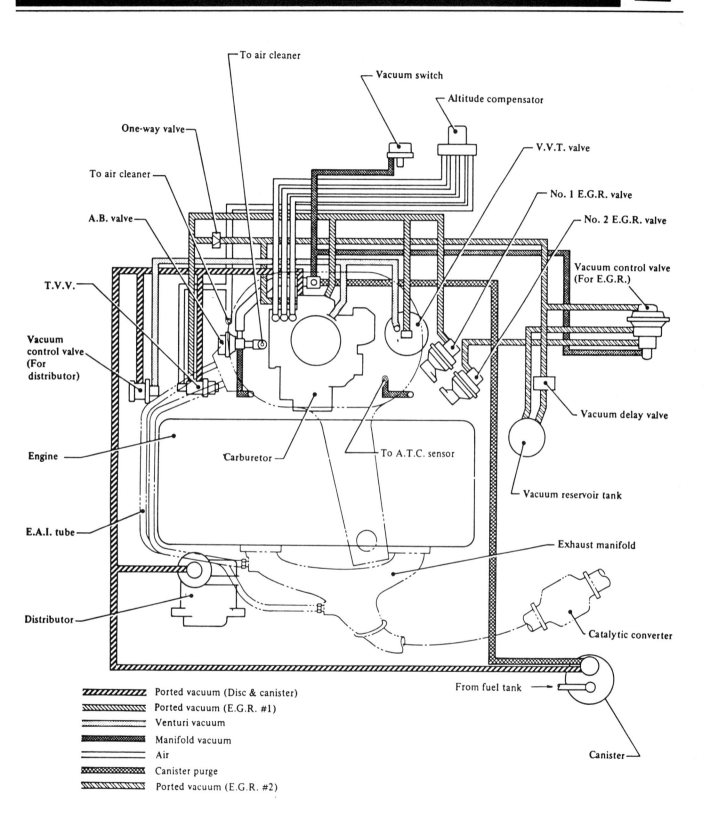

To air cleaner

Vacuum switch

Altitude compensator

One-way valve

V.V.T. valve

To air cleaner

No. 1 E.G.R. valve

A.B. valve

No. 2 E.G.R. valve

Vacuum control valve
(For E.G.R.)

T.V.V.

Vacuum
control valve
(For
distributor)

Vacuum delay valve

Engine

Carburetor

To A.T.C. sensor

Vacuum reservoir tank

E.A.I. tube

Exhaust manifold

Distributor

Catalytic converter

From fuel tank

Canister

| | |
|---|---|
| ▨▨▨ | Ported vacuum (Disc & canister) |
| ▨▨▨ | Ported vacuum (E.G.R. #1) |
| ▦▦▦ | Venturi vacuum |
| ▬▬▬ | Manifold vacuum |
| ── | Air |
| ▨▨▨ | Canister purge |
| ▨▨▨ | Ported vacuum (E.G.R. #2) |

**NISSAN STANZA—CALIFORNIA**

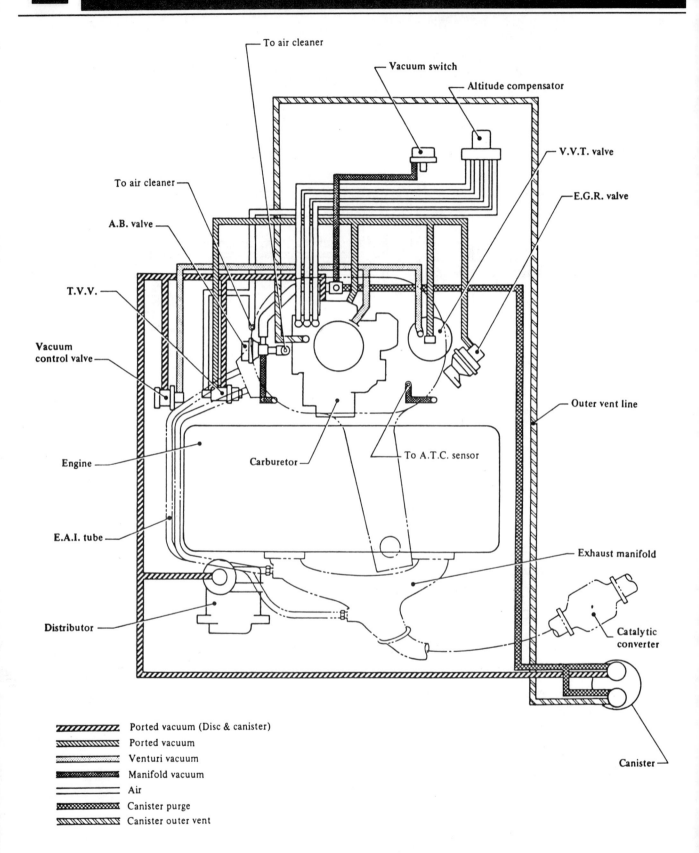

To air cleaner

Vacuum switch

Altitude compensator

To air cleaner

V.V.T. valve

A.B. valve

E.G.R. valve

T.V.V.

Vacuum control valve

Outer vent line

Engine

Carburetor

To A.T.C. sensor

E.A.I. tube

Exhaust manifold

Distributor

Catalytic converter

Canister

| | |
|---|---|
| *ZZZZZZZ* | Ported vacuum (Disc & canister) |
| | Ported vacuum |
| | Venturi vacuum |
| | Manifold vacuum |
| | Air |
| | Canister purge |
| | Canister outer vent |

**NISSAN STANZA—FEDERAL & HIGH ALT.**

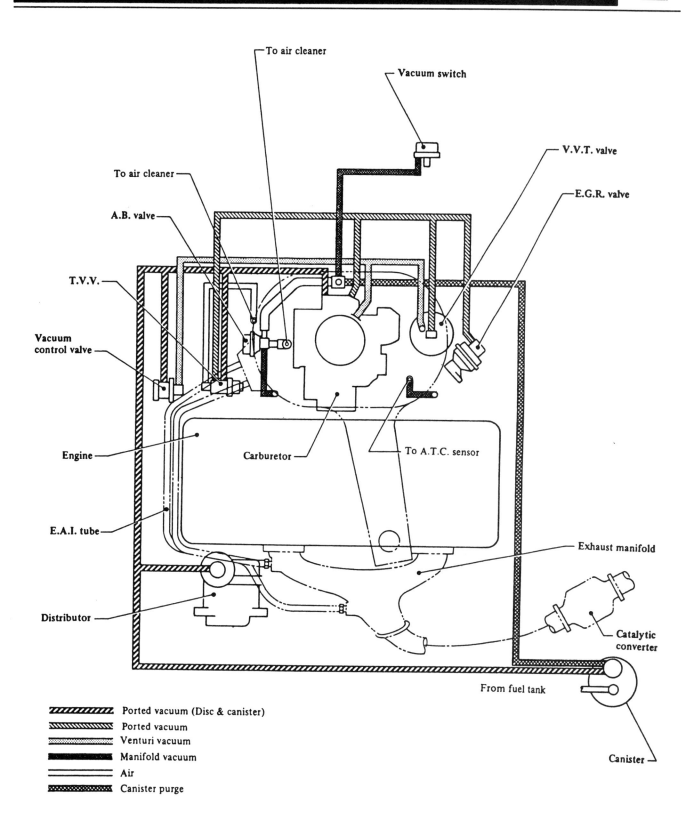

To air cleaner

Vacuum switch

V.V.T. valve

E.G.R. valve

To air cleaner

A.B. valve

T.V.V.

Vacuum control valve

Engine

Carburetor

To A.T.C. sensor

E.A.I. tube

Exhaust manifold

Distributor

Catalytic converter

From fuel tank

Canister

| | |
|---|---|
| ▨▨▨ | Ported vacuum (Disc & canister) |
| ▧▧▧ | Ported vacuum |
| ░░░ | Venturi vacuum |
| ▬▬▬ | Manifold vacuum |
| ═══ | Air |
| ▓▓▓ | Canister purge |

**NISSAN STANZA—EXC. CALIFORNIA**

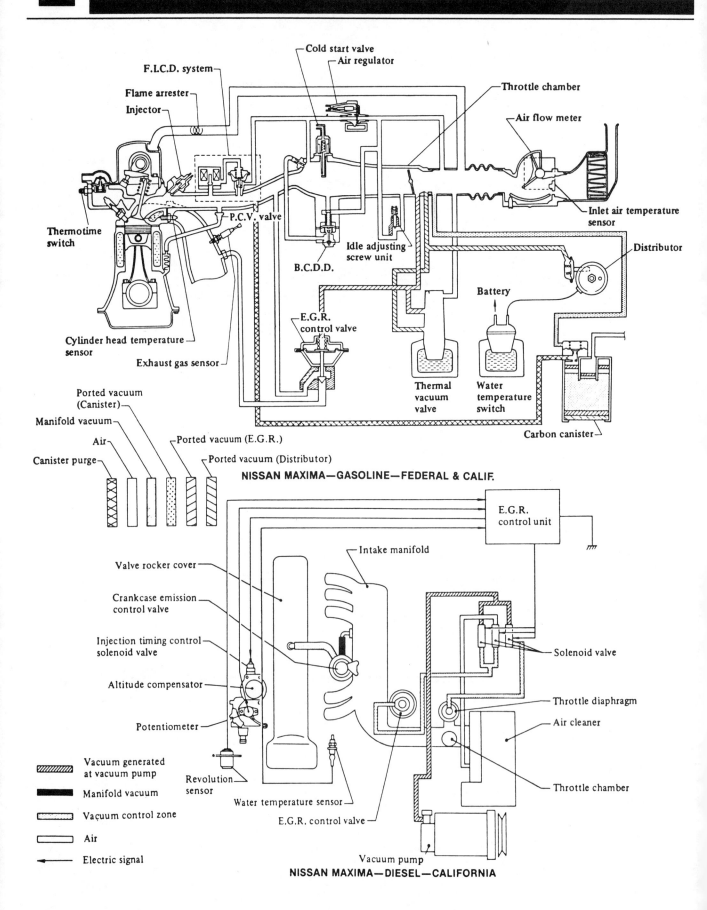

Cold start valve
Air regulator
F.I.C.D. system
Flame arrester
Injector
Throttle chamber
Air flow meter
Thermotime switch
P.C.V. valve
Inlet air temperature sensor
Distributor
Idle adjusting screw unit
B.C.D.D.
Battery
Cylinder head temperature sensor
Exhaust gas sensor
E.G.R. control valve
Thermal vacuum valve
Water temperature switch
Carbon canister

Ported vacuum (Canister)
Manifold vacuum
Air
Ported vacuum (E.G.R.)
Canister purge
Ported vacuum (Distributor)

**NISSAN MAXIMA—GASOLINE—FEDERAL & CALIF.**

E.G.R. control unit
Intake manifold
Valve rocker cover
Crankcase emission control valve
Injection timing control solenoid valve
Solenoid valve
Altitude compensator
Throttle diaphragm
Potentiometer
Air cleaner
Revolution sensor
Water temperature sensor
E.G.R. control valve
Throttle chamber

Vacuum generated at vacuum pump
Manifold vacuum
Vacuum control zone
Air
Electric signal

Vacuum pump
**NISSAN MAXIMA—DIESEL—CALIFORNIA**

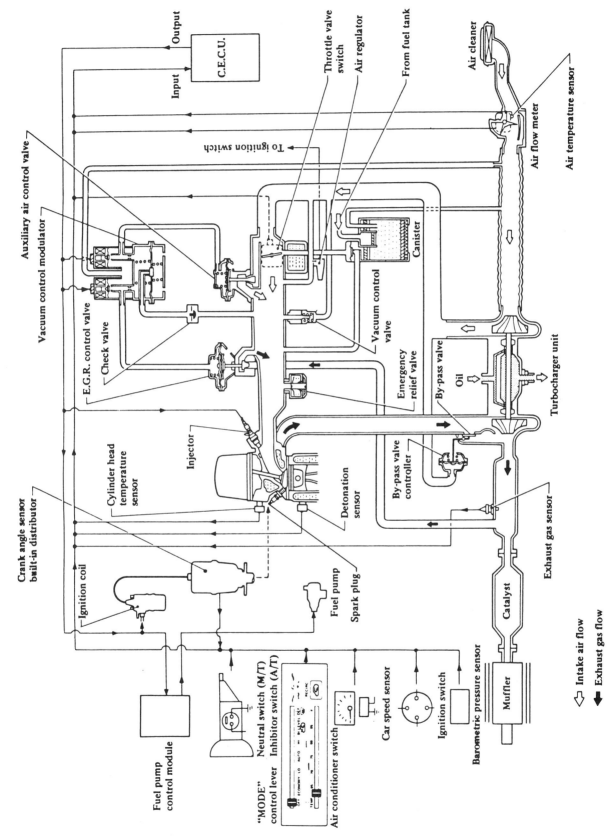

DATSUN 200ZX—E.C.C.S.—FEDERAL & CALIF.

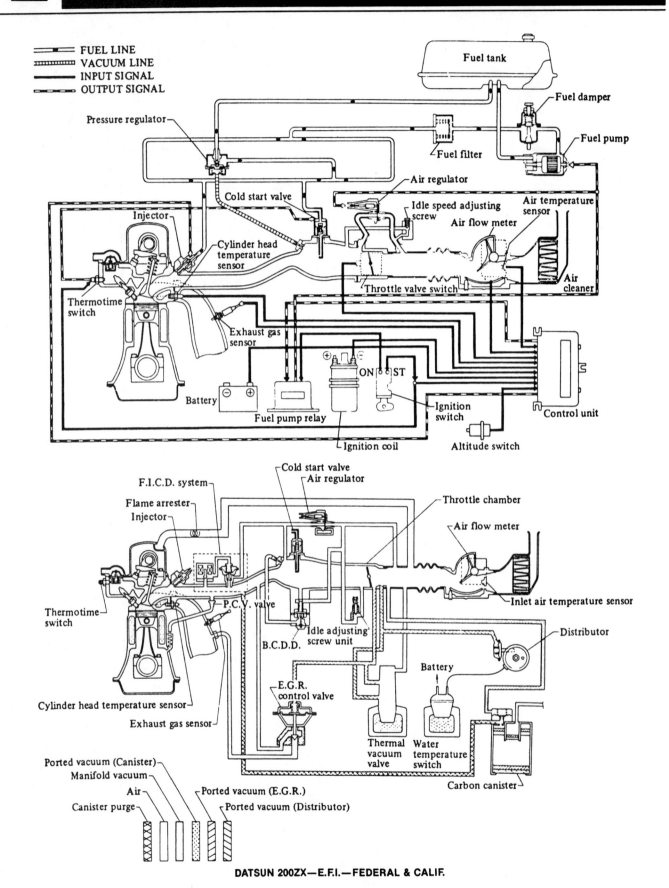

FUEL LINE
VACUUM LINE
INPUT SIGNAL
OUTPUT SIGNAL

Fuel tank

Fuel damper

Pressure regulator

Fuel pump

Fuel filter

Air regulator

Cold start valve

Air temperature sensor

Idle speed adjusting screw

Air flow meter

Injector

Cylinder head temperature sensor

Throttle valve switch

Air cleaner

Thermotime switch

Exhaust gas sensor

Battery

Fuel pump relay

Ignition coil

ON ST

Ignition switch

Control unit

Altitude switch

F.I.C.D. system

Cold start valve
Air regulator

Throttle chamber

Flame arrester
Injector

Air flow meter

Thermotime switch

P.C.V. valve

Inlet air temperature sensor

B.C.D.D.

Idle adjusting screw unit

Distributor

Cylinder head temperature sensor

Battery

Exhaust gas sensor

E.G.R. control valve

Thermal vacuum valve

Water temperature switch

Ported vacuum (Canister)
Manifold vacuum
Air
Canister purge

Ported vacuum (E.G.R.)
Ported vacuum (Distributor)

Carbon canister

**DATSUN 200ZX—E.F.I.—FEDERAL & CALIF.**

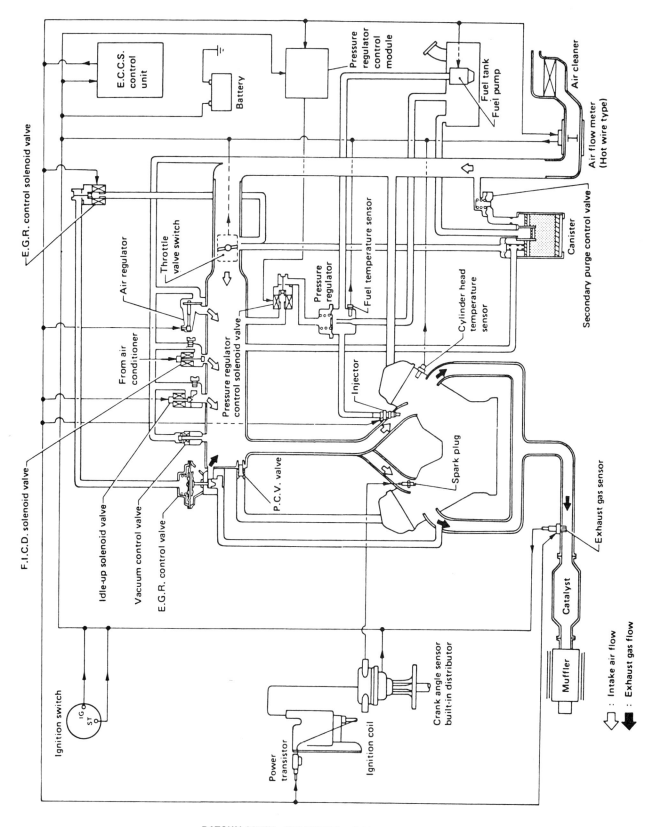

DATSUN 300ZX—WO/TURBO   FEDERAL & CALIF.

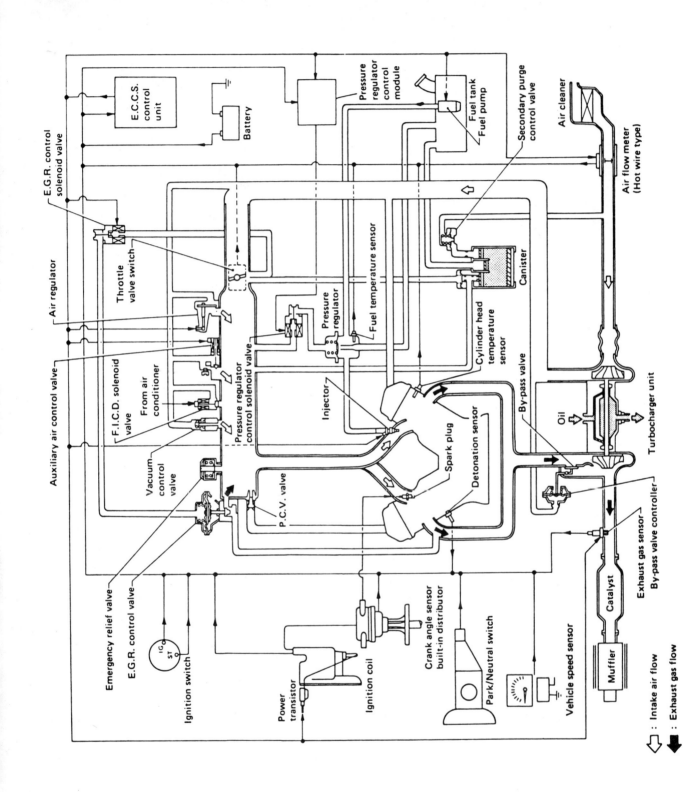

DATSUN 300ZX—W/TURBO—FEDERAL & CALIF.

## ENGINE AND EMISSION CONTROL SYSTEM
## DIAGRAM B OF E16 E.C.C. ENGINE FOR CALIFORNIA

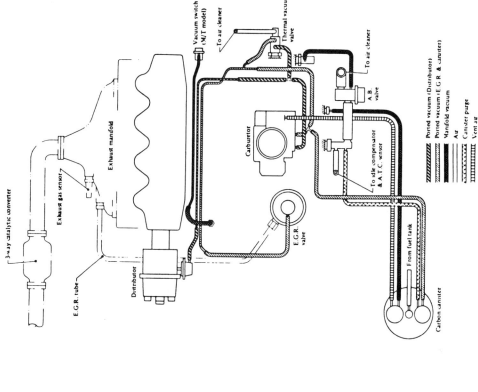

**Vacuum circuit diagram for 1984-85 Sentra—California models**

## ENGINE AND EMISSION CONTROL SYSTEM
## DIAGRAM B OF E16 E.C.C. ENGINE FOR NON-CALIFORNIA

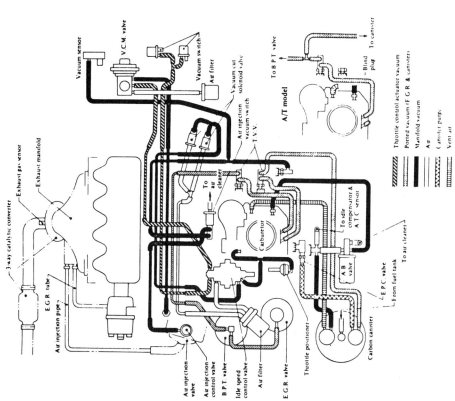

**Vacuum circuit diagram for 1984 Sentra—Federal models**

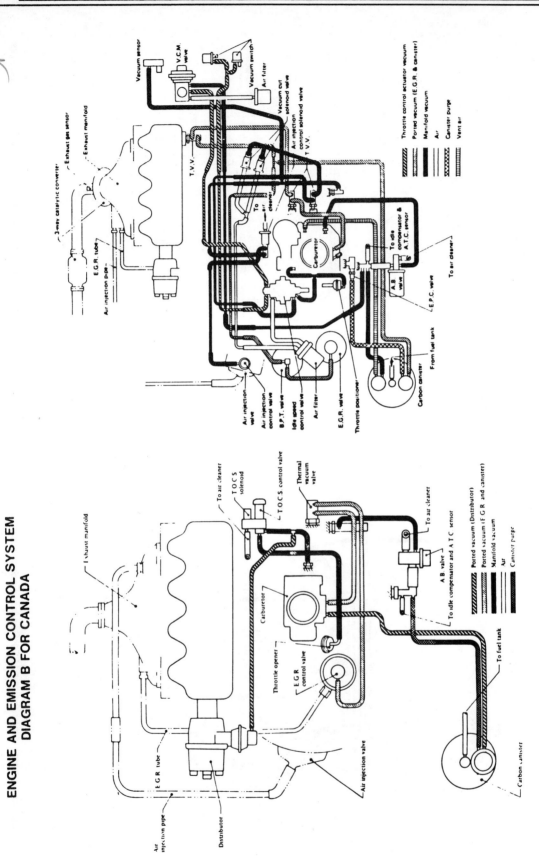

ENGINE AND EMISSION CONTROL SYSTEM
DIAGRAM B FOR CANADA

Vacuum circuit diagram for 1985 Sentra—Federal models

Vacuum circuit diagram for 1984-85 Sentra—Canada models

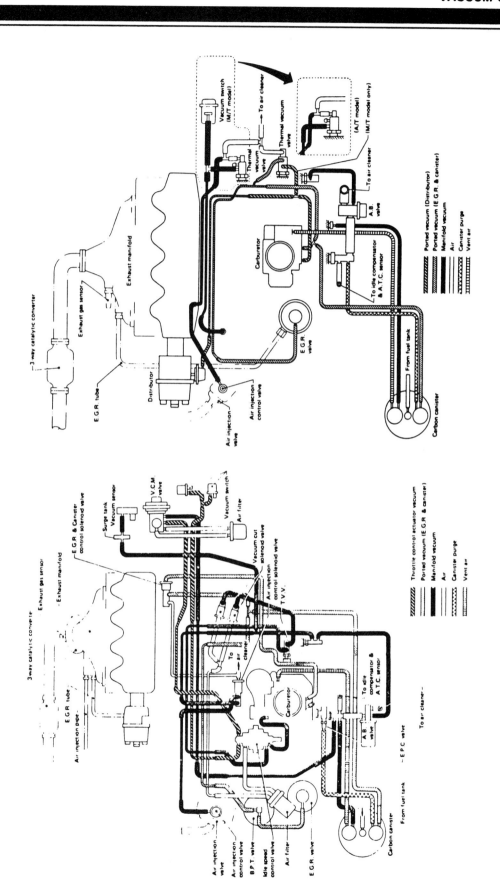

Vacuum circuit diagram for 1986 Sentra–California models

Vacuum circuit diagram for 1986 Sentra–Federal models

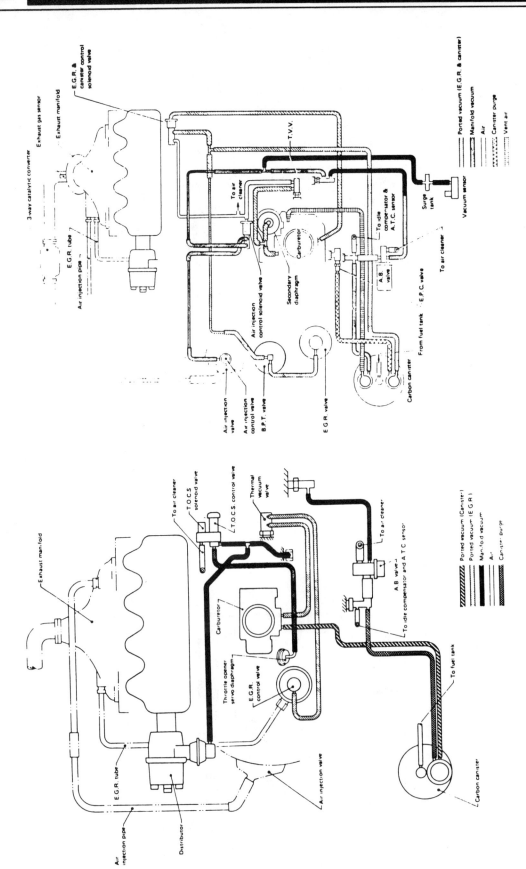

**Vacuum circuit diagram for 1987 Sentra–California and Canada models**

**Vacuum circuit diagram for 1986 Sentra–Canada models**

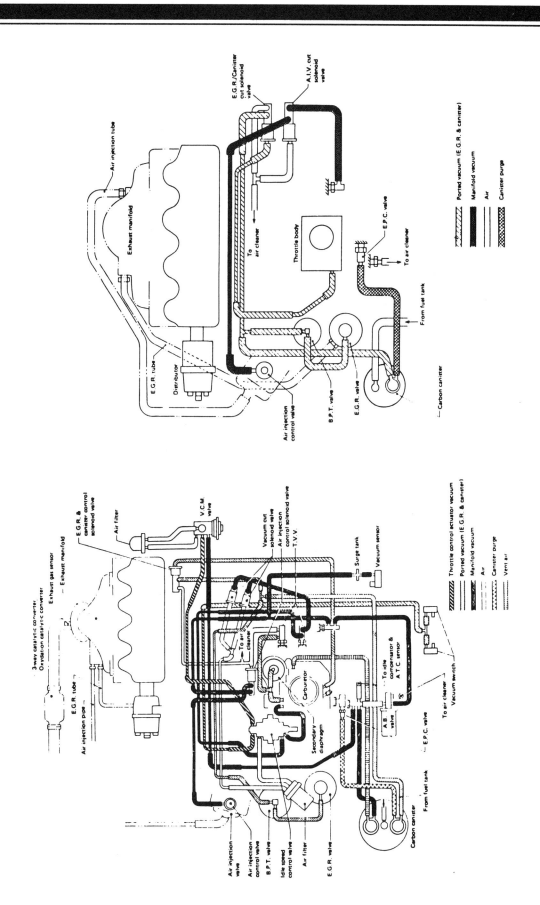

**Vacuum circuit diagram for 1987 Sentra—E16i engine**

**Vacuum circuit diagram for 1987 Sentra—Federal models**

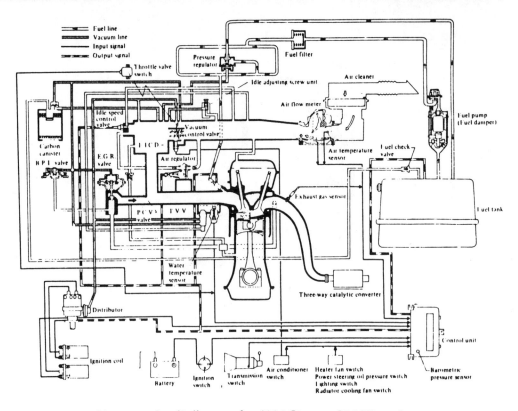

**Vacuum circuit diagram for 1984 Stanza—CA20E engine**

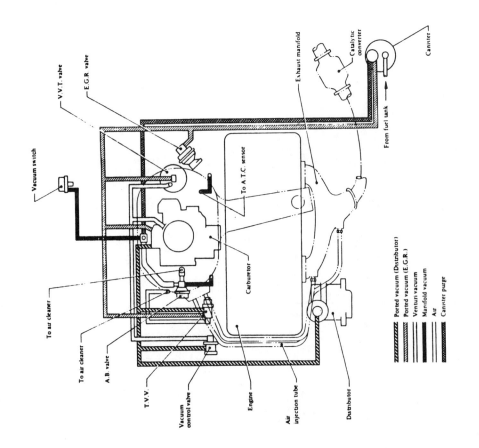

**Vacuum circuit diagram for 1984 Stanza—CA20S engine**

# NISSAN/DATSUN
## VACUUM CIRCUITS

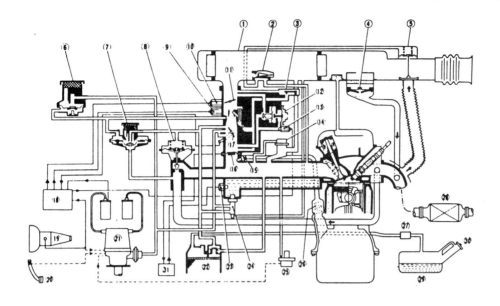

| | | |
|---|---|---|
| 1 A.T.C. air cleaner | 12 B.C.D.D. | 22 Carbon canister |
| 2 Air temperature sensor | 13 B.C.D.D. control solenoid (M/T) | 23 Water temperature switch |
| 3 Hot idle compensator | 14 A.B. valve | 24 T.V.V. |
| 4 A.I.V. valve | 15 P.C.V. valve | 25 Vacuum switch |
| 5 Vacuum motor | 16 Mixture heater | 26 Oil separator |
| 6 Vacuum control valve | 17 Throttle valve switch | 27 Fuel check valve |
| 7 V.V.T valve | 18 Engine revolution unit | 28 Oxidation catalytic converter |
| 8 E.G.R. valve | 19 Neutral switch (M/T)/Inhibitor switch (A/T) | 29 Fuel tank |
| 9 Anti-dieseling solenoid | 20 Clutch switch (M/T) | 30 Fuel filler cap (Vacuum relief valve) |
| 10 Idle speed control solenoid | 21 Distributor (IC ignition unit) | 31 Mixture heater relay |
| 11 P.T.C. auto-choke | | |

**Vacuum circuit diagram for 1985 Stanza–CA20S engine**

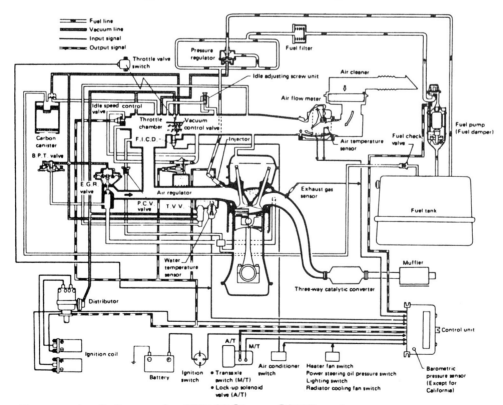

**Vacuum circuit diagram for 1985-86 Stanza–CA20E engine**

**161**

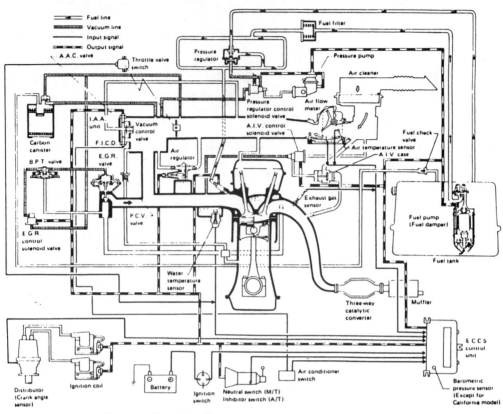

**Vacuum circuit diagram for 1987 Stanza**

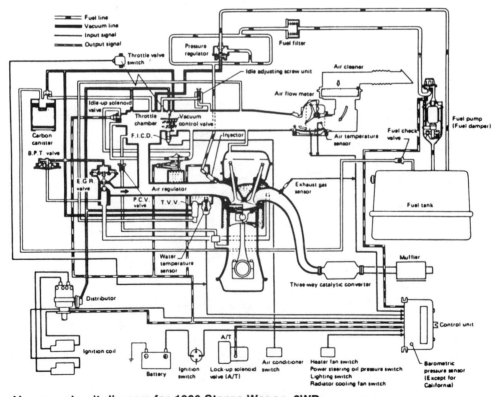

**Vacuum circuit diagram for 1986 Stanza Wagon—2WD**

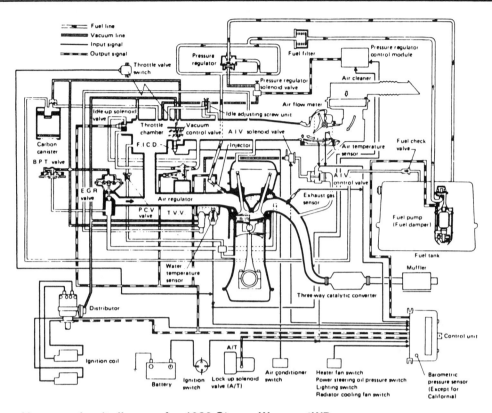

**Vacuum circuit diagram for 1986 Stanza Wagon–4WD**

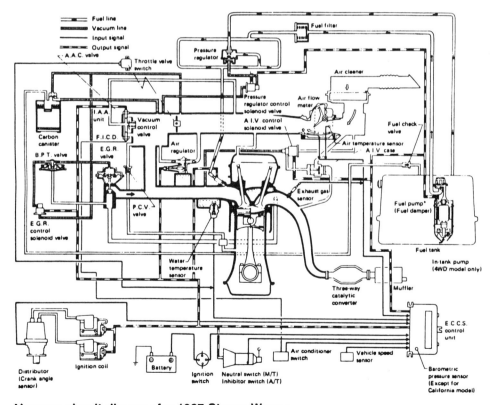

**Vacuum circuit diagram for 1987 Stanza Wagon**

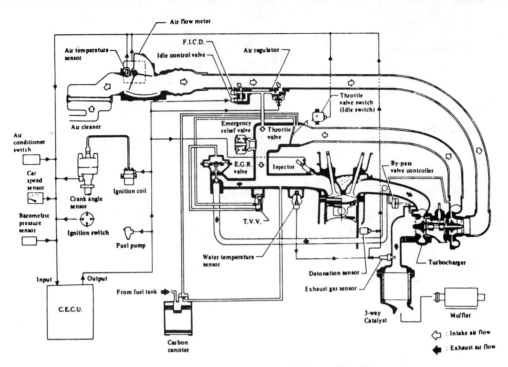

**Engine and emission control diagram for 1984 Pulsar–E15ET engine**

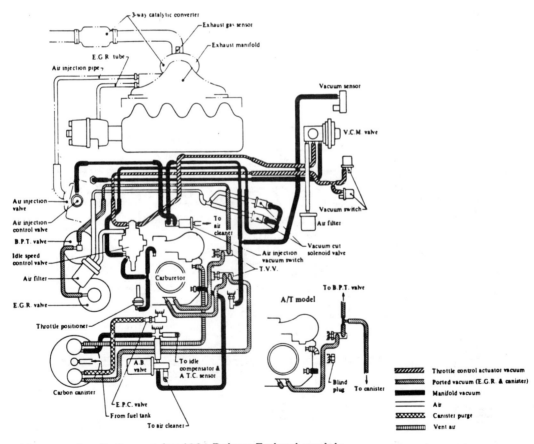

**Vacuum circuit diagram for 1984 Pulsar–Federal models**

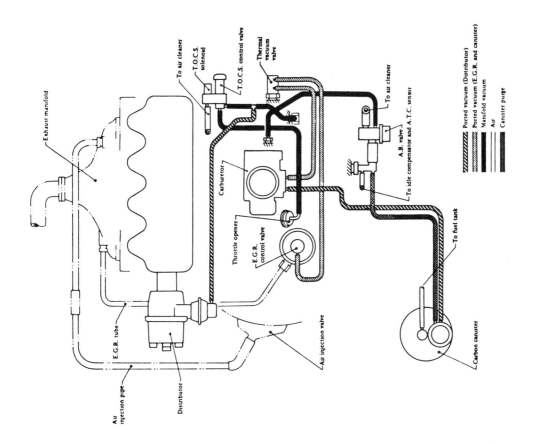

**Vacuum circuit diagram for 1984 Pulsar–Canada models**

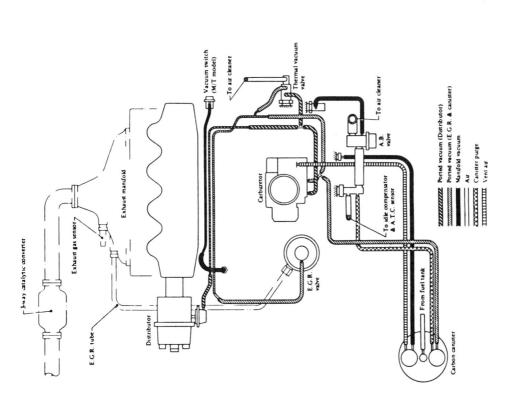

**Vacuum circuit diagram for 1984 Pulsar–California models**

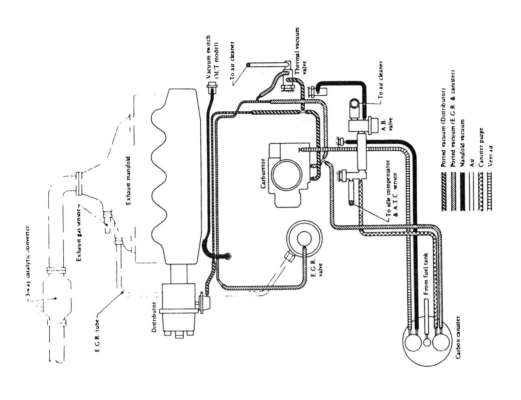

**Vacuum circuit diagram for 1985 Pulsar–California models**

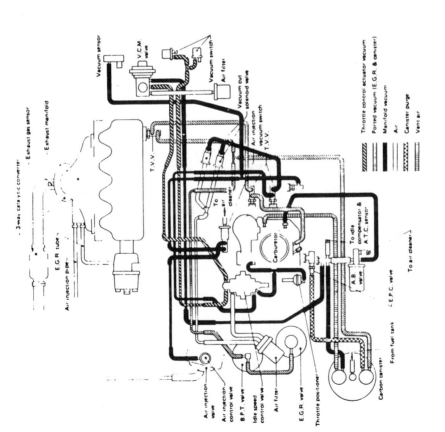

**Vacuum circuit diagram for 1985 Pulsar–Federal models**

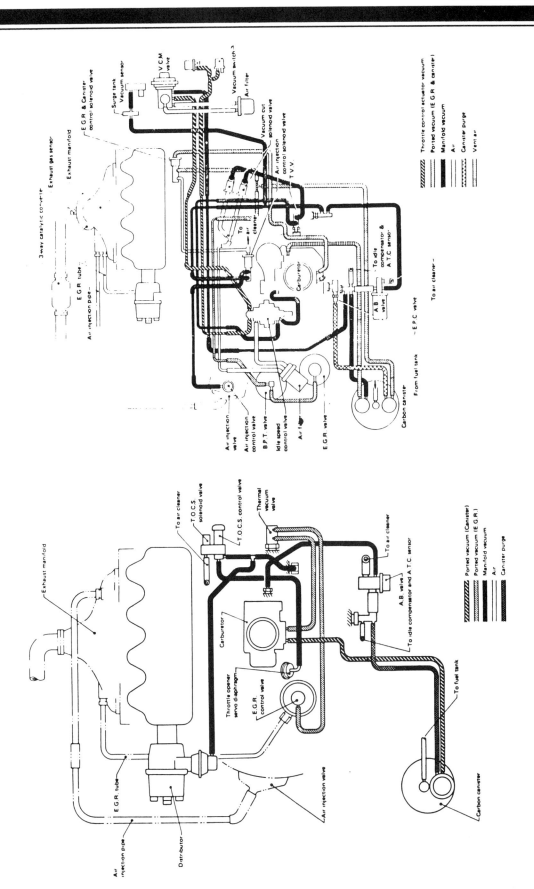

**Vacuum circuit diagram for 1986 Pulsar–Federal models**

**Vacuum circuit diagram for 1985 Pulsar–Canada models**

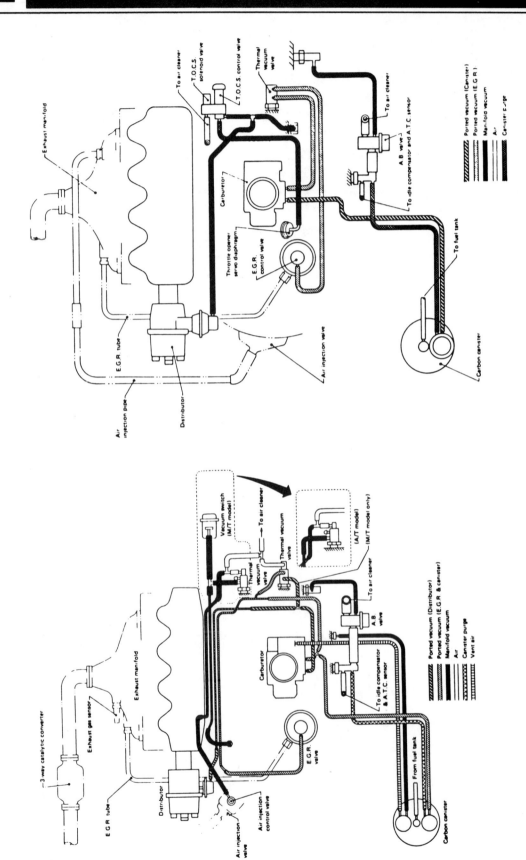

**Vacuum circuit diagram for 1986 Pulsar—Canada models**

**Vacuum circuit diagram for 1986 Pulsar—California models**

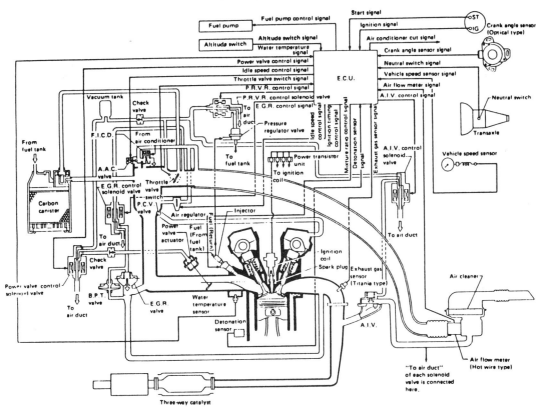

**Vacuum circuit diagram for 1987 Pulsar–CA16DE engine**

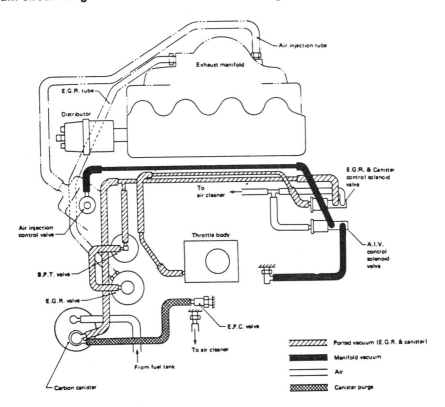

**Vacuum circuit diagram for 1987 Pulsar–E16i engine**

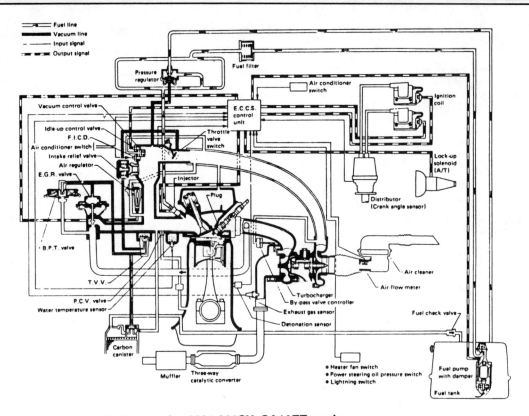

**Vacuum circuit diagram for 1984 200SX–CA18ET engine**

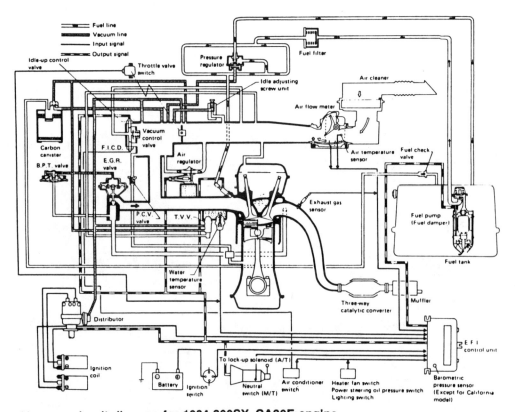

**Vacuum circuit diagram for 1984 200SX–CA20E engine**

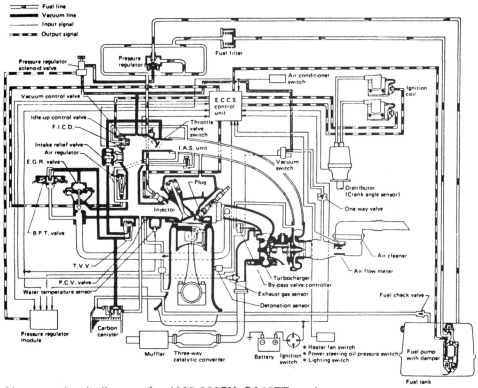

**Vacuum circuit diagram for 1985 200SX–CA18ET engine**

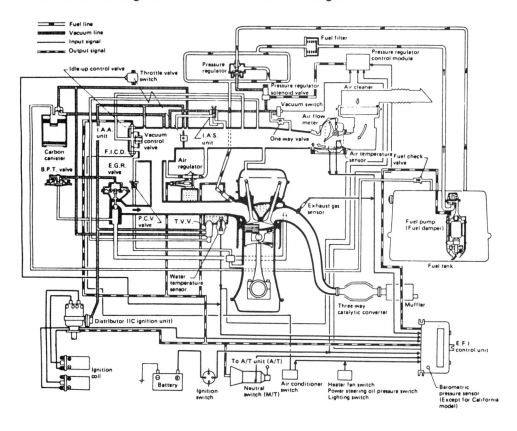

**Vacuum circuit diagram for 1985 200SX–CA20E engine**

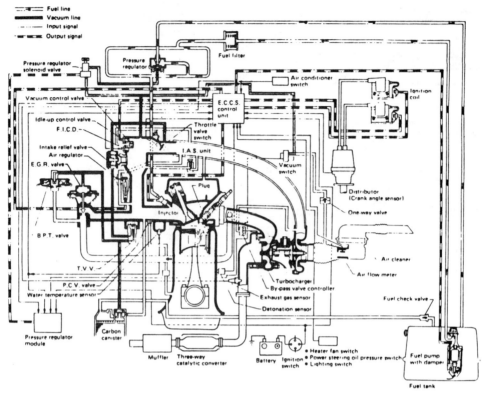

**Vacuum circuit diagram for 1986 200SX–CA18ET engine**

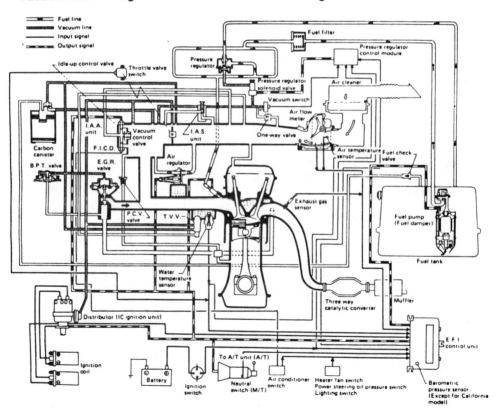

**Vacuum circuit diagram for 1986 200SX–CA20E engine**

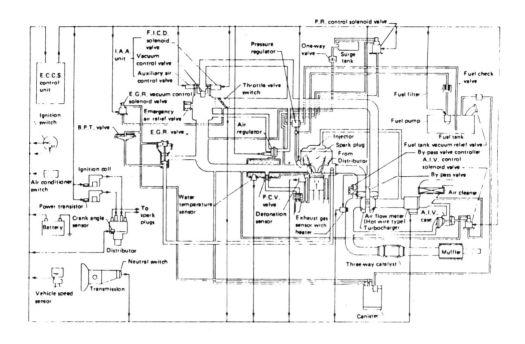

**ECCS diagram for 1987 200SX–CA18ET engine**

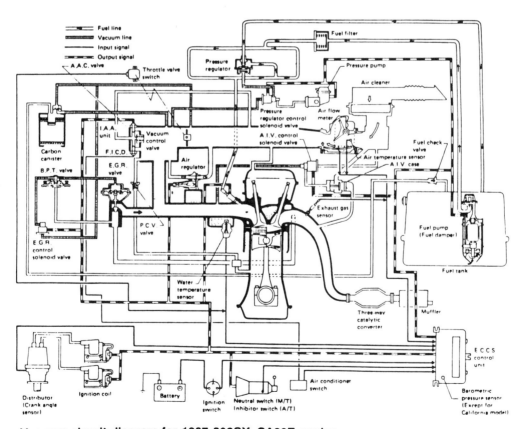

**Vacuum circuit diagram for 1987 200SX–CA20E engine**

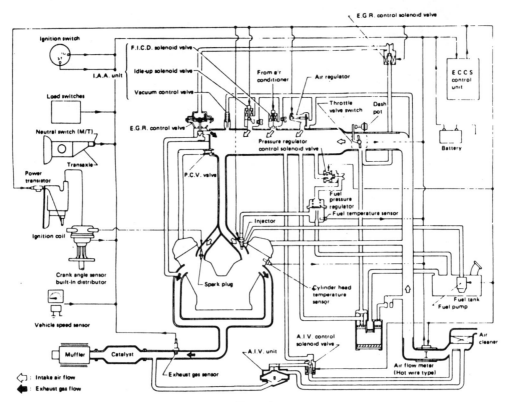

**ECCS diagram for 1987 200SX–VG30E engine**

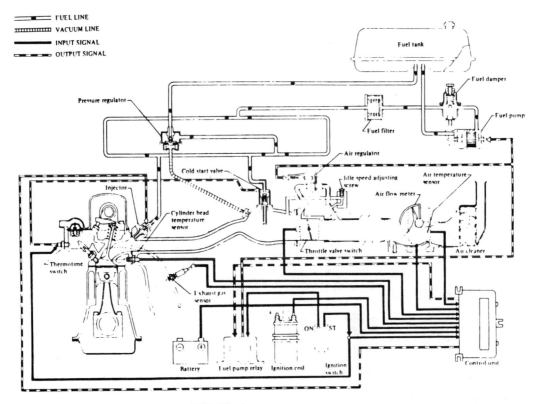

**Vacuum circuit diagram for 1984 Maxima**

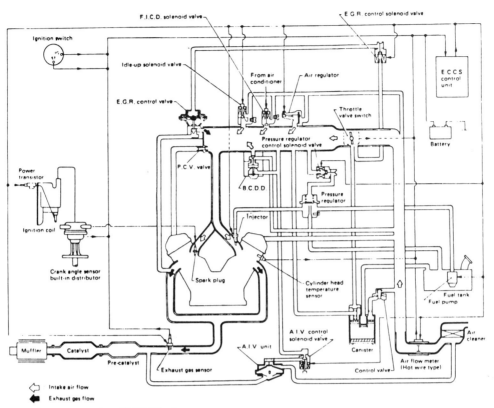

**ECCS diagram for 1985 Maxima**

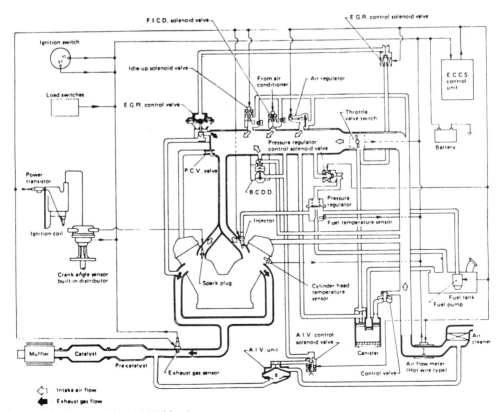

**ECCS diagram for 1986 Maxima**

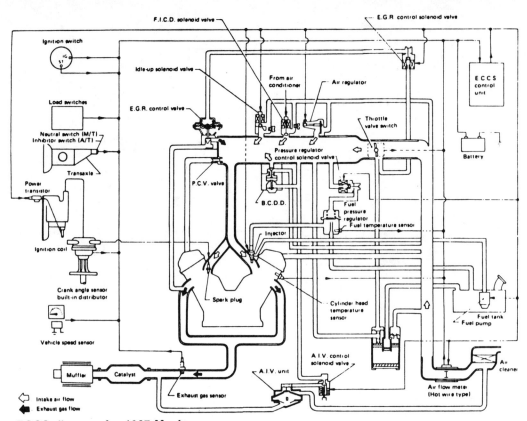

**ECCS diagram for 1987 Maxima**

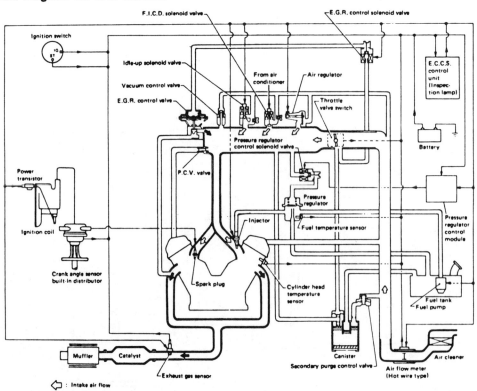

**ECCS diagram for 1984–85 300ZX–VG30E engine**

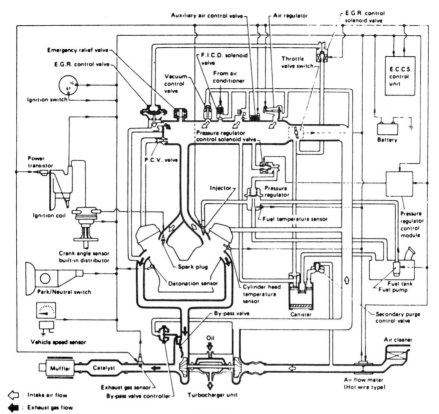

**ECCS diagram for 1984–85 300ZX–VG30ET engine**

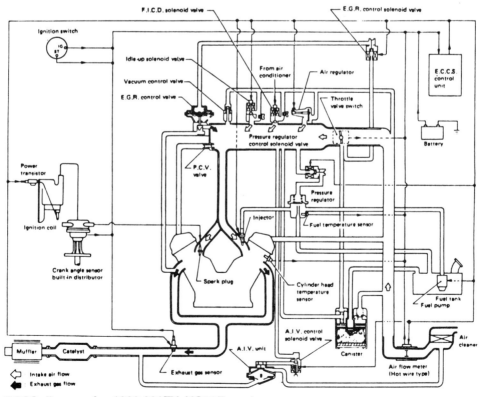

**ECCS diagram for 1986 300ZX–VG30E engine**

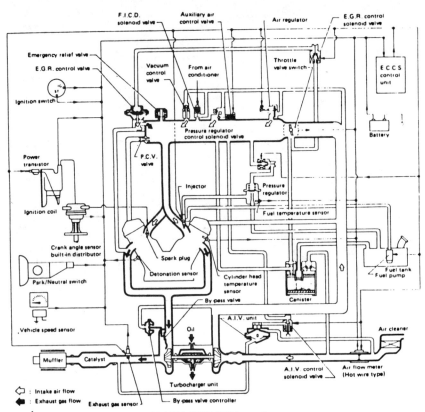

ECCS diagram for 1986 300ZX–VG30ET engine

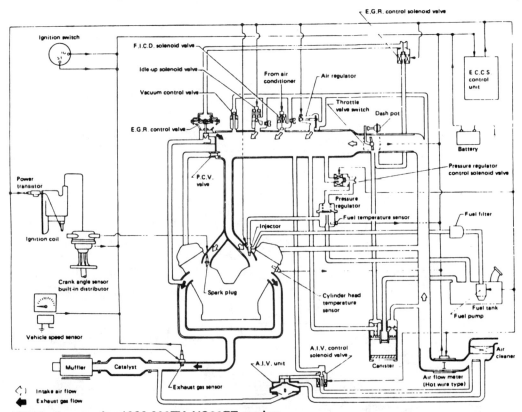

ECCS diagram for 1986 300ZX–VG30ET engine

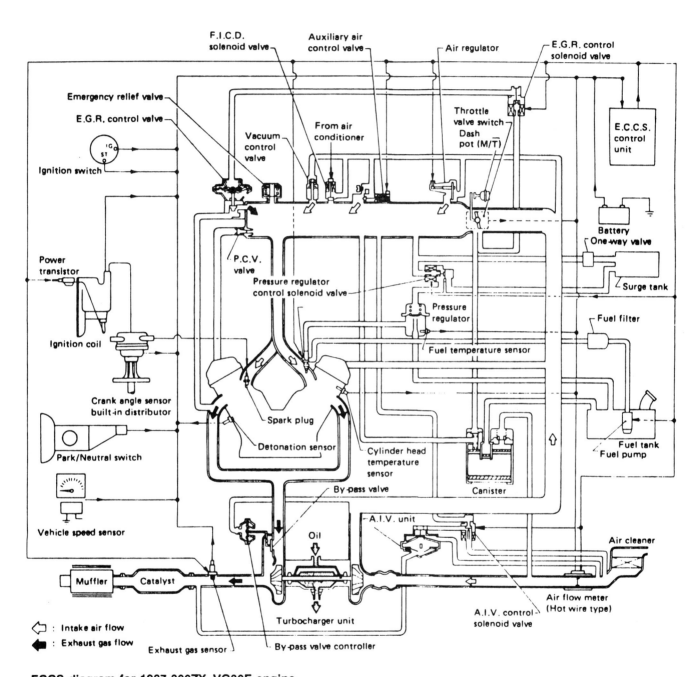

**ECCS diagram for 1987 300ZX–VG30E engine**

# Peugeot

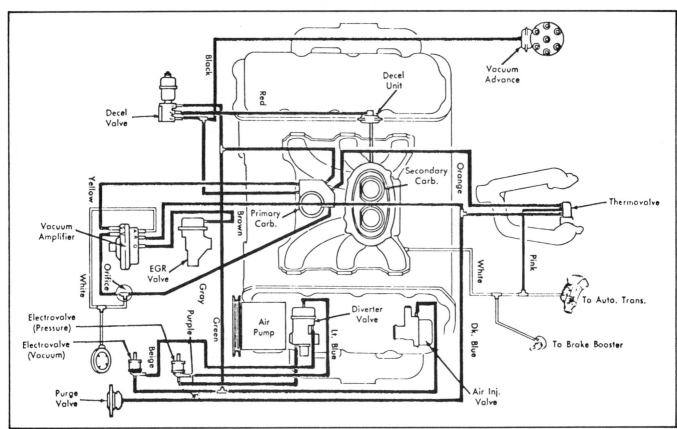

**604 with automatic transmission vacuum diagram**

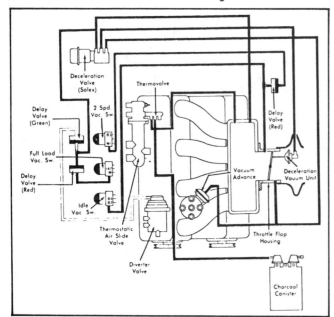

**505 vacuum hose diagram**

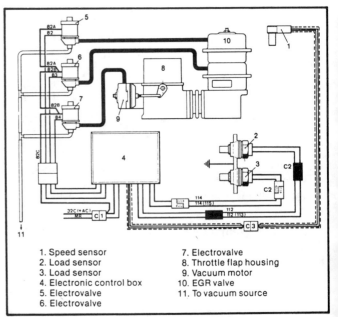

1. Speed sensor
2. Load sensor
3. Load sensor
4. Electronic control box
5. Electrovalve
6. Electrovalve
7. Electrovalve
8. Throttle flap housing
9. Vacuum motor
10. EGR valve
11. To vacuum source

**505 diesel EGR vacuum and wiring diagram**

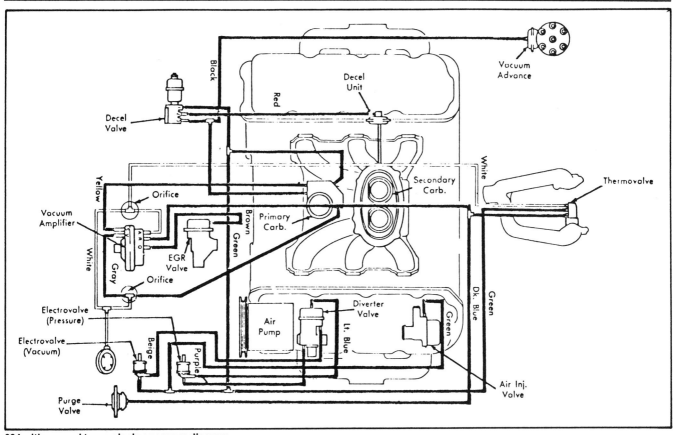

**604 with manual transmission vacuum diagram**

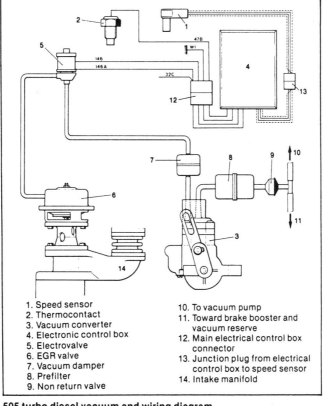

1. Speed sensor
2. Thermocontact
3. Vacuum converter
4. Electronic control box
5. Electrovalve
6. EGR valve
7. Vacuum damper
8. Prefilter
9. Non return valve

10. To vacuum pump
11. Toward brake booster and vacuum reserve
12. Main electrical control box connector
13. Junction plug from electrical control box to speed sensor
14. Intake manifold

**505 turbo diesel vacuum and wiring diagram**

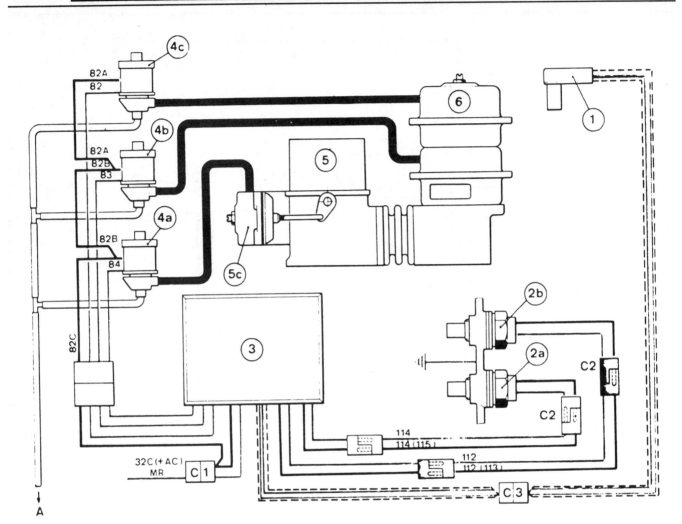

**PEUGEOT DIESEL ENGINE—E.G.R. SYSTEM**

### Component legend

| | | |
|---|---|---|
| — 1 | : | speed sensor |
| — 2a - 2b | : | load sensors |
| — 3 | : | electronic control box |
| — 4a - 4b - 4c | : | electrovalves |
| — 5 | : | throttle flap housing |
| — 5c | : | vacuum motor |
| — 6 | : | EGR valve |
| — A | : | to vacuum source |

### Electrical circuit legend

——— Current supply (+)

——— Ground circuit (—)

Load sensor signal circuit

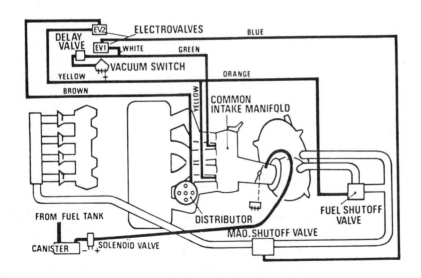

**PEUGEOT 505 MODELS—GASOLINE ENGINE**

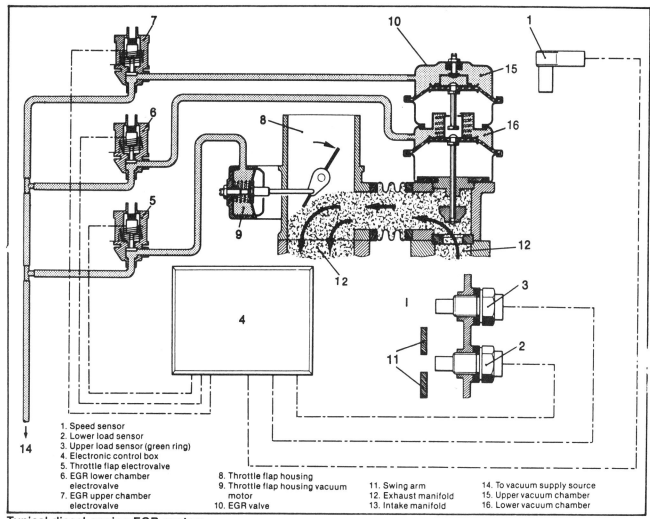

1. Speed sensor
2. Lower load sensor
3. Upper load sensor (green ring)
4. Electronic control box
5. Throttle flap electrovalve
6. EGR lower chamber electrovalve
7. EGR upper chamber electrovalve
8. Throttle flap housing
9. Throttle flap housing vacuum motor
10. EGR valve
11. Swing arm
12. Exhaust manifold
13. Intake manifold
14. To vacuum supply source
15. Upper vacuum chamber
16. Lower vacuum chamber

**Typical diesel engine EGR system**

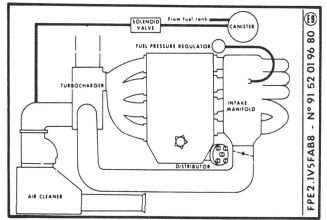

**Typical 1985 turbocharged gasoline engine vacuum hose routing**

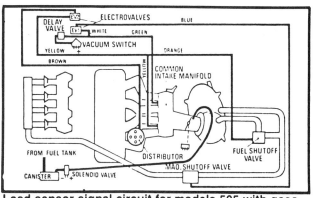

**Load sensor signal circuit for models 505 with gasoline engines**

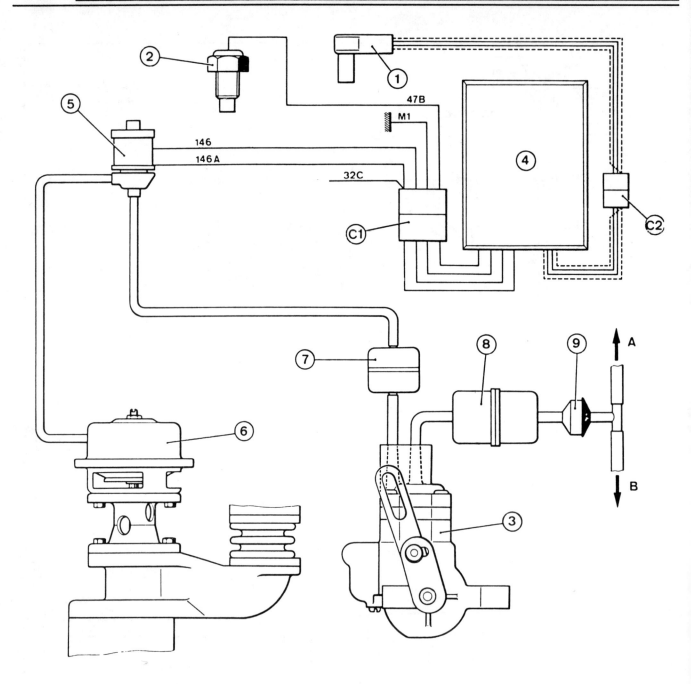

47B

M1

146

146 A

32C

C1

C2

A

B

**Legend :**

1 - Speed sensor
2 - Thermocontact
3 - Converter
4 - Electronic control box
5 - Electrovalve
6 - EGR valve
7 - Vacuum damper

8 - Prefilter
9 - Non return valve
A - To vacuum pump
B - Toward brake booster and vacuum reserve
C1 - Main electrical control box connector
C2 - Junction plug from electrical control box
 to speed sensor

**PEUGEOT TURBO DIESEL—E.G.R. SYSTEM**

# Porsche

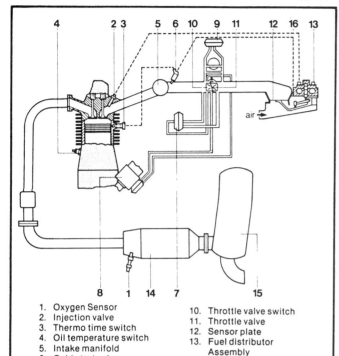

1. Oxygen Sensor
2. Injection valve
3. Thermo time switch
4. Oil temperature switch
5. Intake manifold
6. Cold start valve
7. Vacuum limiter
8. Ignition distributor
9. Auxiliary air valve for  start
10. Throttle valve switch
11. Throttle valve
12. Sensor plate
13. Fuel distributor Assembly
14. Threeway catalyst
15. Muffler
16. Fuel injection line

**1980 911 emission schematic—typical**

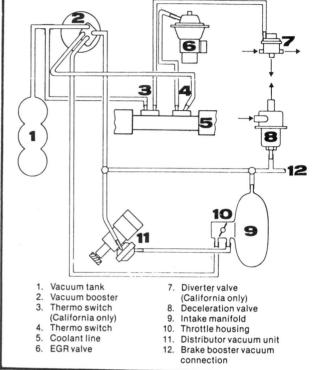

1. Vacuum tank
2. Vacuum booster
3. Thermo switch (California only)
4. Thermo switch
5. Coolant line
6. EGR valve
7. Diverter valve (California only)
8. Deceleration valve
9. Intake manifold
10. Throttle housing
11. Distributor vacuum unit
12. Brake booster vacuum connection

**1977–80 924 vacuum circuits—typical**

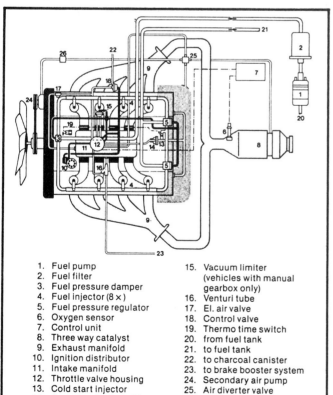

1. Fuel pump
2. Fuel filter
3. Fuel pressure damper
4. Fuel injector (8 ×)
5. Fuel pressure regulator
6. Oxygen sensor
7. Control unit
8. Three way catalyst
9. Exhaust manifold
10. Ignition distributor
11. Intake manifold
12. Throttle valve housing
13. Cold start injector
14. Aux. air valve for cold start
15. Vacuum limiter (vehicles with manual gearbox only)
16. Venturi tube
17. El. air valve
18. Control valve
19. Thermo time switch
20. from fuel tank
21. to fuel tank
22. to charcoal canister
23. to brake booster system
24. Secondary air pump
25. Air diverter valve
26. Check valve

**1982 928 emission system schematic**

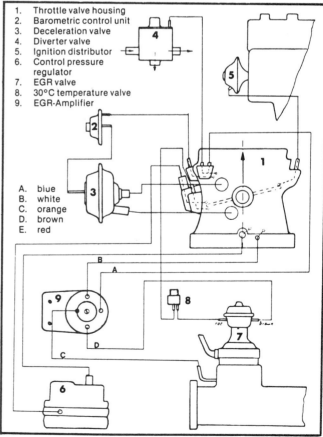

1. Throttle valve housing
2. Barometric control unit
3. Deceleration valve
4. Diverter valve
5. Ignition distributor
6. Control pressure regulator
7. EGR valve
8. 30°C temperature valve
9. EGR-Amplifier

A. blue
B. white
C. orange
D. brown
E. red

**1982 944 vacuum circuits**

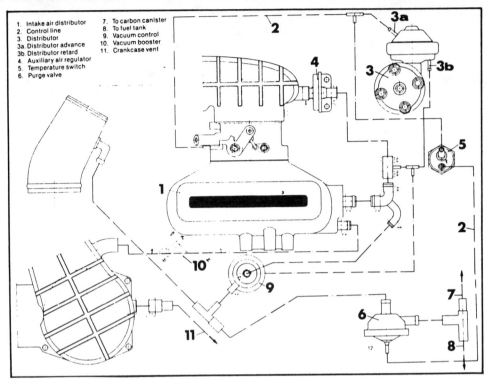

1. Intake air distributor
2. Control line
3. Distributor
3a. Distributor advance
3b. Distributor retard
4. Auxiliary air regulator
5. Temperature switch
6. Purge valve
7. To carbon canister
8. To fuel tank
9. Vacuum control
10. Vacuum booster
11. Crankcase vent

**1982 924 vacuum circuits**

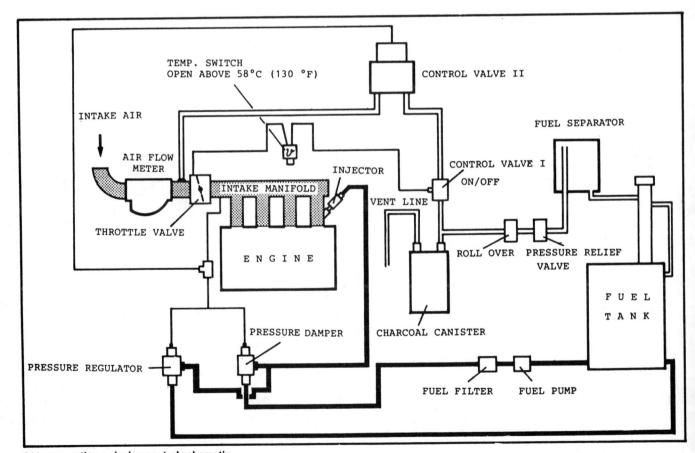

**944 evaporative emission control schematic**

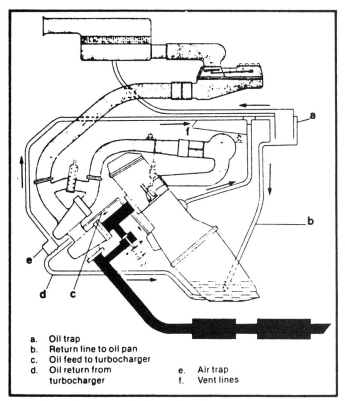

a. Oil trap
b. Return line to oil pan
c. Oil feed to turbocharger
d. Oil return from turbocharger
e. Air trap
f. Vent lines

**924 turbo crankcase ventilation schematic**

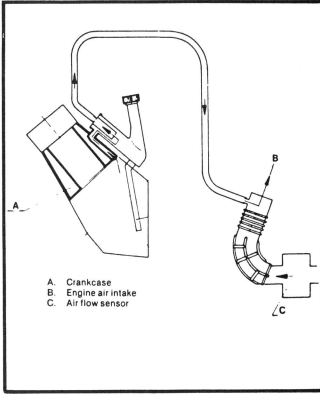

A. Crankcase
B. Engine air intake
C. Air flow sensor

**944 crankcase ventilation schematic**

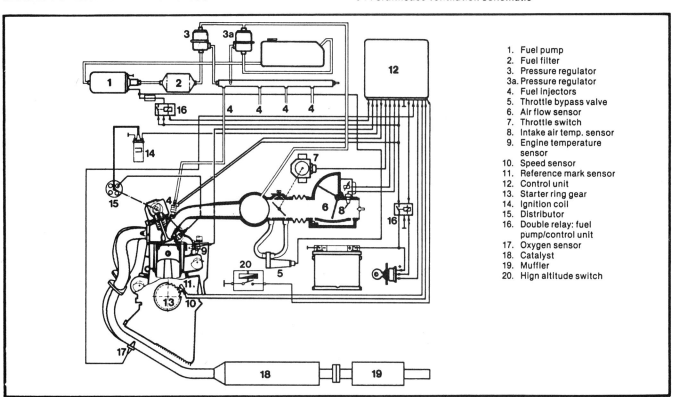

1. Fuel pump
2. Fuel filter
3. Pressure regulator
3a. Pressure regulator
4. Fuel injectors
5. Throttle bypass valve
6. Air flow sensor
7. Throttle switch
8. Intake air temp. sensor
9. Engine temperature sensor
10. Speed sensor
11. Reference mark sensor
12. Control unit
13. Starter ring gear
14. Ignition coil
15. Distributor
16. Double relay: fuel pump/control unit
17. Oxygen sensor
18. Catalyst
19. Muffler
20. High altitude switch

**Schematic of AFC fuel injection—944 shown**

# PORSCHE
## VACUUM CIRCUITS

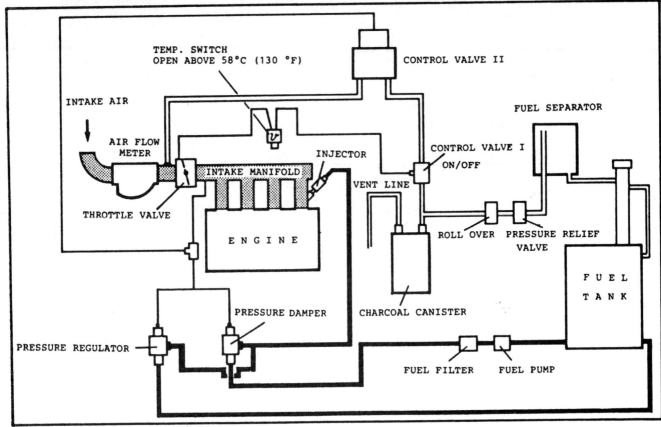

**944 evaporative emission system—others similar**

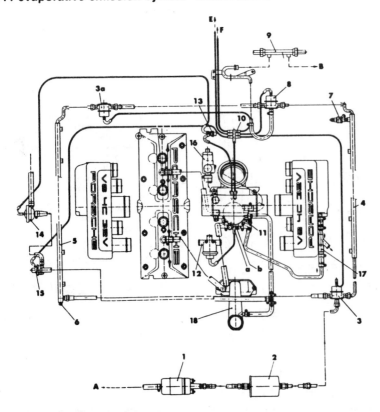

1 — Fuel pump
2 — Fuel filter
3 — Pressure damper
3a — Pressure damper
4 — Fuel line  (cyl. 5 . . . 8)
5 — Fuel line  (cyl. 1 . . . 4)
6 — Fuel pressure test connection
7 — Fuel injectors
8 — Pressure regulator
9 — Fuel cooler
10 — Vacuum distributor
11 — Throttle housing
12 — Diverter valve
13 — Thermo switch
14 — Shift valve
15 — Control valve
16 — Air regulating valve
17 — Vacuum booster venturi
18 — Oil filler neck

a — Connection 49 states
b — Connection California

A — From fuel tank
B — Return to fuel tank
E — To automatic transmission
F — To EZF control unit

**Porsche 928 models**

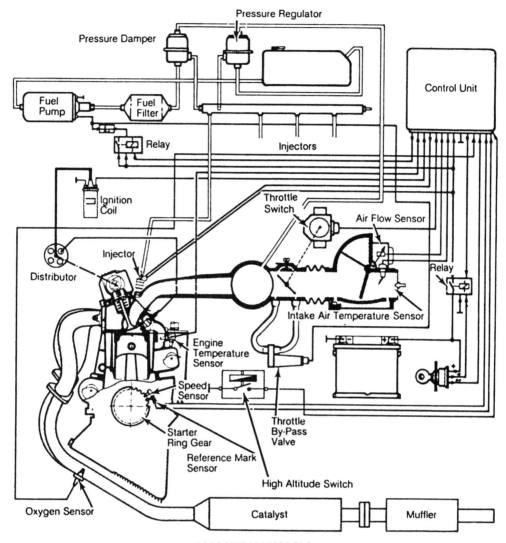

**PORSCHE 944 MODELS**

Pressure Regulator

Pressure Damper

Control Unit

Fuel Pump

Fuel Filter

Relay

Injectors

Ignition Coil

Throttle Switch

Air Flow Sensor

Relay

Injector

Distributor

Intake Air Temperature Sensor

Engine Temperature Sensor

Speed Sensor

Throttle By-Pass Valve

Starter Ring Gear

Reference Mark Sensor

High Altitude Switch

Oxygen Sensor

Catalyst

Muffler

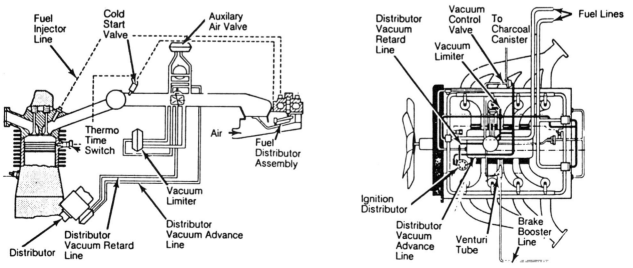

Fuel Injector Line

Cold Start Valve

Auxilary Air Valve

Thermo Time Switch

Air

Fuel Distributor Assembly

Vacuum Limiter

Distributor Vacuum Advance Line

Distributor Vacuum Retard Line

Distributor

**PORSCHE 911SC MODELS**

Distributor Vacuum Retard Line

Vacuum Control Valve

To Charcoal Canister

Fuel Lines

Vacuum Limiter

Ignition Distributor

Distributor Vacuum Advance Line

Venturi Tube

Brake Booster Line

**PORSCHE 928 MODELS**

# Renault

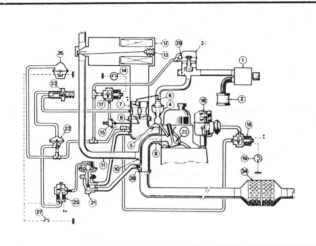

1. Air pump
2. Air pump filter
3. Relief and divertor valve assembly
4. Check valve
5. Air injection manifold
6. Air shut-off valve
7. Carburetor
8. Intake manifold
9. Exhaust manifold
10. Air filter pre-heated air take-off
11. Air filter pre-heated air intake duct
12. Air filter
13. Thermovalve activating sensor
14. Electronic governor
15. Throttle plate opener
16. Distributor

17. Solenoid valve
18. Solenoid valve for vacuum advance capsule
19. Choke plate switch
20. Exhaust valve
21. EGR valve
22. Vacuum amplifier
23. Coolant temperature switch (opens channel at 130° F./45° C.)
24. Catalytic convertor
25. EGR solenoid
26. Vacuum controlled switch (closes as vacuum exceeds 10″ or 254 mm hg.)
27. Transmission switch (contacts closed in 4th gear)
28. Calibrated orifice
29. Calibrated orifice

Emission control schematic, 1976—California LeCar

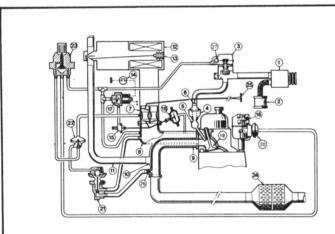

1. Air pump
2. Air pump filter
3. Relief and divertor valve assembly
4. Check valve
5. Air injection manifold
6. Air shut-off valve
7. Carburetor
8. Intake manifold
9. Exhaust manifold
10. Air filter pre-heated air take-off
11. Air filter pre-heated air intake duct
12. Air filter
13. Thermovalve activating sensor

14. Electronic governor
15. Throttle plate opener
16. Distributor
17. Fast idle solenoid valve
18. Vacuum operated throttle plate plunger
19. Exhaust valve
20. Vacuum advance unit
21. EGR valve
22. Vacuum switch
23. Thermovalve
24. Catalytic convertor
25. Choke knob
26. Calibrated orifice
27. Calibrated orifice

Emission control schematic, 1977—California LeCar

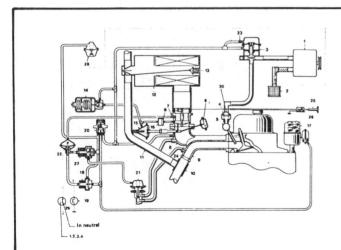

1. Air pump
2. Air pump filter
3. Relief and divertor valve assembly
4. Check valve
5. Air injection manifold
6. Dashpot
7. Carburetor
8. Intake manifold
9. Exhaust manifold
10. Air filter pre-heated air take-off
11. Air filter pre-heated air intake duct
12. Thermostatic air cleaner
13. Thermovalve activating sensor
14. Deceleration valve

15. Throttle plate opener
16. Idle delay valve
17. Distributor
18. Solenoid valve
19. 4th gear switch
20. Thermovalve
21. EGR valve
22. Vacuum amplifier
23. Calibrated orifice
24. Calibrated orifice
25. Choke knob
26. Choke control switch
27. Solenoid valve
28. Electro-vacuum switch
29. Transmission switch
30. Air shut-off valve
B. White side of delay valve

Emission control schematic, 1979—Federal LeCar

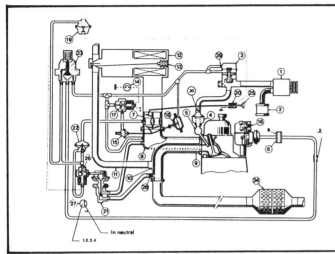

1. Air pump
2. Air pump filter
3. Relief and divertor valve assembly
4. Check valve
5. Air injection manifold
6. Delay valve
7. Carburetor
8. Intake manifold
9. Exhaust manifold
10. Air filter pre-heated air take-off
11. Air filter pre-heated air intake duct
12. Thermostatic air cleaner
13. Thermovalve activating sensor
14. Electronic tachometer switch
15. Throttle plate opener
16. Distributor
17. Throttle plate opening solenoid
18. Throttle plate plunger
19. Electro-vacuum switch
20. Choke control switch
21. EGR valve
22. Vacuum amplifier
23. Thermovalve
24. Catalytic converter
25. Choke knob
26. Solenoid valve
27. Transmission switch
28. Calibrated orifice
29. Calibrated orifice
30. Air shut-off valve
B. Blue side of delay valve
X. Calib.ated orifice

Emission control schematic, 1979—California LeCar

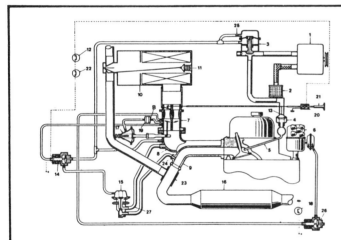

1. Air pump
2. Air pump filter
3. Relief and divertor valve assembly
4. Check valve
5. Air injection manifold
6. Distributor
7. Carburetor
8. Intake manifold
9. Exhaust manifold
10. Thermostatic air cleaner
11. Thermovalve activating sensor
12. Coolant temperature switch
13. Air shut-off valve
14. EGR solenoid valve
15. EGR valve
16. Catalytic converter
17. Throttle plate opener
18. Oil thermoswitch
19. Delay valve
20. Choke control switch
21. Choke control cable
22. Transmission switch
23. Air intake system pre-heated air stove
24. Calibrated orifice
25. Calibrated orifice
26. Solenoid valve (vacuum advance)
27. Calibrated orifice
B. White side of vacuum delay valve

Emission control schematic, 1980—Federal LeCar. Typical of later models

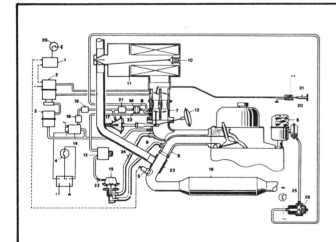

1. Electronic control unit
2. Vacuum solenoid regulator
3. Vacuum tank (fuel control system)
4. Magnetic pick-up
5. Oxygen sensor
6. Distributor
7. Carburetor
8. Intake manifold
9. Exhaust manifold
10. Thermovalve activating sensor
11. Thermostatic air cleaner
12. Coolant temperature switch
13. Dashpot
14. Fast idle solenoid valve
15. EGR valve
16. Catalytic converter
17. Throttle plate opener
18. Vacuum regulator
19. Check valve
20. Choke control switch
21. Vacuum reservoir (fast idle system)
22. Delay valve
23. Calibrated orifice
24. Calibrated orifice
25. Oil thermoswitch
26. Vacuum advance solenoid valve

Emission control schematic, 1980—California LeCar. Typical of later models

# RENAULT
## VACUUM CIRCUITS

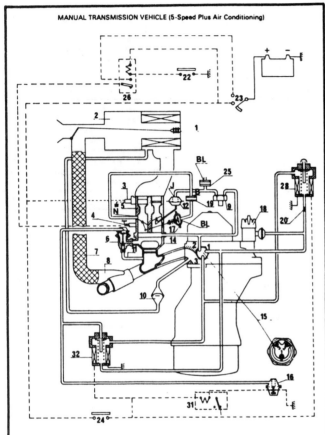

MANUAL TRANSMISSION VEHICLE (5-Speed Plus Air Conditioning)

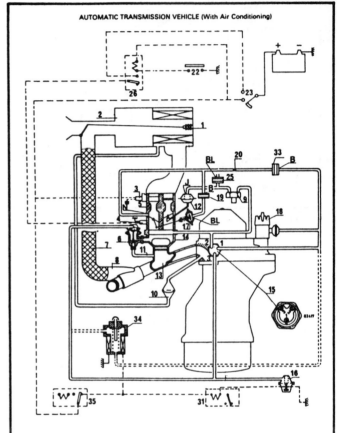

AUTOMATIC TRANSMISSION VEHICLE (With Air Conditioning)

1. Thermostatic component
2. Air filter
3. Anti-dieseling solenoid
4. Mixture control solenoid
5. Carburetor
6. Exhaust gas recycling (EGR) valve
7. Hot air pipe
8. Hot air intake
9. Two-way thermovalve (closed for water temperatures higher than 45°C, or 113°F)
10. Air intake valves
11. Recycling pipe
12. Secondary barrel lock-out
13. Exhaust manifold
14. Intake manifold
15. Three-way thermovalve (1 and 2 open for water temperatures lower than 45°C, or 113°F; 2 and 3 open for water temperatures higher than 45°C, or 113°F)

16. Vacuum switch (closed for a vacuum greater than 460 mbar, or about 14 in. Hg)
17. Throttle plate opener
18. Distributor
19. Delay valve
20. Diameter 0.35 mm (0.014 in.)
22. Ambient cooling liquid temperature switch (closed for temperatures lower than 15°C, or 59°F)
23. Starting switch
24. Switch on transmission (open in 4th)
25. Delay valve
26. Mixture control relay
28. Electrovalve
31. Advance-delay distributor relay
32. Electrovalve
35. Air conditioner relay
Color code system:
B   White
BL  Blue
J   Yellow
N   Black

1. Thermostatic component
2. Air filter
3. Anti-dieseling solenoid
4. Mixture control solenoid
5. Carburetor
6. Exhaust gas recycling (EGR) valve
7. Hot air pipe
8. Hot air intake
9. Two-way thermovalve (closed for water temperatures higher than 45°C, or 113°F)
10. Air intake valves
11. Recycling pipe
12. Secondary barrel lock-out
13. Exhaust manifold
14. Intake manifold
15. Three-way thermovalve (1 and 2 open for water temperatures lower than 45°C, or 113°F; 2 and 3 open for water temperatures higher than 45°C, or 113°F)

16. Vacuum switch (closed for a vacuum greater than 460 mbar, or about 14 in. Hg)
17. Throttle plate opener
18. Distributor
19. Delay valve
20. Diameter 0.35 mm (0.014 in.)
22. Ambient cooling liquid temperature switch (closed for temperatures lower than 15°C, or 59°F)
23. Starting switch
24. Switch on transmission (open in 4th)
25. Delay valve
28. Electrovalve
31. Advance-delay distributor relay
32. Electrovalve
35. Air conditioner relay
Color code system:
B   White
BL  Blue
J   Yellow
N   Black

Emission control schematic, 18i Canadian models with carburetor, manual transmission, 5 speed plus air conditioning

Emission control schematic, 18i Canadian models with carburetor, automatic transmission with air conditioning

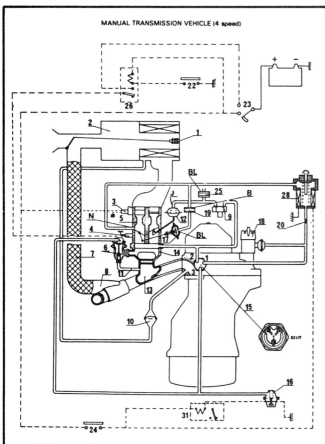

MANUAL TRANSMISSION VEHICLE (4 speed)

MANUAL TRANSMISSION VEHICLE (5 Speed)

1. Thermostatic
   component
2. Air filter
3. Anti-dieseling solenoid
4. Mixture control solenoid
5. Carburetor
6. Exhaust gas recycling
   (EGR) valve
7. Hot air pipe
8. Hot air intake
9. Two-way thermovalve
   (closed for water
   temperatures higher
   than 45°C, or 113°F)
10. Air intake valves
11. Recycling pipe
12. Secondary barrel lock-
   out
13. Exhaust manifold
14. Intake manifold
15. Three-way thermovalve
   (1 and 2 open for water
   temperatures lower than
   45°C, or 113°F; 2 and 3
   open for water
   temperatures higher
   than 45°C, or 113°F)

16. Vacuum switch (closed
   for a vacuum greater
   than 460 mbar, or about
   14 in. Hg)
17. Throttle plate opener
18. Distributor
19. Delay valve
20. Diameter 0.35 mm
   (0.014 in.)
22. Ambient cooling liquid
   temperature switch
   (closed for temperatures
   lower than 15°C, or 59°F)
23. Starting switch
24. Switch on transmission
   (open in 4th)
25. Delay valve
26. Mixture control relay
28. Electrovalve
31. Advance-delay
   distributor relay

Color code system:
B   White
BL  Blue
J   Yellow
N   Black

**Emission control schematic, 18i Canadian models with carburetor, manual transmission—4 speed**

1. Thermostatic
   component
2. Air filter
3. Anti-dieseling solenoid
4. Mixture control solenoid
5. Carburetor
6. Exhaust gas recycling
   (EGR) valve
7. Hot air pipe
8. Hot air intake
9. Two-way thermovalve
   (closed for water
   temperatures higher
   than 45°C, or 113°F)
10. Air intake valves
11. Recycling pipe
12. Secondary barrel
   lock-out
13. Exhaust manifold
14. Intake manifold
15. Three-way thermovalve
   (1 and 2 open for water
   temperatures lower than
   45°C, or 113°F; 2 and 3
   open for water
   temperatures higher
   than 45°C, or 113°F)

16. Vacuum switch (closed
   for a vacuum greater
   than 460 mbar, or about
   14 in. Hg)
17. Throttle plate opener
18. Distributor
19. Delay valve
20. Diameter 0.35 mm
   (0.014 in.)
22. Ambient cooling liquid
   temperature switch
   (closed for temperatures
   lower than 15°C, or 59°F)
23. Starting switch
24. Switch on transmission
   (open in 4th)
25. Delay valve
26. Mixture control relay
28. Electrovalve
31. Advance-delay
   distributor relay
32. Electrovalve

Color code system:
B   White
BL  Blue
J   Yellow
N   Black

**Emission control schematic, 18i Canadian models with carburetor, manual transmission—5 speed**

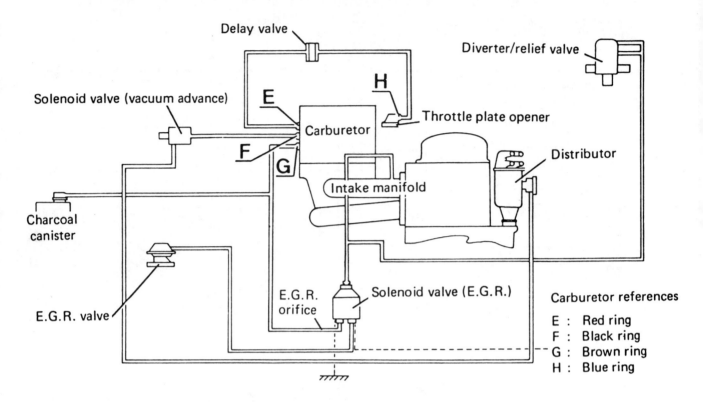

Delay valve

Diverter/relief valve

Solenoid valve (vacuum advance)

E

H

Carburetor

Throttle plate opener

F

G

Distributor

Intake manifold

Charcoal canister

E.G.R. valve

E.G.R. orifice

Solenoid valve (E.G.R.)

Carburetor references

E : Red ring
F : Black ring
G : Brown ring
H : Blue ring

**RENAULT LeCAR—WO/AIR CONDITIONING—49 STATES**

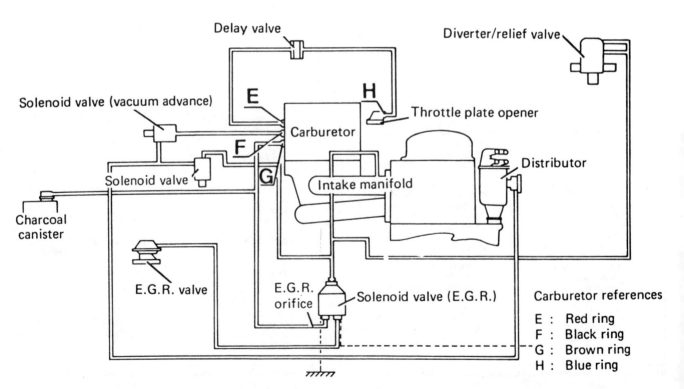

Delay valve

Diverter/relief valve

Solenoid valve (vacuum advance)

E

H

Carburetor

Throttle plate opener

F

Solenoid valve

G

Distributor

Intake manifold

Charcoal canister

E.G.R. valve

E.G.R. orifice

Solenoid valve (E.G.R.)

Carburetor references

E : Red ring
F : Black ring
G : Brown ring
H : Blue ring

**RENAULT LeCAR—W/AIR CONDITIONING—49 STATES**

194

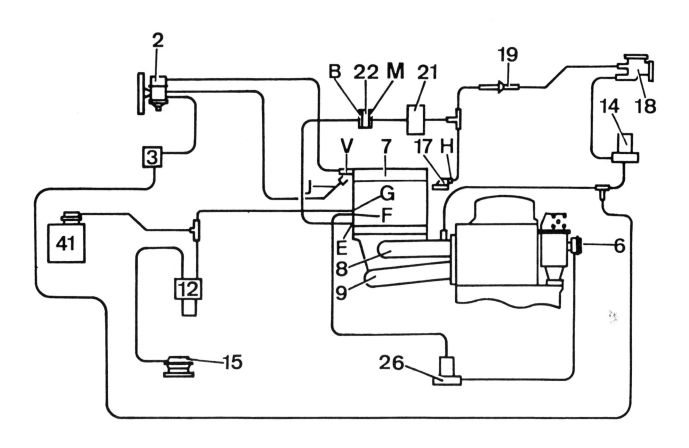

| Item | DESCRIPTION | | Item | DESCRIPTION |
|------|-------------|---|------|-------------|
| 2 | Vacuum solenoid regulator | | | |
| 3 | Vacuum tank (fuel control system) | | 41 | Charcoal cannister |
| 6 | Distributor | | | |
| 7 | Carburetor | | | **Carburetor references** |
| 8 | Intake manifold | | | |
| 9 | Exhaust manifold | | J | Yellow ring |
| 12 | Coolant thermovalve | | V | Green ring |
| 14 | Fast idle solenoid valve | | | |
| 15 | E.G.R. valve | | E | Red ring |
| 17 | Throttle plate opener | | F | Black ring |
| 18 | Vacuum regulator | | G | Brown ring |
| 19 | Check valve | | H | Blue ring |
| 21 | Vacuum reservoir (fast idle system) | | | |
| 22 | Delay valve | | M | Brown side |
| 26 | Vacuum advance solenoid valve | | B | White side |

**RENAULT LeCAR—WO/AIR CONDITIONING—CALIFORNIA**

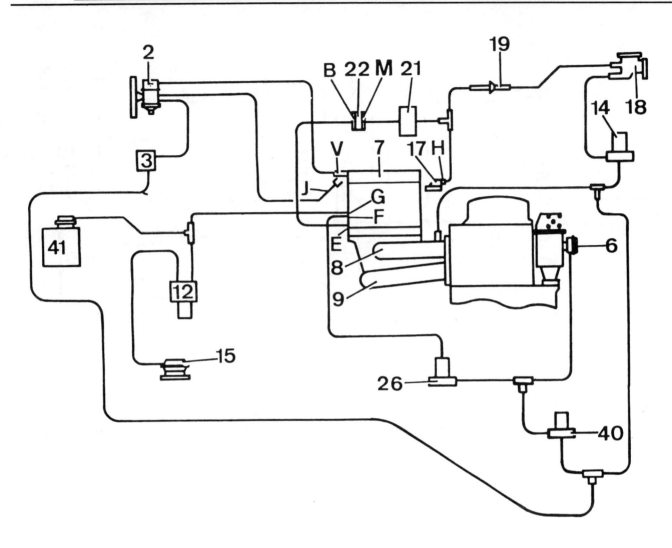

| Item | DESCRIPTION |
|------|-------------|
| 2 | Vacuum solenoid regulator |
| 3 | Vacuum tank (fuel control system) |
| 6 | Distributor |
| 7 | Carburetor |
| 8 | Intake manifold |
| 9 | Exhaust manifold |
| 12 | Coolant thermovalve |
| 14 | Fast idle solenoid valve |
| 15 | E.G.R. valve |
| 17 | Throttle plate opener |
| 18 | Vacuum regulator |
| 19 | Check valve |
| 21 | Vacuum reservoir (fast idle system) |
| 22 | Delay valve |
| 26 | Vacuum advance solenoid valve |

| Item | DESCRIPTION |
|------|-------------|
| 41 | Charcoal cannister |

**Carburetor references**

| | |
|------|-------------|
| J | Yellow ring |
| V | Green ring |
| E | Red ring |
| F | Black ring |
| G | Brown ring |
| H | Blue ring |
| M | Brown side |
| B | White side |

**RENAULT LeCAR—W/AIR CONDITIONING—CALIFORNIA**

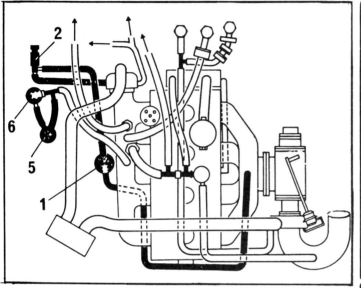

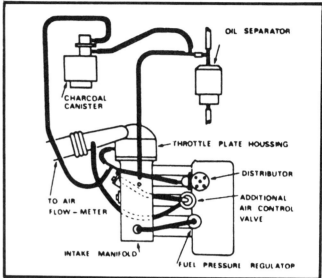

Crankcase ventilation system, typical of 18i and Fuego

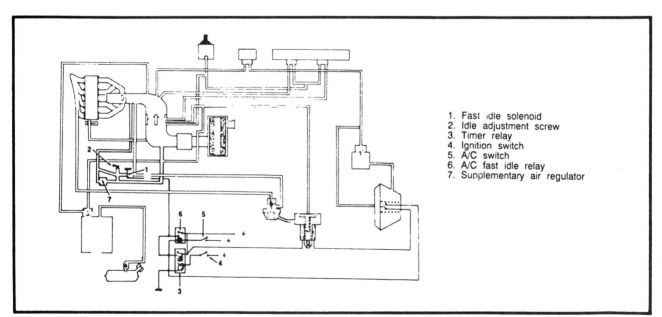

1. Fast idle solenoid
2. Idle adjustment screw
3. Timer relay
4. Ignition switch
5. A/C switch
6. A/C fast idle relay
7. Supplementary air regulator

2.2L engine fast idle schematic

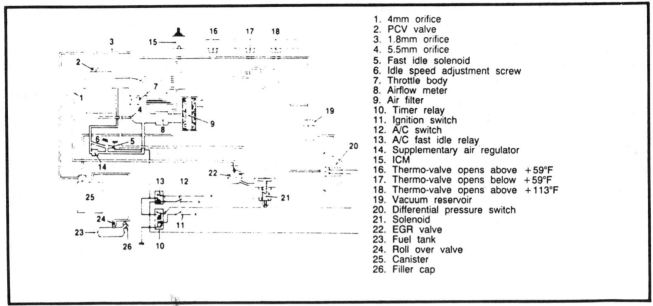

1. 4mm orifice
2. PCV valve
3. 1.8mm orifice
4. 5.5mm orifice
5. Fast idle solenoid
6. Idle speed adjustment screw
7. Throttle body
8. Airflow meter
9. Air filter
10. Timer relay
11. Ignition switch
12. A/C switch
13. A/C fast idle relay
14. Supplementary air regulator
15. ICM
16. Thermo-valve opens above +59°F
17. Thermo-valve opens below +59°F
18. Thermo-valve opens above +113°F
19. Vacuum reservoir
20. Differential pressure switch
21. Solenoid
22. EGR valve
23. Fuel tank
24. Roll over valve
25. Canister
26. Filler cap

2.2L engine emission control system diagram

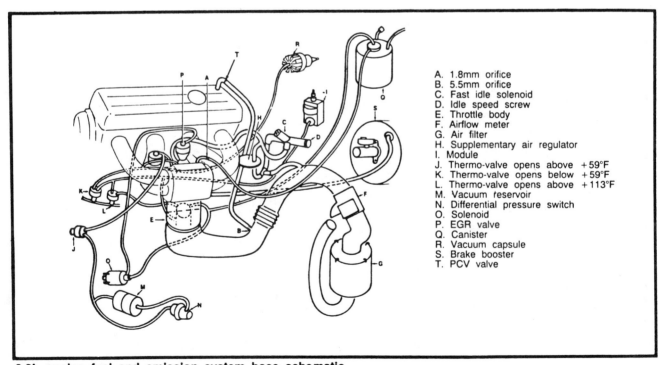

A. 1.8mm orifice
B. 5.5mm orifice
C. Fast idle solenoid
D. Idle speed screw
E. Throttle body
F. Airflow meter
G. Air filter
H. Supplementary air regulator
I. Module
J. Thermo-valve opens above +59°F
K. Thermo-valve opens below +59°F
L. Thermo-valve opens above +113°F
M. Vacuum reservoir
N. Differential pressure switch
O. Solenoid
P. EGR valve
Q. Canister
R. Vacuum capsule
S. Brake booster
T. PCV valve

2.2L engine fuel and emission system hose schematic

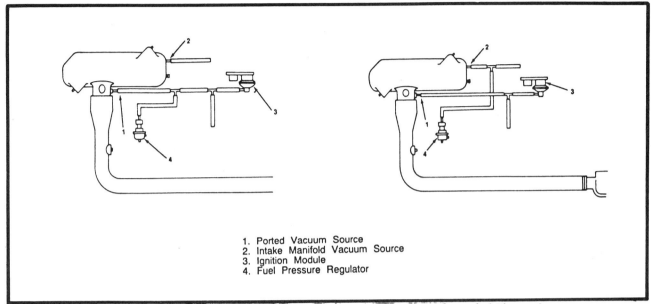

1. Ported Vacuum Source
2. Intake Manifold Vacuum Source
3. Ignition Module
4. Fuel Pressure Regulator

Injection system vacuum lines for multi-point injection on 1984-85 1.4L and 1.7L engines

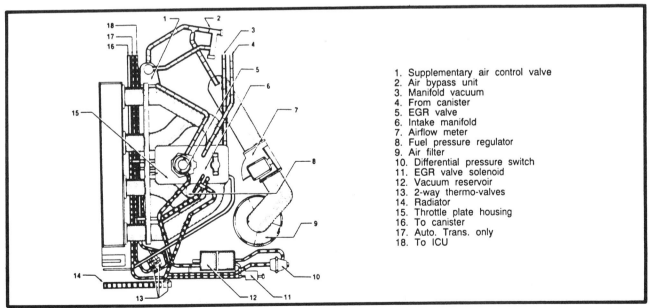

1. Supplementary air control valve
2. Air bypass unit
3. Manifold vacuum
4. From canister
5. EGR valve
6. Intake manifold
7. Airflow meter
8. Fuel pressure regulator
9. Air filter
10. Differential pressure switch
11. EGR valve solenoid
12. Vacuum reservoir
13. 2-way thermo-valves
14. Radiator
15. Throttle plate housing
16. To canister
17. Auto. Trans. only
18. To ICU

2.2L engine emission vacuum hoses

# SAAB

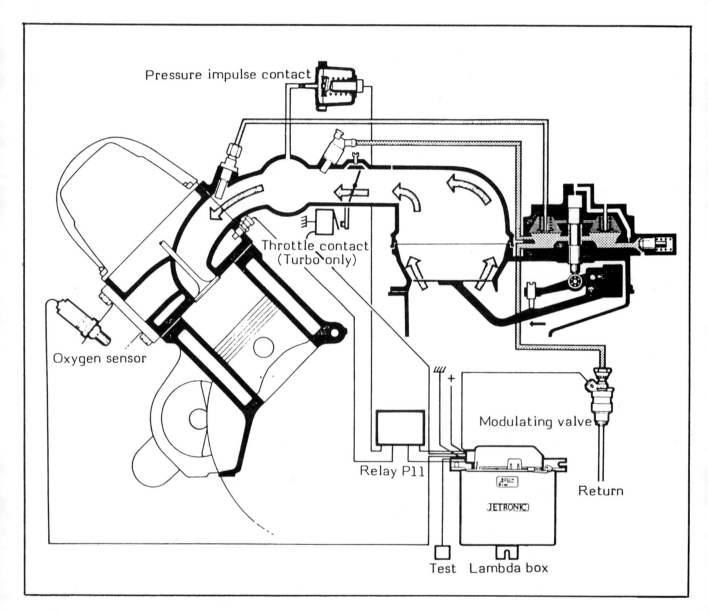

Pressure impulse contact

Throttle contact
(Turbo only)

Oxygen sensor

Modulating valve

Relay P11

Return

Test    Lambda box

JETRONIC

**SAAB 900 MODELS**

# Spectrum

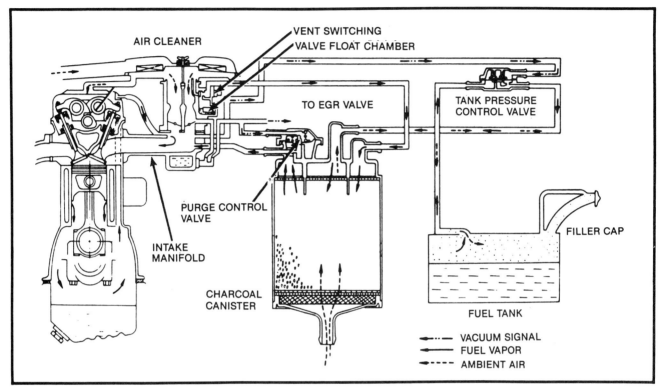

**Evaporative emission control system**

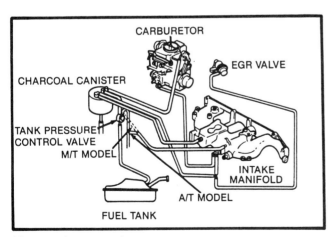

**Vacuum hose routing**

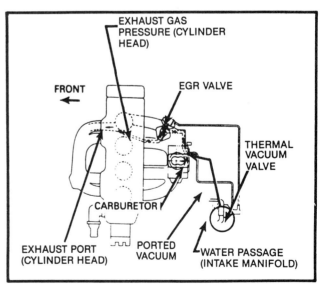

**Exhaust gas recirculation system**

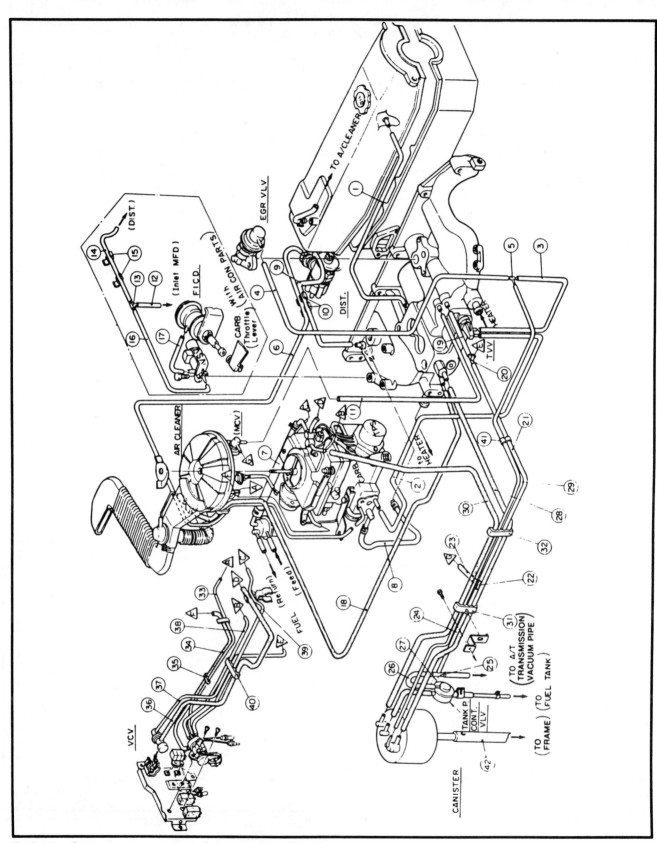

**Emission Control component and vacuum hose locations**

| NO. | CONNECTION | | NO. | CONNECTION | |
|---|---|---|---|---|---|
| 1 | Head Cover — Inlet | | 22 | 3 Way; MCV — VCV | |
| 2 | Carb — TVV | | 23 | 3 Way — MCV | |
| 3 | TVV — 3 Way | | 24 | 3 Way — 3 Way | |
| 4 | 3 Way — EGR VLV | | 25 | 3 Way; A/T Mission | A/T Only |
| 5 | 3 Way; EGR | | 26 | 3 Way — TPC VLV | |
| 6 | Carb — Dist | | 27 | 3 Way — TPC VLV | M/T Only |
| 7 | Carb — F/Pump | | 28 | Canister — Inlet | |
| 8 | Inlet — Carb | (Hot Water) | 29 | 3 Way — Canister | |
| 9 | Inlet — Dist | | 30 | Carb — Canister | |
| 10 | Clip; 2 Way, Dist | | 31 | Clip; 4 Way | |
| 11 | MCV — Inlet | | 32 | Clip; 4 Way | |
| 12 | Inlet — 3 Way | (With A/C) | 33 | Solenoid — Carb; Slow | |
| 13 | 3 Way; Dist — VSV | (With A/C) | 34 | Solenoid — A/Cleaner | |
| 14 | 3 Way — Dist | (With A/C) | 35 | Clip; 2 Way | |
| 15 | Clip; 2 Way, Dist | (With A/C) | 36 | VCV — Carb | |
| 16 | 3 Way — VSV | (With A/C) | 37 | VCV — 3 Way | |
| 17 | VSV — FICD | (With A/C) | 38 | Solenoid — Carb; Main | |
| 18 | ITC VLV — Inlet | | 39 | Solenoid — Carb; SECO | |
| 19 | Inlet — 3 Way | | 40 | Clip; 4 Way | |
| 20 | 3 Way; Inlet — VCV | | 41 | Clip; R/Hose | |
| 21 | 3 Way — 3 Way | | 42 | Canister Drain | |

**HOSE CONNECTIONS IDENTIFICATION**

**Hose Identification**

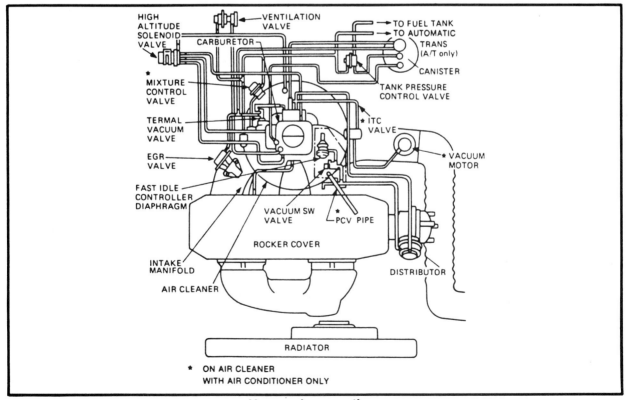

**Vacuum hose routing**

# Sprint

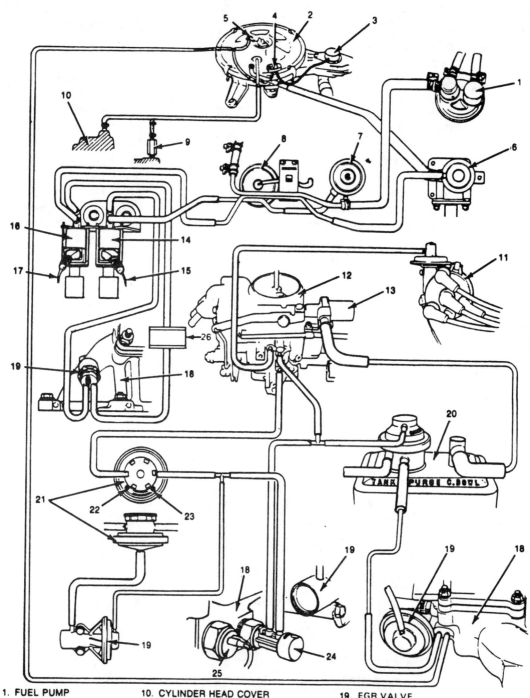

1. FUEL PUMP
2. AIR CLEANER
3. AIR CONTROL ACTUATOR
4. THERMO SENSOR
5. HOT IDLE COMPENSATOR
6. SECOND AIR VALVE
7. IDLE-UP ACTUATOR
8. SECONDARY DIAPHRAGM
9. PCV VALVE
10. CYLINDER HEAD COVER
11. DISTRIBUTOR
12. CARBURETOR
13. SWITCH VENT SOLENOID
14. THREE WAY SOLENOID VALVE (BLACK)
15. BLACK WIRE
16. THREE WAY SOLENOID VALVE (BLUE)
17. BLUE WIRE
18. INTAKE MANIFOLD
19. EGR VALVE
20. CANISTER
21. EGR MODULATOR
22. P
23. Q
24. BI-METAL VACUUM SWITCHING VALVE
25. THERMAL SWITCH
26. VTV (VACUUM TRANSMITTING VALVE)
    A/T ONLY

**Engine emission control systems schematic**

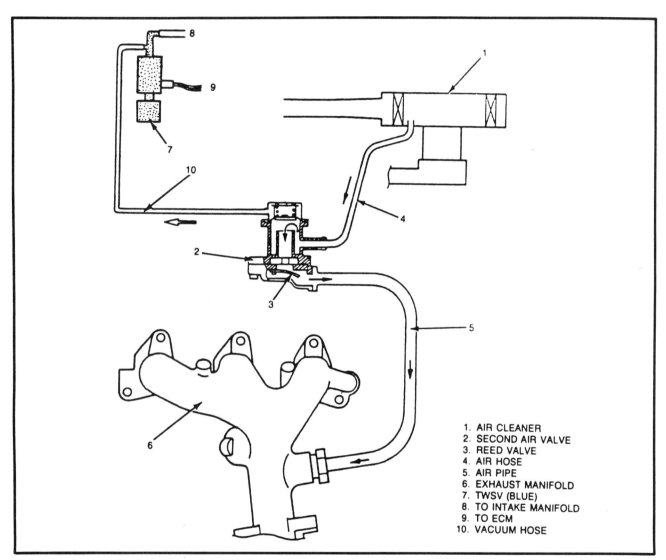

1. AIR CLEANER
2. SECOND AIR VALVE
3. REED VALVE
4. AIR HOSE
5. AIR PIPE
6. EXHAUST MANIFOLD
7. TWSV (BLUE)
8. TO INTAKE MANIFOLD
9. TO ECM
10. VACUUM HOSE

**Pulse Air Control System operation**

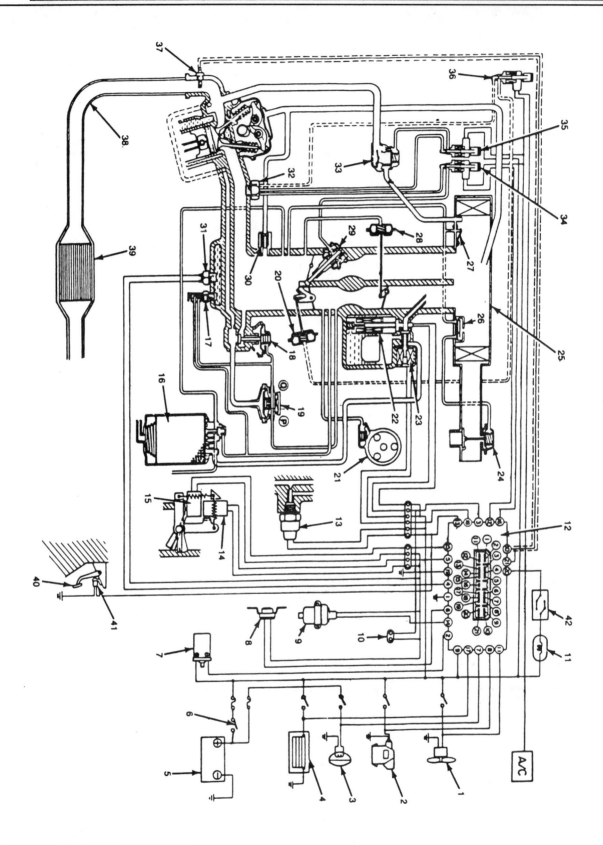

**Engine emission control systems**

1. ENGINE COOLING FAN

2. HEATER FAN

3. SMALL LIGHT, TAIL LIGHT, SIDE MARKER LIGHT & LICENSE LIGHT

4. REAR DEFOGGER

5. BATTERY

6. IGNITION SWITCH

7. IGNITION COIL

8. THERMAL ENGINE ROOM SWITCH

9. HIGH ALTITUDE COMPENSATOR

10. DUTY CHECK CONNECTOR

11. "SENSOR" LIGHT

12. ELECTRONIC CONTROL MODULE (ECM)

13. FUEL CUT SOLENOID VALVE

14. WIDE OPEN MICRO SWITCH

15. IDLE MICRO SWITCH

16. CANISTER

17. BI-METAL VACUUM SWITCHING VALVE ( BVSV )

18. EGR VALVE

19. EGR MODULATOR

20. CAR AIR CON IDLE-UP

21. DISTRIBUTOR

22. MIXTURE CONTROL SOLENOID (MCS) VALVE

23. SWITCH VENT SOLENOID

24. AIR CONTROL ACTUATOR

25. AIR CLEANER

26. THERMO SENSOR

27. HOT IDLE COMPENSATOR

28. CHOKE PISTON

29. IDLE-UP ACTUATOR

30. POSITIVE CRANKCASE VENTILATION (PCV) VALVE

31. THERMAL SWITCH

32. GAS FILTER

33. SECOND AIR VALVE

34. THREE WAY SOLENOID VALVE (WITH BLACK LEAD WIRE)

35. THREE WAY SOLENOID VALVE (WITH BLUE LEAD WIRE)

36. IDLE-UP VACUUM SWITCHING VALVE (FOR A/C)

37. OXYGEN SENSOR

38. EXHAUST NO. 1 PIPE

39. THREE WAY CATALYST

40. CLUTCH PEDAL

41. CLUTCH SWITCH

42. CANCEL SWITCH

Engine Emission Control Systems

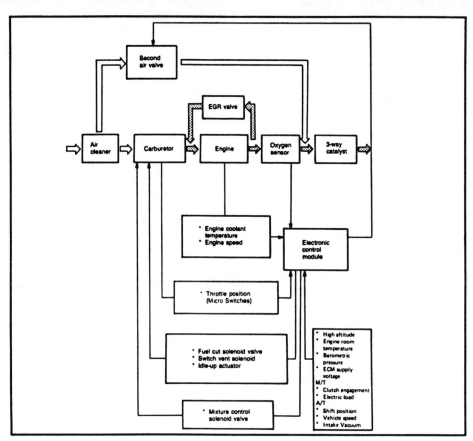

**Computer Controlled Emission Control System**

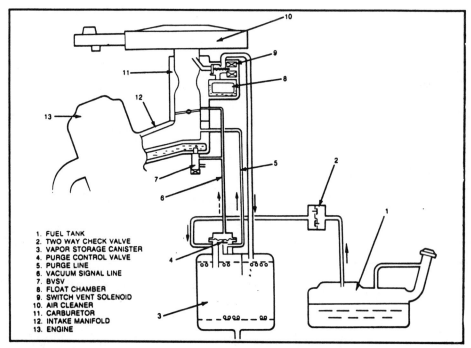

1. FUEL TANK
2. TWO WAY CHECK VALVE
3. VAPOR STORAGE CANISTER
4. PURGE CONTROL VALVE
5. PURGE LINE
6. VACUUM SIGNAL LINE
7. BVSV
8. FLOAT CHAMBER
9. SWITCH VENT SOLENOID
10. AIR CLEANER
11. CARBURETOR
12. INTAKE MANIFOLD
13. ENGINE

**Evaporative Emission Control System**

# Subaru

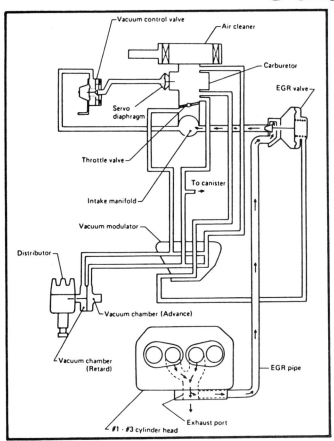

**49 STATE VEHICLES WITH AUTOMATIC TRANSMISSIONS
(EXCEPT CALIFORNIA AND CANADA)**

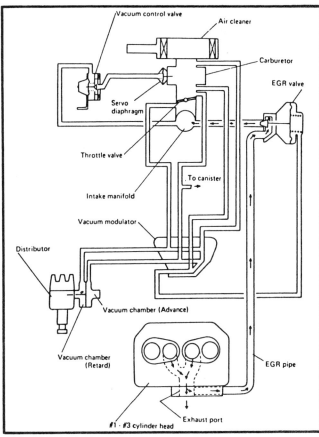

**4WD VEHICLES FOR 49 STATES (EXCEPT CALIFORNIA AND
CANADA)**

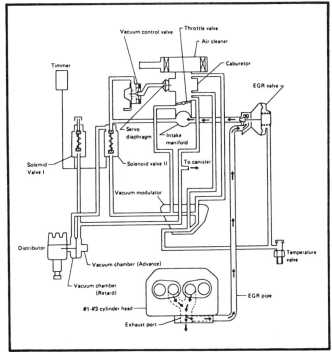

**MANUAL TRANSMISSION VEHICLES FOR CALIFORNIA
(EXCEPT 4WD)**

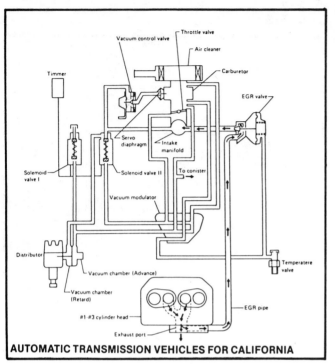

**AUTOMATIC TRANSMISSION VEHICLES FOR CALIFORNIA**

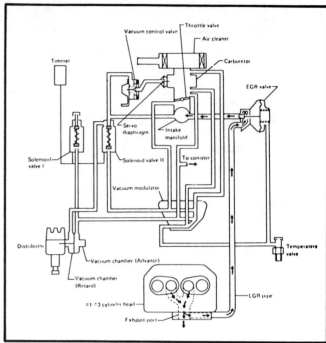

**4WD VEHICLES FOR CALIFORNIA**

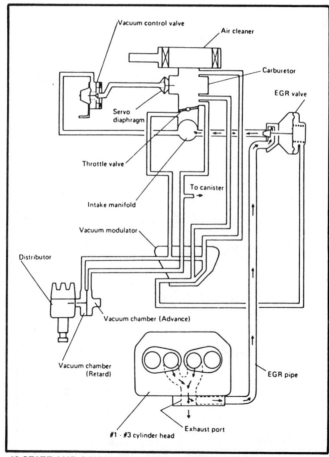

**49 STATE AND CANADIAN MODELS WITH MANUAL
TRANSMISSION (EXCEPT 4WD)**

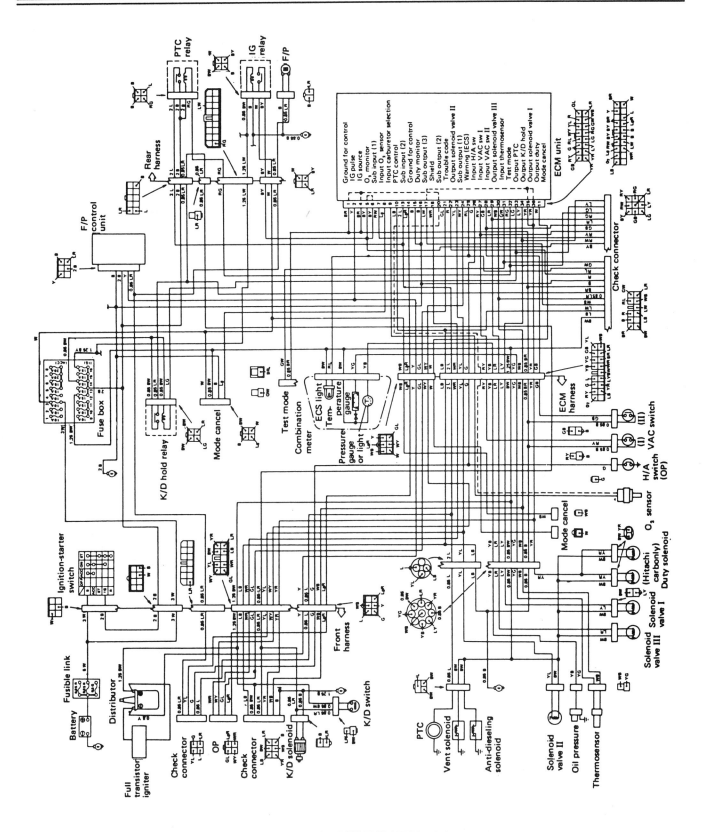

**1983 SUBARU MODELS—EQUIPPED WITH E.C.C. SYSTEM**

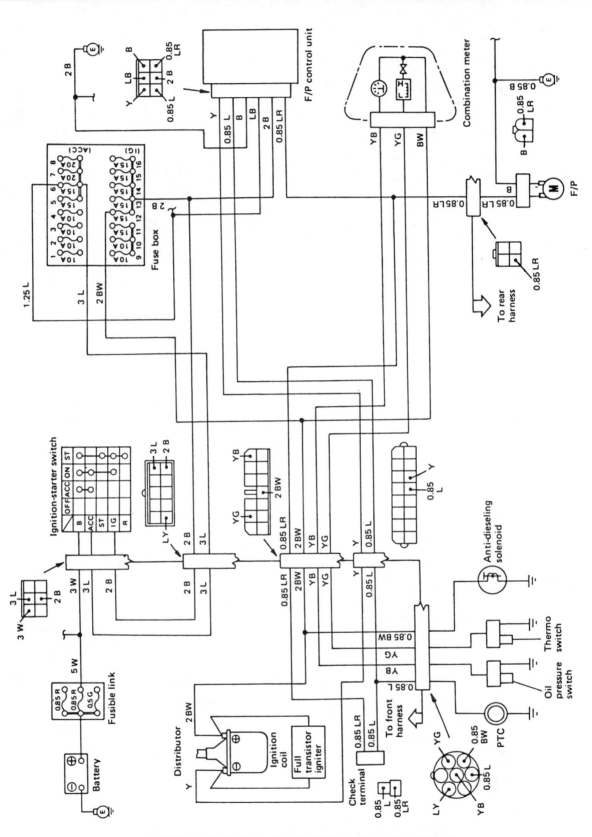

**1983 SUBARU MODELS—NOT EQUIPPED WITH E.C.C. SYSTEM**

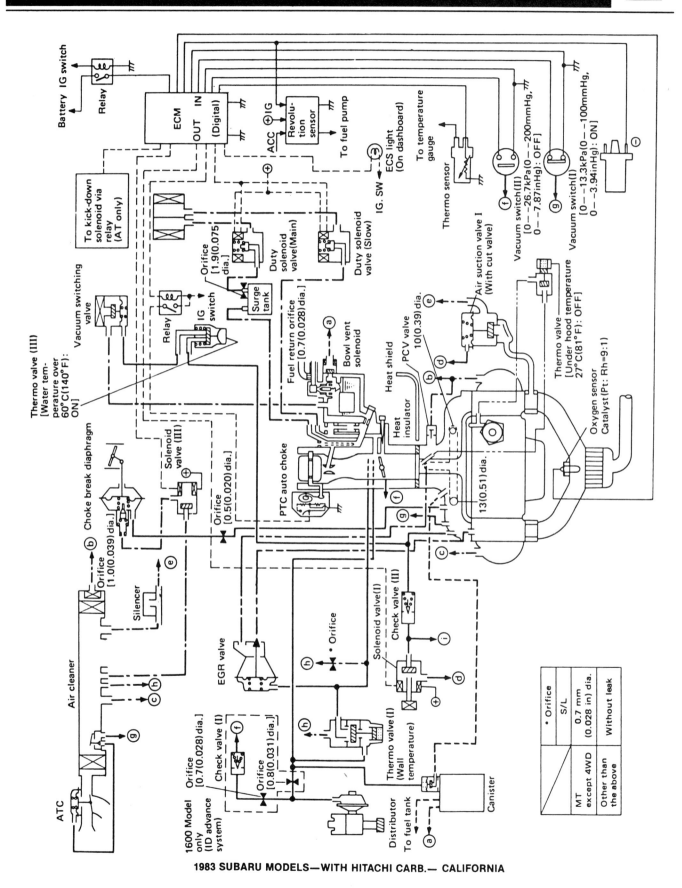

**1983 SUBARU MODELS—WITH HITACHI CARB.— CALIFORNIA**

| | | Orifice | Without leak |
|---|---|---|---|
| MT except 4WD | S/L | 0.7 mm (0.028 in) dia. | |
| Other than the above | | | |

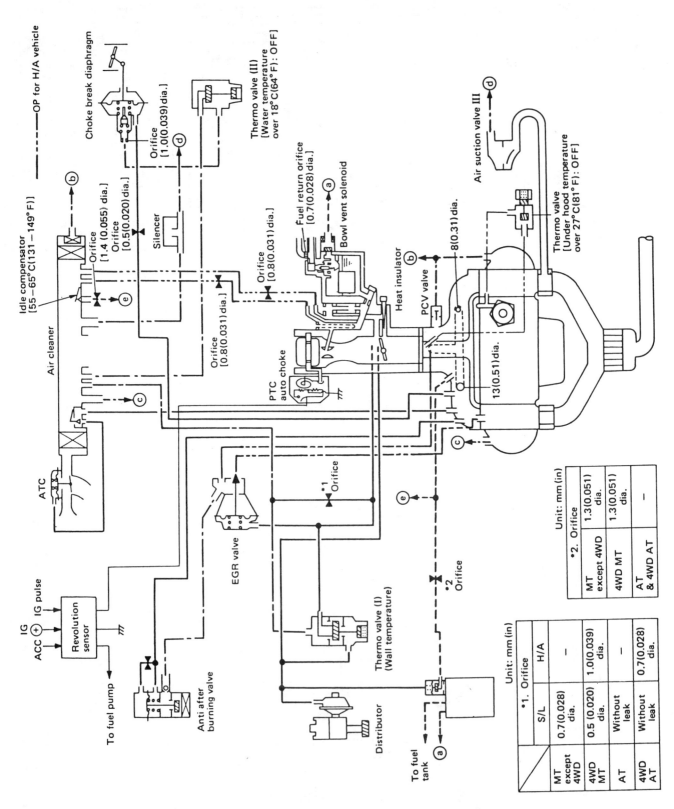

Choke break diaphragm

OP for H/A vehicle

Orifice [1.0(0.039) dia.]

Thermo valve (II) [Water temperature over 18°C(64°F): OFF]

Air suction valve III

Idle compensator [55—65°C(131—149°F)]

Fuel return orifice [0.7(0.028) dia.]

Bowl vent solenoid

Thermo valve [Under hood temperature over 27°C(81°F): OFF]

Orifice [1.4 (0.055) dia.]

Orifice [0.5(0.020) dia.]

Silencer

Orifice [0.8(0.031) dia.]

Heat insulator

8(0.31) dia.

PCV valve

Air cleaner

Orifice [0.8(0.031) dia.]

PTC auto choke

13(0.51) dia.

ATC

Orifice

Orifice

IG pulse

IG

ACC ⊕

Revolution sensor

EGR valve

Thermo valve (I) (Wall temperature)

*2 Orifice

To fuel pump

Anti after burning valve

Distributor

To fuel tank

| Unit: mm (in) |  |  |  |
|---|---|---|---|
| *2. Orifice |  |  |  |
| MT except 4WD | 1.3(0.051) dia. | 4WD MT | 1.3(0.051) dia. |
|  |  | AT & 4WD AT | – |

| Unit: mm (in) |  |  |
|---|---|---|
| *1. Orifice | S/L | H/A |
| MT except 4WD | 0.7(0.028) dia. | – |
| 4WD MT | 0.5 (0.020) dia. | 1.0(0.039) dia. |
| AT | Without leak | – |
| 4WD AT | Without leak | 0.7(0.028) dia. |

**1983 SUBARU MODELS—WITH HITACHI CARB—CANADA AND 4WD MODELS—EXC. CALIFORNIA**

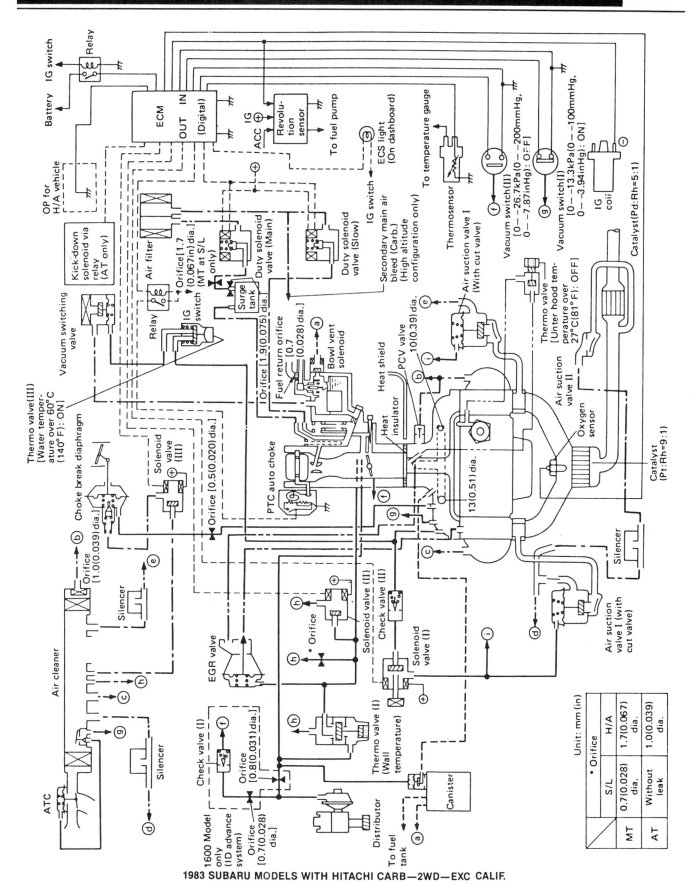

1983 SUBARU MODELS WITH HITACHI CARB—2WD—EXC CALIF.

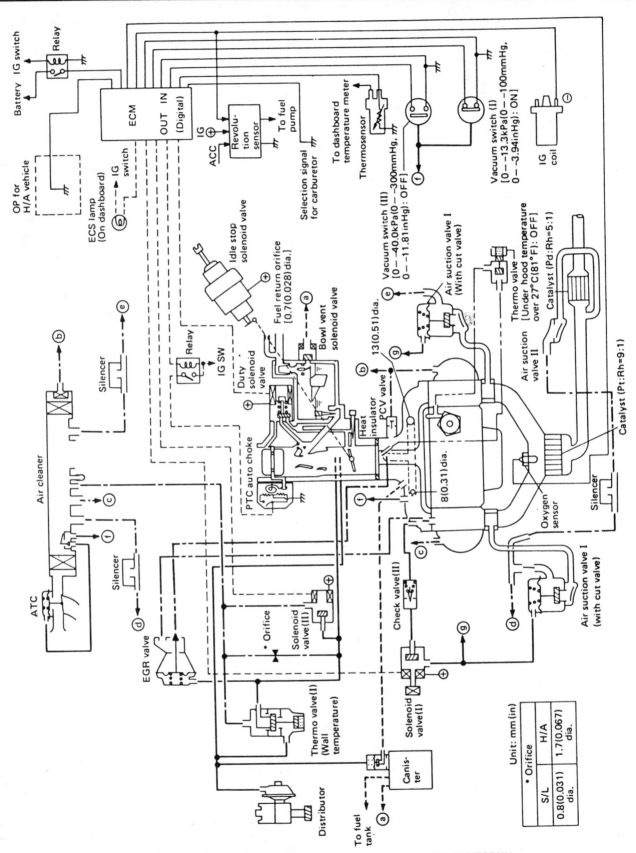

1983 SUBARU MODELS WITH CARTER-WEBER CARB—2WD EXC. CALIFORNIA

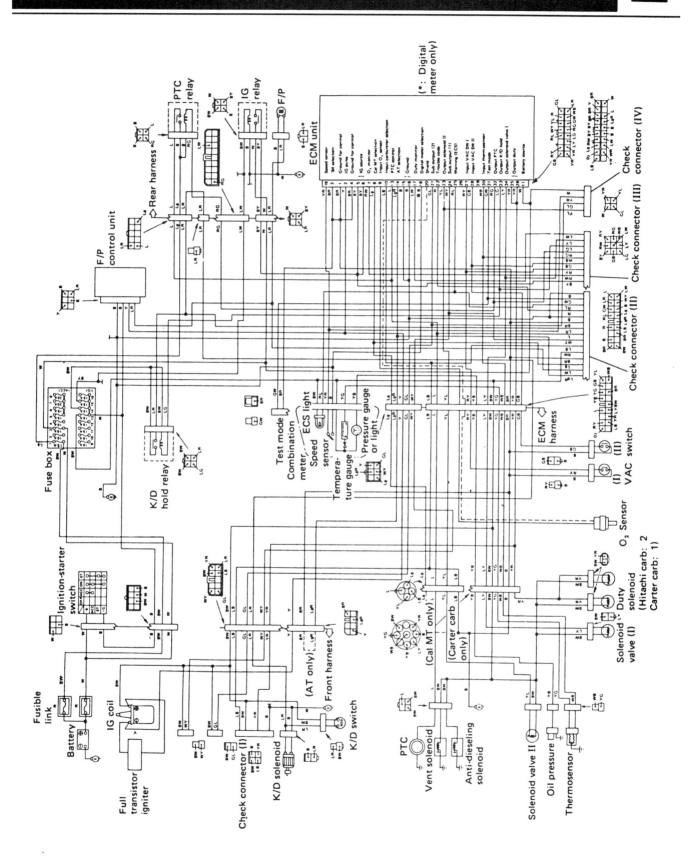

**1984 SUBARU MODELS—EQUIPPED WITH E.C.C. SYSTEM**

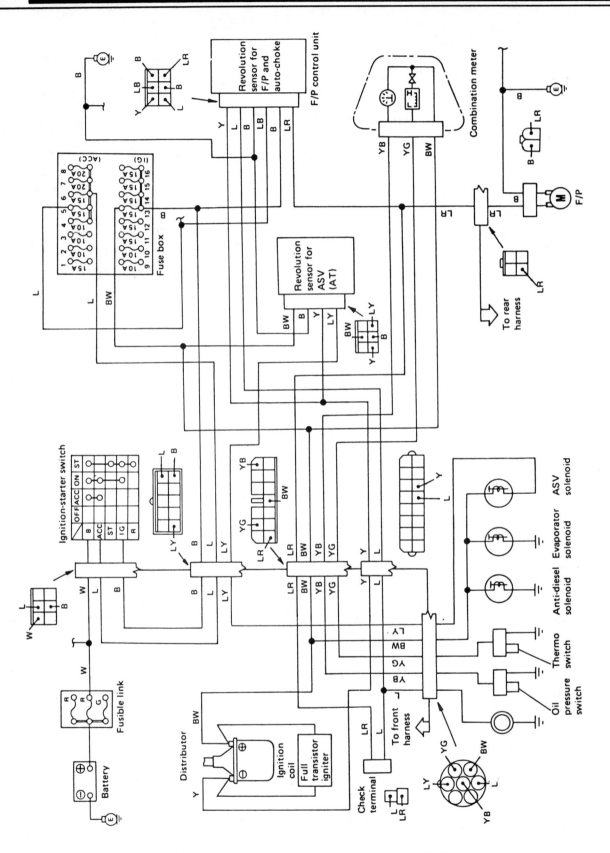

**1984 SUBARU MODELS—NOT EQUIPPED WITH E.C.C. SYSTEM**

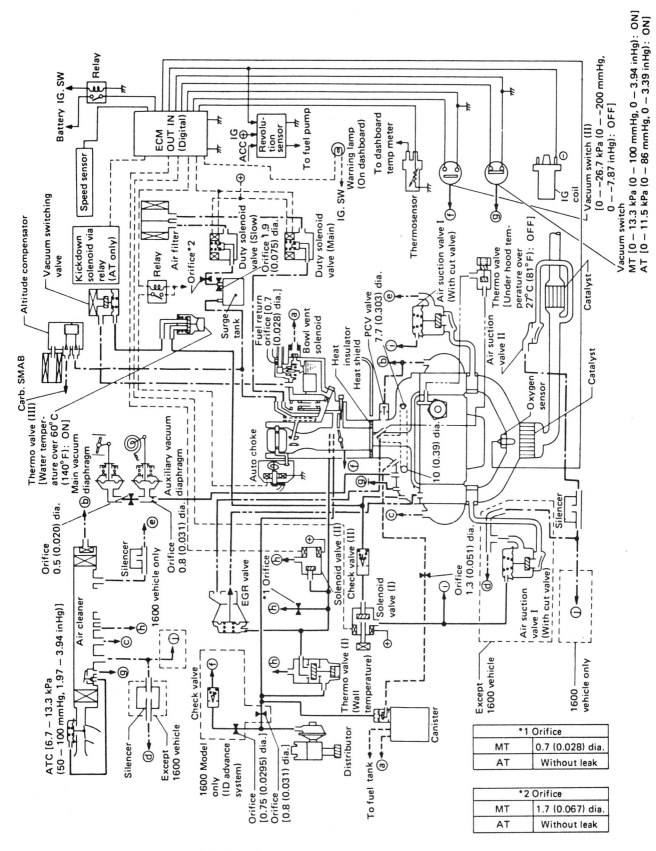

**1984 SUBARU MODELS WITH HITACHI CARB.—2WD—49 STATES**

| *1 Orifice | |
|---|---|
| MT | 0.7 (0.028) dia. |
| AT | Without leak |

| *2 Orifice | |
|---|---|
| MT | 1.7 (0.067) dia. |
| AT | Without leak |

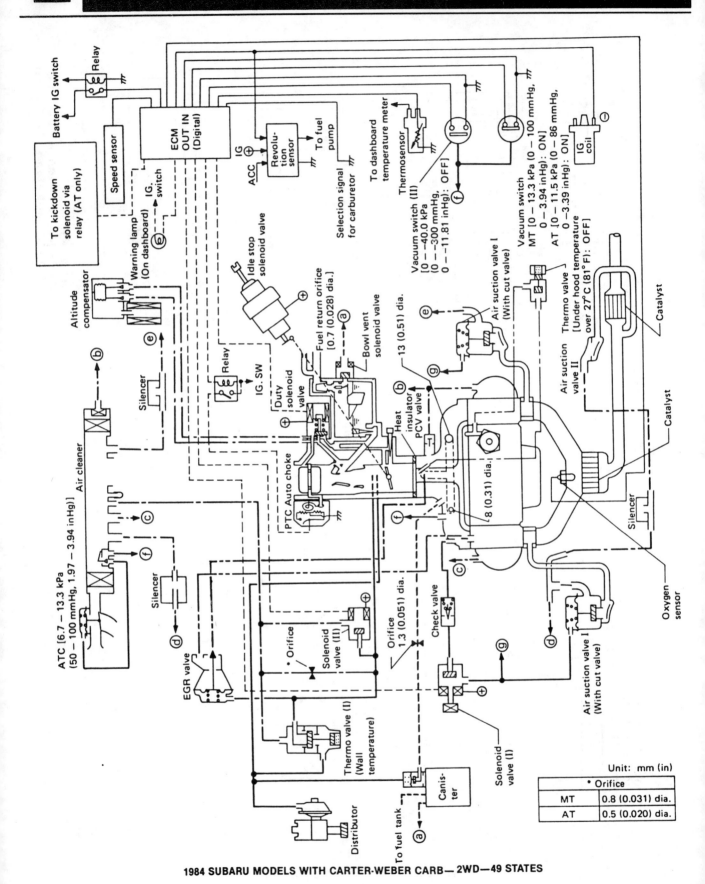

**1984 SUBARU MODELS WITH CARTER-WEBER CARB— 2WD—49 STATES**

Battery IG switch

Relay

To kickdown solenoid via relay (AT only)

Speed sensor

ECM OUT IN (Digital)

IG switch

IG

ACC

Revolution sensor

To fuel pump

Selection signal for carburetor

To dashboard temperature meter

Thermosensor

Vacuum switch (III)
[0 — 40.0 kPa]
(0 — 300 mmHg,
0 —11.81 inHg]: OFF]

Vacuum switch
MT [0 — 13.3 kPa (0 — 100 mmHg,
0 — 3.94 inHg): ON]
AT [0 — 11.5 kPa (0 — 86 mmHg,
0 — 3.39 inHg): ON]

IG coil

Warning lamp (On dashboard)

Altitude compensator

Idle stop solenoid valve

Fuel return orifice [0.7 (0.028) dia.]

Bowl vent solenoid valve

13 (0.51) dia.

Air suction valve I (With cut valve)

Thermo valve [Under hood temperature over 27°C (81°F): OFF]

Air suction valve II

Catalyst

Silencer

Relay

IG. SW

Duty solenoid valve

Heat insulator

PCV valve

8 (0.31) dia.

Catalyst

Air cleaner

PTC Auto choke

Silencer

ATC [6.7 — 13.3 kPa
(50 — 100 mmHg, 1.97 — 3.94 inHg]

Silencer

Orifice

Solenoid valve (II)

Orifice 1.3 (0.051) dia.

Check valve

Air suction valve I (With cut valve)

Oxygen sensor

EGR valve

Thermo valve (I) (Wall temperature)

Solenoid valve (I)

Canister

Distributor

To fuel tank

| Unit: mm (in) | |
|---|---|
| • Orifice | |
| MT | 0.8 (0.031) dia. |
| AT | 0.5 (0.020) dia. |

220

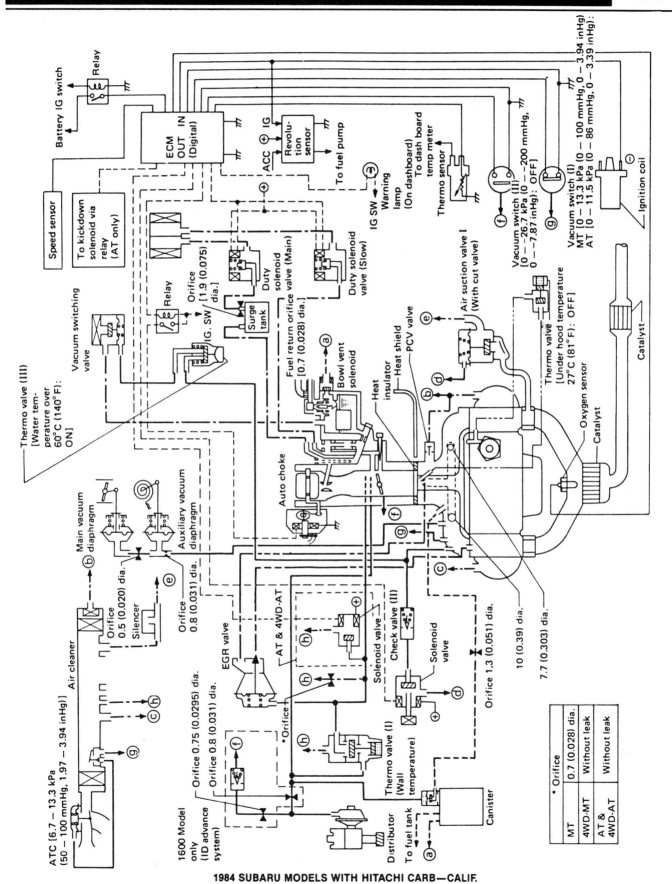

**1984 SUBARU MODELS WITH HITACHI CARB—CALIF.**

|  | • Orifice | 0.7 (0.028) dia. |
|---|---|---|
| MT | 4WD-MT | Without leak |
| AT & 4WD-AT |  | Without leak |

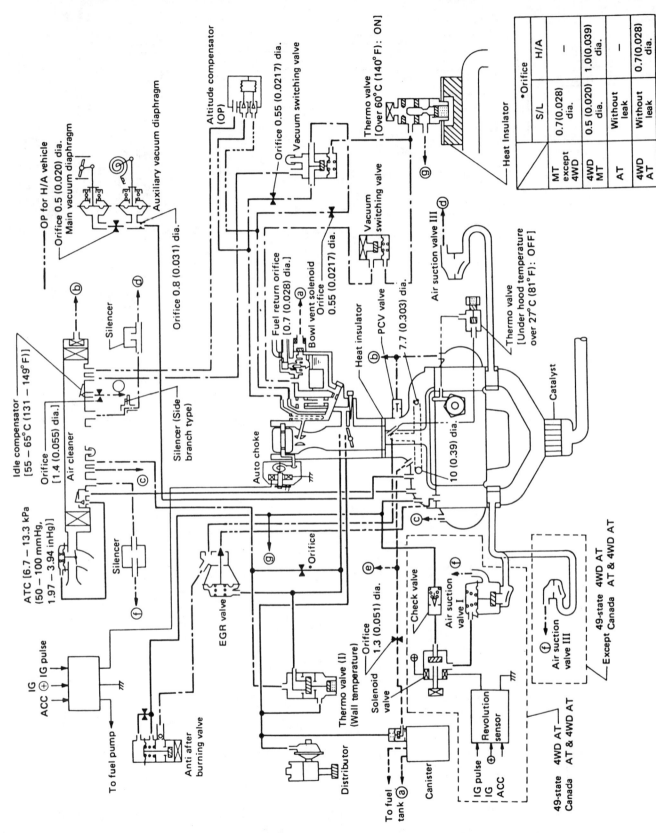

| *Orifice | | S/L | H/A |
|---|---|---|---|
| MT except 4WD | | 0.7(0.028) dia. | — |
| 4WD MT | | 0.5 (0.020) dia. | 1.0(0.039) dia. |
| AT | | Without leak | — |
| 4WD AT | | Without leak | 0.7(0.028) dia. |

**1984 SUBARU MODELS WITH HITACHI CARB.—CANADA
AND 4WD MODELS—49 STATES**

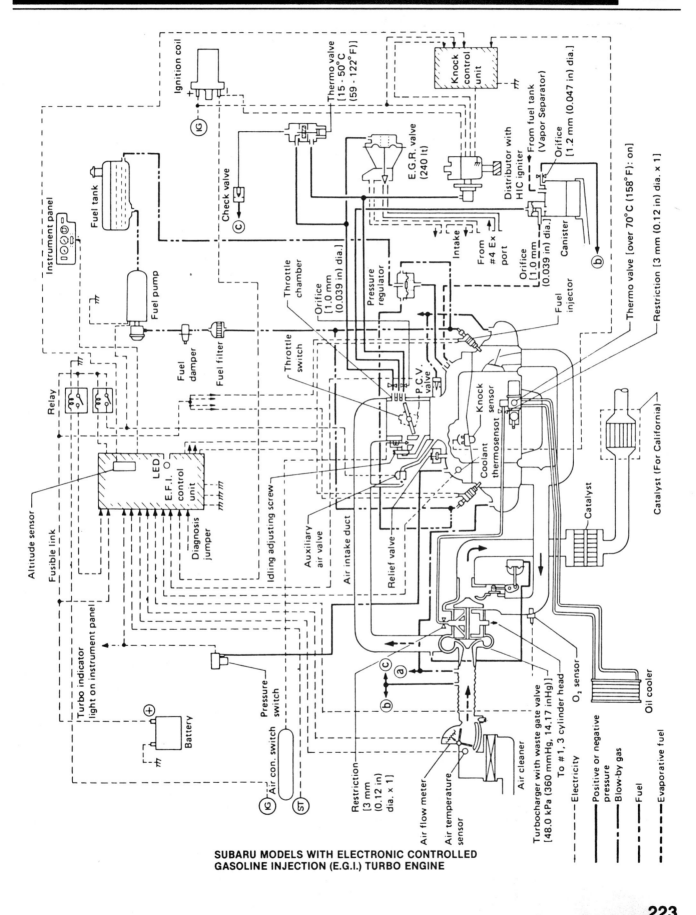

**SUBARU MODELS WITH ELECTRONIC CONTROLLED GASOLINE INJECTION (E.G.I.) TURBO ENGINE**

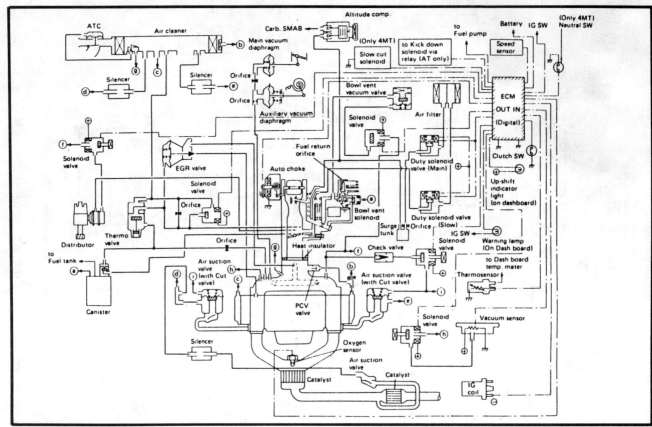

**Vacuum schematic-Carb. 49 states 2WD**

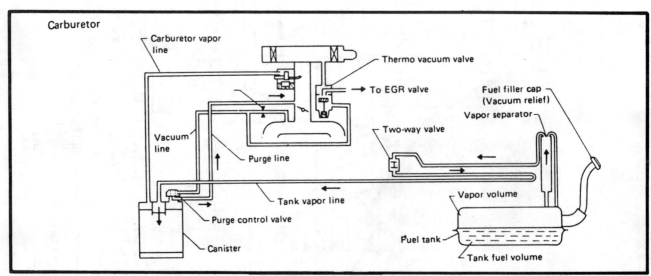

**Evaporative emission control system — carburetor models**

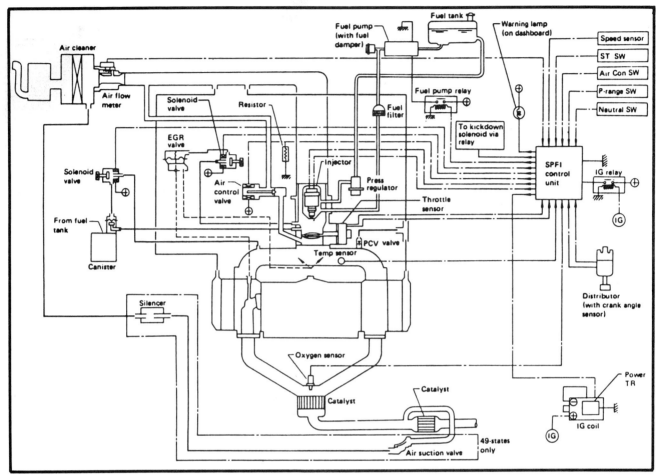

**Vacuum schematic-SPFI**

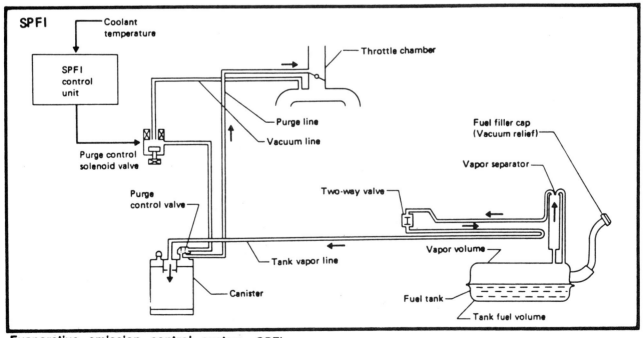

**Evaporative emission control system–SPFI**

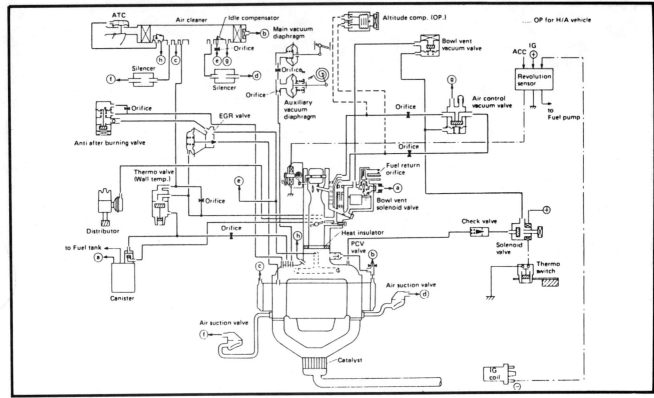

**Vacuum schematic-Carb. 49 states 4WD and Canada**

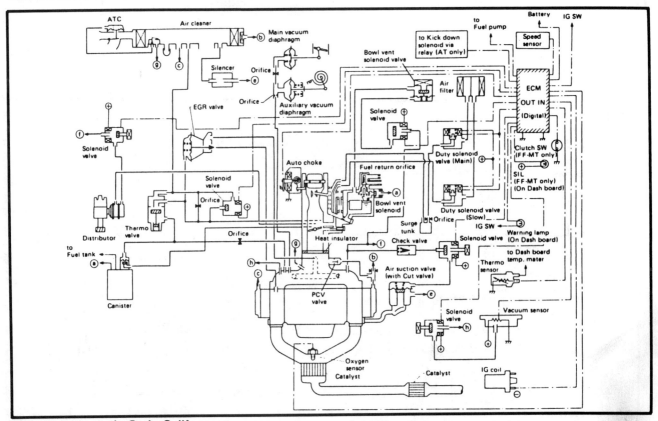

**Vacuum schematic-Carb. Calif.**

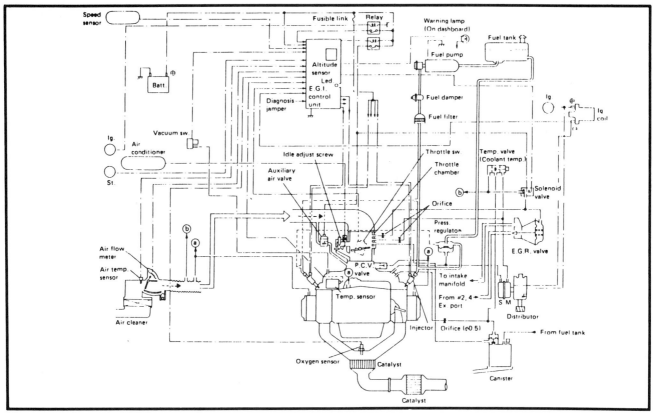

**Vacuum schematic-MFPI non-turbo**

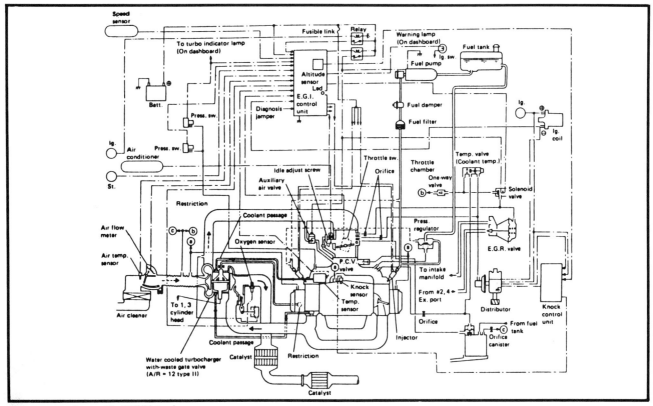

**Vacuum schematic-MFPI turbo**

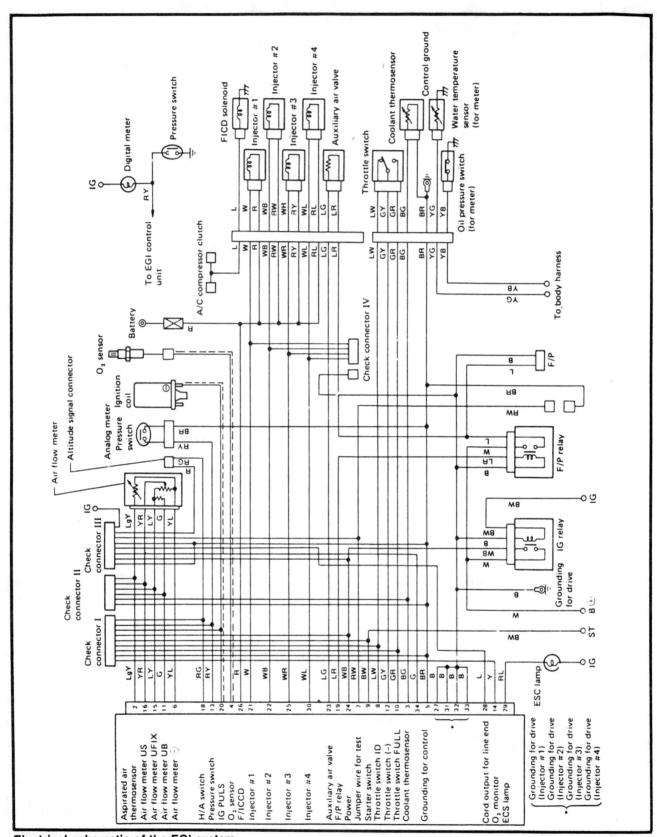

**Electrical schematic of the EGI system**

# Toyota

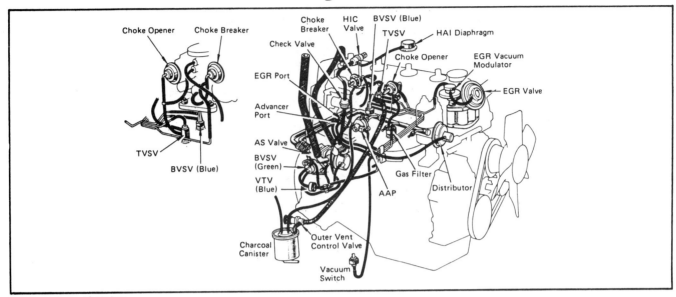

**2T-C engine—49 states**

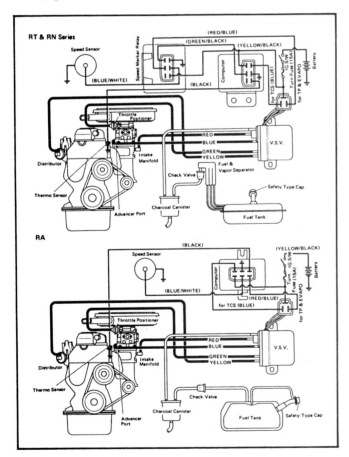

**RT & RN Series**

**RA**

**18R-C engine**

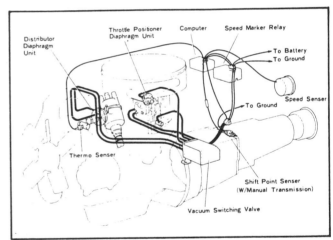

**8R-C engine**

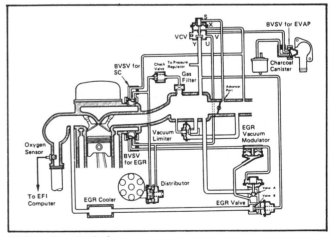

**4M-E engine—typical**

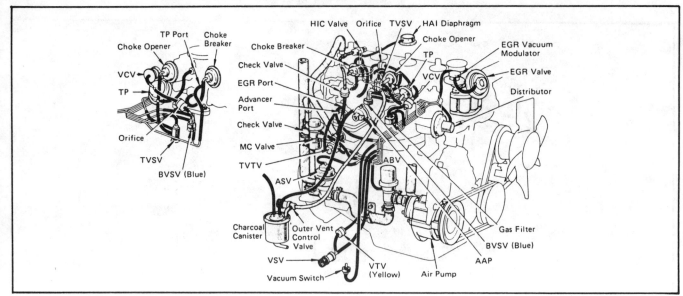

**2T-C engine—Calif.**

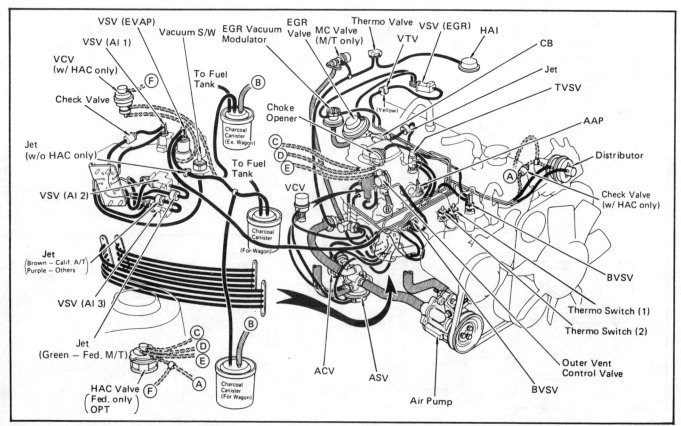

**22R engine—typical**

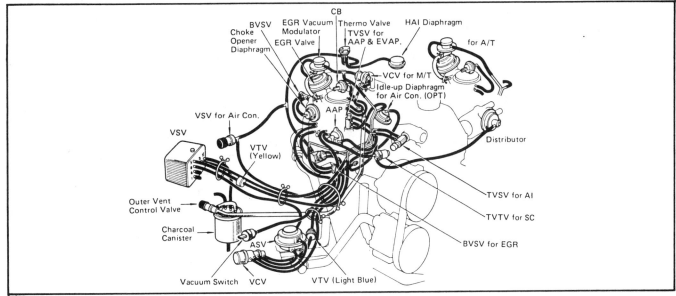

**20R engine—49 states**

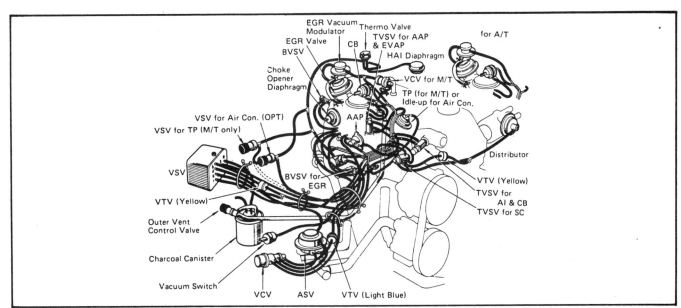

**20R engine—Calif.**

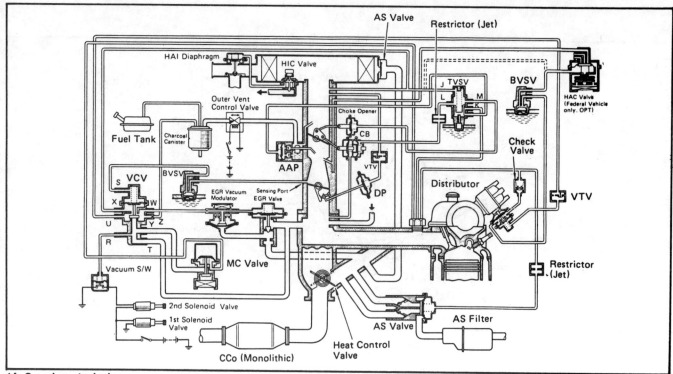

**1A-C engine—typical**

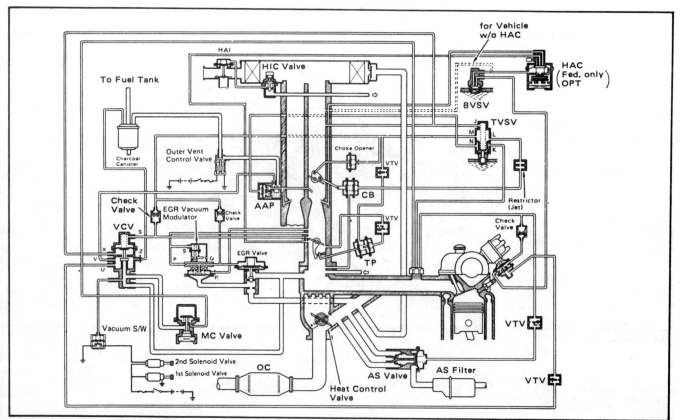

**3A-C engine—49 states and Canada**

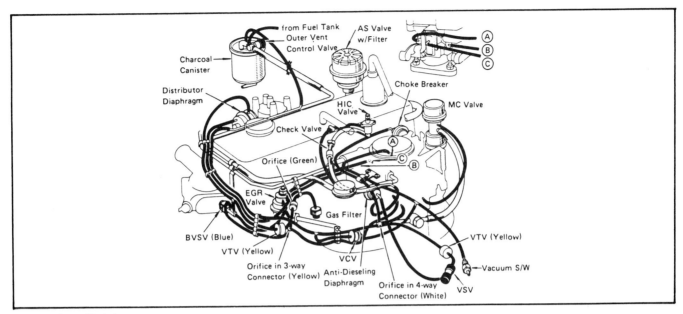

**3K-C engine—49 states**

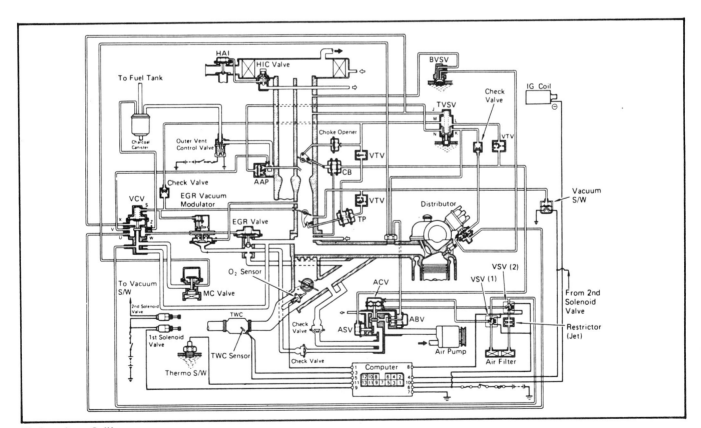

**3A-C engine—Calif.**

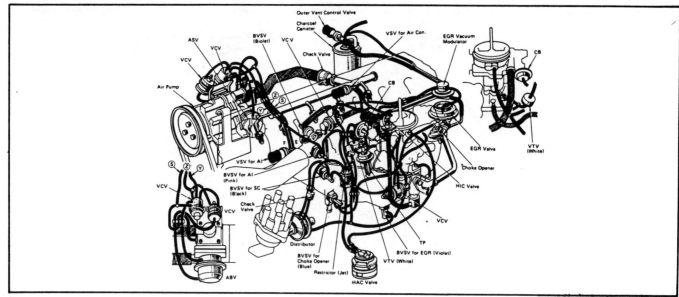

4M engine—typical

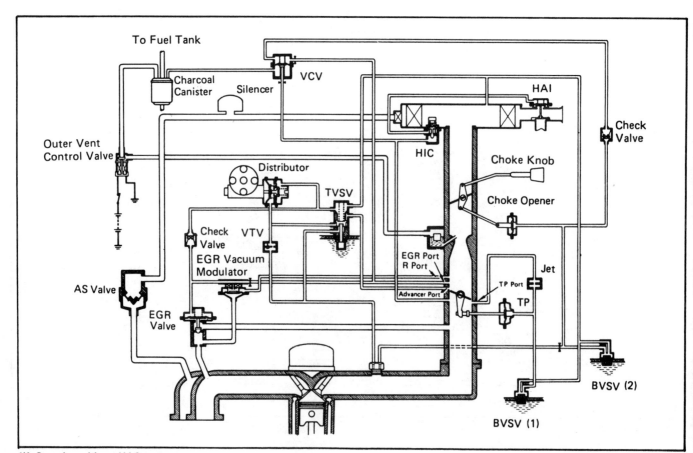

4K-C engine without HAC system

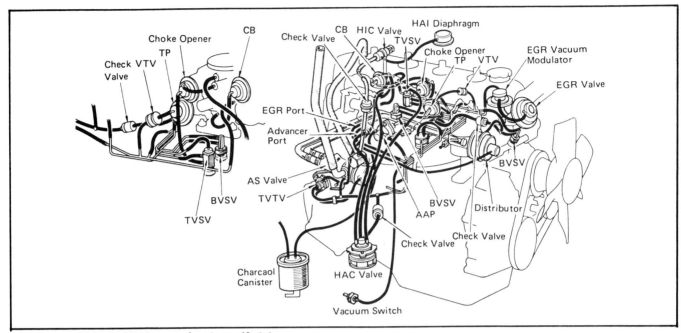

**3T-C engine with high altitude control system—49 states**

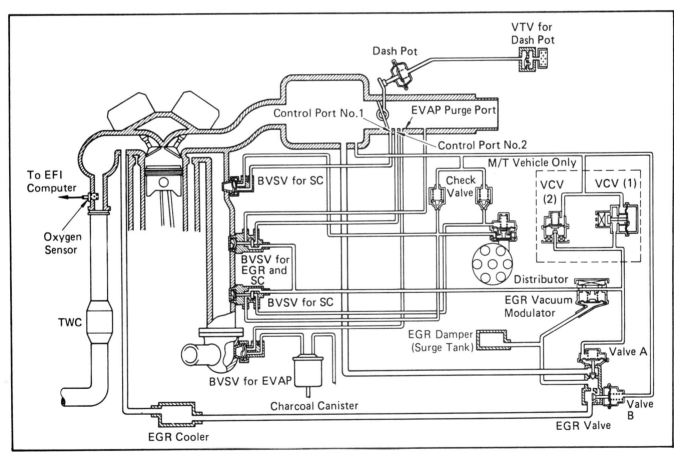

**5M-GE engine—typical**

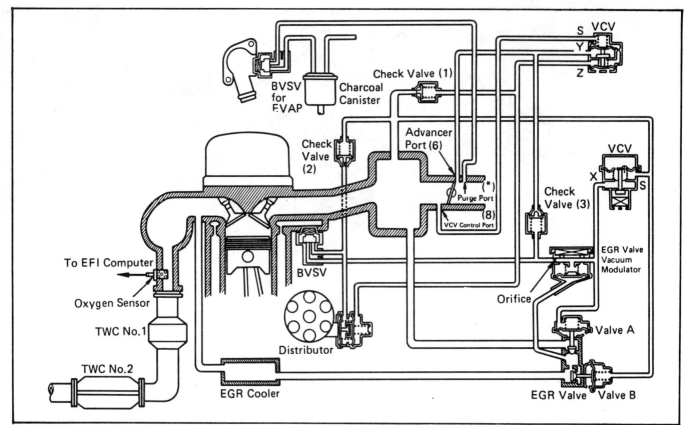

**5M-E engine—typical**

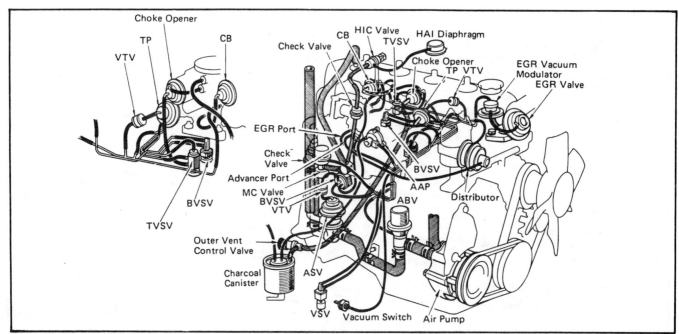

**3T-C engine—Calif.**

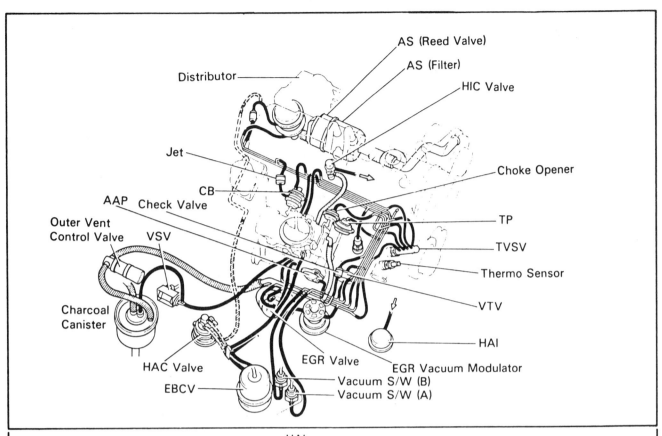

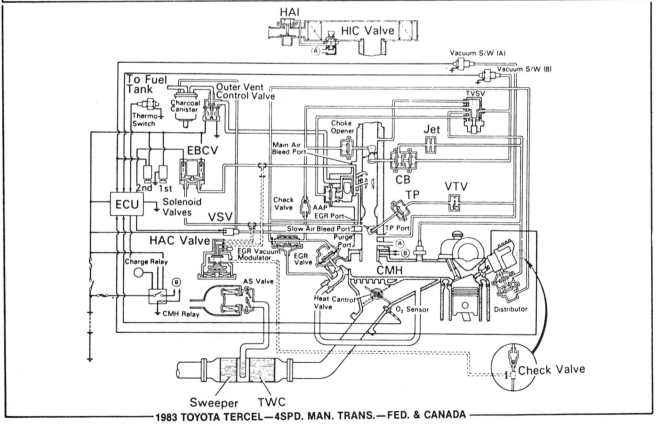

1983 TOYOTA TERCEL—4SPD. MAN. TRANS.—FED. & CANADA

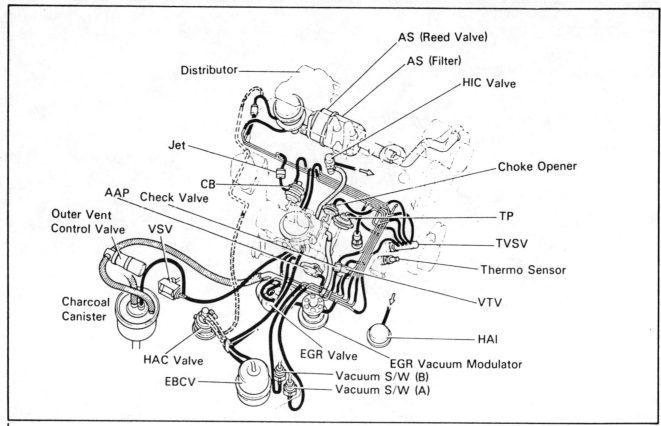

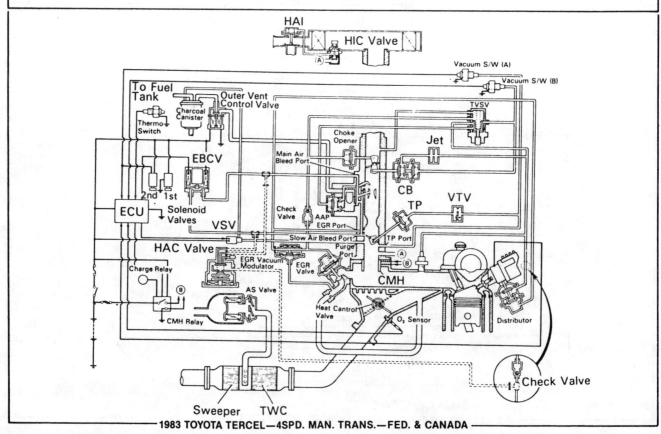

**1983 TOYOTA TERCEL—4SPD. MAN. TRANS.—FED. & CANADA**

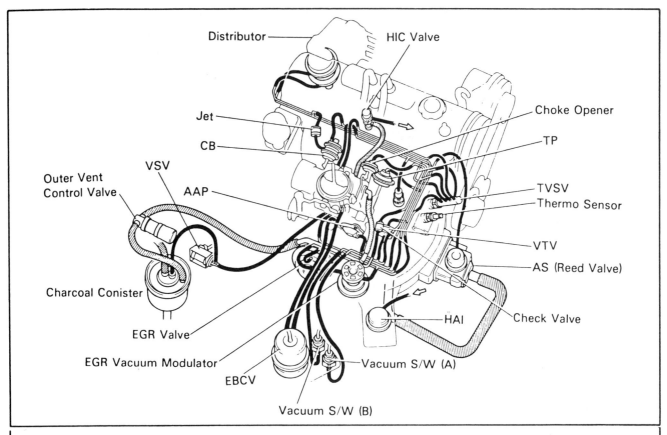

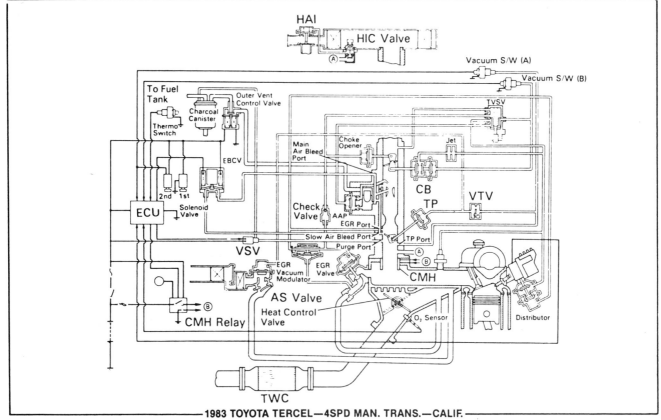

**1983 TOYOTA TERCEL—4SPD MAN. TRANS.—CALIF.**

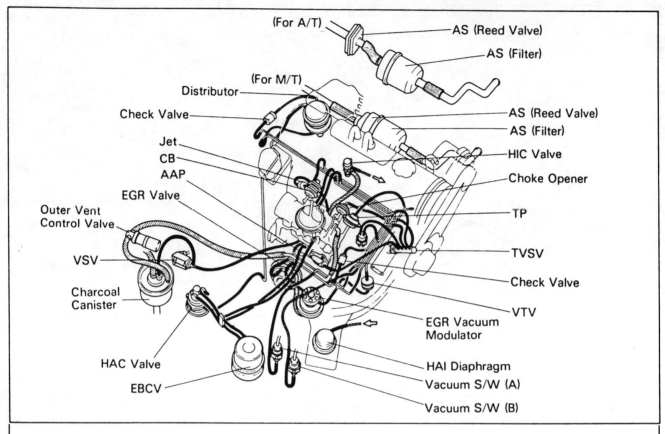

(For A/T) —————— AS (Reed Valve)

—————— AS (Filter)

(For M/T)

Distributor

Check Valve —————— AS (Reed Valve)

—————— AS (Filter)

Jet

CB —————— HIC Valve

AAP —————— Choke Opener

EGR Valve

Outer Vent
Control Valve —————— TP

VSV —————— TVSV

Charcoal —————— Check Valve
Canister

—————— VTV

EGR Vacuum
Modulator

HAC Valve

EBCV —————— HAI Diaphragm

—————— Vacuum S/W (A)

—————— Vacuum S/W (B)

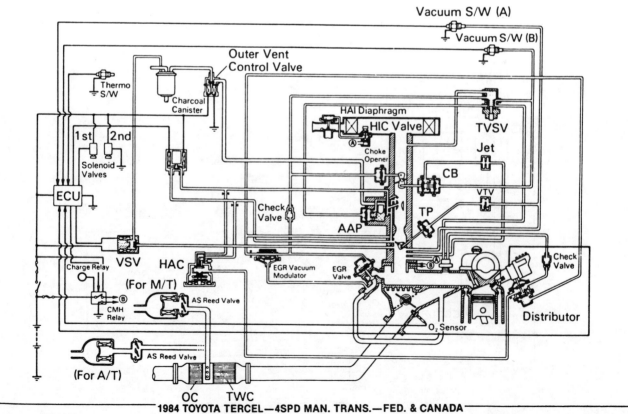

Vacuum S/W (A)

Vacuum S/W (B)

Outer Vent
Control Valve

Thermo
S/W

Charcoal
Canister

HAI Diaphragm

HIC Valve

TVSV

Choke
Opener

1st   2nd

Jet

Solenoid
Valves

CB

VTV

ECU

Check
Valve

TP

Check
Valve

AAP

VSV   HAC

EGR Vacuum
Modulator

EGR
Valve

Distributor

Charge Relay

(For M/T)

CMH
Relay

AS Reed Valve

O₂ Sensor

(For A/T)

AS Reed Valve

OC    TWC

**1984 TOYOTA TERCEL—4SPD MAN. TRANS.—FED. & CANADA**

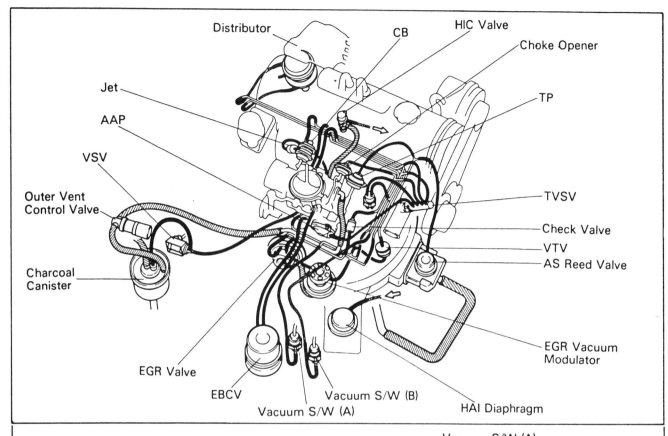

Distributor · CB · HIC Valve · Choke Opener
Jet · TP
AAP
VSV · TVSV
Outer Vent Control Valve · Check Valve · VTV · AS Reed Valve
Charcoal Canister
EGR Valve · EBCV · Vacuum S/W (A) · Vacuum S/W (B) · HAI Diaphragm · EGR Vacuum Modulator

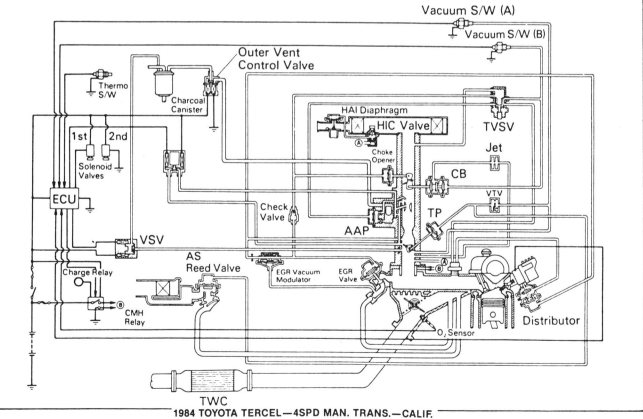

Vacuum S/W (A)
Vacuum S/W (B)
Outer Vent Control Valve
Thermo S/W · Charcoal Canister · HAI Diaphragm · HIC Valve · TVSV
1st · 2nd · Choke Opener · Jet
Solenoid Valves · CB · VTV
ECU · Check Valve · AAP · TP
VSV · AS Reed Valve
Charge Relay · EGR Vacuum Modulator · EGR Valve · Distributor
CMH Relay · O₂ Sensor
TWC

**1984 TOYOTA TERCEL—4SPD MAN. TRANS.—CALIF.**

**241**

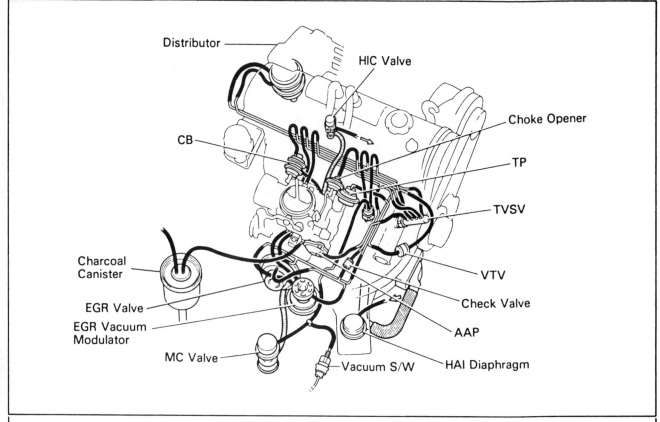

Distributor

HIC Valve

Choke Opener

CB

TP

TVSV

Charcoal
Canister

VTV

EGR Valve

Check Valve

EGR Vacuum
Modulator

AAP

MC Valve

HAI Diaphragm

Vacuum S/W

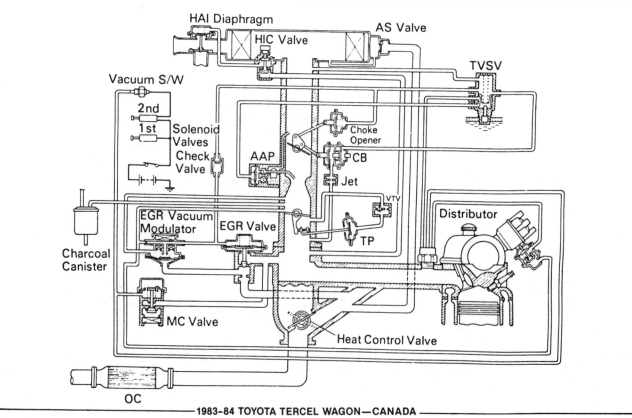

HAI Diaphragm

AS Valve

HIC Valve

TVSV

Vacuum S/W

2nd

1st

Solenoid
Valves

Choke
Opener

Check
Valve

AAP

CB

Jet

VTV

Distributor

EGR Vacuum
Modulator

EGR Valve

Charcoal
Canister

TP

MC Valve

Heat Control Valve

OC

**— 1983-84 TOYOTA TERCEL WAGON—CANADA —**

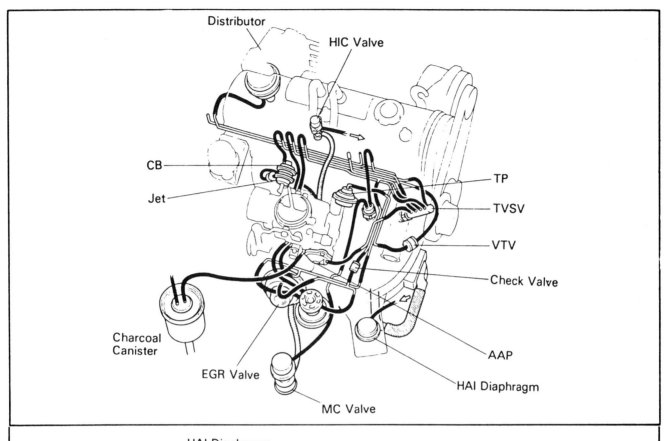

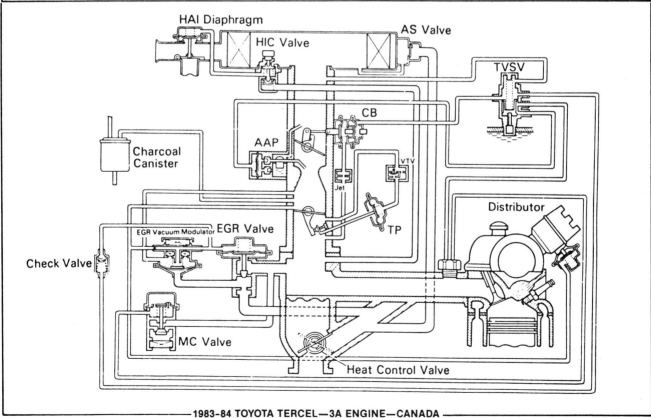

**1983-84 TOYOTA TERCEL—3A ENGINE—CANADA**

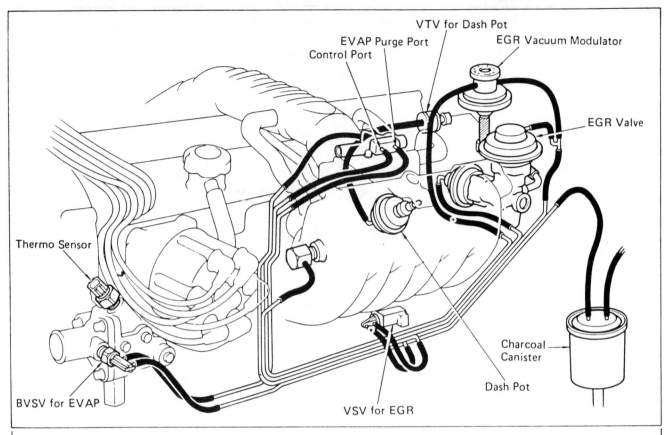

VTV for Dash Pot

EVAP Purge Port

Control Port

EGR Vacuum Modulator

EGR Valve

Thermo Sensor

Charcoal Canister

Dash Pot

BVSV for EVAP

VSV for EGR

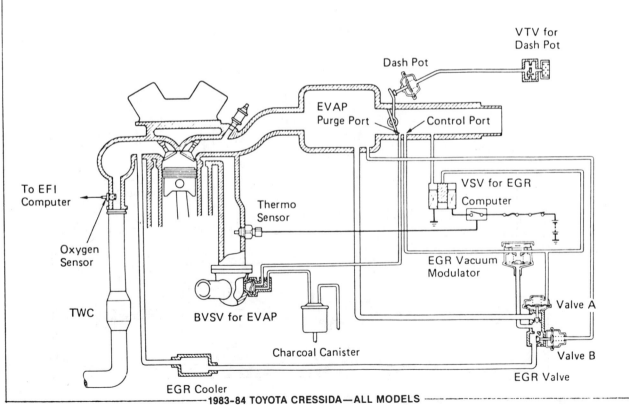

VTV for Dash Pot

Dash Pot

EVAP Purge Port

Control Port

To EFI Computer

VSV for EGR Computer

Thermo Sensor

Oxygen Sensor

EGR Vacuum Modulator

TWC

Valve A

BVSV for EVAP

Charcoal Canister

Valve B

EGR Valve

EGR Cooler

**1983-84 TOYOTA CRESSIDA—ALL MODELS**

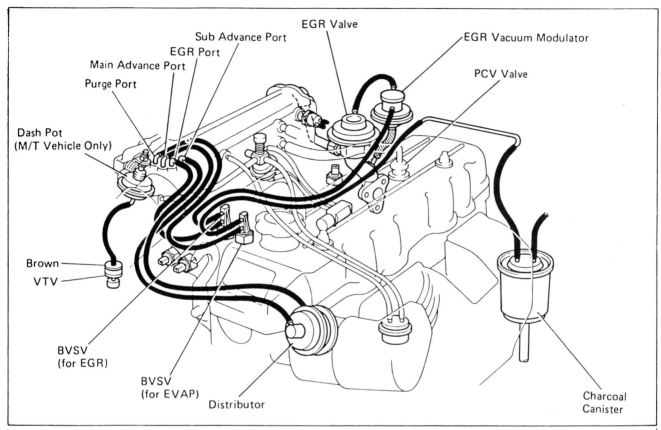

Sub Advance Port
EGR Port
Main Advance Port
Purge Port
EGR Valve
EGR Vacuum Modulator
PCV Valve
Dash Pot (M/T Vehicle Only)
Brown
VTV
BVSV (for EGR)
BVSV (for EVAP)
Distributor
Charcoal Canister

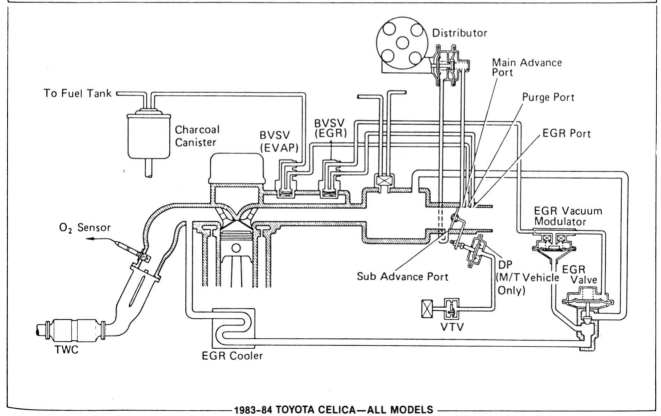

To Fuel Tank
Charcoal Canister
BVSV (EVAP)
BVSV (EGR)
Distributor
Main Advance Port
Purge Port
EGR Port
EGR Vacuum Modulator
O₂ Sensor
Sub Advance Port
DP (M/T Vehicle Only)
EGR Valve
VTV
TWC
EGR Cooler

**1983-84 TOYOTA CELICA—ALL MODELS**

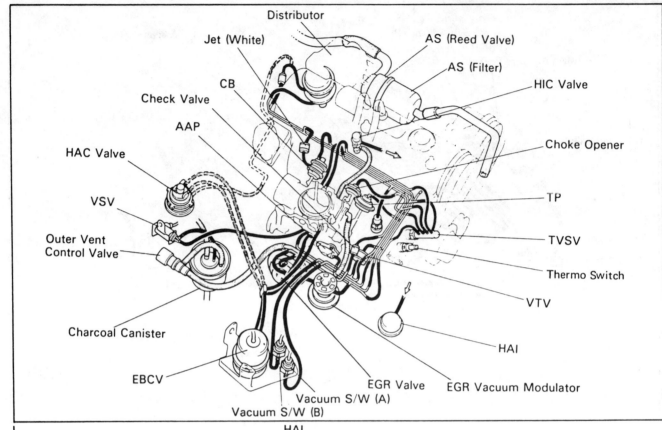

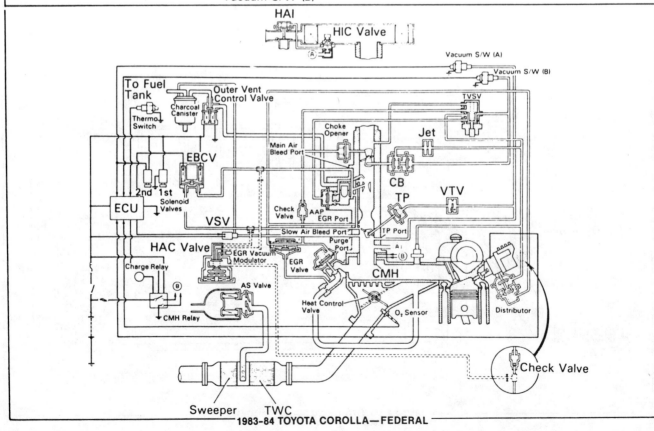

**1983-84 TOYOTA COROLLA—FEDERAL**

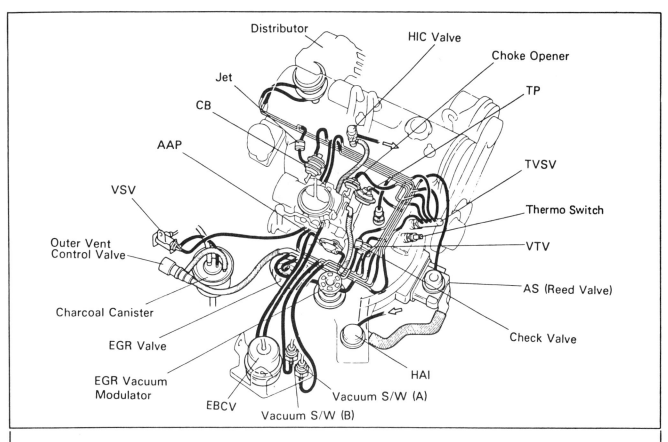

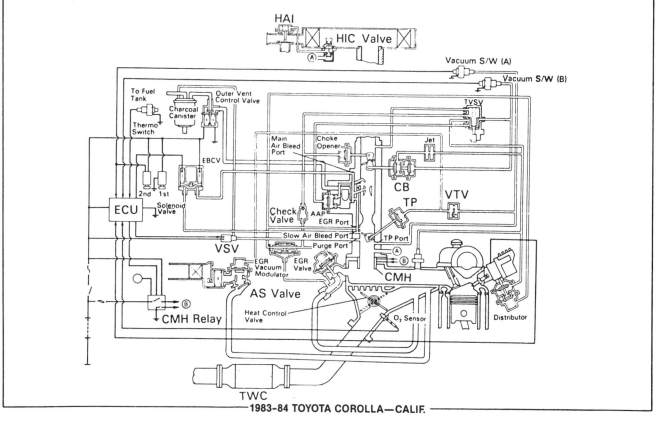

1983-84 TOYOTA COROLLA—CALIF.

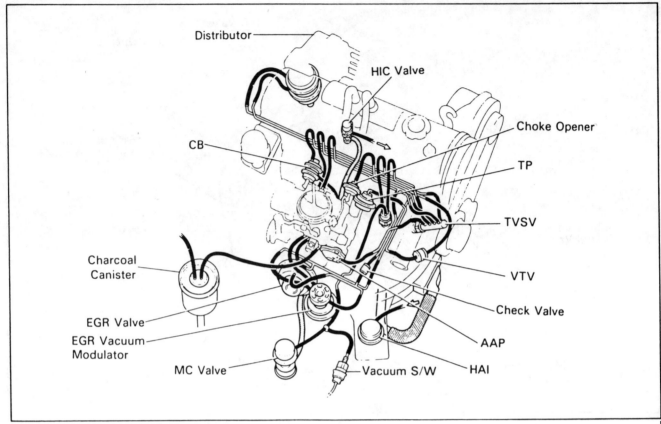

Distributor

HIC Valve

Choke Opener

CB

TP

TVSV

VTV

Charcoal Canister

Check Valve

EGR Valve

AAP

EGR Vacuum Modulator

MC Valve

Vacuum S/W

HAI

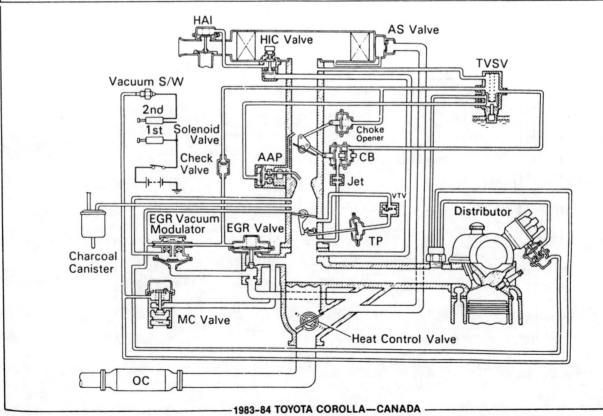

HAI

HIC Valve

AS Valve

TVSV

Vacuum S/W

2nd

1st

Solenoid Valve

Choke Opener

Check Valve

AAP

CB

Jet

VTV

Distributor

EGR Vacuum Modulator

EGR Valve

TP

Charcoal Canister

MC Valve

Heat Control Valve

OC

1983-84 TOYOTA COROLLA—CANADA

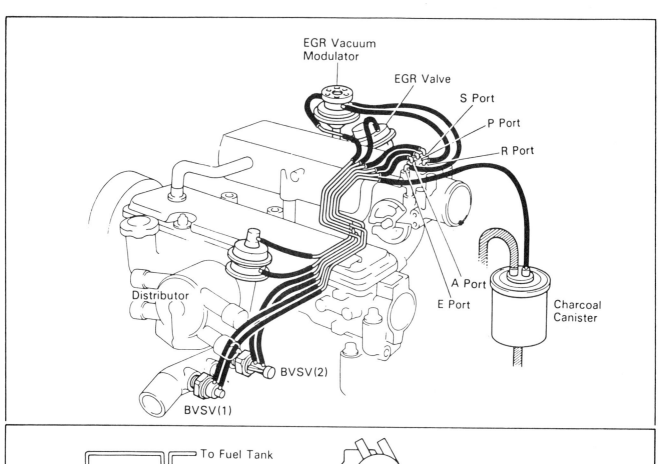

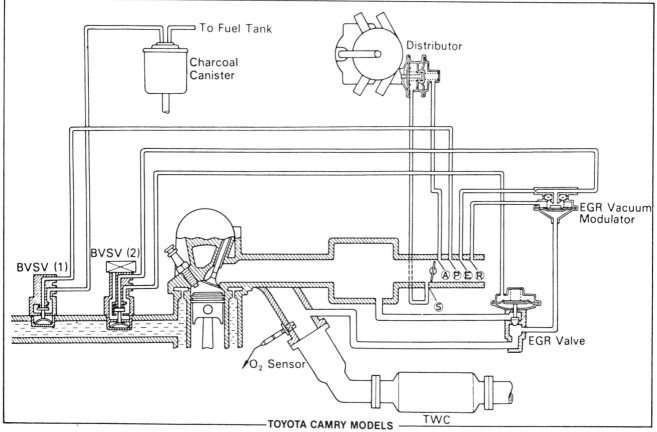

TOYOTA CAMRY MODELS

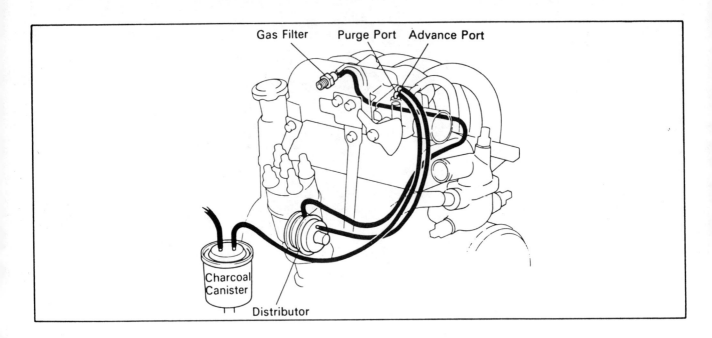

Gas Filter  Purge Port  Advance Port

Charcoal Canister

Distributor

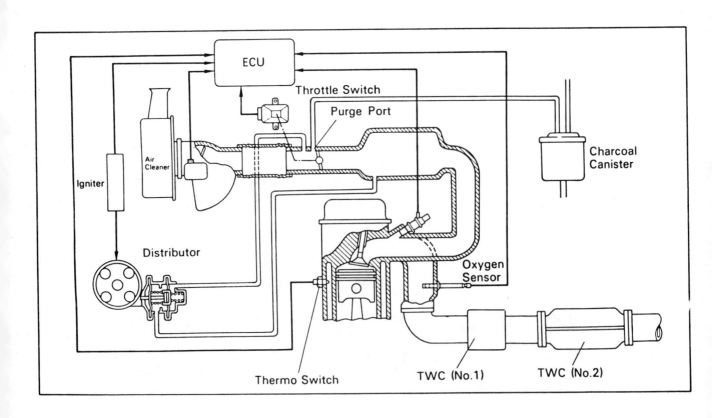

ECU

Throttle Switch

Purge Port

Air Cleaner

Igniter

Distributor

Charcoal Canister

Oxygen Sensor

Thermo Switch

TWC (No.1)

TWC (No.2)

**1984 TOYOTA STARLET MODELS**

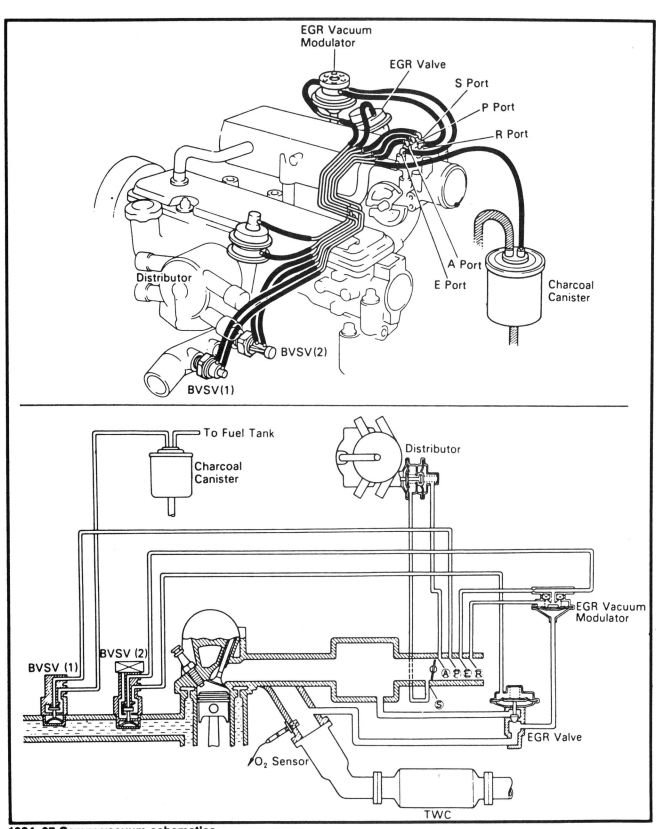

**1984–87 Camry vacuum schematics**

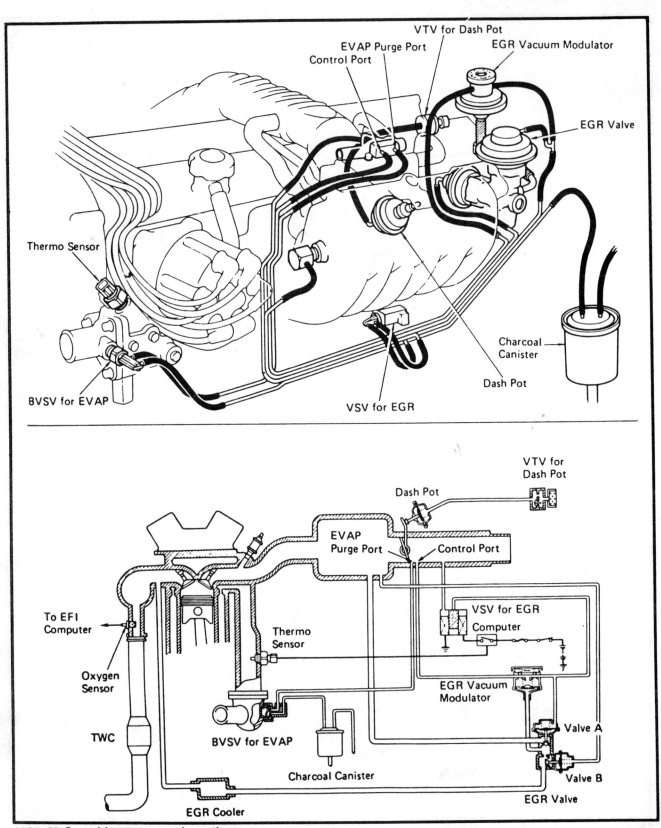

VTV for Dash Pot

EVAP Purge Port
Control Port

EGR Vacuum Modulator

EGR Valve

Thermo Sensor

EGR Valve

Charcoal Canister

BVSV for EVAP

VSV for EGR

Dash Pot

VTV for Dash Pot

Dash Pot

EVAP Purge Port

Control Port

VSV for EGR

Computer

To EFI Computer

Thermo Sensor

Oxygen Sensor

EGR Vacuum Modulator

TWC

BVSV for EVAP

Valve A

Charcoal Canister

Valve B

EGR Cooler

EGR Valve

**1984–87 Cressida vacuum schematics**

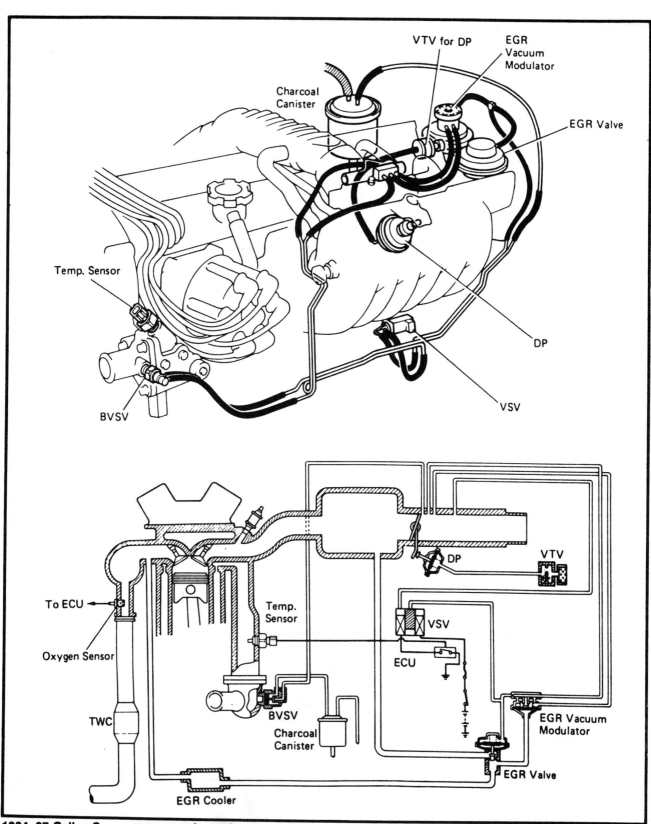

VTV for DP

EGR
Vacuum
Modulator

Charcoal
Canister

EGR Valve

Temp. Sensor

DP

BVSV

VSV

To ECU

Temp.
Sensor

VTV

DP

Oxygen Sensor

VSV

ECU

TWC

BVSV

Charcoal
Canister

EGR Vacuum
Modulator

EGR Valve

EGR Cooler

**1984–87 Celica Supra vacuum schematics**

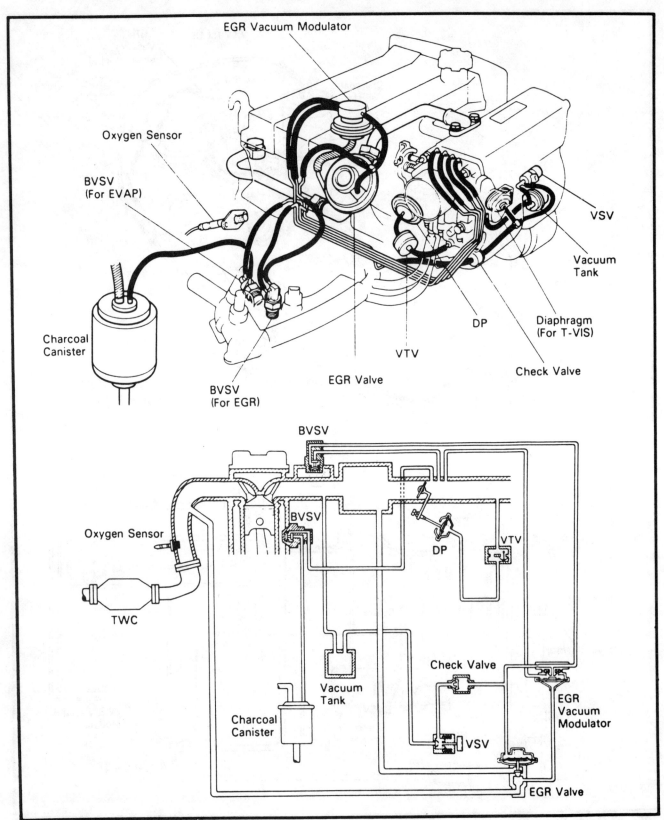

EGR Vacuum Modulator

Oxygen Sensor

BVSV
(For EVAP)

Charcoal
Canister

BVSV
(For EGR)

EGR Valve

VTV

DP

VSV

Vacuum
Tank

Diaphragm
(For T-VIS)

Check Valve

BVSV

Oxygen Sensor

BVSV

DP

VTV

TWC

Charcoal
Canister

Vacuum
Tank

Check Valve

VSV

EGR
Vacuum
Modulator

EGR Valve

**1985–87 MR–2 vacuum schematics**

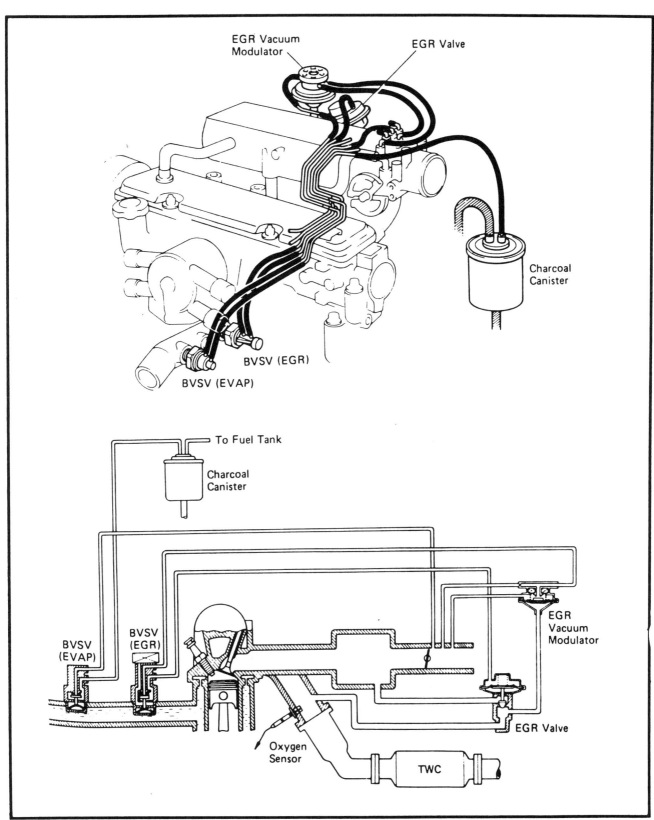

EGR Vacuum Modulator

EGR Valve

Charcoal Canister

BVSV (EGR)

BVSV (EVAP)

To Fuel Tank

Charcoal Canister

BVSV (EVAP)

BVSV (EGR)

EGR Vacuum Modulator

EGR Valve

Oxygen Sensor

TWC

**1985–87 Celica 2S–E engine vacuum schematics**

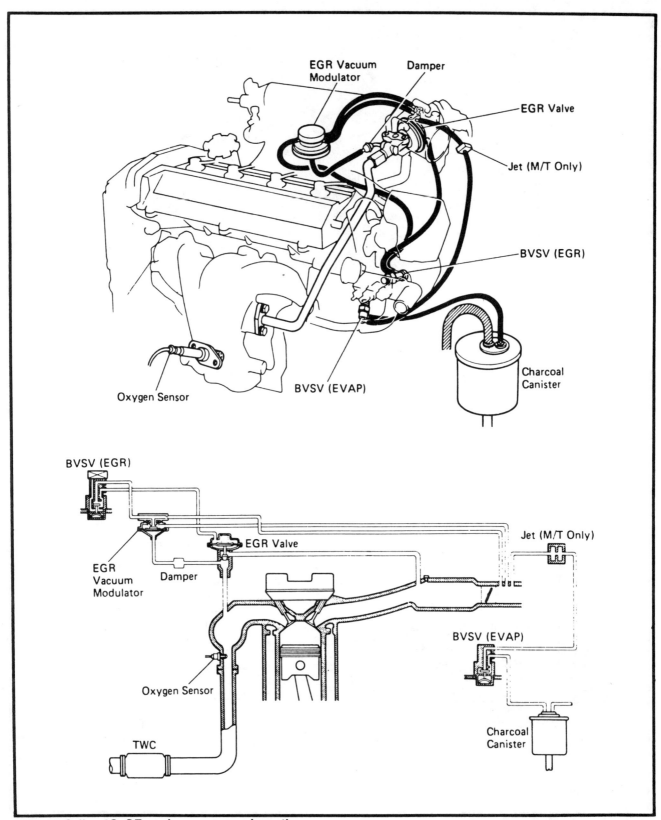

EGR Vacuum Modulator

Damper

EGR Valve

Jet (M/T Only)

BVSV (EGR)

Charcoal Canister

Oxygen Sensor

BVSV (EVAP)

BVSV (EGR)

Jet (M/T Only)

EGR Valve

EGR Vacuum Modulator

Damper

BVSV (EVAP)

Oxygen Sensor

Charcoal Canister

TWC

**1985–87 Celica 3S–GE engine vacuum schematics**

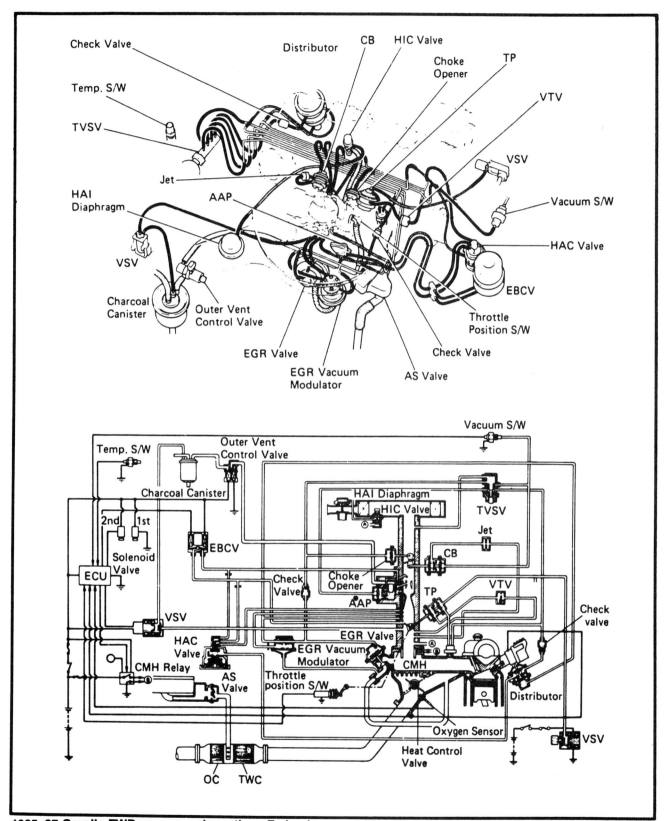

**1985–87 Corolla FWD vacuum schematics—Federal**

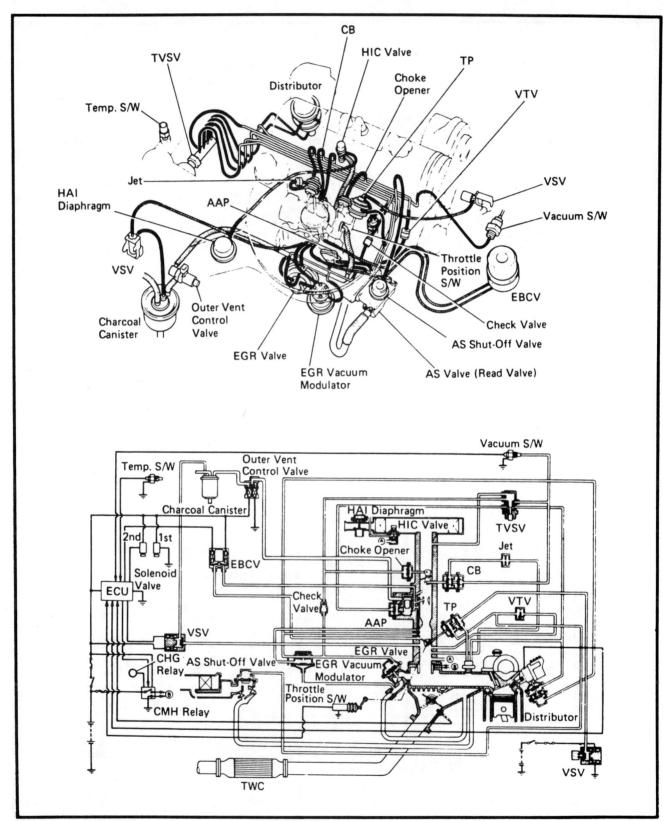

CB

TVSV

HIC Valve

TP

Distributor

Choke Opener

VTV

Temp. S/W

VSV

Jet

Vacuum S/W

HAI Diaphragm

AAP

VSV

Throttle Position S/W

EBCV

Charcoal Canister

Outer Vent Control Valve

Check Valve

AS Shut-Off Valve

EGR Valve

AS Valve (Read Valve)

EGR Vacuum Modulator

Vacuum S/W

Temp. S/W

Outer Vent Control Valve

HAI Diaphragm

HIC Valve

TVSV

Charcoal Canister

Choke Opener

Jet

2nd   1st

CB

Solenoid Valve

EBCV

ECU

Check Valve

VTV

TP

VSV

AAP

CHG Relay

AS Shut-Off Valve

EGR Valve

EGR Vacuum Modulator

Distributor

CMH Relay

Throttle Position S/W

VSV

TWC

**1985–87 Corolla FWD vacuum schematics – California**

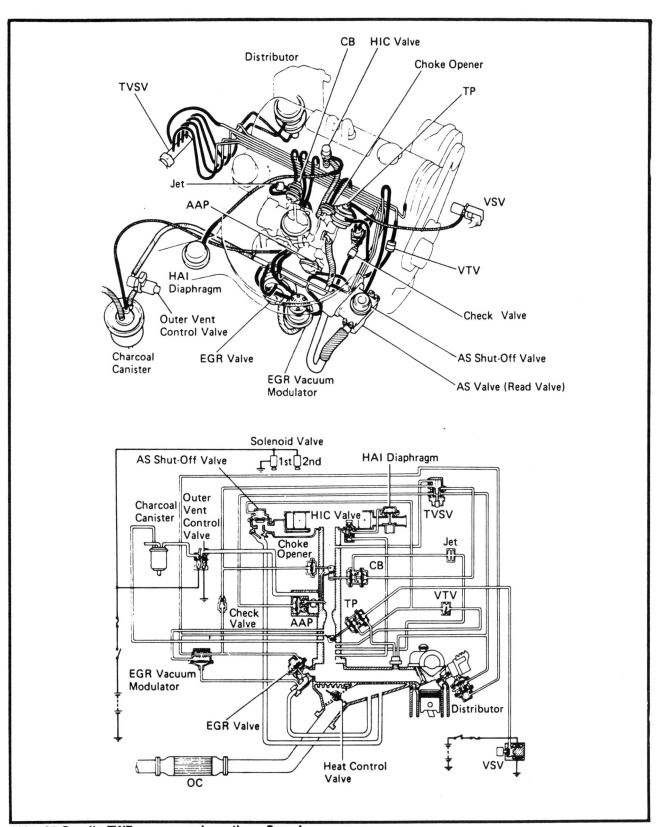

Distributor
CB  HIC Valve
Choke Opener
TVSV
TP
Jet
VSV
AAP
VTV
HAI Diaphragm
Check Valve
Outer Vent Control Valve
Charcoal Canister
EGR Valve
AS Shut-Off Valve
AS Valve (Read Valve)
EGR Vacuum Modulator

Solenoid Valve
AS Shut-Off Valve
1st 2nd
HAI Diaphragm
Charcoal Canister
Outer Vent Control Valve
HIC Valve
TVSV
Choke Opener
Jet
CB
Check Valve
AAP
TP
VTV
EGR Vacuum Modulator
Distributor
EGR Valve
Heat Control Valve
OC
VSV

**1985–87 Corolla FWD vacuum schematics — Canada**

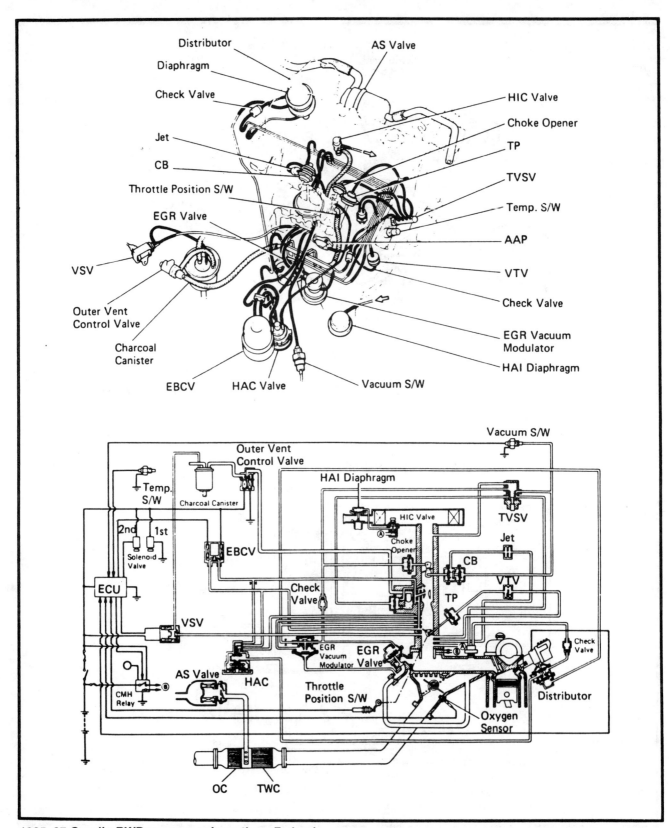

**1985–87 Corolla RWD vacuum schematics—Federal**

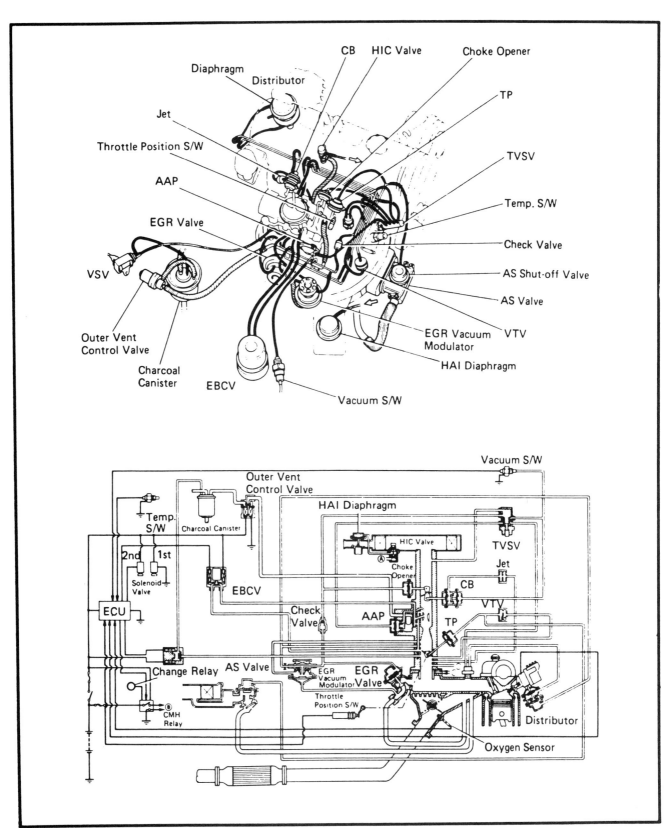

Diaphragm
Distributor
CB  HIC Valve  Choke Opener
Jet
TP
Throttle Position S/W
TVSV
AAP
Temp. S/W
EGR Valve
Check Valve
VSV
AS Shut-off Valve
AS Valve
Outer Vent
Control Valve
EGR Vacuum  VTV
Modulator
Charcoal
Canister
HAI Diaphragm
EBCV
Vacuum S/W

Vacuum S/W
Outer Vent
Control Valve
HAI Diaphragm
Temp.
S/W
HIC Valve
TVSV
Charcoal Canister
Choke
Opener
Jet
2nd  1st
CB
Solenoid
Valve
EBCV
VTV
ECU
Check
Valve
AAP
TP
Change Relay  AS Valve
EGR
Vacuum
Modulator
EGR
Valve
CMH
Relay
Throttle
Position S/W
Distributor
Oxygen Sensor

**1985–87 Corolla RWD vacuum schematics—California**

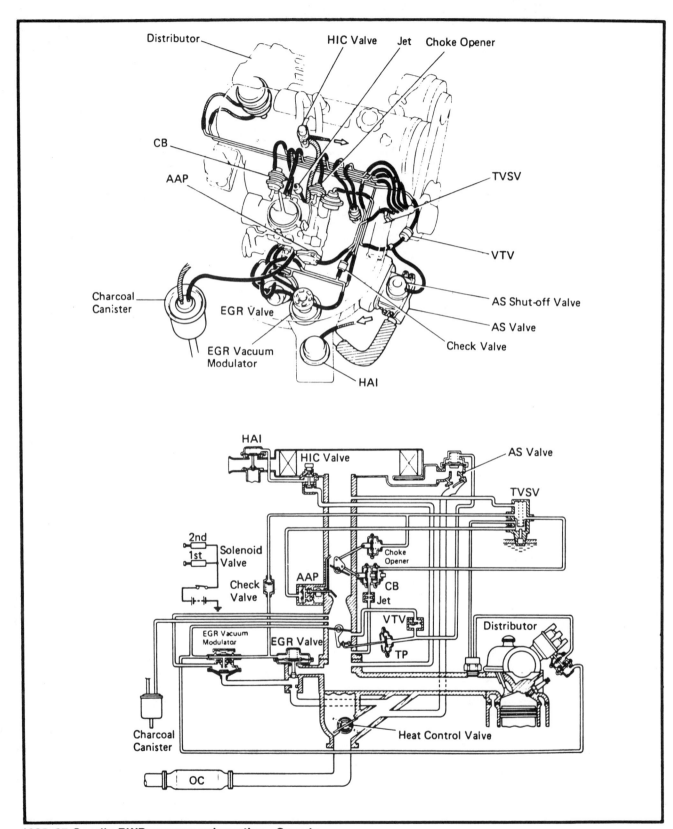

Distributor · HIC Valve · Jet · Choke Opener

CB

AAP

TVSV

Charcoal Canister

EGR Valve

VTV

AS Shut-off Valve

AS Valve

Check Valve

EGR Vacuum Modulator

HAI

HAI

HIC Valve

AS Valve

TVSV

2nd

1st · Solenoid Valve

Check Valve

AAP

Choke Opener

CB

Jet

VTV

Distributor

EGR Vacuum Modulator

EGR Valve

TP

Charcoal Canister

Heat Control Valve

OC

**1985–87 Corolla RWD vacuum schematics—Canada**

# Volkswagen

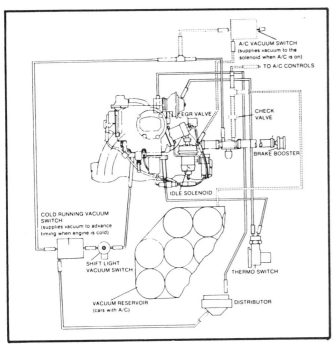

**1982 Carbureted Rabbit**

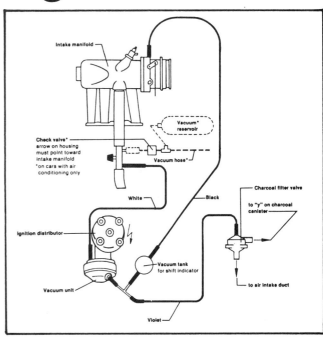

**1982 Quantum**

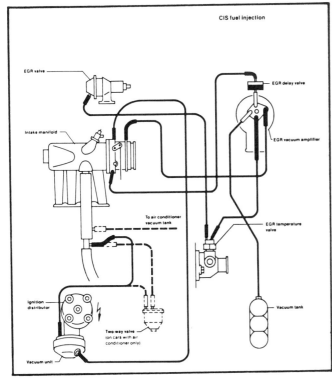

**1978 CIS fuel injection models**

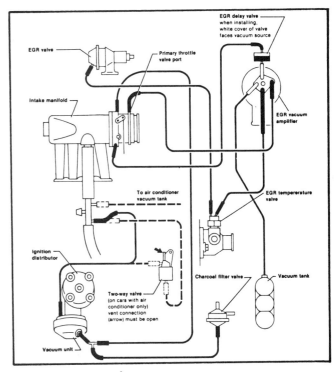

**1979 CIS fuel injection models with automatic transmission**

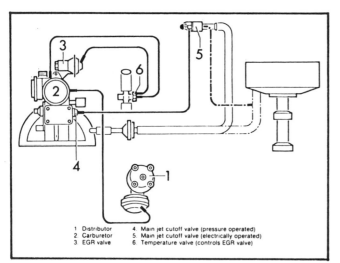

1. Distributor
2. Carburetor
3. EGR valve
4. Main jet cutoff valve (pressure operated)
5. Main jet cutoff valve (electrically operated)
6. Temperature valve (controls EGR valve)

**1978 Carbureted Rabbit**

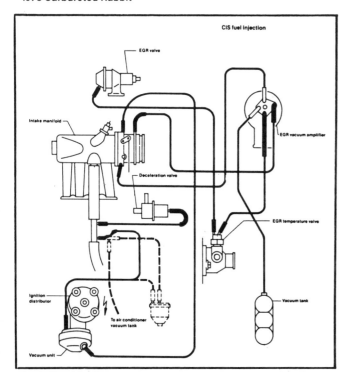

**1976 CIS fuel injection models**

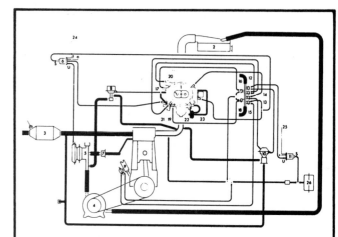

1. Carburetor
2. Air cleaner
3. Catalytic converter
4. Air pump
5. Diverter valve
6. Two way valve for air injection
7. Check valve for air injection
8. Anti-backfire valve for air injection
9. Ignition distributor
10. EGR valve
11. Two way valve for EGR second stage (California only)
12. Temperature valve for EGR second stage (California only)
13. Temperature valve for EGR first stage
14. Temperature valve for carburetor second stage
15. Temperature valve for ignition advance cutoff
16. Temperature valve for temperature controlled injection quantity
17. Check-valve for temperature controlled injection quantity
18. Temperature valve for cold idle valve
19. Cold idle valve
20. Vacuum unit for carburetor second stage
21. Vacuum unit for choke pull-down (first stage)
22. Vacuum unit for choke pull-down (second-stage)
23. Thermo-time valve for choke pull-down (second stage)
24. Electrical wire to relay
25. Electrical wire to micro switch on throttle valve (California only)
26. Brake booster

**1976 Carbureted Rabbit and Scirocco**

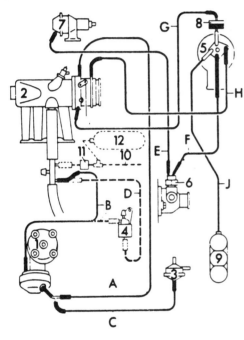

Manual transmission – U.S.A. (except Calif.)
Auto. transmission – U.S.A. (except Calif.)

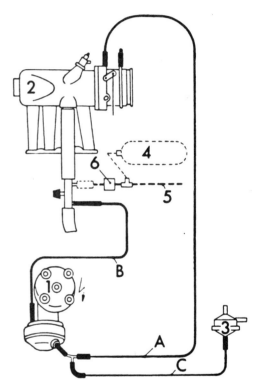

Manual transmission – California only
Auto. transmission – California only

1. Ignition distributor
2. Intake manifold
3. Charcoal filter valve
4. Two-way valve (A/C cars only)
5. Vacuum booster
6. EGR temperature valve
7. EGR valve
8. Deceleration valve (49 states autom. transm. only)

8. Deceleration valve (49 states autom.transm.only)

9. Vacuum tank

10. Hose to air conditioner (A/C cars only)
11. Check valve (A/C cars only)
A. Black
B. White
C. Violet
D. Pink
E. Yellow
F. Light blue
G. Gray
H. Red
I. Light green

1. Ignition distributor
2. Intake manifold

3. Charcoal filter valve
4. Air conditioner vacuum tank (A/C cars only)
5. Hose to air conditioner (A/C cars only)
6. Check valve (A/C cars only)
A. Black
B. White
C. Violet

**VOLKSWAGEN—JETTA, RABBIT AND SCIROCCO MODELS**

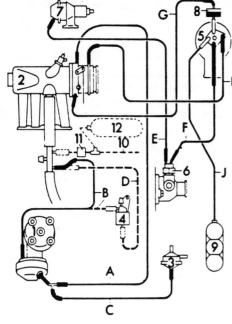

Manual transmission – U.S.A. (except Calif.)
Auto. transmission  – U.S.A. (except Calif.)

1. Ignition distributor
2. Intake manifold
3. Charcoal filter valve
4. Two-way valve (A/C cars only)
5. Vacuum booster
6. EGR temperature valve
7. EGR valve
8. Deceleration valve (49 states autom. transm. only)
8. Deceleration valve (49 states autom.transm.only)
9. Vacuum tank
10. Hose to air conditioner (A/C cars only)
11. Check valve (A/C cars only)

| | | | |
|---|---|---|---|
| A. | Black | F. | Light blue |
| B. | White | G. | Gray |
| C. | Violet | H. | Red |
| D. | Pink | I. | Light green |
| E. | Yellow | | |

**RABBIT MODELS**

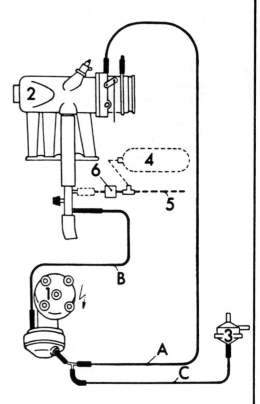

Manual transmission – California only
Auto. transmission  – California only

1. Ignition distributor
2. Intake manifold
3. Charcoal filter valve
4. Air conditioner vacuum tank (A/C cars only)
5. Hose to air conditioner (A/C cars only)
6. Check valve (A/C cars only)

| | |
|---|---|
| A. | Black |
| B. | White |
| C. | Violet |

A/C VACUUM SWITCH
(supplies vacuum to the solenoid when A/C is on)

TO A/C CONTROLS

EGR VALVE

CHECK VALVE

BRAKE BOOSTER

IDLE SOLENOID

COLD RUNNING VACUUM SWITCH
(supplies vacuum to advance timing when engine is cold)

SHIFT LIGHT VACUUM SWITCH

THERMO SWITCH

VACUUM RESERVOIR
(cars with A C)

DISTRIBUTOR

**CARBURETED ENGINE**

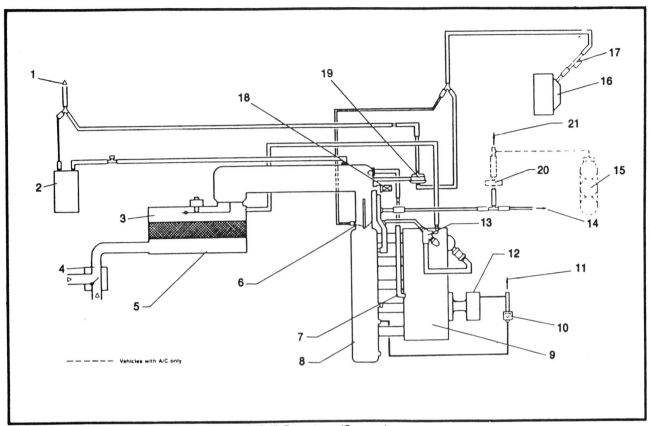

------ Vehicles with A/C only

**Vacuum schematics for the five cylinder CIS-E Quantum (Syncro)**

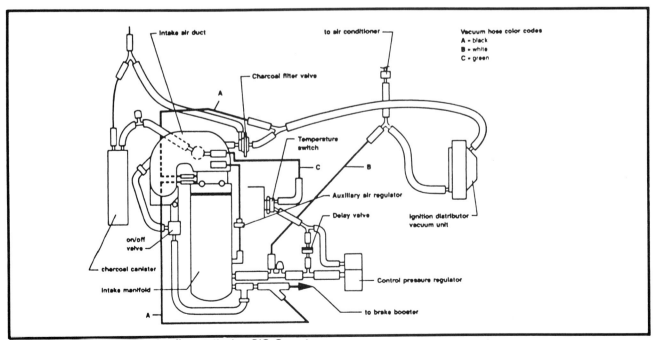

Intake air duct

to air conditioner

Vacuum hose color codes
A = black
B = white
C = green

Charcoal filter valve

A

Temperature switch

C          B

Auxiliary air regulator

Delay valve

Ignition distributor vacuum unit

on/off valve

charcoal canister

Control pressure regulator

intake manifold

A

to brake booster

**Vacuum schematics for the five cylinder CIS Quantum**

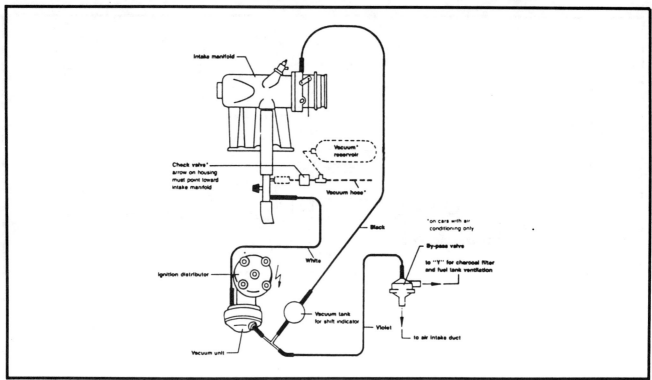

**Vacuum schematics for the four cylinder CIS Quantum**

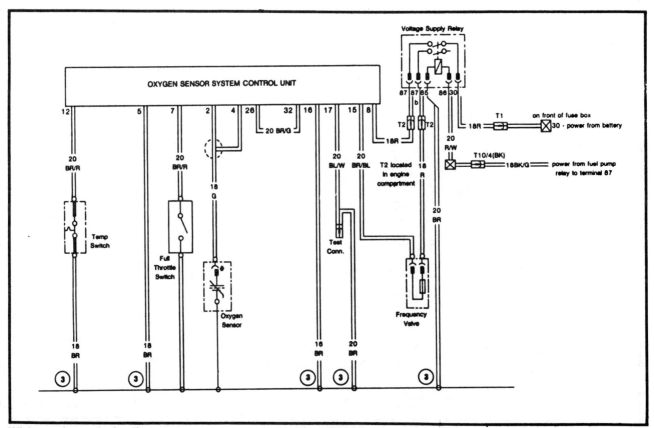

**Wiring schematic for the oxygen sensor system—1984 GTI**

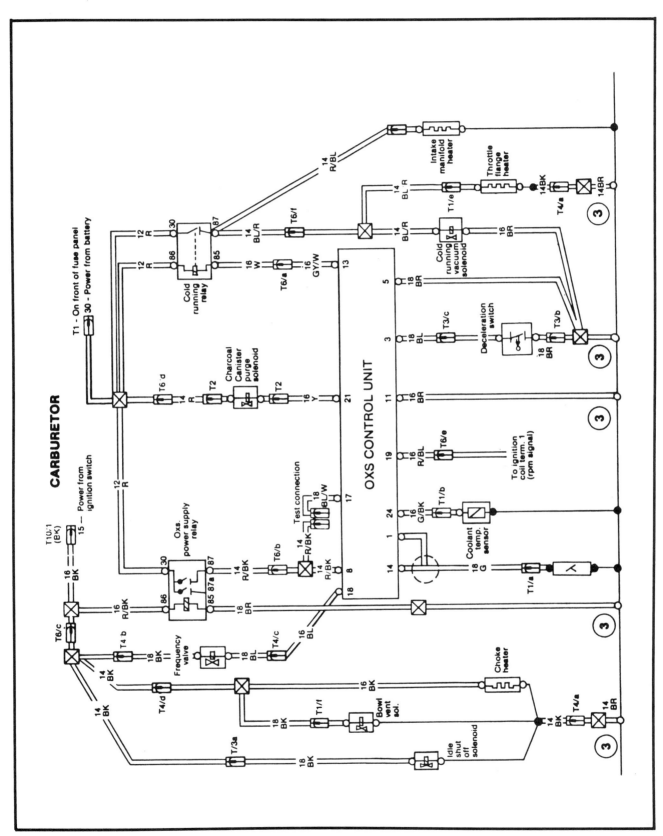

**Wiring schematic for the oxygen sensor system—1984 Rabbit (carb)**

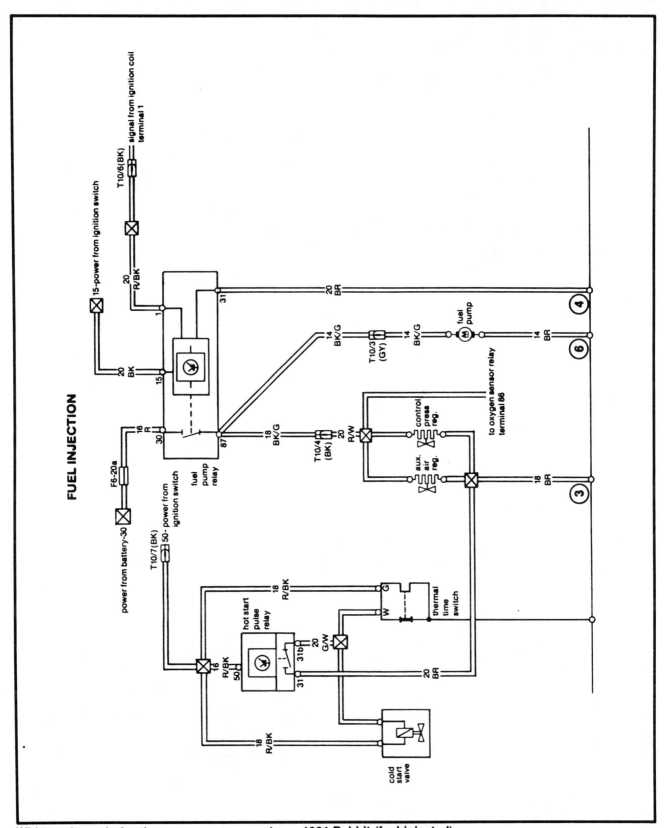

**FUEL INJECTION**

Wiring schematic for the oxygen sensor system—1984 Rabbit (fuel injected)

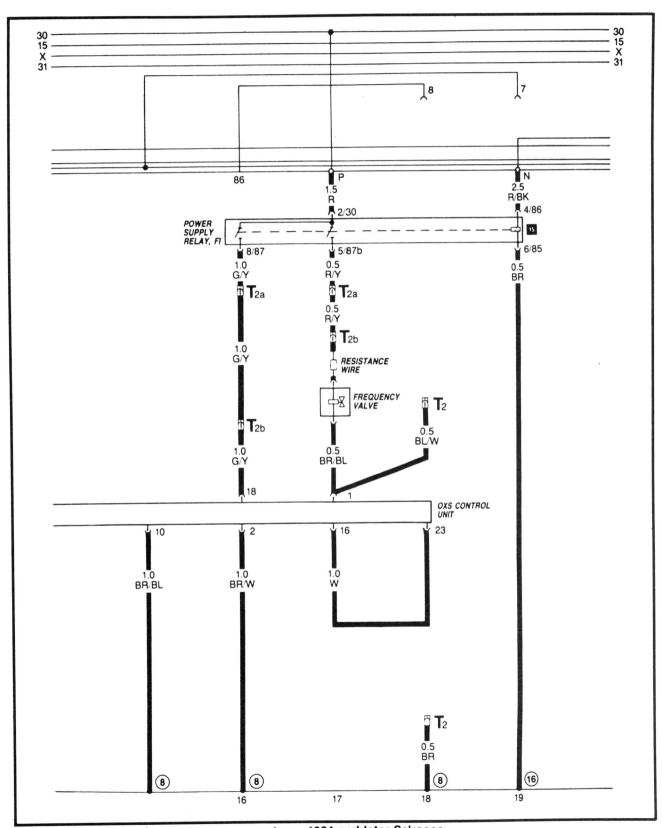

Wiring schematic for the oxygen sensor system — 1984 and later Scirocco

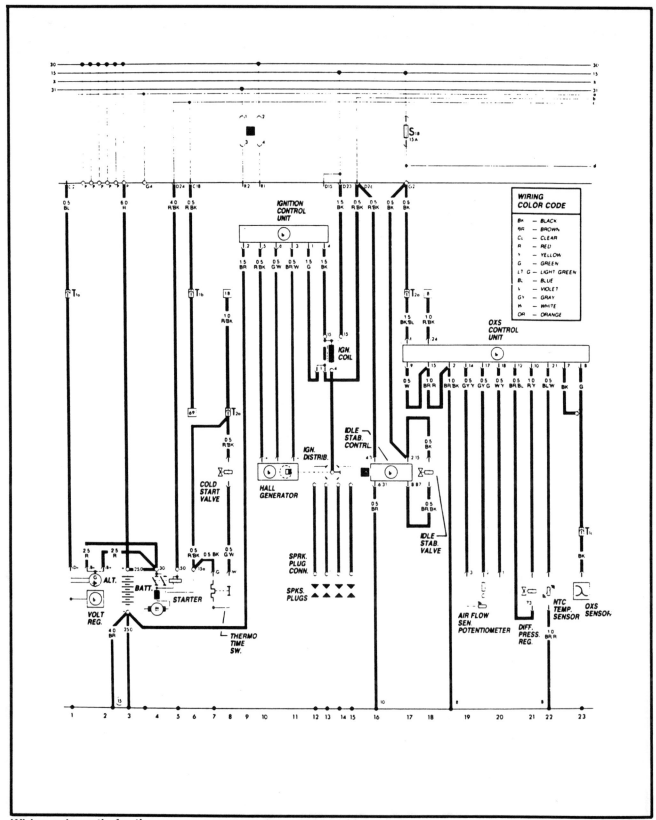

**Wiring schematic for the oxygen sensor system—1984 and later Jetta**

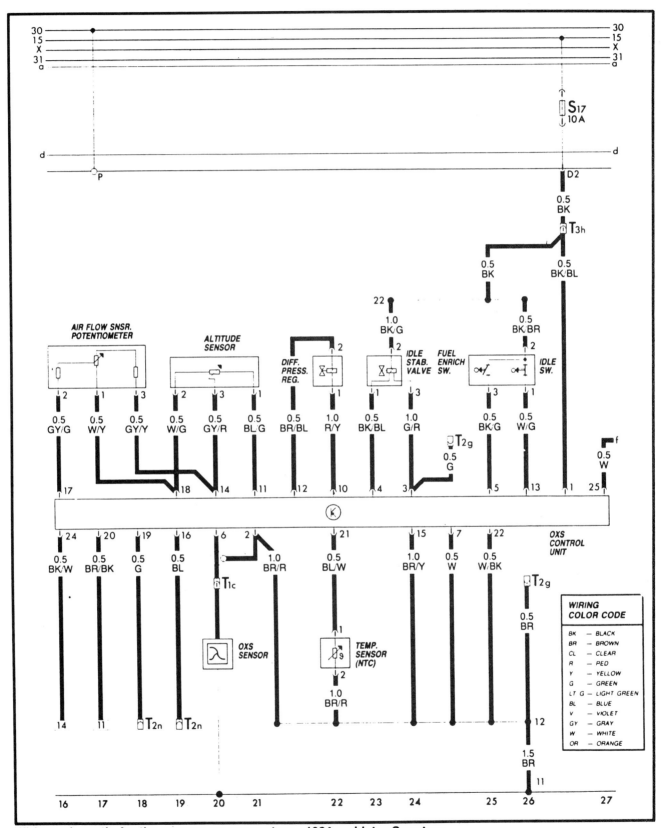

**Wiring schematic for the oxygen sensor system—1984 and later Quantum**

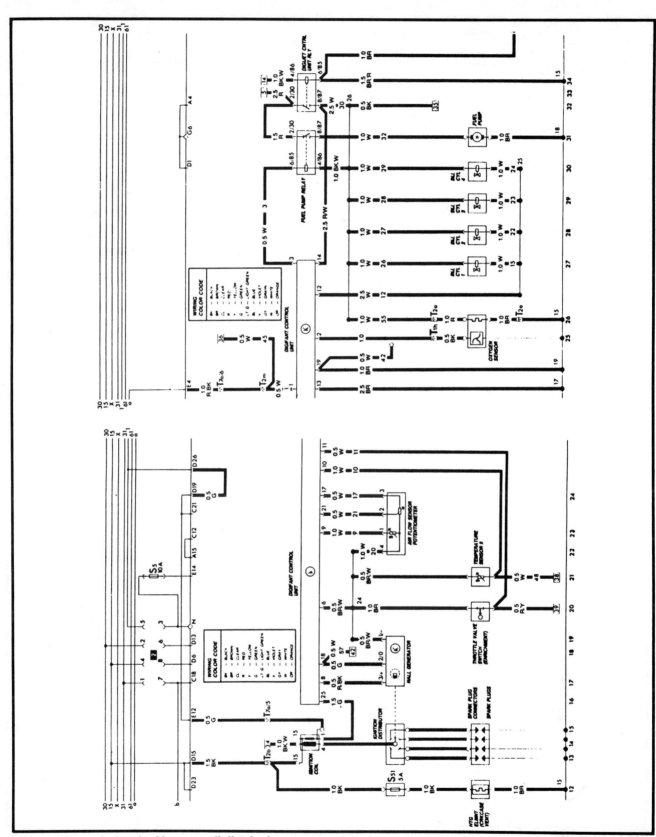

Wiring schematic for the Vanagon digijet fuel system

# Isuzu Pick Up

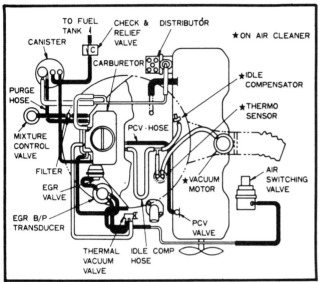

**Vacuum hose routing – 4DZ1 engine (Federal)**

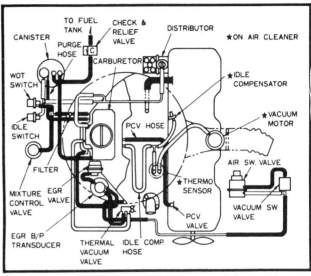

**Vacuum hose routing – 4DZ1 engine (California)**

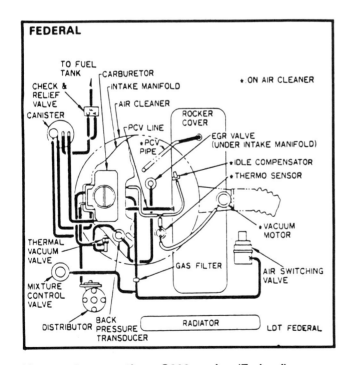

**Vacuum hose routing – G200 engine (Federal)**

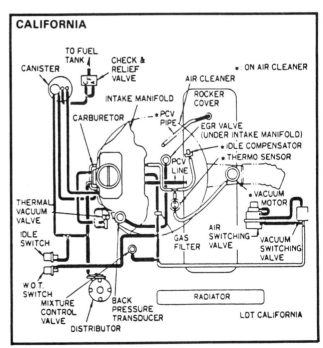

**Vacuum hose routing – G200 engine (California)**

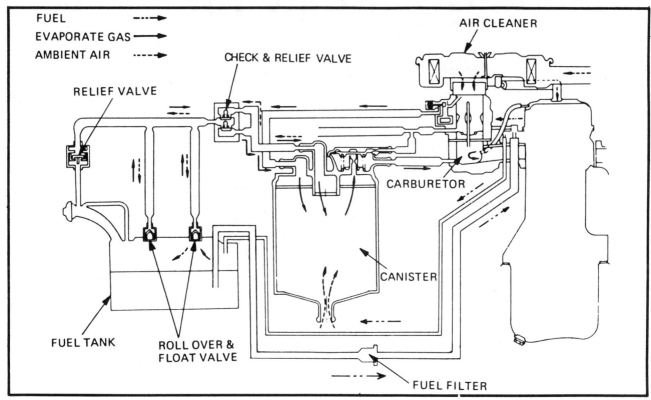

**FUEL** ----▶

**EVAPORATE GAS** ——▶

**AMBIENT AIR** ----▶

RELIEF VALVE

CHECK & RELIEF VALVE

AIR CLEANER

CARBURETOR

CANISTER

FUEL TANK

ROLL OVER & FLOAT VALVE

FUEL FILTER

**Typical evaporative emission control system**

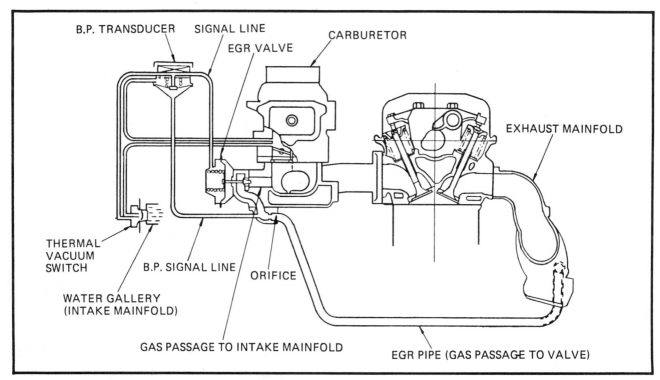

B.P. TRANSDUCER    SIGNAL LINE    CARBURETOR

EGR VALVE

EXHAUST MAINFOLD

THERMAL VACUUM SWITCH

B.P. SIGNAL LINE

ORIFICE

WATER GALLERY (INTAKE MAINFOLD)

GAS PASSAGE TO INTAKE MAINFOLD

EGR PIPE (GAS PASSAGE TO VALVE)

**Exhaust gas recirculation system – 4ZD1 engine**

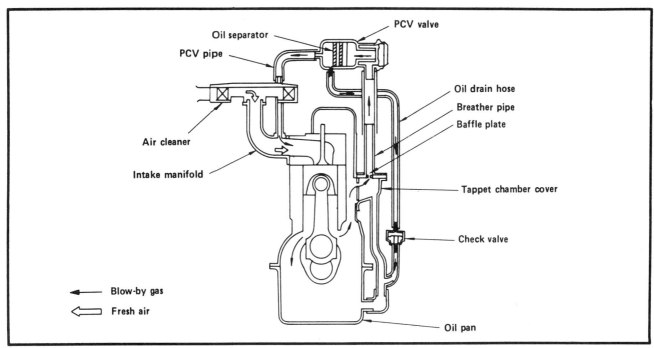

**P.C.V. system diesel engine without turbocharger**

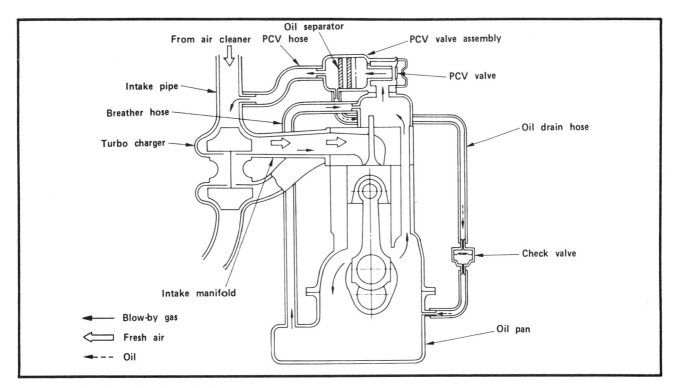

**P.C.V. system diesel engine with turbocharger**

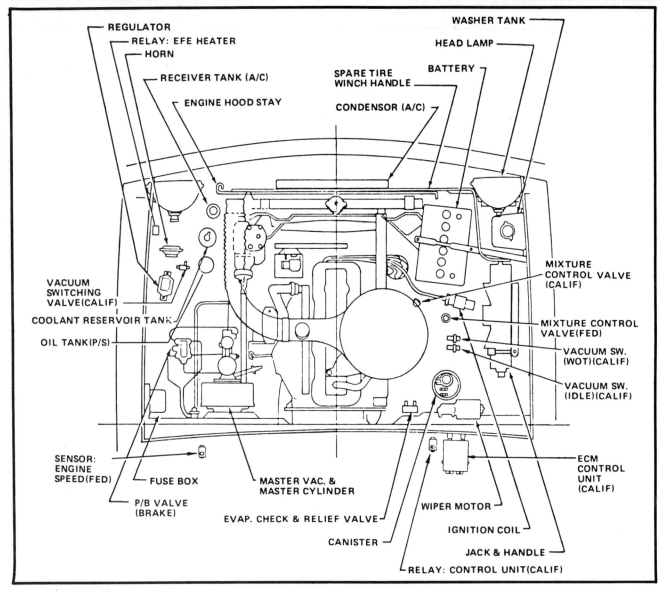

**Emission control system — G200 engine**

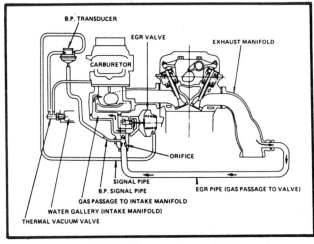

**Exhaust gas recirculation system — G200 engine**

# Mazda Pick Up

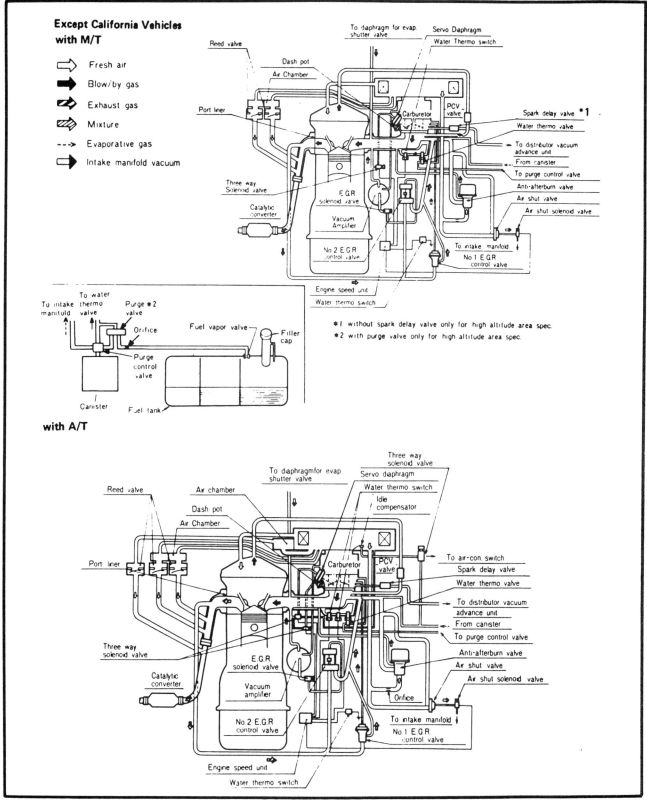

**Except California Vehicles with M/T**

- Fresh air
- Blow/by gas
- Exhaust gas
- Mixture
- Evaporative gas
- Intake manifold vacuum

*1 without spark delay valve only for high altitude area spec.
*2 with purge valve only for high altitude area spec.

**with A/T**

**Emission component and vacuum hose schematic for 1984 B–2000 Federal models**

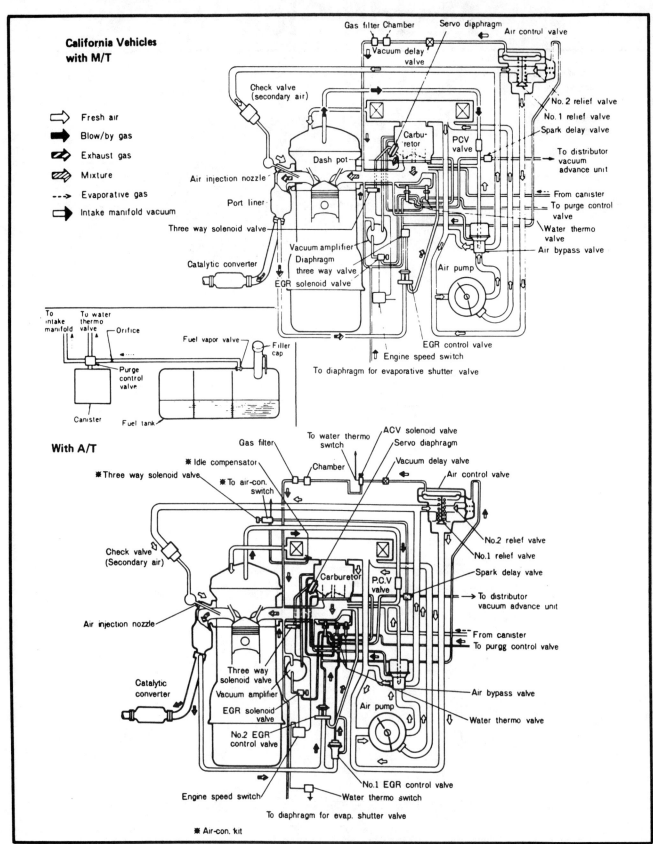

**California Vehicles with M/T**

⟹ Fresh air

⟹ Blow/by gas

⟹ Exhaust gas

⟹ Mixture

--→ Evaporative gas

⟹ Intake manifold vacuum

Gas filter Chamber
Servo diaphragm
Air control valve
Vacuum delay valve
Check valve (secondary air)
Carburetor
PCV valve
No. 2 relief valve
No. 1 relief valve
Spark delay valve
To distributor vacuum advance unit
Dash pot
Air injection nozzle
Port liner
From canister
To purge control valve
Three way solenoid valve
Water thermo valve
Air bypass valve
Vacuum amplifier
Diaphragm three way valve
Catalytic converter
EGR solenoid valve
Air pump
To intake manifold
To water thermo valve
Orifice
Fuel vapor valve
Filler cap
Purge control valve
Canister
Fuel tank
EGR control valve
Engine speed switch
To diaphragm for evaporative shutter valve

**With A/T**

To water thermo switch
ACV solenoid valve
Servo diaphragm
Gas filter
※ Idle compensator
Chamber
Vacuum delay valve
Air control valve
※ Three way solenoid valve
※ To air-con. switch
No. 2 relief valve
No. 1 relief valve
Check valve (Secondary air)
Carburetor
P.C.V valve
Spark delay valve
To distributor vacuum advance unit
Air injection nozzle
From canister
To purge control valve
Three way solenoid valve
Vacuum amplifier
E.GR solenoid valve
Air bypass valve
Catalytic converter
Water thermo valve
No.2 EGR control valve
Air pump
No.1 EGR control valve
Engine speed switch
Water thermo switch
To diaphragm for evap. shutter valve
※ Air-con. kit

**Emission component and vacuum hose schematic for 1984 B–2000 California models**

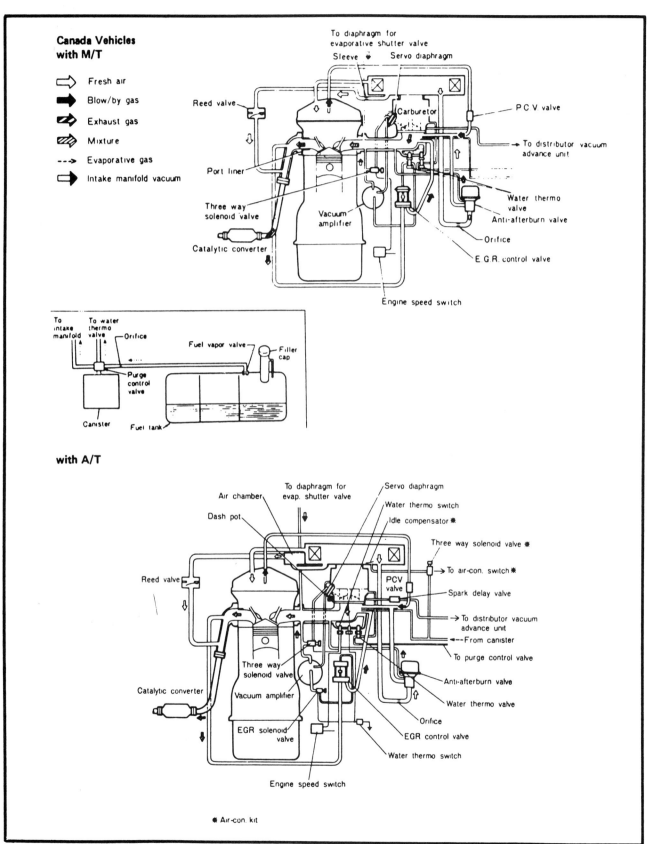

**Canada Vehicles
with M/T**

⇨ Fresh air

➡ Blow/by gas

⬈ Exhaust gas

⬈ Mixture

--→ Evaporative gas

⇨ Intake manifold vacuum

To diaphragm for
evaporative shutter valve

Sleeve · Servo diaphragm

Reed valve

Carburetor

P.C.V. valve

To distributor vacuum
advance unit

Port liner

Three way
solenoid valve

Vacuum
amplifier

Water thermo
valve

Anti-afterburn valve

Orifice

E.G.R. control valve

Catalytic converter

Engine speed switch

To
intake
manifold

To water
thermo
valve

Orifice

Fuel vapor valve

Filler
cap

Purge
control
valve

Canister

Fuel tank

**with A/T**

Air chamber

Dash pot

To diaphragm for
evap. shutter valve

Servo diaphragm

Water thermo switch

Idle compensator ✱

Three way solenoid valve ✱

To air-con. switch ✱

Reed valve

PCV
valve

Spark delay valve

To distributor vacuum
advance unit

From canister

To purge control valve

Three way
solenoid valve

Anti-afterburn valve

Catalytic converter

Vacuum amplifier

Water thermo valve

Orifice

EGR solenoid
valve

EGR control valve

Water thermo switch

Engine speed switch

✱ Air-con. kit

**Emission component and vacuum hose schematic for 1984 B–2000 Canadian models**

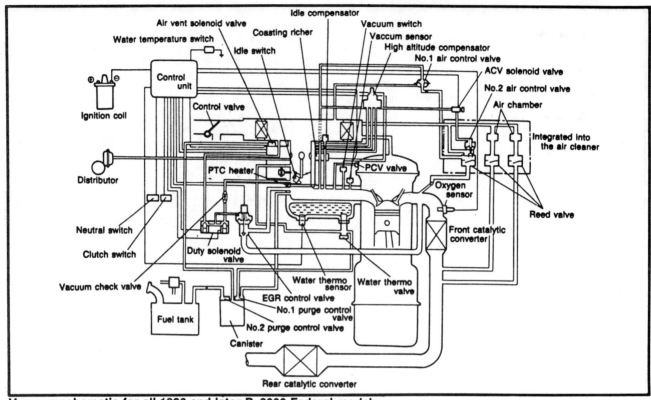

**Vacuum schematic for all 1986 and later B–2000 Federal models**

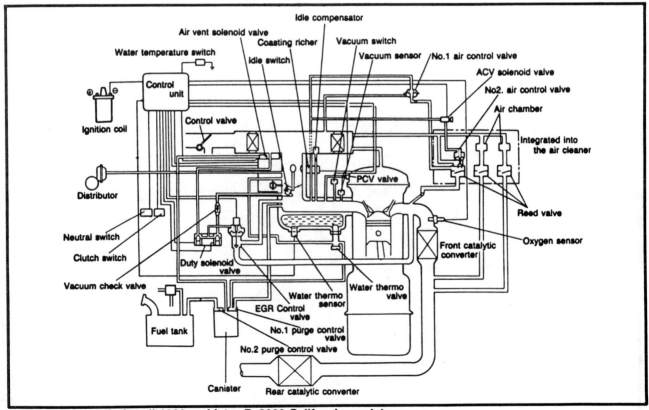

**Vacuum schematic for all 1986 and later B–2000 California models**

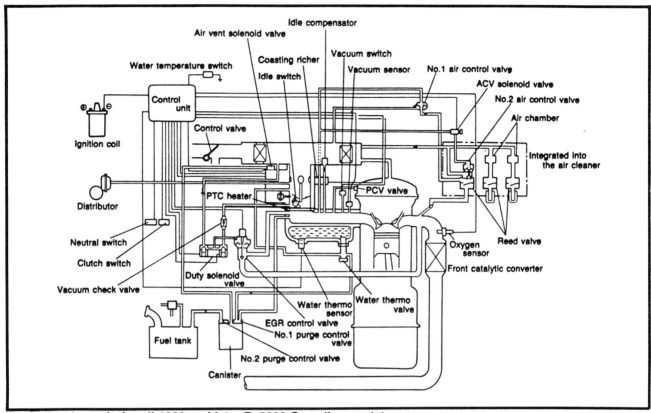

Vacuum schematic for all 1986 and later B–2000 Canadian models

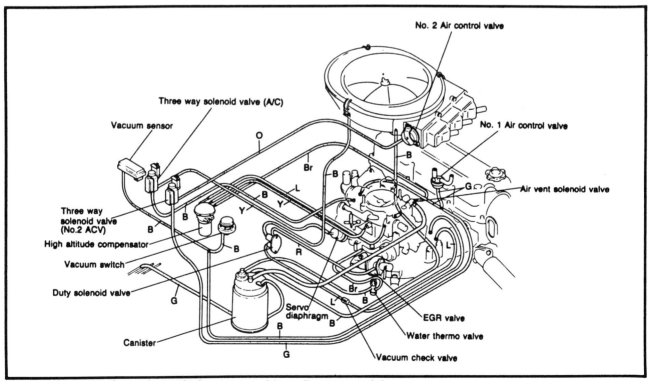

Vacuum hose routing schematic for 1986 and later B–2000 models

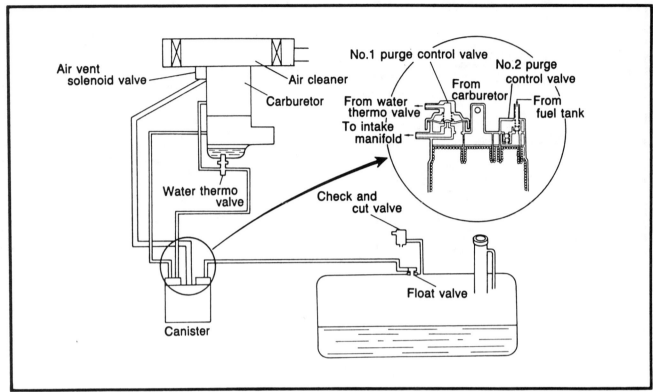

Fuel evaporative emission system schematic

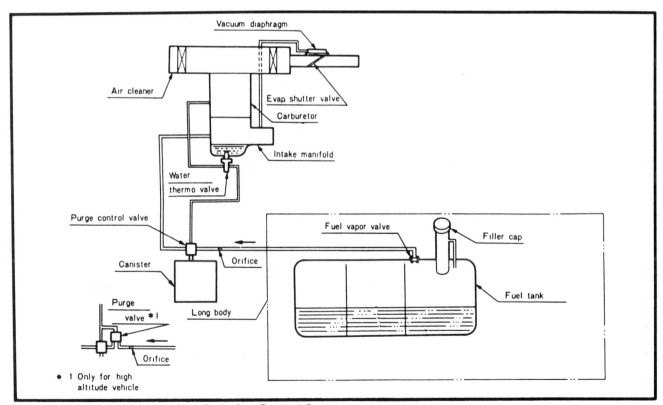

1984 B–2000 Model Evaporative Emission Control System

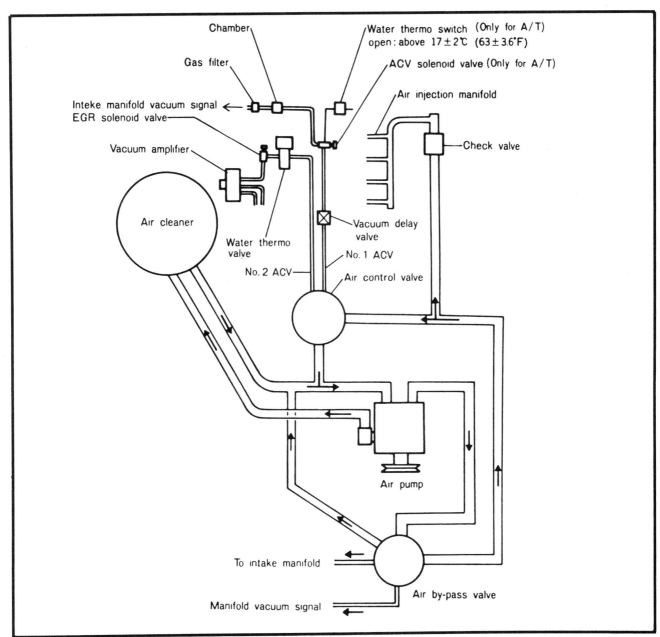

**Air Injection System for 1984 B–2000 California models**

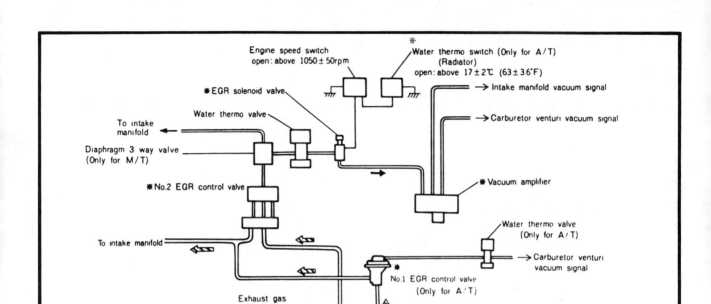

EGR System, 1984 B–2000 California models

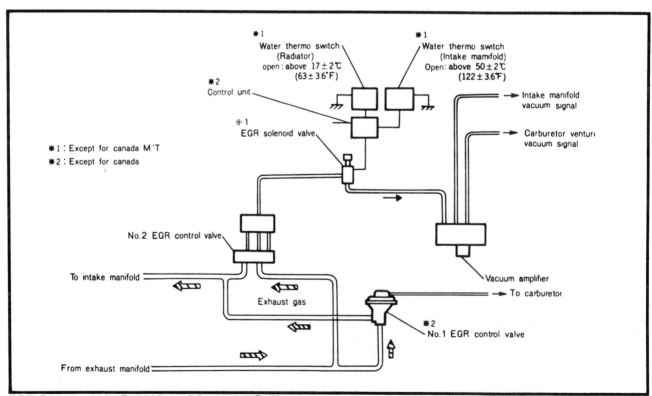

EGR System, 1984 B–2000 models except California

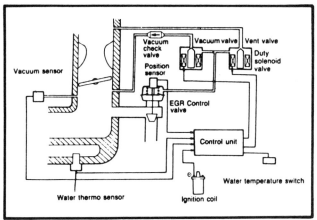

EGR System schematic, 1986 and later B–2000 models

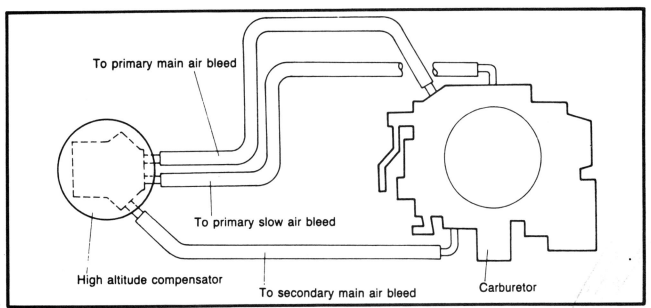

Altitude Compensation System schematic

# Mitsubishi Pick Up

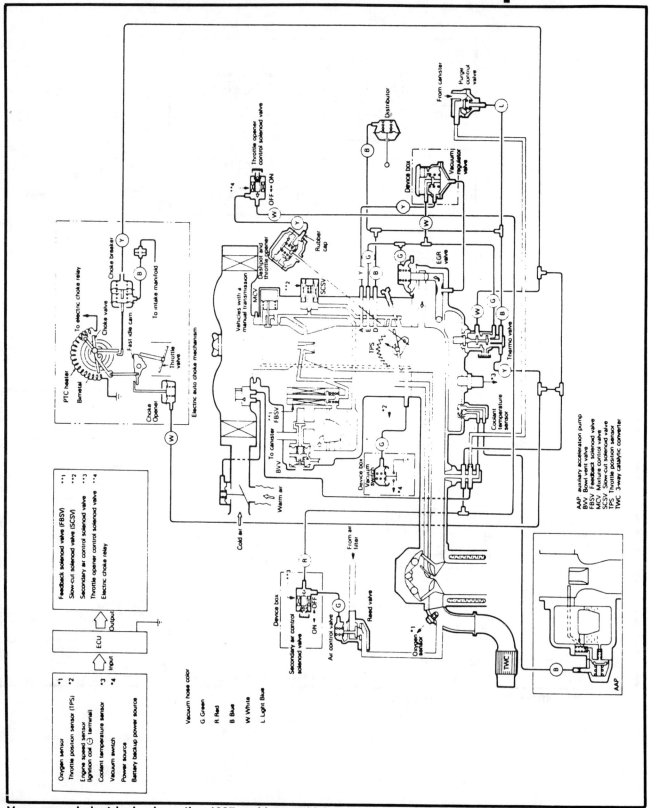

**Vacuum and electrical schematic—1987 and later vehicles except California and high altitude**

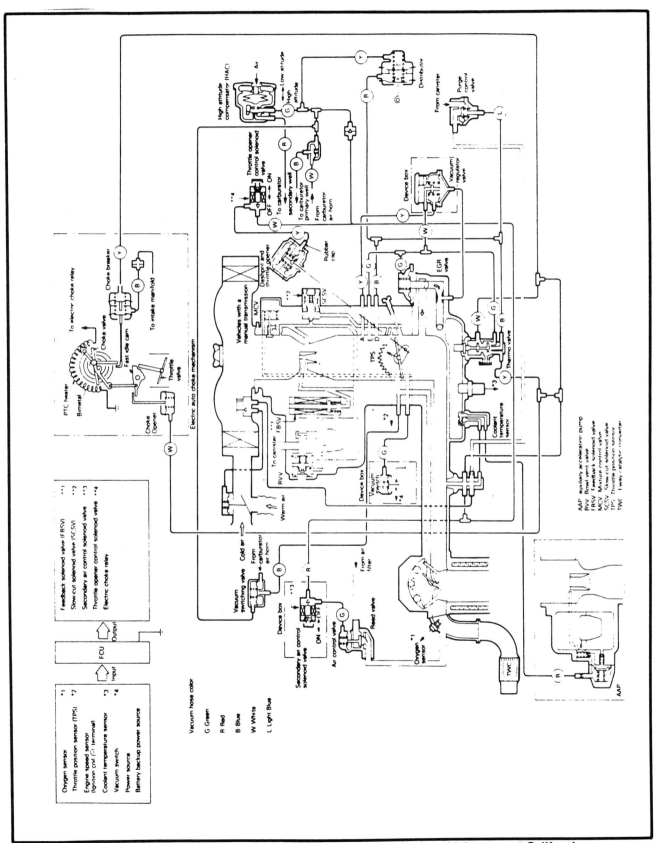

**Vacuum and electrical schematic schematic 1987 and later high altitude vehicles except California**

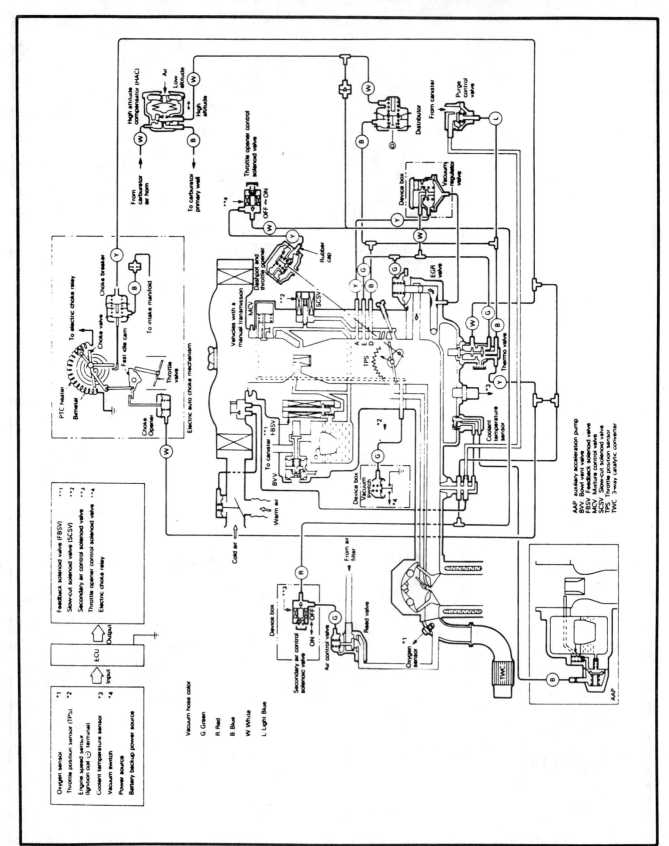

**Vacuum and electrical schematic 1987 and later California vehicles**

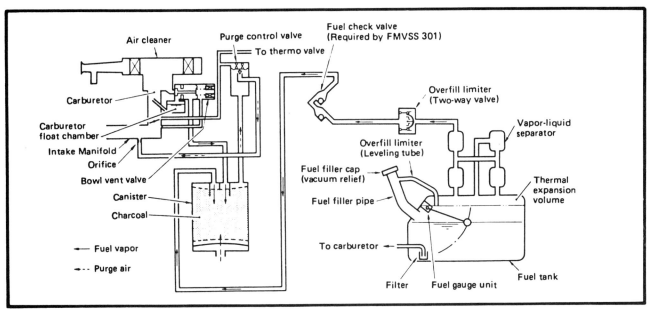

**Evaporative emission control system**

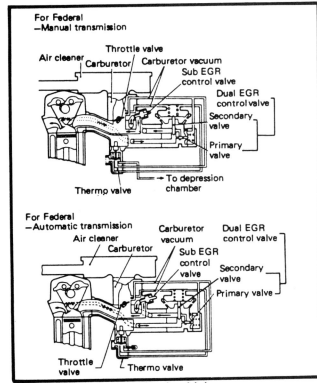

**EGR system—1984 Federal vehicles**

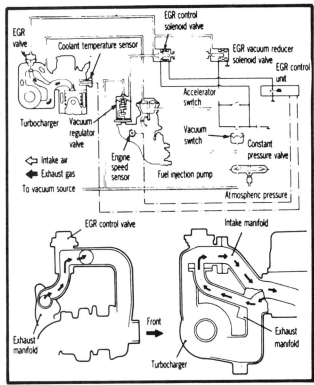

**EGR system—diesel engine**

# Nissan/Datsun Pick Up

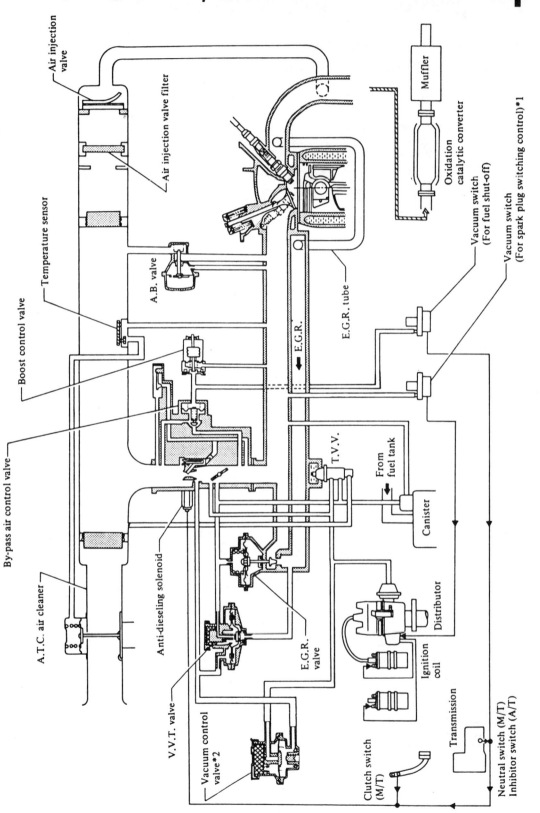

Air injection valve

Air injection valve filter

Temperature sensor

Boost control valve

By-pass air control valve

A.T.C. air cleaner

Anti-dieseling solenoid

V.V.T. valve

Vacuum control valve*2

A.B. valve

E.G.R.

E.G.R. tube

E.G.R. valve

T.V.V.

From fuel tank

Canister

Ignition coil

Distributor

Transmission

Clutch switch (M/T)

Neutral switch (M/T) Inhibitor switch (A/T)

Muffler

Oxidation catalytic converter

Vacuum switch (For fuel shut-off)

Vacuum switch (For spark plug switching control)*1

*1: Except MPG model
*2: Except MPG and heavy duty models

**DATSUN PICKUP Z-20 ENGINE—EXC. CALIF. AND CANADA.**

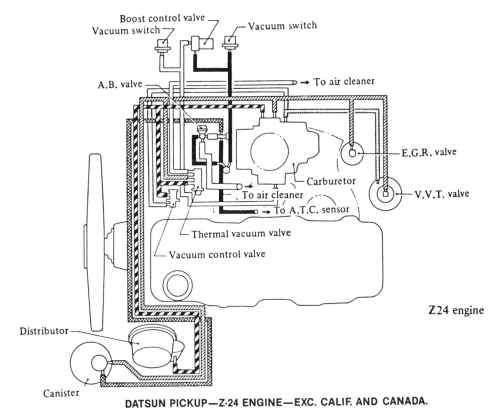

Boost control valve
Vacuum switch
Vacuum switch
A.B. valve
To air cleaner
E.G.R. valve
V.V.T. valve
Carburetor
To air cleaner
To A.T.C. sensor
Thermal vacuum valve
Vacuum control valve
Z24 engine
Distributor
Canister

**DATSUN PICKUP—Z-24 ENGINE—EXC. CALIF. AND CANADA.**

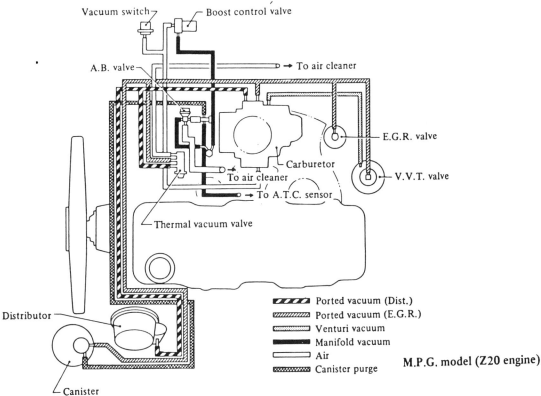

Vacuum switch
Boost control valve
A.B. valve
To air cleaner
E.G.R. valve
V.V.T. valve
Carburetor
To air cleaner
To A.T.C. sensor
Thermal vacuum valve
Distributor
Canister

Ported vacuum (Dist.)
Ported vacuum (E.G.R.)
Venturi vacuum
Manifold vacuum
Air
Canister purge
M.P.G. model (Z20 engine)

**DATSUN PICKUP Z-20 M.P.G. ENGINE—EXC. CALIF. AND CANADA**

**295**

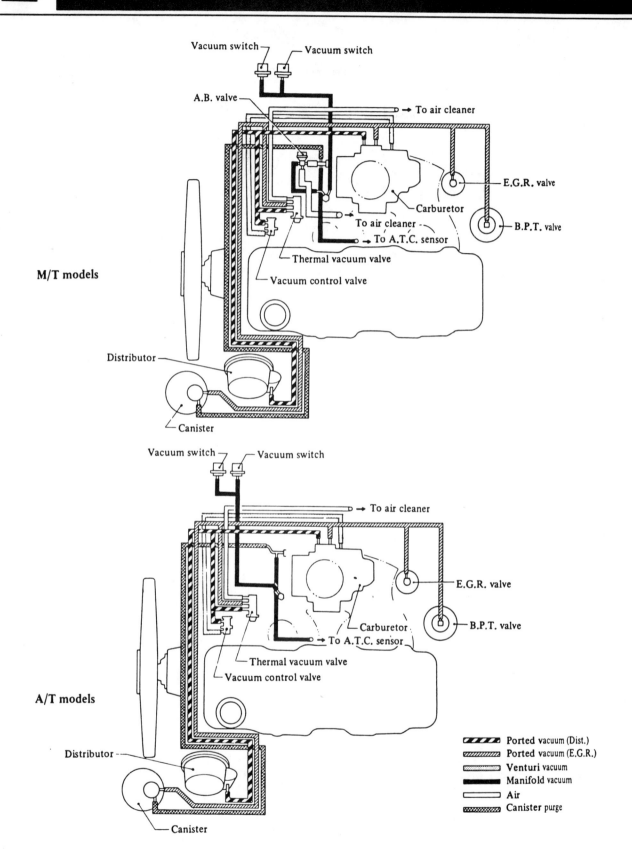

M/T models

A/T models

| | |
|---|---|
| ⬜ | Ported vacuum (Dist.) |
| ⬜ | Ported vacuum (E.G.R.) |
| ⬜ | Venturi vacuum |
| ⬛ | Manifold vacuum |
| ⬜ | Air |
| ⬜ | Canister purge |

**DATSUN PICKUP Z-20 & Z-24 ENGINES—CALIFORNIA**

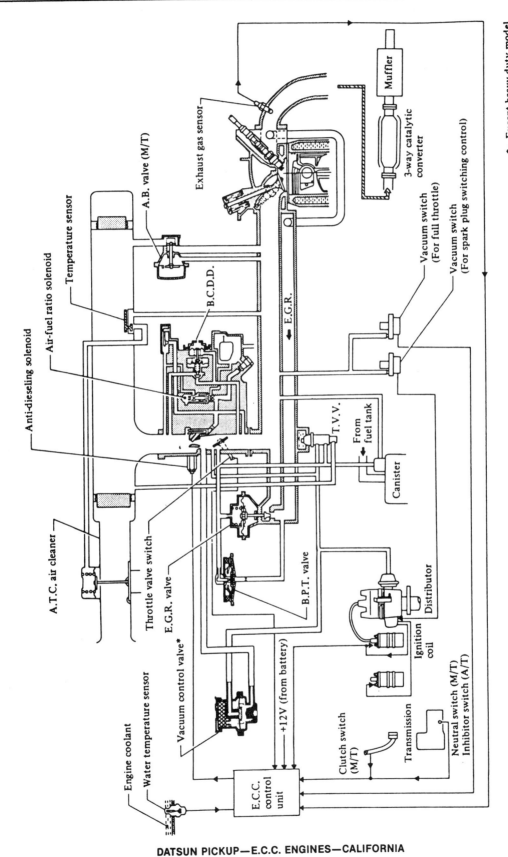

*: Except heavy duty model

DATSUN PICKUP—E.C.C. ENGINES—CALIFORNIA

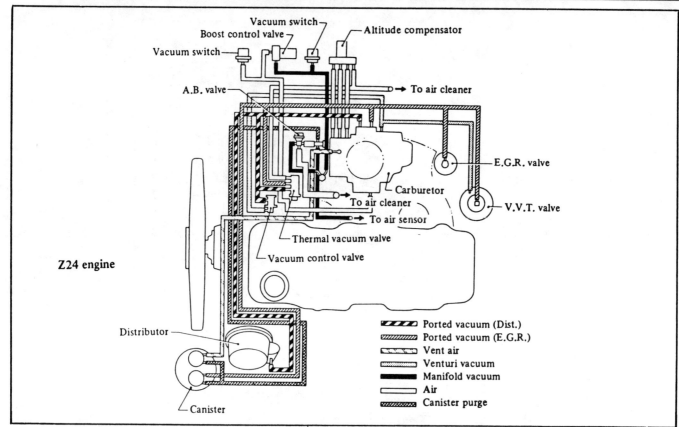

| | |
|---|---|
| Ported vacuum (Dist.) | |
| Ported vacuum (E.G.R.) | |
| Vent air | |
| Venturi vacuum | |
| Manifold vacuum | |
| Air | |
| Canister purge | |

**DATSUN PICKUP Z-24 ENGINE—FEDERAL & HIGH ALT.**

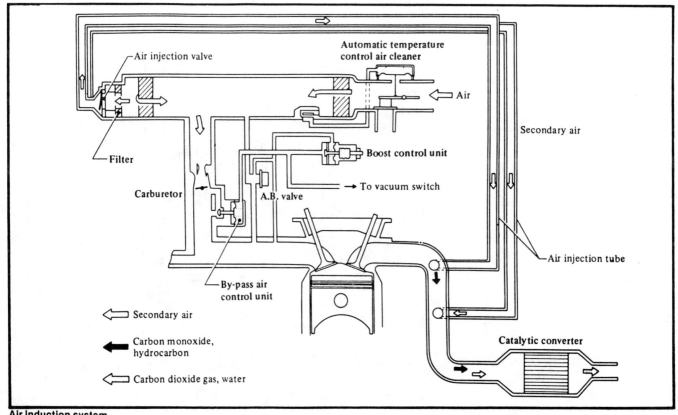

⇨ Secondary air

⬅ Carbon monoxide, hydrocarbon

⇦ Carbon dioxide gas, water

**Air Induction system**

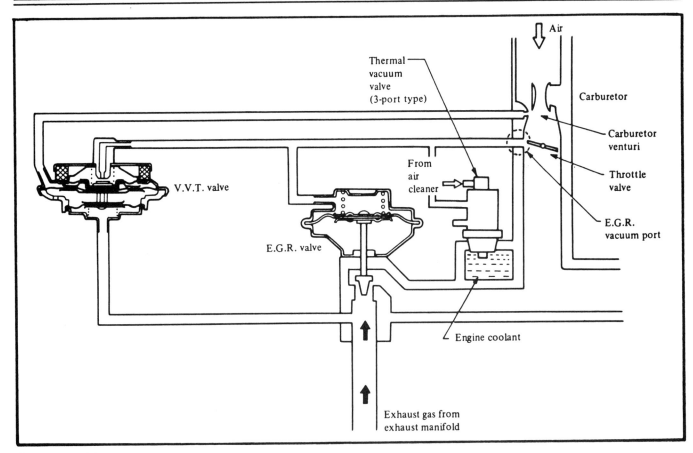

**Gas engine—EGR system**

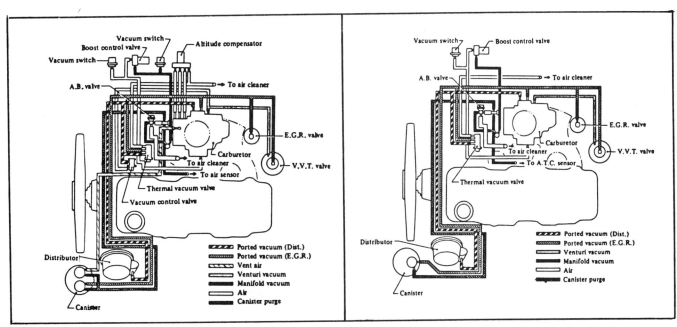

**Vacuum circuits for 1984-86 Z24 engine—Federal models**

**Vacuum circuits for 1984-86 Z20 engine—Federal models**

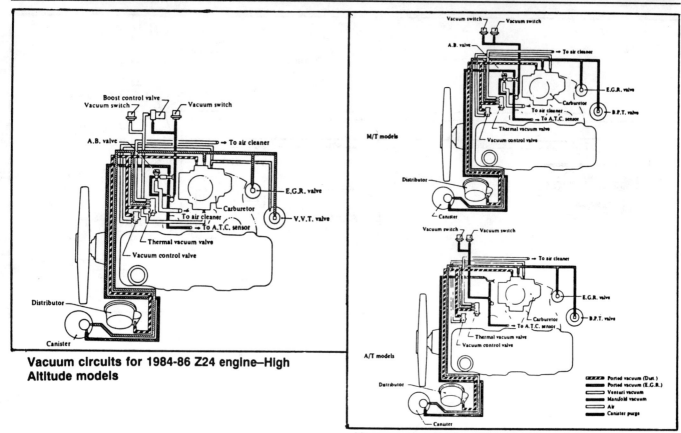

**Vacuum circuits for 1984-86 Z24 engine—High Altitude models**

**Vacuum circuits for 1984-86 Z20 and A24 engines—California models**

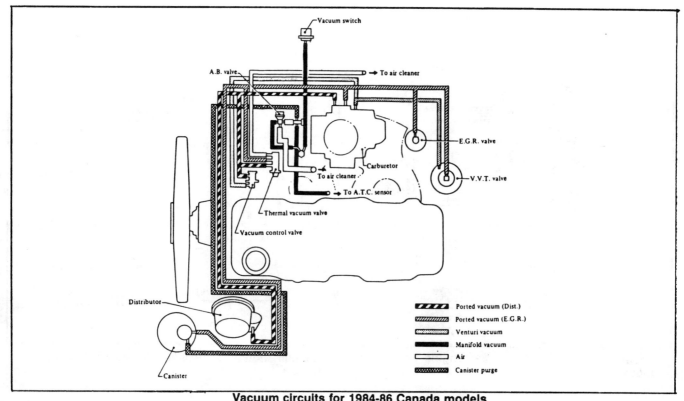

**Vacuum circuits for 1984-86 Canada models**

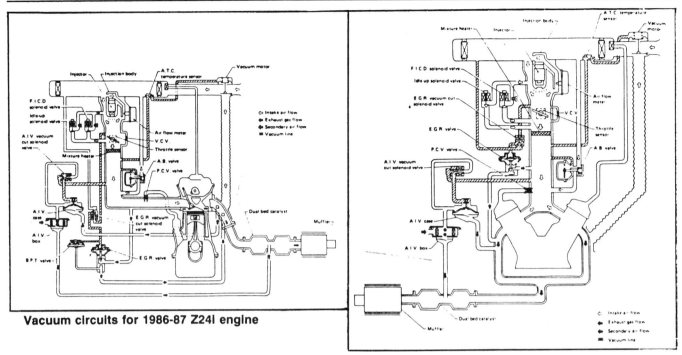

**Vacuum circuits for 1986-87 Z24i engine**

**Vacuum circuits for 1986-87 VG30i engine**

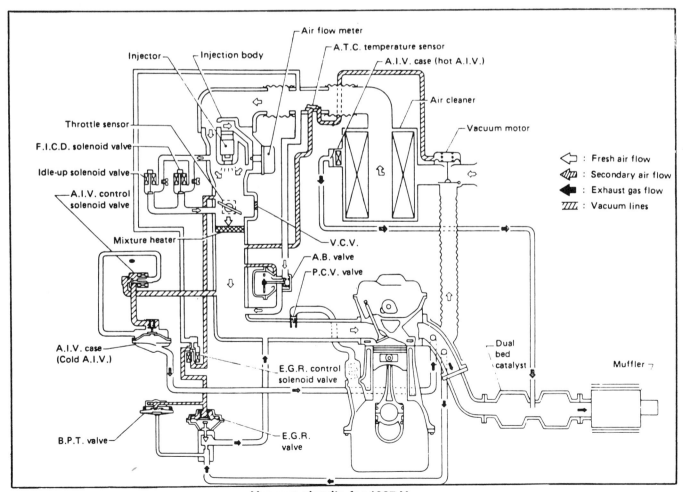

**Vacuum circuits for 1987 Van**

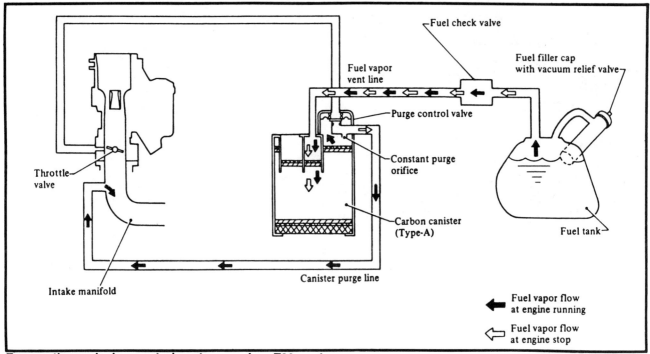

Evaporative emission control system used on Z20 engine

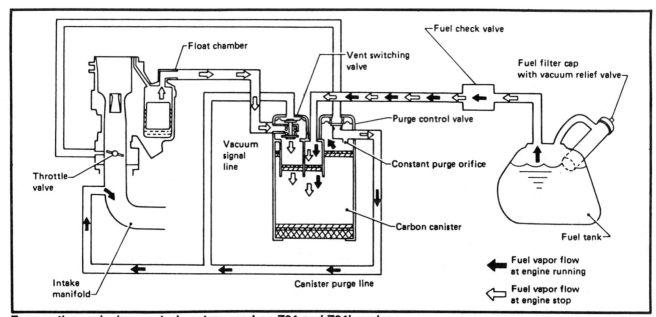

Evaporative emission control system used on Z24 and Z24i engines

# Toyota Pick Up

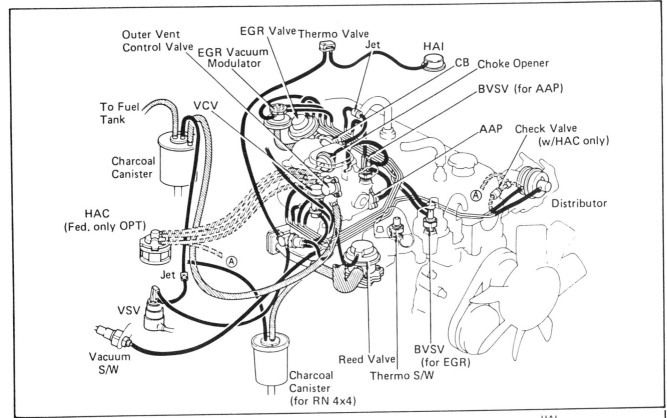

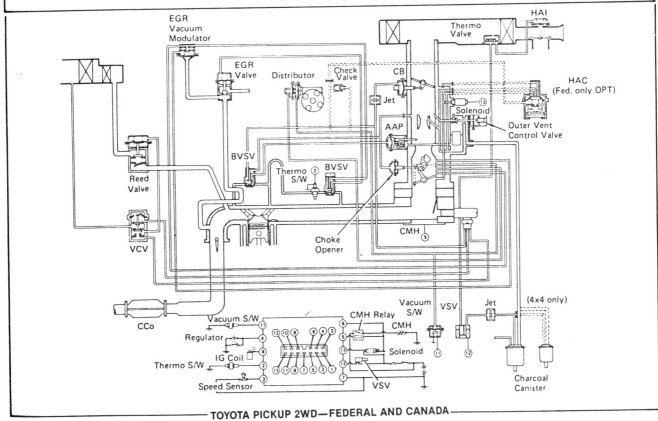

TOYOTA PICKUP 2WD—FEDERAL AND CANADA

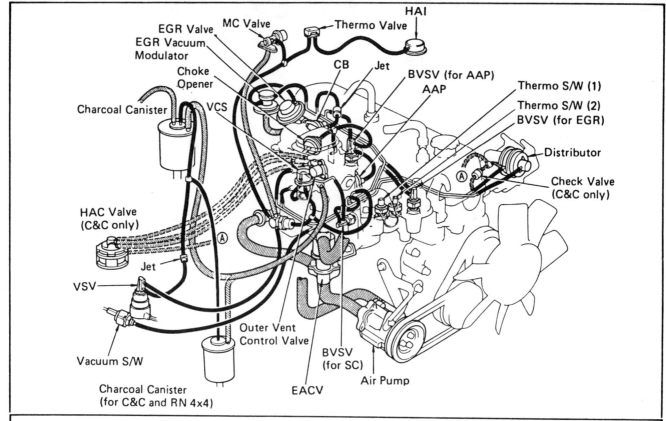

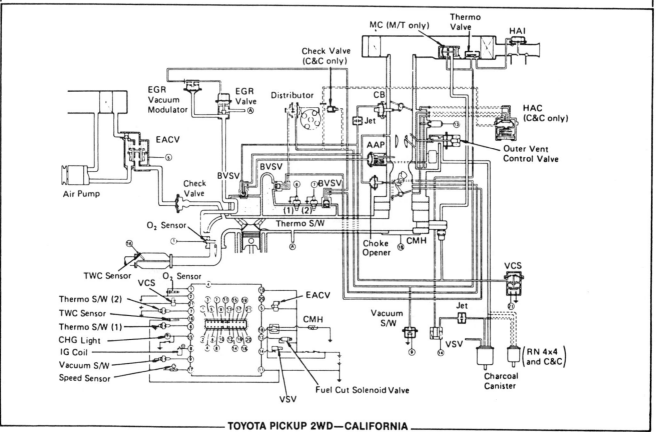

TOYOTA PICKUP 2WD—CALIFORNIA

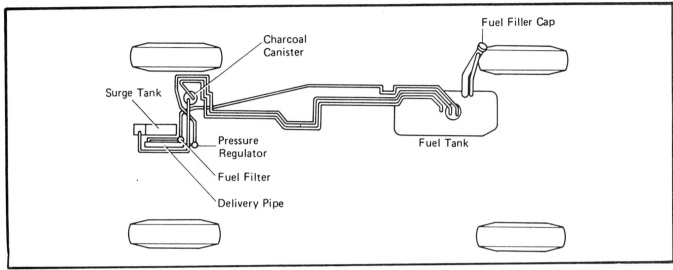

**Fuel Evaporative Emission Control System (EVAP)—Pick-up (EFI)**

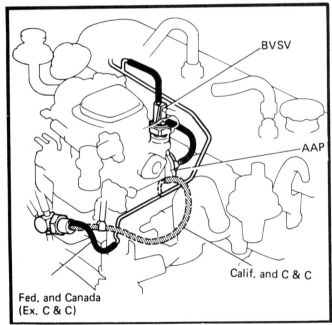

**Auxiliary Accelerator Pump (AAP) System—Pick-up (Carb.)**

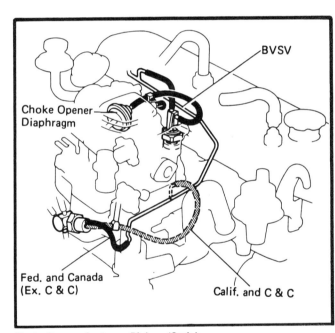

**Choke Opener System—Pick-up (Carb.)**

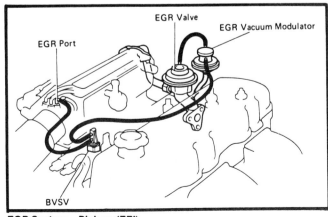

**EGR System—Pick-up (EFI)**

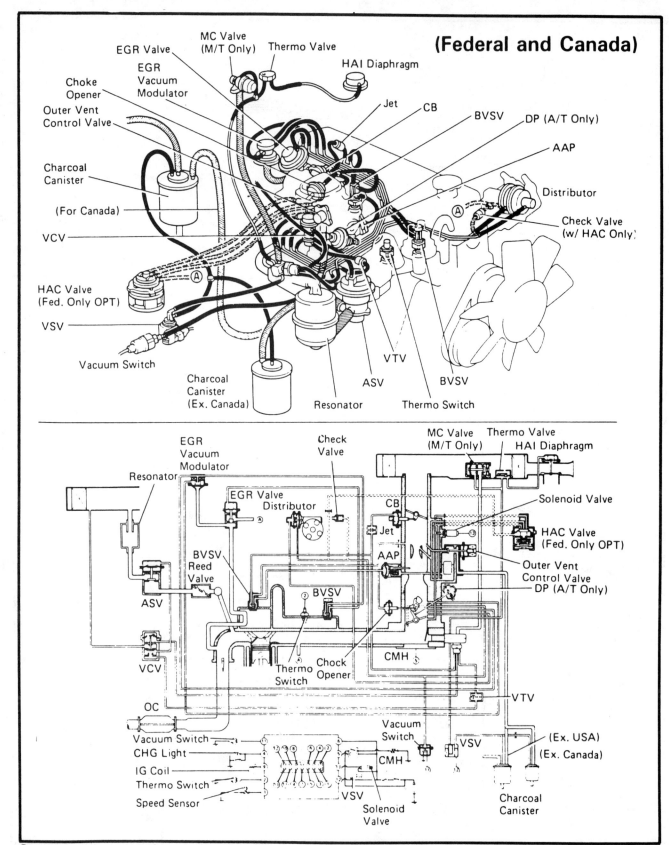

**(Federal and Canada)**

EGR Valve

MC Valve (M/T Only)

Thermo Valve

HAI Diaphragm

EGR Vacuum Modulator

Choke Opener

Outer Vent Control Valve

Jet

CB

BVSV

DP (A/T Only)

AAP

Charcoal Canister

(For Canada)

Distributor

Check Valve (w/ HAC Only)

VCV

HAC Valve (Fed. Only OPT)

VSV

Vacuum Switch

Charcoal Canister (Ex. Canada)

Resonator

ASV

VTV

BVSV

Thermo Switch

EGR Vacuum Modulator

Check Valve

MC Valve (M/T Only)

Thermo Valve

HAI Diaphragm

Resonator

EGR Valve

Distributor

CB

Jet

Solenoid Valve

HAC Valve (Fed. Only OPT)

AAP

BVSV Reed Valve

Outer Vent Control Valve

DP (A/T Only)

ASV

BVSV

VCV

Thermo Switch

Chock Opener

CMH

OC

VTV

Vacuum Switch

CHG Light

IG Coil

Thermo Switch

Speed Sensor

Vacuum Switch

CMH

VSV

Solenoid Valve

VSV

(Ex. USA)

(Ex. Canada)

Charcoal Canister

**Component layout and vacuum schematic for the 1984 and later Trucks and 4Runner**

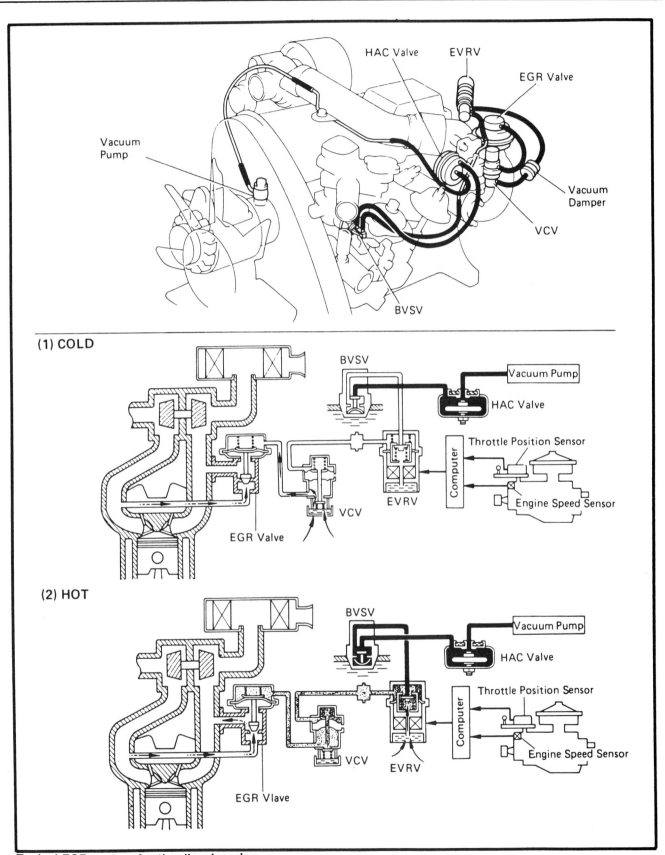

HAC Valve

EVRV

EGR Valve

Vacuum Pump

Vacuum Damper

VCV

BVSV

**(1) COLD**

BVSV

Vacuum Pump

HAC Valve

Throttle Position Sensor

Computer

Engine Speed Sensor

EVRV

EGR Valve

VCV

**(2) HOT**

BVSV

Vacuum Pump

HAC Valve

Throttle Position Sensor

Computer

Engine Speed Sensor

VCV

EVRV

EGR Vlave

**Typical EGR system for the diesel engine**

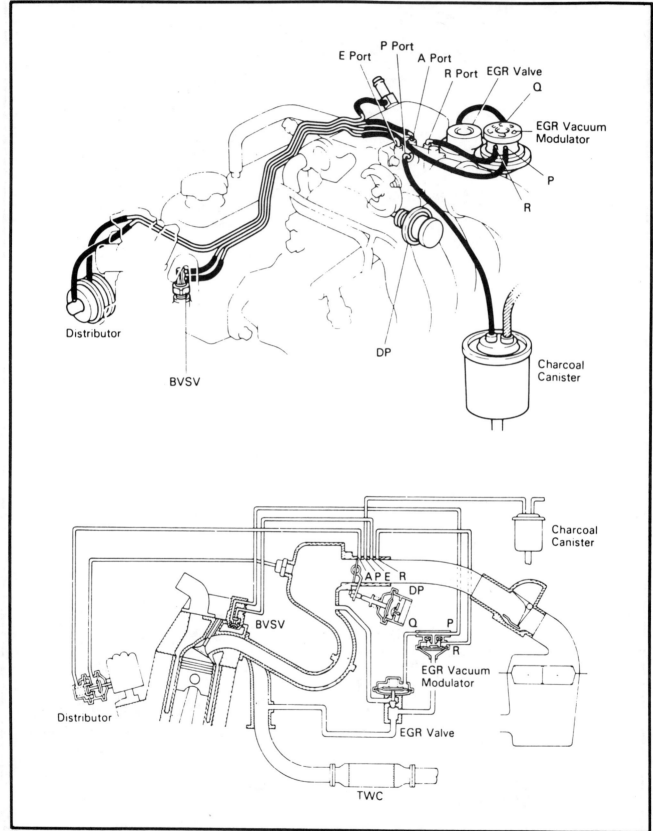

Component layout and vacuum schematic for the 1984 and later Van

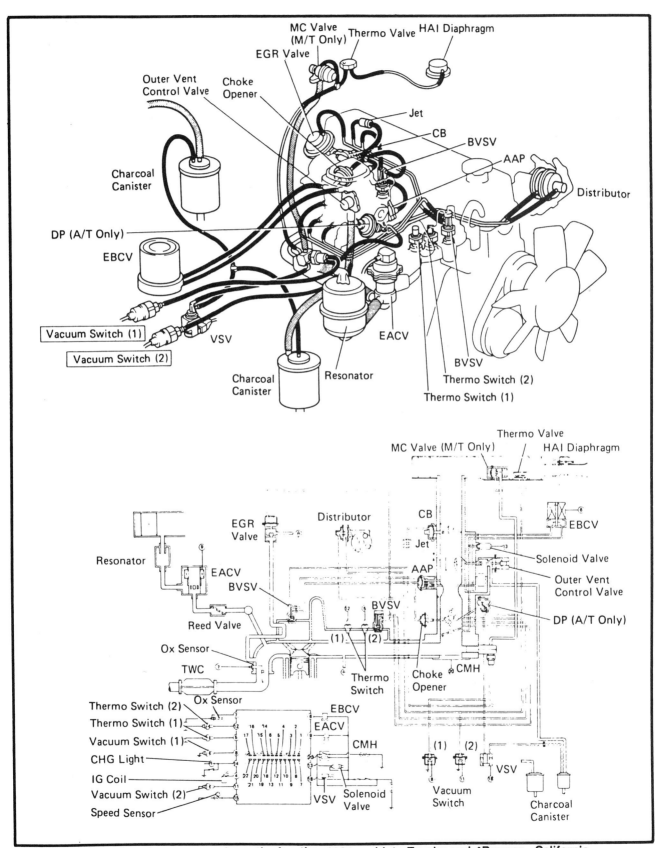

Component layout and vacuum schematic for the 1984 and laterTrucks and 4Runner—California

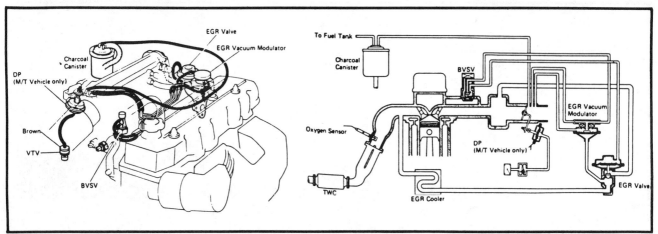

Component layout and vacuum schematic for the 1985 and later Trucks and 4Runner—22R-E engine

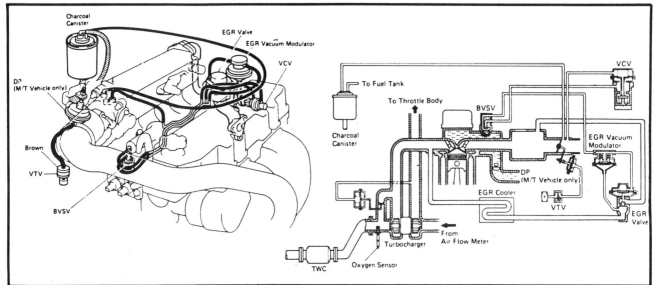

Component layout and vacuum schematic for the 1985 and later Trucks and 4Runner—22R-ET engine

# Mechanics' Data

## SI METRIC TABLES

The following tables are given in SI (International System) metric units. SI units replace both customary (English) and the older gavimetric units. The use of SI units as a new worldwide standard was set by the International Committee of Weights and Measures in 1960. SI has since been adopted by most countries as their national standard.

These tables are general conversion tables which will allow you to convert customary units, which appear in the text, into SI units.

The following are a list of SI units and the customary units, used in this book, which they replace:

| To measure: | Use SI units: | Which replace (customary units): |
|---|---|---|
| mass | kilograms (kg) | pounds (lbs) |
| temperature | Celsius (°C) | Fahrenheit (°F) |
| length | millimeters (mm) | inches (in.) |
| force | newtons (N) | pounds force (lbs) |
| capacities | liters (l) | pints/quarts/gallons (pts/qts/gals) |
| torque | newton-meters (N·m) | foot pounds (ft lbs) |
| pressure | kilopascals (kPa) | pounds per square inch (psi) |
| volume | cubic centimeters (cm³) | cubic inches (cu in.) |
| power | kilowatts (kW) | horsepower (hp) |

If you have had any prior experience with the metric system, you may have noticed units in this chart which are not familiar to you. This is because, in some cases, SI units differ from the older gravimetric units which they replace. For example, newtons (N) replace kilograms (kg) as a force unit, kilopascals (kPa) replace atmos- pheres or bars as a unit of pressure, and, although the units are the same, the name Celsius replaces centigrade for temperature measurement.

If you are not using the SI tables, have a look at them anyway; you will be seeing a lot more of them in the future.

# MECHANIC'S DATA

## ENGLISH TO METRIC CONVERSION: MASS (WEIGHT)

Current mass measurement is expressed in pounds and ounces (lbs. & ozs.). The metric unit of mass (or weight) is the kilogram (kg). Even although this table does not show conversion of masses (weights) larger than 15 lbs, it is easy to calculate larger units by following the data immediately below.

To convert ounces (oz.) to grams (g): multiply th number of ozs. by 28
To convert grams (g) to ounces (oz.): multiply the number of grams by .035

To convert pounds (lbs.) to kilograms (kg): multiply the number of lbs. by .45
To convert kilograms (kg) to pounds (lbs.): multiply the number of kilograms by 2.2

| lbs | kg | lbs | kg | oz | kg | oz | kg |
|-----|------|-----|-----|-----|-------|-----|-------|
| 0.1 | 0.04 | 0.9 | 0.41 | 0.1 | 0.003 | 0.9 | 0.024 |
| 0.2 | 0.09 | 1 | 0.4 | 0.2 | 0.005 | 1 | 0.03 |
| 0.3 | 0.14 | 2 | 0.9 | 0.3 | 0.008 | 2 | 0.06 |
| 0.4 | 0.18 | 3 | 1.4 | 0.4 | 0.011 | 3 | 0.08 |
| 0.5 | 0.23 | 4 | 1.8 | 0.5 | 0.014 | 4 | 0.11 |
| 0.6 | 0.27 | 5 | 2.3 | 0.6 | 0.017 | 5 | 0.14 |
| 0.7 | 0.32 | 10 | 4.5 | 0.7 | 0.020 | 10 | 0.28 |
| 0.8 | 0.36 | 15 | 6.8 | 0.8 | 0.023 | 15 | 0.42 |

## ENGLISH TO METRIC CONVERSION: TEMPERATURE

To convert Fahrenheit (°F) to Celsius (°C): take number of °F and subtract 32; multiply result by 5; divide result by 9

To convert Celsius (°C) to Fahrenheit (°F): take number of °C and multiply by 9; divide result by 5; add 32 to total

| Fahrenheit (F) | Celsius (C) | | | Fahrenheit (F) | Celsius (C) | | | Fahrenheit (F) | Celsius (C) | | |
|------|------|------|------|------|------|------|------|------|-------|------|------|
| °F | °C | °C | °F | °F | °C | °C | °F | °F | °C | °C | °F |
| −40 | −40 | −38 | −36.4 | 80 | 26.7 | 18 | 64.4 | 215 | 101.7 | 80 | 176 |
| −35 | −37.2 | −36 | −32.8 | 85 | 29.4 | 20 | 68 | 220 | 104.4 | 85 | 185 |
| −30 | −34.4 | −34 | −29.2 | 90 | 32.2 | 22 | 71.6 | 225 | 107.2 | 90 | 194 |
| −25 | −31.7 | −32 | −25.6 | 95 | 35.0 | 24 | 75.2 | 230 | 110.0 | 95 | 202 |
| −20 | −28.9 | −30 | −22 | 100 | 37.8 | 26 | 78.8 | 235 | 112.8 | 100 | 212 |
| −15 | −26.1 | −28 | −18.4 | 105 | 40.6 | 28 | 82.4 | 240 | 115.6 | 105 | 221 |
| −10 | −23.3 | −26 | −14.8 | 110 | 43.3 | 30 | 86 | 245 | 118.3 | 110 | 230 |
| −5 | −20.6 | −24 | −11.2 | 115 | 46.1 | 32 | 89.6 | 250 | 121.1 | 115 | 239 |
| 0 | −17.8 | −22 | −7.6 | 120 | 48.9 | 34 | 93.2 | 255 | 123.9 | 120 | 248 |
| 1 | −17.2 | −20 | −4 | 125 | 51.7 | 36 | 96.8 | 260 | 126.6 | 125 | 257 |
| 2 | −16.7 | −18 | −0.4 | 130 | 54.4 | 38 | 100.4 | 265 | 129.4 | 130 | 266 |
| 3 | −16.1 | −16 | 3.2 | 135 | 57.2 | 40 | 104 | 270 | 132.2 | 135 | 275 |
| 4 | −15.6 | −14 | 6.8 | 140 | 60.0 | 42 | 107.6 | 275 | 135.0 | 140 | 284 |
| 5 | −15.0 | −12 | 10.4 | 145 | 62.8 | 44 | 112.2 | 280 | 137.8 | 145 | 293 |
| 10 | −12.2 | −10 | 14 | 150 | 65.6 | 46 | 114.8 | 285 | 140.6 | 150 | 302 |
| 15 | −9.4 | −8 | 17.6 | 155 | 68.3 | 48 | 118.4 | 290 | 143.3 | 155 | 311 |
| 20 | −6.7 | −6 | 21.2 | 160 | 71.1 | 50 | 122 | 295 | 146.1 | 160 | 320 |
| 25 | −3.9 | −4 | 24.8 | 165 | 73.9 | 52 | 125.6 | 300 | 148.9 | 165 | 329 |
| 30 | −1.1 | −2 | 28.4 | 170 | 76.7 | 54 | 129.2 | 305 | 151.7 | 170 | 338 |
| 35 | 1.7 | 0 | 32 | 175 | 79.4 | 56 | 132.8 | 310 | 154.4 | 175 | 347 |
| 40 | 4.4 | 2 | 35.6 | 180 | 82.2 | 58 | 136.4 | 315 | 157.2 | 180 | 356 |
| 45 | 7.2 | 4 | 39.2 | 185 | 85.0 | 60 | 140 | 320 | 160.0 | 185 | 365 |
| 50 | 10.0 | 6 | 42.8 | 190 | 87.8 | 62 | 143.6 | 325 | 162.8 | 190 | 374 |
| 55 | 12.8 | 8 | 46.4 | 195 | 90.6 | 64 | 147.2 | 330 | 165.6 | 195 | 383 |
| 60 | 15.6 | 10 | 50 | 200 | 93.3 | 66 | 150.8 | 335 | 168.3 | 200 | 392 |
| 65 | 18.3 | 12 | 53.6 | 205 | 96.1 | 68 | 154.4 | 340 | 171.1 | 205 | 401 |
| 70 | 21.1 | 14 | 57.2 | 210 | 98.9 | 70 | 158 | 345 | 173.9 | 210 | 410 |
| 75 | 23.9 | 16 | 60.8 | 212 | 100.0 | 75 | 167 | 350 | 176.7 | 215 | 414 |

## ENGLISH TO METRIC CONVERSION: LENGTH

To convert inches (ins.) to millimeters (mm): multiply number of inches by 25.4

To convert millimeters (mm) to inches (ins.): multiply number of millimeters by .04

| Inches | Decimals | Milli-meters | Inches to millimeters inches | mm | Inches | Decimals | Milli-meters | Inches to millimeters inches | mm |
|---|---|---|---|---|---|---|---|---|---|
| 1/64 | 0.051625 | 0.3969 | 0.0001 | 0.00254 | 33/64 | 0.515625 | 13.0969 | 0.6 | 15.24 |
| 1/32 | 0.03125 | 0.7937 | 0.0002 | 0.00508 | 17/32 | 0.53125 | 13.4937 | 0.7 | 17.78 |
| 3/64 | 0.046875 | 1.1906 | 0.0003 | 0.00762 | 35/64 | 0.546875 | 13.8906 | 0.8 | 20.32 |
| 1/16 | 0.0625 | 1.5875 | 0.0004 | 0.01016 | 9/16 | 0.5625 | 14.2875 | 0.9 | 22.86 |
| 5/64 | 0.078125 | 1.9844 | 0.0005 | 0.01270 | 37/64 | 0.578125 | 14.6844 | 1 | 25.4 |
| 3/32 | 0.09375 | 2.3812 | 0.0006 | 0.01524 | 19/32 | 0.59375 | 15.0812 | 2 | 50.8 |
| 7/64 | 0.109375 | 2.7781 | 0.0007 | 0.01778 | 39/64 | 0.609375 | 15.4781 | 3 | 76.2 |
| 1/8 | 0.125 | 3.1750 | 0.0008 | 0.02032 | 5/8 | 0.625 | 15.8750 | 4 | 101.6 |
| 9/64 | 0.140625 | 3.5719 | 0.0009 | 0.02286 | 41/64 | 0.640625 | 16.2719 | 5 | 127.0 |
| 5/32 | 0.15625 | 3.9687 | 0.001 | 0.0254 | 21/32 | 0.65625 | 16.6687 | 6 | 152.4 |
| 11/64 | 0.171875 | 4.3656 | 0.002 | 0.0508 | 43/64 | 0.671875 | 17.0656 | 7 | 177.8 |
| 3/16 | 0.1875 | 4.7625 | 0.003 | 0.0762 | 11/16 | 0.6875 | 17.4625 | 8 | 203.2 |
| 13/64 | 0.203125 | 5.1594 | 0.004 | 0.1016 | 45/64 | 0.703125 | 17.8594 | 9 | 228.6 |
| 7/32 | 0.21875 | 5.5562 | 0.005 | 0.1270 | 23/32 | 0.71875 | 18.2562 | 10 | 254.0 |
| 15/64 | 0.234375 | 5.9531 | 0.006 | 0.1524 | 47/64 | 0.734375 | 18.6531 | 11 | 279.4 |
| 1/4 | 0.25 | 6.3500 | 0.007 | 0.1778 | 3/4 | 0.75 | 19.0500 | 12 | 304.8 |
| 17/64 | 0.265625 | 6.7469 | 0.008 | 0.2032 | 49/64 | 0.765625 | 19.4469 | 13 | 330.2 |
| 9/32 | 0.28125 | 7.1437 | 0.009 | 0.2286 | 25/32 | 0.78125 | 19.8437 | 14 | 355.6 |
| 19/64 | 0.296875 | 7.5406 | 0.01 | 0.254 | 51/64 | 0.796875 | 20.2406 | 15 | 381.0 |
| 5/16 | 0.3125 | 7.9375 | 0.02 | 0.508 | 13/16 | 0.8125 | 20.6375 | 16 | 406.4 |
| 21/64 | 0.328125 | 8.3344 | 0.03 | 0.762 | 53/64 | 0.828125 | 21.0344 | 17 | 431.8 |
| 11/32 | 0.34375 | 8.7312 | 0.04 | 1.016 | 27/32 | 0.84375 | 21.4312 | 18 | 457.2 |
| 23/64 | 0.359375 | 9.1281 | 0.05 | 1.270 | 55/64 | 0.859375 | 21.8281 | 19 | 482.6 |
| 3/8 | 0.375 | 9.5250 | 0.06 | 1.524 | 7/8 | 0.875 | 22.2250 | 20 | 508.0 |
| 25/64 | 0.390625 | 9.9219 | 0.07 | 1.778 | 57/64 | 0.890625 | 22.6219 | 21 | 533.4 |
| 13/32 | 0.40625 | 10.3187 | 0.08 | 2.032 | 29/32 | 0.90625 | 23.0187 | 22 | 558.8 |
| 27/64 | 0.421875 | 10.7156 | 0.09 | 2.286 | 59/64 | 0.921875 | 23.4156 | 23 | 584.2 |
| 7/16 | 0.4375 | 11.1125 | 0.1 | 2.54 | 15/16 | 0.9375 | 23.8125 | 24 | 609.6 |
| 29/64 | 0.453125 | 11.5094 | 0.2 | 5.08 | 61/64 | 0.953125 | 24.2094 | 25 | 635.0 |
| 15/32 | 0.46875 | 11.9062 | 0.3 | 7.62 | 31/32 | 0.96875 | 24.6062 | 26 | 660.4 |
| 31/64 | 0.484375 | 12.3031 | 0.4 | 10.16 | 63/64 | 0.984375 | 25.0031 | 27 | 690.6 |
| 1/2 | 0.5 | 12.7000 | 0.5 | 12.70 | | | | | |

## ENGLISH TO METRIC CONVERSION: TORQUE

To convert foot-pounds (ft. lbs.) to Newton-meters: multiply the number of ft. lbs. by 1.3

To convert inch-pounds (in. lbs.) to Newton-meters: multiply the number of in. lbs. by .11

| in lbs | N·m | in lbs | N·m | in lbs | N·m | in lbs | N·m | in lbs | N·m |
|---|---|---|---|---|---|---|---|---|---|
| 0.1 | 0.01 | 1 | 0.11 | 10 | 1.13 | 19 | 2.15 | 28 | 3.16 |
| 0.2 | 0.02 | 2 | 0.23 | 11 | 1.24 | 20 | 2.26 | 29 | 3.28 |
| 0.3 | 0.03 | 3 | 0.34 | 12 | 1.36 | 21 | 2.37 | 30 | 3.39 |
| 0.4 | 0.04 | 4 | 0.45 | 13 | 1.47 | 22 | 2.49 | 31 | 3.50 |
| 0.5 | 0.06 | 5 | 0.56 | 14 | 1.58 | 23 | 2.60 | 32 | 3.62 |
| 0.6 | 0.07 | 6 | 0.68 | 15 | 1.70 | 24 | 2.71 | 33 | 3.73 |
| 0.7 | 0.08 | 7 | 0.78 | 16 | 1.81 | 25 | 2.82 | 34 | 3.84 |
| 0.8 | 0.09 | 8 | 0.90 | 17 | 1.92 | 26 | 2.94 | 35 | 3.95 |
| 0.9 | 0.10 | 9 | 1.02 | 18 | 2.03 | 27 | 3.05 | 36 | 4.0/ |

## ENGLISH TO METRIC CONVERSION: TORQUE

Torque is now expressed as either foot-pounds (ft./lbs.) or inch-pounds (in./lbs.). The metric measurement unit for torque is the Newton-meter (Nm). This unit—the Nm—will be used for all SI metric torque references, both the present ft./lbs. and in./lbs.

| ft lbs | N-m | ft lbs | N-m | ft lbs | N-m | ft lbs | N-m |
|--------|-----|--------|-----|--------|-----|--------|-----|
| 0.1 | 0.1 | 33 | 44.7 | 74 | 100.3 | 115 | 155.9 |
| 0.2 | 0.3 | 34 | 46.1 | 75 | 101.7 | 116 | 157.3 |
| 0.3 | 0.4 | 35 | 47.4 | 76 | 103.0 | 117 | 158.6 |
| 0.4 | 0.5 | 36 | 48.8 | 77 | 104.4 | 118 | 160.0 |
| 0.5 | 0.7 | 37 | 50.7 | 78 | 105.8 | 119 | 161.3 |
| 0.6 | 0.8 | 38 | 51.5 | 79 | 107.1 | 120 | 162.7 |
| 0.7 | 1.0 | 39 | 52.9 | 80 | 108.5 | 121 | 164.0 |
| 0.8 | 1.1 | 40 | 54.2 | 81 | 109.8 | 122 | 165.4 |
| 0.9 | 1.2 | 41 | 55.6 | 82 | 111.2 | 123 | 166.8 |
| 1 | 1.3 | 42 | 56.9 | 83 | 112.5 | 124 | 168.1 |
| 2 | 2.7 | 43 | 58.3 | 84 | 113.9 | 125 | 169.5 |
| 3 | 4.1 | 44 | 59.7 | 85 | 115.2 | 126 | 170.8 |
| 4 | 5.4 | 45 | 61.0 | 86 | 116.6 | 127 | 172.2 |
| 5 | 6.8 | 46 | 62.4 | 87 | 118.0 | 128 | 173.5 |
| 6 | 8.1 | 47 | 63.7 | 88 | 119.3 | 129 | 174.9 |
| 7 | 9.5 | 48 | 65.1 | 89 | 120.7 | 130 | 176.2 |
| 8 | 10.8 | 49 | 66.4 | 90 | 122.0 | 131 | 177.6 |
| 9 | 12.2 | 50 | 67.8 | 91 | 123.4 | 132 | 179.0 |
| 10 | 13.6 | 51 | 69.2 | 92 | 124.7 | 133 | 180.3 |
| 11 | 14.9 | 52 | 70.5 | 93 | 126.1 | 134 | 181.7 |
| 12 | 16.3 | 53 | 71.9 | 94 | 127.4 | 135 | 183.0 |
| 13 | 17.6 | 54 | 73.2 | 95 | 128.8 | 136 | 184.4 |
| 14 | 18.9 | 55 | 74.6 | 96 | 130.2 | 137 | 185.7 |
| 15 | 20.3 | 56 | 75.9 | 97 | 131.5 | 138 | 187.1 |
| 16 | 21.7 | 57 | 77.3 | 98 | 132.9 | 139 | 188.5 |
| 17 | 23.0 | 58 | 78.6 | 99 | 134.2 | 140 | 189.8 |
| 18 | 24.4 | 59 | 80.0 | 100 | 135.6 | 141 | 191.2 |
| 19 | 25.8 | 60 | 81.4 | 101 | 136.9 | 142 | 192.5 |
| 20 | 27.1 | 61 | 82.7 | 102 | 138.3 | 143 | 193.9 |
| 21 | 28.5 | 62 | 84.1 | 103 | 139.6 | 144 | 195.2 |
| 22 | 29.8 | 63 | 85.4 | 104 | 141.0 | 145 | 196.6 |
| 23 | 31.2 | 64 | 86.8 | 105 | 142.4 | 146 | 198.0 |
| 24 | 32.5 | 65 | 88.1 | 106 | 143.7 | 147 | 199.3 |
| 25 | 33.9 | 66 | 89.5 | 107 | 145.1 | 148 | 200.7 |
| 26 | 35.2 | 67 | 90.8 | 108 | 146.4 | 149 | 202.0 |
| 27 | 36.6 | 68 | 92.2 | 109 | 147.8 | 150 | 203.4 |
| 28 | 38.0 | 69 | 93.6 | 110 | 149.1 | 151 | 204.7 |
| 29 | 39.3 | 70 | 94.9 | 111 | 150.5 | 152 | 206.1 |
| 30 | 40.7 | 71 | 96.3 | 112 | 151.8 | 153 | 207.4 |
| 31 | 42.0 | 72 | 97.6 | 113 | 153.2 | 154 | 208.8 |
| 32 | 43.4 | 73 | 99.0 | 114 | 154.6 | 155 | 210.2 |

## ENGLISH TO METRIC CONVERSION: FORCE

Force is presently measured in pounds (lbs.). This type of measurement is used to measure spring pressure, specifically how many pounds it takes to compress a spring. Our present force unit (the pound) will be replaced in SI metric measurements by the Newton (N). This term will eventually see use in specifications for electric motor brush spring pressures, valve spring pressures, etc.

To convert pounds (lbs.) to Newton (N): multiply the number of lbs. by **4.45**

| lbs | N | lbs | N | lbs | N | oz | N |
|---|---|---|---|---|---|---|---|
| 0.01 | 0.04 | 21 | 93.4 | 59 | 262.4 | 1 | 0.3 |
| 0.02 | 0.09 | 22 | 97.9 | 60 | 266.9 | 2 | 0.6 |
| 0.03 | 0.13 | 23 | 102.3 | 61 | 271.3 | 3 | 0.8 |
| 0.04 | 0.18 | 24 | 106.8 | 62 | 275.8 | 4 | 1.1 |
| 0.05 | 0.22 | 25 | 111.2 | 63 | 280.2 | 5 | 1.4 |
| 0.06 | 0.27 | 26 | 115.6 | 64 | 284.6 | 6 | 1.7 |
| 0.07 | 0.31 | 27 | 120.1 | 65 | 289.1 | 7 | 2.0 |
| 0.08 | 0.36 | 28 | 124.6 | 66 | 293.6 | 8 | 2.2 |
| 0.09 | 0.40 | 29 | 129.0 | 67 | 298.0 | 9 | 2.5 |
| 0.1 | 0.4 | 30 | 133.4 | 68 | 302.5 | 10 | 2.8 |
| 0.2 | 0.9 | 31 | 137.9 | 69 | 306.9 | 11 | 3.1 |
| 0.3 | 1.3 | 32 | 142.3 | 70 | 311.4 | 12 | 3.3 |
| 0.4 | 1.8 | 33 | 146.8 | 71 | 315.8 | 13 | 3.6 |
| 0.5 | 2.2 | 34 | 151.2 | 72 | 320.3 | 14 | 3.9 |
| 0.6 | 2.7 | 35 | 155.7 | 73 | 324.7 | 15 | 4.2 |
| 0.7 | 3.1 | 36 | 160.1 | 74 | 329.2 | 16 | 4.4 |
| 0.8 | 3.6 | 37 | 164.6 | 75 | 333.6 | 17 | 4.7 |
| 0.9 | 4.0 | 38 | 169.0 | 76 | 338.1 | 18 | 5.0 |
| 1 | 4.4 | 39 | 173.5 | 77 | 342.5 | 19 | 5.3 |
| 2 | 8.9 | 40 | 177.9 | 78 | 347.0 | 20 | 5.6 |
| 3 | 13.4 | 41 | 182.4 | 79 | 351.4 | 21 | 5.8 |
| 4 | 17.8 | 42 | 186.8 | 80 | 355.9 | 22 | 6.1 |
| 5 | 22.2 | 43 | 191.3 | 81 | 360.3 | 23 | 6.4 |
| 6 | 26.7 | 44 | 195.7 | 82 | 364.8 | 24 | 6.7 |
| 7 | 31.1 | 45 | 200.2 | 83 | 369.2 | 25 | 7.0 |
| 8 | 35.6 | 46 | 204.6 | 84 | 373.6 | 26 | 7.2 |
| 9 | 40.0 | 47 | 209.1 | 85 | 378.1 | 27 | 7.5 |
| 10 | 44.5 | 48 | 213.5 | 86 | 382.6 | 28 | 7.8 |
| 11 | 48.9 | 49 | 218.0 | 87 | 387.0 | 29 | 8.1 |
| 12 | 53.4 | 50 | 224.4 | 88 | 391.4 | 30 | 8.3 |
| 13 | 57.8 | 51 | 226.9 | 89 | 395.9 | 31 | 8.6 |
| 14 | 62.3 | 52 | 231.3 | 90 | 400.3 | 32 | 8.9 |
| 15 | 66.7 | 53 | 235.8 | 91 | 404.8 | 33 | 9.2 |
| 16 | 71.2 | 54 | 240.2 | 92 | 409.2 | 34 | 9.4 |
| 17 | 75.6 | 55 | 244.6 | 93 | 413.7 | 35 | 9.7 |
| 18 | 80.1 | 56 | 249.1 | 94 | 418.1 | 36 | 10.0 |
| 19 | 84.5 | 57 | 253.6 | 95 | 422.6 | 37 | 10.3 |
| 20 | 89.0 | 58 | 258.0 | 96 | 427.0 | 38 | 10.6 |

**MECHANIC'S DATA**

## ENGLISH TO METRIC CONVERSION: LIQUID CAPACITY

Liquid or fluid capacity is presently expressed as pints, quarts or gallons, or a combination of all of these. In the metric system the liter (I) will become the basic unit. Fractions of a liter would be expressed as deciliters, centiliters, or most frequently (and commonly) as milliliters.

To convert pints (pts.) to liters (I): multiply the number of pints by .47
To convert liters (I) to pints (pts.): multiply the number of liters by 2.1
To convert quarts (qts.) to liters (I): multiply the number of quarts by .95

To convert liters (I) to quarts (qts.): multiply the number of liters by 1.06
To convert gallons (gals.) to liters (I): multiply the number of gallons by 3.8
To convert liters (I) to gallons (gals.): multiply the number of liters by .26

| gals | liters | qts | liters | pts | liters |
|------|--------|-----|--------|-----|--------|
| 0.1 | 0.38 | 0.1 | 0.10 | 0.1 | 0.05 |
| 0.2 | 0.76 | 0.2 | 0.19 | 0.2 | 0.10 |
| 0.3 | 1.1 | 0.3 | 0.28 | 0.3 | 0.14 |
| 0.4 | 1.5 | 0.4 | 0.38 | 0.4 | 0.19 |
| 0.5 | 1.9 | 0.5 | 0.47 | 0.5 | 0.24 |
| 0.6 | 2.3 | 0.6 | 0.57 | 0.6 | 0.28 |
| 0.7 | 2.6 | 0.7 | 0.66 | 0.7 | 0.33 |
| 0.8 | 3.0 | 0.8 | 0.76 | 0.8 | 0.38 |
| 0.9 | 3.4 | 0.9 | 0.85 | 0.9 | 0.43 |
| 1 | 3.8 | 1 | 1.0 | 1 | 0.5 |
| 2 | 7.6 | 2 | 1.9 | 2 | 1.0 |
| 3 | 11.4 | 3 | 2.8 | 3 | 1.4 |
| 4 | 15.1 | 4 | 3.8 | 4 | 1.9 |
| 5 | 18.9 | 5 | 4.7 | 5 | 2.4 |
| 6 | 22.7 | 6 | 5.7 | 6 | 2.8 |
| 7 | 26.5 | 7 | 6.6 | 7 | 3.3 |
| 8 | 30.3 | 8 | 7.6 | 8 | 3.8 |
| 9 | 34.1 | 9 | 8.5 | 9 | 4.3 |
| 10 | 37.8 | 10 | 9.5 | 10 | 4.7 |
| 11 | 41.6 | 11 | 10.4 | 11 | 5.2 |
| 12 | 45.4 | 12 | 11.4 | 12 | 5.7 |
| 13 | 49.2 | 13 | 12.3 | 13 | 6.2 |
| 14 | 53.0 | 14 | 13.2 | 14 | 6.6 |
| 15 | 56.8 | 15 | 14.2 | 15 | 7.1 |
| 16 | 60.6 | 16 | 15.1 | 16 | 7.6 |
| 17 | 64.3 | 17 | 16.1 | 17 | 8.0 |
| 18 | 68.1 | 18 | 17.0 | 18 | 8.5 |
| 19 | 71.9 | 19 | 18.0 | 19 | 9.0 |
| 20 | 75.7 | 20 | 18.9 | 20 | 9.5 |
| 21 | 79.5 | 21 | 19.9 | 21 | 9.9 |
| 22 | 83.2 | 22 | 20.8 | 22 | 10.4 |
| 23 | 87.0 | 23 | 21.8 | 23 | 10.9 |
| 24 | 90.8 | 24 | 22.7 | 24 | 11.4 |
| 25 | 94.6 | 25 | 23.6 | 25 | 11.8 |
| 26 | 98.4 | 26 | 24.6 | 26 | 12.3 |
| 27 | 102.2 | 27 | 25.5 | 27 | 12.8 |
| 28 | 106.0 | 28 | 26.5 | 28 | 13.2 |
| 29 | 110.0 | 29 | 27.4 | 29 | 13.7 |
| 30 | 113.5 | 30 | 28.4 | 30 | 14.2 |

## ENGLISH TO METRIC CONVERSION: PRESSURE

The basic unit of pressure measurement used today is expressed as pounds per square inch (psi). The metric unit for psi will be the kilopascal (kPa). This will apply to either fluid pressure or air pressure, and will be frequently seen in tire pressure readings, oil pressure specifications, fuel pump pressure, etc.

To convert pounds per square inch (psi) to kilopascals (kPa): multiply the number of psi by 6.89

| Psi | kPa | Psi | kPa | Psi | kPa | Psi | kPa |
|-----|-----|-----|-----|-----|-----|-----|-----|
| 0.1 | 0.7 | 37 | 255.1 | 82 | 565.4 | 127 | 875.6 |
| 0.2 | 1.4 | 38 | 262.0 | 83 | 572.3 | 128 | 882.5 |
| 0.3 | 2.1 | 39 | 268.9 | 84 | 579.2 | 129 | 889.4 |
| 0.4 | 2.8 | 40 | 275.8 | 85 | 586.0 | 130 | 896.3 |
| 0.5 | 3.4 | 41 | 282.7 | 86 | 592.9 | 131 | 903.2 |
| 0.6 | 4.1 | 42 | 289.6 | 87 | 599.8 | 132 | 910.1 |
| 0.7 | 4.8 | 43 | 296.5 | 88 | 606.7 | 133 | 917.0 |
| 0.8 | 5.5 | 44 | 303.4 | 89 | 613.6 | 134 | 923.9 |
| 0.9 | 6.2 | 45 | 310.3 | 90 | 620.5 | 135 | 930.8 |
| 1 | 6.9 | 46 | 317.2 | 91 | 627.4 | 136 | 937.7 |
| 2 | 13.8 | 47 | 324.0 | 92 | 634.3 | 137 | 944.6 |
| 3 | 20.7 | 48 | 331.0 | 93 | 641.2 | 138 | 951.5 |
| 4 | 27.6 | 49 | 337.8 | 94 | 648.1 | 139 | 958.4 |
| 5 | 34.5 | 50 | 344.7 | 95 | 655.0 | 140 | 965.2 |
| 6 | 41.4 | 51 | 351.6 | 96 | 661.9 | 141 | 972.2 |
| 7 | 48.3 | 52 | 358.5 | 97 | 668.8 | 142 | 979.0 |
| 8 | 55.2 | 53 | 365.4 | 98 | 675.7 | 143 | 985.9 |
| 9 | 62.1 | 54 | 372.3 | 99 | 682.6 | 144 | 992.8 |
| 10 | 69.0 | 55 | 379.2 | 100 | 689.5 | 145 | 999.7 |
| 11 | 75.8 | 56 | 386.1 | 101 | 696.4 | 146 | 1006.6 |
| 12 | 82.7 | 57 | 393.0 | 102 | 703.3 | 147 | 1013.5 |
| 13 | 89.6 | 58 | 399.9 | 103 | 710.2 | 148 | 1020.4 |
| 14 | 96.5 | 59 | 406.8 | 104 | 717.0 | 149 | 1027.3 |
| 15 | 103.4 | 60 | 413.7 | 105 | 723.9 | 150 | 1034.2 |
| 16 | 110.3 | 61 | 420.6 | 106 | 730.8 | 151 | 1041.1 |
| 17 | 117.2 | 62 | 427.5 | 107 | 737.7 | 152 | 1048.0 |
| 18 | 124.1 | 63 | 434.4 | 108 | 744.6 | 153 | 1054.9 |
| 19 | 131.0 | 64 | 441.3 | 109 | 751.5 | 154 | 1061.8 |
| 20 | 137.9 | 65 | 448.2 | 110 | 758.4 | 155 | 1068.7 |
| 21 | 144.8 | 66 | 455.0 | 111 | 765.3 | 156 | 1075.6 |
| 22 | 151.7 | 67 | 461.9 | 112 | 772.2 | 157 | 1082.5 |
| 23 | 158.6 | 68 | 468.8 | 113 | 779.1 | 158 | 1089.4 |
| 24 | 165.5 | 69 | 475.7 | 114 | 786.0 | 159 | 1096.3 |
| 25 | 172.4 | 70 | 482.6 | 115 | 792.9 | 160 | 1103.2 |
| 26 | 179.3 | 71 | 489.5 | 116 | 799.8 | 161 | 1110.0 |
| 27 | 186.2 | 72 | 496.4 | 117 | 806.7 | 162 | 1116.9 |
| 28 | 193.0 | 73 | 503.3 | 118 | 813.6 | 163 | 1123.8 |
| 29 | 200.0 | 74 | 510.2 | 119 | 820.5 | 164 | 1130.7 |
| 30 | 206.8 | 75 | 517.1 | 120 | 827.4 | 165 | 1137.6 |
| 31 | 213.7 | 76 | 524.0 | 121 | 834.3 | 166 | 1144.5 |
| 32 | 220.6 | 77 | 530.9 | 122 | 841.2 | 167 | 1151.4 |
| 33 | 227.5 | 78 | 537.8 | 123 | 848.0 | 168 | 1158.3 |
| 34 | 234.4 | 79 | 544.7 | 124 | 854.9 | 169 | 1165.2 |
| 35 | 241.3 | 80 | 551.6 | 125 | 861.8 | 170 | 1172.1 |
| 36 | 248.2 | 81 | 558.5 | 126 | 868.7 | 171 | 1179.0 |

## ENGLISH TO METRIC CONVERSION: PRESSURE

The basic unit of pressure measurement used today is expressed as pounds per square inch (psi). The metric unit for psi will be the kilopascal (kPa). This will apply to either fluid pressure or air pressure, and will be frequently seen in tire pressure readings, oil pressure specifications, fuel pump pressure, etc.

To convert pounds per square inch (psi) to kilopascals (kPa): multiply the number of psi by 6.89

| Psi | kPa | Psi | kPa | Psi | kPa | Psi | kPa |
|-----|-----|-----|-----|-----|-----|-----|-----|
| 172 | 1185.9 | 216 | 1489.3 | 260 | 1792.6 | 304 | 2096.0 |
| 173 | 1192.8 | 217 | 1496.2 | 261 | 1799.5 | 305 | 2102.9 |
| 174 | 1199.7 | 218 | 1503.1 | 262 | 1806.4 | 306 | 2109.8 |
| 175 | 1206.6 | 219 | 1510.0 | 263 | 1813.3 | 307 | 2116.7 |
| 176 | 1213.5 | 220 | 1516.8 | 264 | 1820.2 | 308 | 2123.6 |
| 177 | 1220.4 | 221 | 1523.7 | 265 | 1827.1 | 309 | 2130.5 |
| 178 | 1227.3 | 222 | 1530.6 | 266 | 1834.0 | 310 | 2137.4 |
| 179 | 1234.2 | 223 | 1537.5 | 267 | 1840.9 | 311 | 2144.3 |
| 180 | 1241.0 | 224 | 1544.4 | 268 | 1847.8 | 312 | 2151.2 |
| 181 | 1247.9 | 225 | 1551.3 | 269 | 1854.7 | 313 | 2158.1 |
| 182 | 1254.8 | 226 | 1558.2 | 270 | 1861.6 | 314 | 2164.9 |
| 183 | 1261.7 | 227 | 1565.1 | 271 | 1868.5 | 315 | 2171.8 |
| 184 | 1268.6 | 228 | 1572.0 | 272 | 1875.4 | 316 | 2178.7 |
| 185 | 1275.5 | 229 | 1578.9 | 273 | 1882.3 | 317 | 2185.6 |
| 186 | 1282.4 | 230 | 1585.8 | 274 | 1889.2 | 318 | 2192.5 |
| 187 | 1289.3 | 231 | 1592.7 | 275 | 1896.1 | 319 | 2199.4 |
| 188 | 1296.2 | 232 | 1599.6 | 276 | 1903.0 | 320 | 2206.3 |
| 189 | 1303.1 | 233 | 1606.5 | 277 | 1909.8 | 321 | 2213.2 |
| 190 | 1310.0 | 234 | 1613.4 | 278 | 1916.7 | 322 | 2220.1 |
| 191 | 1316.9 | 235 | 1620.3 | 279 | 1923.6 | 323 | 2227.0 |
| 192 | 1323.8 | 236 | 1627.2 | 280 | 1930.5 | 324 | 2233.9 |
| 193 | 1330.7 | 237 | 1634.1 | 281 | 1937.4 | 325 | 2240.8 |
| 194 | 1337.6 | 238 | 1641.0 | 282 | 1944.3 | 326 | 2247.7 |
| 195 | 1344.5 | 239 | 1647.8 | 283 | 1951.2 | 327 | 2254.6 |
| 196 | 1351.4 | 240 | 1654.7 | 284 | 1958.1 | 328 | 2261.5 |
| 197 | 1358.3 | 241 | 1661.6 | 285 | 1965.0 | 329 | 2268.4 |
| 198 | 1365.2 | 242 | 1668.5 | 286 | 1971.9 | 330 | 2275.3 |
| 199 | 1372.0 | 243 | 1675.4 | 287 | 1978.8 | 331 | 2282.2 |
| 200 | 1378.9 | 244 | 1682.3 | 288 | 1985.7 | 332 | 2289.1 |
| 201 | 1385.8 | 245 | 1689.2 | 289 | 1992.6 | 333 | 2295.9 |
| 202 | 1392.7 | 246 | 1696.1 | 290 | 1999.5 | 334 | 2302.8 |
| 203 | 1399.6 | 247 | 1703.0 | 291 | 2006.4 | 335 | 2309.7 |
| 204 | 1406.5 | 248 | 1709.9 | 292 | 2013.3 | 336 | 2316.6 |
| 205 | 1413.4 | 249 | 1716.8 | 293 | 2020.2 | 337 | 2323.5 |
| 206 | 1420.3 | 250 | 1723.7 | 294 | 2027.1 | 338 | 2330.4 |
| 207 | 1427.2 | 251 | 1730.6 | 295 | 2034.0 | 339 | 2337.3 |
| 208 | 1434.1 | 252 | 1737.5 | 296 | 2040.8 | 240 | 2344.2 |
| 209 | 1441.0 | 253 | 1744.4 | 297 | 2047.7 | 341 | 2351.1 |
| 210 | 1447.9 | 254 | 1751.3 | 298 | 2054.6 | 342 | 2358.0 |
| 211 | 1454.8 | 255 | 1758.2 | 299 | 2061.5 | 343 | 2364.9 |
| 212 | 1461.7 | 256 | 1765.1 | 300 | 2068.4 | 344 | 2371.8 |
| 213 | 1468.7 | 257 | 1772.0 | 301 | 2075.3 | 345 | 2378.7 |
| 214 | 1475.5 | 258 | 1778.8 | 302 | 2082.2 | 346 | 2385.6 |
| 215 | 1482.4 | 259 | 1785.7 | 303 | 2089.1 | 347 | 2392.5 |

7926 44 89